Van Halen 101

Foreword by
Brian May

by
Abel Sanchez

authorHOUSE™

1663 LIBERTY DRIVE, SUITE 200
BLOOMINGTON, INDIANA 47403
(800) 839-8640
WWW.AUTHORHOUSE.COM

First published by AuthorHouse 09/07/05

ISBN: 1-4208-7886-7 (sc)

Printed in the United States of America
Bloomington, Indiana

This book is printed on acid-free paper.

Cover photograph provided by Neil Zlozower

prod·i·gy \'prä-d*&*-jE\ *noun, pl* -**gies** [L *prodigium* omen, monster, fr. *pro-, prod- + -igium* (akin to *aio* **I** say) – more at ADAGE] **1 a :** a portentous event **:** OMEN **b :** something extraordinary or inexplicable **2 a :** an extraordinary, marvelous, or unusual accomplishment, deed, or event **b :** a highly talented child or youth

Merriam-Webster Dictionary

Table of Contents

Simply put, over 100 of the world's finest musicians - including the world's greatest guitar players, of course - came forward to personally share their thoughts, memories and stories about Edward Van Halen

Foreword

My memories of Edward are all great. I first saw him in action when Tony Iommi invited me to a Black Sabbath concert in which Van Halen were the support act. It was a bit like seeing Jimi Hendrix for the first time. I couldn't quite believe it – Edward's fabulous technique, his effortless dexterity and invention, the sheer joy of that wonderful waterfall of notes that poured from him. It was like some wonderful conjuring trick. Like watching Michael Jordan, so skillful everyone else seemed to be standing still. For me it was time to reassess (again) what I thought I knew about guitar playing.

We became friends, and I saw quite a few VH gigs, notably their first night at the Forum, L.A. which was something extraordinary. It was one of those moments when you know you are witnessing a phenomenon at its absolute perfect peak. Every move, every note from the whole band seemed like it was hooked straight into the audience. An amazing experience.

One day I woke up in L.A. when there was a rare lull in Queen activity, and thought... wouldn't it be great to create a moment with my friends in this city, and spontaneously make music. I rang Edward and bounced the idea off him. He was up for it. I played him over the phone a tune my small son had become fond of (Star Fleet), and told Ed I had an idea for an arrangement, which would start us off. I booked the Record Plant, a great studio where we all felt at home (long since sadly demolished to make a mini-mall) and in we went for an afternoon. We played the Star Fleet track and rolled tape. You can hear the results on the (now rare) vinyl album.

Spontaneously, now that we were on a roll, we launched into some blues. Edward had played one of his timelessly brilliant solos on SF – tapping magically into the stratosphere. For the blues he played absolutely as he had grown up playing, he later told me – pure blues, no tapping, just feel. And finally there was a song I'd written specially for the occasion, called "Let Me

Out." Alan Gratzer, my friend who played drums on the sessions, said – it feels like cheating on your wife! It was a day in a million.

Of course the biggest thrill for me was the stuff EVH played, with me, playing together. The live track was amazing, and I mixed it very simple and true to the occasion, but we actually overdubbed a double run together in harmony, as the icing on the cake. We were all fired up being around Ed – sparks flew. We saw each other a fair bit every time I came back to L.A., but recently I haven't seen my great old friend Edward. There has been much water under the bridge, and sometimes events seem to cut you off from the past. I miss him very much.

What a wonderful musician…absolutely the pinnacle of guitar playing in our lifetime. In my view Edward Van Halen broadened the spectrum of electric guitar playing as much as Jimi Hendrix, almost a generation before, and no one would have thought that possible, until the first Van Halen album was born.

A prodigy, and his playing is a joy forever…

Brian May

History...

Prodigy from Pasadena

The story of Van Halen unfolds in Pasadena, California by way of Nijmegen, the Netherlands. Here's a quick geography lesson for you. The Netherlands is located in Western Europe. Nijmegen is a small city – population 160,000 – located in the east of the Netherlands, near the German border, in the province of Gelderland. Or you could just say that Nijmegen is east of South Holland and southeast of Amsterdam, dig?

From this small city of Nijmegen came the nucleus of one of the most important and influential bands the world has ever known. This is owed to Jan and Eugenia Van Halen. During the 1940s, Jan Van Halen was a professional musician in his twenties, touring around Europe. He'd been classically trained in music and played the clarinet, as well as the saxophone. The man would play everything from live radio broadcasts to gigs with a circus troupe. Jan was a cool guy and a smokin' musician. Basically, the kind of cat who cut class, smoked cigarettes, and absolutely lived for music. Ever wonder where Edward and Alex Van Halen got it from? They got it from that man, right there.

Well, around this time, Jan cruised on over to Indonesia. While there, he met a lady named Eugenia van Beers. They fell in love and got married, eventually leaving Indonesia and moving to Nijmegen. This is where they would settle down and start a family. Their first son, Alexander Arthur Van Halen, came into this world on May 8, 1953. Almost two years later, his brother and musical soul mate followed when the couple had their second son, Edward Lodewijk Van Halen, on January 26, 1955.

I believe the Van Halen family resided on Rozemarijnstreet 59 in Nijmegen. By all accounts, they were a tight-knit and happy family. Jan continued to gig professionally and, from what I understand, music was

3

something that was *always* around the house. You know, to this day, I've heard people cite many different musical influences for the Van Halen brothers, from Mozart and Beethoven to the Beatles, Cream, Led Zeppelin, Black Sabbath, the Who, and many more. And yes, all of those artists inspired and influenced them – later on. But before any of those artists came into their lives, their very first musical influence and inspiration was their dad.

The earliest sounds Edward and Alex ever heard came from a little practice room their dad had in the downstairs section of their home in back in Nijmegen. Jan would chill in his little practice room and sit there going through scales. But he wouldn't just play them. No, he would actually hold each note for as long as he could. Apparently, their old man was going after something his sons would later seek out as well: *tone.* He wasn't just sitting there dickin' around. No, he was going after the *tone.* Jan had managed to achieve a wonderful, warm sound. Edward and Alex would listen to their dad play long, sustained notes – dripping with *tone.*

Here's where their education began. Way before anyone else made their way into their lives and ears, it was Jan Van Halen who gave his sons their first taste of music. I honestly believe this is the man they owe their career to. Jan was not only their first musical influence, but also the driving force behind the brothers' music as well. Edward and Alex would basically spend the rest of their lives trying to do what many sons do – make their father proud. It's that simple. They didn't do it for anyone else, really. They dedicated their entire lives to music to make their father proud and to uphold the Van Halen family name. You know, to keep the family's music tradition alive.

What was really cool about their father was despite the fact that he was a professional musician, he *never* pushed his kids into playing music at all. No, apparently Momma Van Halen handled that department. Eugenia was definitely the one who cracked down on her sons to practice. She was all about heavy-duty practice, instilling a major work ethic in her two young boys. Between wanting to make their father proud and Mom's heavy-duty practice routine, their musical foundation was set. This is really what drove the brothers from early childhood through the rest of their lives, and to this very day. Wanna know what *really* drives these guys? Family.

It ain't about money, fame, women, or anything else. Sure, those things are quite nice and Lord knows they eventually got plenty of each. But that is not the reason the brothers picked up their instruments and dedicated their entire lives to their craft. It was for their parents and to uphold the family name. Music is just something they were born with. It is in their blood, their bones, their DNA. Hearing their old man play just set them on their path. Once they decided they wanted to play, Dad fully supported them and Mom made sure they practiced their ass off. If you could give a Platinum award to a set of parents, Jan and Eugenia deserve one, not only for supporting their sons, but for recognizing how much of an interest in music they displayed at such an early age. So they went out and brought in a music teacher. Funny thing is, they brought a guy in to train their sons to become…classical pianists?

Yes, folks, believe it or not, the Van Halen brothers began their music career as classical pianists. Their parents wanted them to be concert pianists, like the next Vladimir Horowitz! So a teacher was brought into the family home and boy, was this man ever a sweetheart. Apparently, the teacher was a Russian concert pianist who spoke absolutely no English. On top of that, the guy used to sit there with a ruler, ready to slap Edward's face if he made a mistake! That is where their training began. Edward and Alex, about five or six years old, getting schooled as classical pianists. Basically, this is where Edward got his fingers movin' and became exposed to music theory. He began to fine tune his ear at this point as well. The same goes for Alex, too. Well, it wasn't long before little Edward was already playing half-hour compositions by Mozart and Beethoven on his family's German-made Rippen piano. The kid had the knack…big time.

Their training continued up until the beginning of 1962. I imagine the boys had no clue that their lives were about to drastically change. By that time, Jan and Eugenia had already been receiving letters from relatives in America speaking of all the incredible opportunity over here. Like many people, they decided the opportunity was simply too good to pass up. So in February of 1962, the Van Halen family immigrated to America with seventy-five guilders and a piano. In other words, the family boarded a ship and came to America with nothing more than a piano and the equivalent of about fifteen American dollars. Basically, the family was flat broke. It was a nine-day boat ride to America, and to help pay their fare, Jan, Edward, and Alex provided the ship's musical entertainment. After arriving in New York, the family took a four-day train ride to their final destination: Pasadena, California.

It was in Pasadena the family set their new roots. One of the first things they did was change the spelling of their name. The family name is actually spelled "van Halen." You know, it should actually read "Jan van Halen" or "Edward van Halen." After arriving in America, they changed the spelling to "Van Halen." Work was obviously at the top of the list, especially since the family was pretty much broke when they arrived in America. Jan immediately began seeking out jobs and gigs. He worked as a janitor for a Masonic temple, and also washed dishes at the Methodist Hospital. Of course, he also continued to be a professional musician. Jan gigged on the weekends and played everything from weddings and oompah bands to bar mitzvahs. Eugenia did her share as well, going out and cleaning people's houses to help bring in some extra income.

This is how life in America began, and they all worked their ass off to get their family situated. Meanwhile, Edward and Alex began attending Hamilton Elementary School in Pasadena. I imagine the term "culture shock" would apply here. They didn't speak English, and you know how kids can be. Needless to say, little Edward got welcomed to America by getting his ass kicked all over the schoolyard. It's tough enough being the new kid in school, but being the new kid who also happens to be from another country *and* who does not speak English? Well, the ass whoopin's came, big time. Sometimes Alex was able to save his hide, sometimes he wasn't. Alex was always the bigger one, so I guess the kids wouldn't really mess with him.

Other than Alex, the only kids at school who'd actually hang out with Edward and stick up for him were the black kids. It was the early '60s and times were very rough, especially for minorities. Apparently, there was a special place on the playground of the elementary school where they use to hang out—"they" being Edward and the black kids, of course.

As if they weren't tight enough, Edward and Alex got tighter. Being in this strange new land, they really turned to each other, along with Mom and Dad, for support. Once again, it was a very tight-knit family. The boys also continued their music education. As soon as the family settled in, they brought in another music teacher. This new teacher was a Lithuanian cat named Stoskovitis. Just like their first teacher back in Nijmegen, Stoskivitis was good and very strict.

Like the teacher in the movie *Shine,* he was one of those cats who made you play and master an entire piece, and then forget it. Stoskivitis would make Edward practice one song for an entire year! This was also done so that Edward could eventually put his chops on display in a live setting, of course. Over at Long Beach City College, they would hold a music competition for kids. The competition was pretty well known locally, and you'd have over a thousand kids show up. So Edward would practice his one song for an entire year and then swing down to the LBCC competition and play the piece in a little practice room in front of three judges.

Well, Edward won first prize at the competition. In fact, he won first prize in that competition at LBCC three years in a row. But in all honesty, I don't think Edward enjoyed this very much. I believe he did enjoy classical music far as listening to it and playing it, but the whole part about competing and being judged, well, I don't think so. He would get very nervous, as I imagine many kids would. Part of his nerves also had to do with the fact that he'd never really learned to read music. Edward would always fool his teacher by just watching his fingers and listening to the melody. In doing this, he would end up playing the piece, but playing it in his own way. The kid had a good enough ear to where he could more or less get the piece down.

Apparently, the judges at the LBCC competitions actually enjoyed this and would even compliment Edward for his "very interesting interpretation" of the piece he was playing. But the whole competition thing never really appealed to him. Who is anyone to judge someone else, you know? Music is *not* a competition. Plus, the strict rules of the classical world didn't appeal much to him, either. You're to play the piece precisely as written, period. Even though Edward got away with it during all those early piano competitions, there really wasn't much room for improvisation and for your own ideas or identity. Classical music is definitely not free-form music, to put it mildly. Regardless, he forged on.

From the moment they got to America, the brothers continued to be all over that piano. Lots of practice and absorbing that music theory that would come in pretty handy down the road. It was all about classical music until just a few years after they arrived. By the mid 1960s, a wild new form of music caught Edward and Alex's ear and they would never be the same again.

Rock 'n' Roll

By the mid 1960s, rock 'n' roll was exploding. This musical revolution was sparked by the Beatles' appearance on *The Ed Sullivan Show* in February of 1964. America had been blown away and the Van Halen brothers were no different than any other kid out there. They heard rock 'n' roll and immediately took to it. Soon after the Beatles' earth-shaking debut, many other cool bands quickly followed, like the Kinks, the Animals, and the Rolling Stones. I believe that's what was known as the "British Invasion."

These bands were exploding everywhere and the Van Halen brothers were all over it. They continued their classical piano training, but it wouldn't be long now before they'd leave it behind for good. Rock 'n' roll was wild and crazy music, and it made the brothers want to go nuts! No longer did they want to be chained to a piano. More than anything else, it was the beat, the groove, the *rhythm* of rock music that really took them over. In fact, the one band that may really have set them on their rock 'n' roll path, along with the Beatles, was none other than the Dave Clark Five.

The DC5 was another British group that came over to America and was really kickin' ass. Edward really loved DC5 tunes like "Glad All Over," "Bits and Pieces," and "Any Way You Want It." He also really dug the classic Surfaris tune, "Wipeout." What grabbed him about all of these songs were the drums, so he would actually set up some cardboard boxes and bang on them like drums! Once again it was the beat, the groove, the rhythm of this music that grabbed him. In fact, he got off on 'em so much, he actually went out and got a paper route so he could save up some dough and buy himself a drum kit. While payin' his dues delivering newspapers at five in the morning on a flimsy bike, come rain or shine, Edward was finally able to purchase a $125 St. George Japanese Drum Kit. The funny thing is that delivering papers would be the only honest job Edward ever held in his life. And what was it for? To buy a musical instrument, of course.

So make note of that. 1965 is when Edward bought his drum kit. It was also when he'd get the first and *only* honest job in he ever had in his entire life, delivering papers. And it was also the year that Edward and Alex formed their very first band, the Broken Combs. This band consisted of Edward on piano and Alex on saxophone, along with several other friends handling the drum, bass, and guitar duties.

The Broken Combs made their debut during lunchtime at Hamilton Elementary School in Pasadena. It wasn't exactly Madison Square Garden, but hey, they were just kids, you know? The school was nice enough to let them perform gigs during lunchtime and apparently they did well. No word about what the groupie scene around the band was like back then, but rumor has it the lunch lady slipped Alex her phone number.

All kidding aside, this is where it all started out as far as the rock 'n' roll thang goes. The brothers were already showing versatility as musicians, too. On certain Broken Combs originals, like the classic "Boogie Booger," Edward actually played drums while Alex played piano. Another classic was a tune called "Rumpus." Yeah, ok, those song titles aren't exactly up there with "Runnin' with the Devil" and "Panama," but again, they were just kids.

So that first big wave of rock 'n' roll that exploded during the mid-1960s would change their lives forever. However, their classical training would remain with them as well. The brothers had, no pun intended, the best of both worlds. And though Edward never really learned to read music per se, his years of classical training and absorbing theory were huge in terms of having a solid musical foundation. However, while the classical training taught him theory and got his fingers movin', the drums is where he got his rhythm, baby.

Man, the importance of that musical foundation and work ethic which had been instilled in them by their parents and music teachers cannot be overstated. It would remain with Edward and Alex throughout the rest of their lives.

The Switch

"I went to grade school with Ed at Marshall Junior High and then at Pasadena High. We had an English class together taught by Miss Azalena, this foxy teacher who always wore these really short skirts. I think she was the inspiration for 'Hot for Teacher.' By the time he was in seventh grade, he was already playing Hendrix and Cream."

– Martin Clarke

By 1967, the Van Halen brothers were entering what was to be the very last stage of their classical training. The end was near and the second wave of rock 'n' roll that came down the pike during the late '60s pretty much sealed their fate and set them on a rock 'n' roll path forever. At the time, Edward was still pretty new on the drums. Meanwhile, Alex, having been convinced by Momma Van Halen, was actually taking flamenco guitar lessons! Who knows, perhaps Alex was on the road to becoming, like, that "Esteban" character you see hawking guitars on late-night television nowadays. Oh well, the infomercial world's loss was rock 'n' roll's gain.

Along with their drums and guitar, Edward and Alex also began playing violin around this time as well. In fact, they ended up playing violin for about three years. Edward thought the violin was all right, but he didn't really enjoy the tunes they would make him play, so he just kinda lost interest. Meanwhile, Alex was really kickin' ass, even making All City Orchestra on violin. Man, is there anything these guys couldn't play?

In early 1967, Edward and Alex switched instruments. Edward had actually begun messing around on his brother's acoustic guitar in 1966, but the beginning of 1967 was when they switched permanently, forever. This single move can be considered the birth of what would eventually become the band, Van Halen. The manner in which this happened is pretty funny.

Apparently, while Edward was out on his paper route, still trying to pay off that drum kit, Alex would actually get on his kit and mess around. Well, it went from Alex messing around to Alex getting *real* good, *real* quick. In fact, it wasn't long before Alex could play "Wipeout" on the drums. This was one of the songs that caused Edward to buy a drum kit in the first place, and yet it was a song he just could not seem to master.

Edward noticed that his brother was a natural on the drums and came to the conclusion they should switch instruments. What the hell, he'd already been messing around with Alex's guitar a bit and noticed he felt much more comfortable on it than Alex ever had. So they both agreed and it was done. Edward had just turned twelve and Alex was almost fourteen. Say bye-bye to classical music, it was all 'bout rock 'n' roll now. The nucleus of VH truly began *right there* with that switch. From here on out, Edward Van Halen has never played with another drummer. It was just Edward and Alex, constantly jamming. This is what makes Van Halen so special. Call it that whole "blood is thicker than water" thing, but the bond between these two cats – personally, as well as musically – is like that of no other.

They made the switch and the timing of it was perfect for several reasons. Soon after the switch came, Edward went out and got his first electric guitar. With all due respect to Alex's acoustic guitar, that simply was not gonna cut it. So in early 1967, Edward's parents purchased his first electric guitar. It was a $70 Teisco Del Ray four-pickup model guitar they bought for him at Sears in Pasadena. Yes, Sears use to sell musical instruments (I believe some still do).

Here begins the lifelong musical journey of Edward Van Halen and his guitar. It began at the age of twelve and it will continue until the man takes his final breath. During interviews, he's always stated that he began smoking, drinking, and playing guitar at age twelve. Right here, you could say any future social life the kid would have was now officially over. What followed was years and years of Edward locked in his bedroom, playing that guitar. Alex managed to have some kind of a social life during his junior high and high school years, but Edward really didn't.

For example, during high school, here's what would go down on a typical Friday night at the Van Halen household. At 7 P.M. Alex would be all set to go out, party, get laid and whatever, while Edward would be sitting at the edge of his bed playing guitar. When Alex would get home around 3 A.M., guess who was still sitting at the edge of his bed playing the guitar? That was a ritual that repeated itself like clockwork, although it was not only relegated to Friday nights.

Fact is, Edward played all day, every day, from eight to ten hours a day and much more. His friends thought he was weird, cuz he wouldn't go hang out with them. Apparently, they never saw Edward hangin' out anywhere, period. Even when it came to cutting school, while most kids cut to go to the mall or the beach, Edward actually cut school to go and play guitar. Man, I believe this clearly shows one of the few, but *major* differences between Edward and his brother Alex. The difference being that Edward is pretty much a total introvert. I mean, it's bloody obvious, isn't it?

Meanwhile, all of Edward's girlfriends back then would really have fits. Apparently, he would take his guitar everywhere, including over to his girlfriend's house. The story goes that after a while, Edward would be sittin' in his girlfriend's bedroom, off in his own world, playin' his guitar while she sat by, becoming increasingly jealous of that "damn guitar." Every now and then, one of his girls would finally snap and scold him with, "You love your guitar more than me!" Apparently, Edward would usually respond with, "I'm sorry, but you're right!"

From junior high through high school, Edward basically locked himself away in his bedroom – occasionally, in his girlfriend's bedroom – with his guitar. I guess you could say the kid had already found his passion in life. He'd always known he wanted to be a professional musician since he was a little kid, but when he discovered the guitar, he realized this was the instrument he could truly express himself with. Folks, I truly believe this is something that can't be taught. That desire, that fire to want to master something, has to come from within.

Is Edward Van Halen gifted? Absolutely. However, you have to work that gift. The key to the whole thing is for the kid to respect the gift and to realize the gift alone is simply not enough. You have to nurture that gift and work at it. No one gets by on talent alone. *No one.* Sorry, but the gift alone is not enough. I don't care if we are talkin' Beethoven, Picasso, DeNiro, or Michael Jordan, you'll find that while the majority of the great ones did have certain natural gifts, they also possessed an insane amount of drive, along with an obsessive work ethic. These people can be considered "compulsive" artists. No doubt, Edward is a "compulsive" artist, too.

In those six years he spent locked up in his bedroom from junior high through high school (1967-1973), Edward went from being a total beginner to pretty much creating his own signature style and reinventing the instrument. He went from learning a G chord to "Eruption" in about four years. No bullshit. I believe Edward composed "Eruption" when he was around sixteen years of age. Before he'd even finished high school, he had already become Eddie *motherfuckin'* Van Halen.

Sure, the rest of the world wouldn't hear him until Van Halen's debut album came out at the beginning of 1978. However, that ferocious signature sound and style you hear on Van Halen's debut album, well, Edward was already playing like *that* before he even finished high school. When you think about it, man, that's absolutely staggering. Actually, that's a *prodigy*, baby. You know, there is no logical explanation for anyone being that good, that young. Hell, even Edward Van Halen himself can't explain it!

For example, during countless interviews throughout his life, one of the most common questions thrown at Edward Van Halen has always been: "How do you do what you do?" Well, the man's response has always been the same: "Fuck if I know?" And he's not tryin' to be funny or clever or whatever. The man is being sincere. He has absolutely no clue where "it" comes from – "it" being all of his music, ideas, and so forth. His whole approach has always been to just keep jammin' constantly and keep his chops up. This way, when "it" comes, he'll be ready to receive.

So Edward got his first electric guitar at age twelve back in 1967. Well, the first step of his musical journey was to immediately refuse to take guitar lessons. He'd already been slaving on the piano for six long years and wanted no more of being taught and told how to approach an instrument. Edward simply saw the guitar as something new on which he could truly express himself without being told what to do or how to do it. It may come as a shock to many, but the fact is, Edward Van Halen never had so much as a single guitar lesson in his entire life. Not one.

However, his mom did buy him a Mel Bay book, which is a music book for guitar. The funny thing is, Edward couldn't even get past the first page! You see, the first page of the book showed you how you're supposed to hold the guitar pick, which is between your thumb and index finger. Simple enough, right? Well, being an original from the start, Edward would instead hold the pick between his thumb and middle finger. His mom would tell him he was doing it wrong, but Edward didn't seem to care. It felt right to him and that's all that mattered. I believe he still holds it like that to this very day.

One of the first songs, if not *the* first song Edward ever mastered on the guitar was the classic "Walk, Don't Run" by the legendary instrumental group, the Ventures. I believe the song "Pipeline" was also one of the earliest tunes he mastered on guitar as well. The first solo he ever mastered was from the garage rock classic, "Pushin' Too Hard," by the Seeds.

Well, Alex was totally blown away! He'd sit back and listen to his little brother and realize this guy somehow knew what the hell he was doing! Edward was all over the rock music that was out at the time. All those bands he'd first heard that had made him want to play drums became his source for guitar as well, along with the bands that were all over the radio at the time, as well. He continued woodshedding and jamming all through junior high.

During this time, the second major wave of rock music came rollin' in, led by such legendary groups as Led Zeppelin, the Jimi Hendrix Experience,

Ten Years After, the Who, Black Sabbath, Deep Purple, ZZ Top, and Cream. Each and every single one of these bands was a huge influence and inspiration for Edward and Alex. (I believe they really dug Creedence Clearwater Revival as well.) Man, it's hard to pick just one band, because they were all incredibly important to their musical development. Of course, everyone has that one favorite band, and for the Van Halen brothers, that band would be Cream.

Cream was a power trio that came roaring out of England in the fall of 1966. It was Ginger Baker on drums, Jack Bruce on bass, and Eric Clapton on guitar. These three men had come together to form what many consider to be rock 'n' roll's first "supergroup." You had these three cats in one band, and each was considered to be the best on his respective instrument at the time. And while Cream only lasted for just over two years, their impact was *huge.* This was at the time the famous "Clapton is God" graffiti sprang up on that wall in London. Simply put, all three of these cats were *"the shit"* at what they did. Baker is a phenomenal, groundbreaking drummer. Bruce is a phenomenal bassist, and a damn fine vocalist, too.

The Van Halen brothers took to Cream *immediately.* Edward was all over what Clapton was doing. He really loved Clapton's feel. You know, that bluesy type of feel he had. It wasn't about technique or anything like that, really. I mean, Eric Clapton is not a fast guitar player. After all, his nickname is "Slowhand" for crissake. Although, if you listen to Cream's live material, man, Clapton and the boys revved it up pretty damn good (the Who's *Live at Leeds* is another live album the VH brothers loved and mastered as well).

But more than anything, it was Eric Clapton's *feel* that really grabbed Edward. Clapton's killer *tone* was huge for him as well. Edward really loved the fact that Clapton went straight into the amp with absolutely no distortion pedals or boost. And Cream's blues-rock excursions were just what the Van Halen brothers were looking for. Over the course of Edward's life, there have been many great players who've impacted and influenced him, but none so much as Eric Clapton. That was Edward's first real "guitar hero."

Edward was also a fan of Clapton's work on the *Blues Breakers* album he did with John Mayall. You know, the album that shows Eric Clapton reading the *Beano* comic book on the cover? This is a classic album that was actually released right after Clapton quit the band and just prior to Cream's debut. In fact, I believe Edward actually heard Cream first, then went back and discovered the *Blues Breakers* album. This led to him researching the blues. Edward Van Halen quickly fell in love with the blues and ended up spending an entire year doing nothing but playing blues!

However, once again, even more than Cream's studio material, it was their live material that may have had the biggest impact on Edward and Alex. The way Cream would start jamming during their concerts and how it would turn into an amazing cluster-fuck! Alex was definitely into the insane rhythm playing of Bruce and Baker, but Edward was just as into it as well. How Bruce was pumping his bass through a Marshall stack, or how Baker would twist the rhythm around constantly. Baker and Bruce influenced Edward as much as Clapton did. The way those two guys would push Clapton is a fact that was never lost on Edward.

While Edward's playing would eventually morph and evolve into a signature style we all know today, back then he sounded *exactly* like Eric Clapton. He became locally famous around Pasadena for it. When you start out, you always look for someone to cop. You know, to imitate. That is how *everybody* learns. For Edward, it just so happened to be Clapton. It wasn't long after the brothers had switched instruments that Edward was copping Clapton licks note-for-note, along with the licks off records from all of those other groups I mentioned, too. Edward actually did this by ear and in a way that many others at that time would do. You have to remember it's 1967 and all you had out there was vinyl and cassettes. Oh, eight-track tapes too, of course.

Edward would plop a Cream album down on his record player and turn the speed down from 33 to 16. In doing this he would slow the album down enough to start picking out Eric Clapton's parts. You could also pan your stereo to the left or right – a concept that may be totally foreign to kids today – and in doing this, you could pretty much isolate a certain instrument. For example, if you panned the stereo to the left while listening to those Cream albums, you'd mainly just hear Clapton's guitar coming out of that one speaker. Edward would turn the speed down, pan hard left, then dissect and learn *everything* that Clapton was playing.

Now you gotta remember that Edward was barely into junior high school. On top of that, he really hadn't even been playing the guitar that long. Not to mention Cream was one of the baddest bands out there at the time. Many would say they were the baddest out there, period. And until Jimi Hendrix hit the scene, Eric Clapton had been "GOD." Yet there was little Edward, with the guitar almost as big as he was, busting out with Clapton licks all over the damn place. And it wasn't just that he could cop a few licks, he could play entire Cream songs – solos included – note-for-note. Studio material, live material, didn't matter. Edward knew it all.

In fact, it wasn't uncommon to stroll into a music store in Pasadena or Hollywood and find little Edward sitting in a corner, guitar in hand, tearing off record-perfect renditions of Cream's "Crossroads," "I'm So Glad," "Spoonful," and more. Usually, the owner of the music store would just sit there, jaw on the floor, staring in disbelief.

Well, aside from blowin' minds, Edward's already insane chops helped his old man out quite a bit. You see, when it came time to purchase a guitar or an amp, and his old man would start talking dollars and cents with the owner, well, more often than not, Jan managed to cut a sweet deal. A big part of that had to do with little Edward. The way most of the owners saw it, any kid who could already play that freakin' well deserved a break.

So again, by slowing the speed down on the turntable and panning hard left, Edward was able to learn everything, *verbatim*. Well, that along with the fact that he has an amazing ear. I don't believe he has what is known in music circles as "perfect pitch," but it can't be that far off, either. The guy has an absolutely insane ear.

Meanwhile, Alex was all over Ginger Baker. Sure, he had plenty of different influences, from John Bonham and Keith Moon to Ringo Starr. But as Edward had taken to Clapton, you could say Ginger Baker was Alex's main guy. It wasn't long before Alex was playing Baker's signature solo piece, "Toad," note-for-note. It's funny, just a couple years before, they were playing lunchtime gigs with their first band, the Broken Combs. Now, Edward and Alex, armed with a guitar and drums, were playing Cream and Hendrix tunes during lunchtime gigs at Marshall Junior High School with their new band, Genesis.

Needless to say, people were absolutely stunned – *especially* all their friends and classmates. Rudy Leiren was a classmate of Edward's at Marshall Junior High. He'd eventually end up becoming Edward's friend and first real guitar tech. Well, Rudy got to witness one of those early gigs and vividly recalls how mind-blowing the brothers already were back then.

Rudy Leiren: "The first time I saw them, they were in white T-shirts and jeans, playing at an assembly at Marshall Junior High School. This is when they were Genesis. I was up in the balcony, and they didn't have much equipment, but I was blown away! They were playing Cream and a bunch of songs on the radio. I remember thinking to myself that Eddie was going to become famous. Here he was, a kid my age, up on stage, playing Clapton riffs note for note. I was awed."

Cream, the Who, the Jimi Hendrix Experience, Ten Years After, Led Zeppelin, Deep Purple, ZZ Top, and Black Sabbath were the baddest groups out there at the time. I mean, look at the guitar players in these bands: Eric Clapton, Pete Townshend, Jimi Hendrix, Alvin Lee, Jimmy Page, Ritchie Blackmore, Billy Gibbons, and Tony Iommi. Holy shit! Oh, and we can't forget the great Jeff Beck and Allan Holdsworth. While they are basically solo artists, these two legendary players had a monstrous impact on Edward as well.

Then look at the drummers in these bands: Ginger Baker, Keith Moon, Mitch Mitchell, John Bonham, Ian Pace, and Bill Ward. Again, holy shit! These are some of the most legendary and groundbreaking musicians in the history of rock music, and the brothers were all over 'em, learning their music by ear and playing the hell out of it as soon as it would come out on the radio or hit the record store. Man, it was pretty wild. To this very day, I believe the Van Halen brothers still jam on the music of all these bands. In fact, it's not uncommon for them to break this music out during a sound check.

Edward and Alex still really love all that music and still get off on playing those songs. It's their foundation, man. If you wanna learn about a musician, I mean, *really learn* about them, go back and check out their influences. For Edward and Alex, it began with their dad. Then came the years of classical training. Then came rock 'n' roll. First there was the Beatles, the Dave Clark Five, the Kinks, the Animals, and the Ventures. Then came the Who, Cream, Black Sabbath, Led Zeppelin, Ten Years After, Deep Purple, and the Jimi Hendrix Experience.

While they listened to many different styles of music and bands, these are really all the ones that shaped them. If you look closely, it will make sense to you. The first set of rock bands that came out around 1964 and 1965, many of which, in fact, were actually considered "pop music" by most people at the time, displayed plenty of pop sensibility, melody, hooks, great harmonies and background vocals.

The next set of rock bands that came out from about 1966-1969 were really all about heavy instrumentation, guitar solos, and jamming. Somehow, the brothers were able to fuse these two worlds together, sprinkle in a little blues and funk, and eventually, it became their signature sound. Cuz you can't forget the blues. Edward and Alex *love* the blues. Remember, Edward spent his first year on the guitar pretty much playing and jamming nothing but blues. Of course, he would eventually turn it into something much wilder and more aggressive.

The brothers really dig R&B/funk music, too. Artists like the Isley Brothers, Stevie Wonder, and James Brown. Those guys really touched the brothers as well. They had so many different influences, yet Edward and Alex somehow managed to absorb it all. They began to study it, dissect it, and morph it into what would become a signature sound all their own.

It must have been interesting to see just who the other cats in their new bands were because, musically speaking, the brothers were so far ahead of everyone else their age. Remember, at the age of twelve or thirteen, most people are sitting there trying to figure out a damn G chord or something. These guys were playing on a level that was pretty rare for kids, to put it mildly. Regardless, they'd get out there and put a band together so they could get gigs. That's what it was really about for them: "the gig." Even at such an early age, they wanted to get out and perform. There would be some nerves, but the cure for that was pretty simple. Whenever Edward got nervous, his dad would just give him a shot of vodka and, well, bye-bye nerves.

In fact, one of their very first gigs after having switched instruments was with their old man at a place called the La Mareda Country Club. While their dad's band would take a break, Edward and Alex would perform. They'd set up in the middle of the dance floor and just begin to play. Well, people would quickly gather around to watch and listen. So Jan, being a musician *and* businessman, would pass the hat around to collect some dough from the crowd.

When they finished playing, they counted the money and discovered they'd earned $22 and change. So Jan gives Edward $5, and then he gives Alex $5. Well, this didn't sit too well with Alex, who quickly pointed out to Edward there had been $22 in the hat, but yet they're each standing there with just $5? Five and five adds up to ten, so where's the rest of the dough? Alex looks at his dad and Jan says, "Welcome to the music business, boys..."

Mammoth

"I knew early on they were both virtuosos."
– Mark Stone, original bassist for Mammoth

In the fall of 1969 Edward Van Halen entered Pasadena High School. You could say he and Alex were already veteran musicians. Though they'd only begun to play the guitar and drums in 1967, they'd started their music training around five or six years of age. By 1969, they'd been working at it for almost a decade now. Remember, they had their first band, the Broken Combs, in 1965. Then came Genesis, which began in junior high around the fall of 1967 and continued as Edward started high school.

Picking up where they'd left off at John Marshall Junior High, Genesis immediately made their presence felt. It didn't matter that they'd just started high school; Edward and Alex could already play the hell outta *anything*. Almost immediately, they began scoring gigs and showcasing their chops playing dances at Pasadena High School. I also believe 1969 was the year Edward Van Halen purchased his legendary Marshall amplifier. Yes, *the* Marshall. You know, the one he used to record "Eruption" and many other classic Van Halen songs. Well, it used to be the house amp at a place called the Pasadena Rose Palace, but now it belonged to Edward. And yes, he still owns it to this very day. Man, as far as I'm concerned, that baby should be in the Smithsonian.

Anyhow, the beginning of high school was important, because this is when they began playing the backyard party circuit. Even more so than the high school dances at Pasadena High, playing backyard parties is where the boys earned their reputation and really began to establish themselves. You have to understand that these backyard parties were huge. The positive word of mouth they got from playing these parties is how they learned their reputation in and all around Pasadena.

Word of "the amazing VH brothers" began to spread in junior high, but their reputation was truly solidified in high school, playing backyard parties. And while they would go through several different lineups, the kids at Pasadena High School didn't really care. Long as the VH brothers were playing somewhere, people showed up. In fact, most of the kids who attended these parties would eventually follow the band out of the backyards and right on to the Sunset Strip after they had all finally graduated high school and VH began playing clubs.

But those backyard parties, man, it was pretty damn wild. Some poor kid would volunteer his house while his parents were away or something, and literally hundreds of kids would show up. They'd hire Genesis and set up a little stage in their backyard for the band to play on. So when a Friday or Saturday night rolled around, it wasn't uncommon to hear the end of the world comin' out of someone's backyard in Pasadena, cuz you'd have hundreds of kids and one insane band goin' ballistic. Could you imagine? The VH brothers were putting on full-fledged concerts in people's backyards! They would tear through cover tunes with ease, everything from Cream to Sabbath, of course. I believe Edward's signature tune around this time was "Goin' Home," by Alvin Lee and Ten Years After. Quite often, he would close out these parties with that tune and just play the hell out of it. And if you've ever heard it, man, it's humbling to think a guy who'd just started high school could play that song *verbatim*.

All the kids at these parties would already be rowdy enough from drinking, smoking, or whatever. After Genesis would get on stage and start to tear shit up, well, it would often escalate into a riot. On top of that, the band would be playing so damn loud, you could hear 'em from blocks away. Kids would be screaming and singing along, and you know, sometimes fights would break out. These parties were so wild and caused such a ruckus that, of course, the police would sometimes be called in to break it up.

Now I'm sure this happens all over the world, but not quite how it happened here. The difference here is the police would have to show up in full force and led by their police helicopter. Basically, it was a raid! There would be so many people at these parties, they would spill out from the backyard into the front yard and right out into the street. There were people everywhere. It was insane! You couldn't send just one police car to issue a warning. No, you better send a few cuz you were dealing with large numbers here. Sometimes there were so many people, the cops couldn't do anything other than ask the band to please stop playing after a few more songs. Meanwhile, the police chopper hovered overhead, shining its spotlight down on the party as hundreds of kids simultaneously flipped 'em off. This scenario would repeat itself weekend after weekend, all through high school. Legend has it, there is even video of this. Apparently, the police would videotape many of their raids and word is, quite a few of these backyard parties were raided *and* videotaped.

Needless to say, before they even graduated high school, the Van Halen brothers were already legends in and around Pasadena. All this really began with their band, Genesis. And while I could poke a little fun at the "groupie scene" surrounding the Broken Combs, when it came to Genesis, they had absolutely no problem in that department. The boys at Pasadena High immediately learned two things: If you wanted to hear killer music, go see Genesis. If you wanted to find chicks, the answer was the same.

> **Rudy Leiren:** "The next time I saw them, they were playing at a dance at PHS [Pasadena High School]. We were down there and I remember it was the same thing: 'These guys are great, they're really good.' Lots of girls. That was pretty much the diet—when you wanted to go out and look for girls, you asked where Genesis was playing."

Already the dudes wanted to be like them and the chicks wanted to be with them…and they were just high school kids! Basically, Edward and Alex were already the top cats and everyone knew it. Word of their killer musicianship and wild backyard parties began to spread like wildfire. Unfortunately, just like the Broken Combs, Genesis didn't last too long either.

When Genesis ended, the brothers formed another band called the Trojan Rubber Company in 1971 (please feel free to do the Beavis and Butt-Head laugh anytime you like). The TRC consisted of Edward, Alex, and several other members, one of which was a cat named Dennis Travis.

> **Dennis Travis:** "I walk into some places and tell people that I used to be in Van Halen and they laugh at me. The thing they don't understand is that Eddie and Alex were kids once, too. They grew up and had friends, you know, and I was one of them."

As a sophomore at Pasadena High School, Dennis apparently tried to impress Alex Van Halen with his new blues band. Alex gave 'em a listen but wasn't really interested. Instead, he suggested Travis hear his little brother, Eddie, who was tearing up the local garage-band scene with record-perfect cover tunes. Several months later, Travis stumbled upon the Van Halen brothers jamming in their high school gymnasium.

Dennis Travis: "I heard some music that sounded like a Cream album going full tilt and became curious. Back in those days, Cream was mostly instrumental, with big jams and no singing, and I couldn't tell if it was Cream or not. They were that good. As I got closer, I realized that it was Ed and Al doing Cream tunes note-for-note with no bass player. I asked, 'What happened to your bass player?' and they told me they had to get rid of him because he wasn't serious. I asked them if they needed somebody and they jumped back and said, 'Let's go get your equipment!'"

Dennis immediately became a member of the TRC. He played bass and occasionally guitar. They even competed in a Battle of the Bands and placed high despite the fact that they were all about fifteen or sixteen years of age, while the other bands consisted of musicians who were already in their twenties! He was with the TRC for one year until his dad, who was a minister, got a job at a church 300 miles away, and so his family had to move. Nonetheless, Dennis vividly recalls his TRC days and how Edward and Alex were already blowing minds even back then.

Dennis Travis: "I remember Eddie practicing that old James Gang song 'Walk Away.' He started copying it note-for-note from the record, and he had it down instantly. Look at it this way, there were people that tried harder than he did and never got good. Eddie could pick things up so easily, and it was like he already had it in him. He was born with it, and Alex was the same way on drums. When Eddie played, he sounded like Eric Clapton. I mean, if you took out the other guys, it sounded like Clapton was standing right there. I was really surprised, because a lot of guys his age couldn't even play."

What's even wilder is the fact that during their search for a singer, the TRC actually auditioned a skinny, long-haired kid named David Roth. The brothers felt that he looked really cool and carried himself with a certain confidence. Unfortunately, they also felt he couldn't sing for shit. Needless to say, David Roth was quickly rejected following his TRC audition. Oh, but they'd hear from David again in the very near future.

After being the TRC, they became the Space Brothers. By now, you may be wondering what the hell was up with all the name changes? Well, the boys had quite a reputation from their days as Genesis. They were known to be so wild and crazy, the schools would no longer hire them for parties and dances. People would love to have them play their backyard parties, but the schools didn't want anything to do with them! In order to continue getting gigs, they'd have to change their band name once word got out that they were out of control and too rowdy. After all these different bands/lineups, the brothers would finally form the band that would be just one step away from becoming the original Van Halen lineup. That band was known as Mammoth.

Mammoth was formed in 1972 and consisted of Alex on drums, a cat named Mark Stone on bass, and Edward on guitar and...lead vocals! I think this truly shows their Cream influence right here. In fact, many people called Mammoth "Junior Cream." This was a pure power trio, with Edward up front handling the guitar and vocals. But while Edward was already moving air with his guitar, his lead vocals weren't cutting it. He tried his best and handled the vocal duties just so they could get gigs and play. I believe the fact that he had to play *and* sing at the same time didn't really appeal to him. Edward's always been solid at background vocals, but lead vocals just weren't his thing. Honestly, most people didn't seem to mind because their musicianship was already mind-blowing. Edward and Alex were already monsters, and Mark Stone was a fine bass player. So despite Edward's lackluster lead vocals, Mammoth was playing everything from dances to backyard parties and getting a whole lot of attention locally. They definitely continued the tradition started by Genesis and were just tearing up the backyard party circuit.

But Alex Van Halen knew what had to be done. Big brother had to put personal feelings aside here and suggest to Edward they go out and look for a frontman. I don't think Edward fought the decision at all. I think the guy was relieved he could now just focus on writing songs and playing the guitar. So as Edward graduated high school in 1973, the search for a frontman began. After a little while, take a wild guess as to who shows up to audition? A certain skinny long-haired kid named David Roth.

By now, Edward and Alex know who he is. Not just from his first audition for the Trojan Rubber Company in 1971, but because they had also been renting Dave's PA system from him. You see, at this time, David Roth had his own band called Red Ball Jet. He also had his own PA, and the brothers used to rent it from him. Apparently, they would give David $10 every time they rented his PA for gigs. This had been going on for months now. I believe they would also run into David at local Battle of the Bands contests, as well as over at Pasadena Community College. While they were getting into music as a full-time career, the brothers also managed to somehow squeeze in a few music courses at PCC, as did David Roth.

Ever the wise man, Alex figures screw it, why should we pay David ten bucks every time we rent his PA from him? Let's just get him in the band and then we get his PA for free! Edward agreed with Alex, also noting that David's vocal abilities had vastly improved since his first audition two years before. But David brought much more to the table than just decent vocals and swagger. Lord, how in the world do you even begin to describe this man?

David Roth is an Indiana boy, born in Bloomington back on October 10, 1954. So he was just about nineteen years old when he hooked up with Mammoth. He is the son of Nathan and Sybil Roth. He has two sisters, Linda and Allison. His father served in the air force and would later become an eye surgeon and prominent physician. In fact, Dr. Roth eventually became chief of opthalmology at Huntington Memorial in Pasadena. The Roth family moved around a bit, first from Indiana to Massachusetts, then finally to Los Angeles in 1963. I know David also spent a bit of time in New York City, where his Uncle Manny owned the legendary "Café Wha?"

David is a well-read guy who truly loves rock 'n' roll *and* show business. His musical heroes and influences range from Al Jolson, Elvis Presley, and Louis Prima to the Beatles, Jimi Hendrix, the Ohio Players and, of course, the amazing Jim Dandy. 'Ole Jim Dandy was the bad-assed frontman for Black Oak Arkansas. His non-musical influences range from Genghis Khan, Lenny Bruce, and Muhammad Ali to Bruce Lee, Hugh Hefner and *Playboy* magazine, *MAD* magazine, and Mark Twain. The martial arts have always played a big role in David's life as well. Later on, during the Classic Van Halen era and then his solo career, David would actually incorporate some of his martial arts training and moves into his concerts and music videos. I believe this was inspired by one of Dave's musical heroes, Elvis Presley, who was also into the martial arts and incorporated some of that into his Vegas-era shows, too.

Basically, David would go on to combine rock and showbiz in a way unlike anyone had ever seen. This skinny, long-haired kid would one day go on to become the biggest frontman on the planet. David was the kinda guy all the dudes wanted to be like and hang out with. The cool dude you'd want as an older brother cuz you knew he could score weed and chicks. Speaking of which, women loved everything from his looks and wit to his insane energy on stage. Over the years, he's always joked that he's a black man trapped inside the body of a Jewish man. I wouldn't doubt it, cuz man, David Roth could really move. I mean he had rhythm to spare. In fact, his amazing sense of rhythm brought the crucial element of danceability to a good portion of Van Halen's music. In turn, this helped the band to finally begin scoring club gigs!

And not only could he move and dance his ass off, man, he could do things with his body that would land most people in the intensive care unit. Seriously, it's like he was part man, part 'toon. Just imagine Bugs Bunny with long blonde hair and a bottle of Jack – *that's* David. Just like Bugs, David ruled the world with a wink and a smirk, baby.

While fronting the mighty Van Halen, David was pimpin' around the world, armed with an endless supply of booze, krell, hot babes, witty one-liners, choppers, the red-white-and-blue, and a couple of midget bodyguards, to boot. You know, by 1979 he was David Lee Roth, a.k.a. Diamond Dave. Basically, David Lee Roth was the *original* "American Badass." Man, he created and perfected that whole thing *waaay* back when many of today's so-called "rock stars" were wasting away in elementary school learning how to rap or break dance or whatever.

Now that David was in the band, Mammoth was no longer a power trio. The band was now more like a Led Zeppelin, the Who, or Black Sabbath. You know, in the sense that it was a power trio with a man up front solely handling all of the vocal duties. That's really what a four-man band is, when you think about it: a power trio plus mouth. Now that they have their frontman, they were set to do what all bands do: play clubs and look to score a record deal.

Time to pay dues, baby...

The Club Days

*"And when Van Halen came out, it was such a mind-blowing thing—
and everybody decided to go there. Within hours of Van Halen first
playing at the Starwood, there were fifty guys trying to do that whole
'Eddie Van Halen guitar playing' thing, copping his whole trip. When I
saw Van Halen, I was like, 'Wow! That's brilliant!'"*

– Slash

As 1974 began, Mammoth had already auditioned for about nineteen
different clubs in and around Hollywood. Not a single one would hire 'em.
The first guy to finally give the band a shot was a cat named Bill Gazzarri.
This gentleman was quite a character. He may have been into the club and
music thing, but he dressed like a total mobster. Sporting nice suits and a
fedora hat, his nickname wasn't "The Godfather" for nothing. In fact, you
can actually catch a glimpse of 'ole Bill in the classic 1988 Penelope Spheeris
film, *The Decline of Western Civilization Part II: The Metal Years*.

Well, Bill had opened his club, Gazzarri's, on Sunset Boulevard in West
Hollywood back in the early 1960s. You know, on the legendary Sunset Strip.
He was always cool about giving unsigned bands a shot at playing in his
club. Funny thing is, he'd already rejected Mammoth a couple times before.
Part of the reason was the fact that Edward played so damn loud. In fact,
Edward's volume is what had basically gotten the band rejected by nineteen
different clubs! He would start playing and right in the middle of a song,
someone would run up on stage screaming and yelping for him to "turn it
down!" They'd also tell him his playing was "too psychedelic." I guess some
people just couldn't understand what the hell he was doing.

At the time, Edward was also handling the lead vocals. These would be
two major problems, but he was able to solve both. Basically, bringing in

David Roth solved the lead vocal/frontman problem. Far as his volume went, well, he solved his volume problem by discovering he could hook up a device called a Variac to his amp. Without getting too technical, this device, which is basically an industrial light dimmer, would allow Edward to raise or lower the voltage on his amp. So a good Marshall plexi, with a Variac starving it at precisely 92 volts, will scream like a bitch in heat.

You see, a Marshall amp sounds its best when it is cranked to "10" (well, to "11" if you're Nigel Tufnel). In other words, all the way up! With the Variac, he was able to spank the tubes as if the amp was on "10," but it wasn't. In other words, you get the sound/tone of an amp at full volume without actually having it at full volume. Kids, *do not* try this at home. For starters, in doing this, Edward was pushing the amp so hard, the tubes would literally melt! On top of that, if you hook it up incorrectly, um, you basically risk electrocuting yourself.

Anyhow, this is what it was all about. High school is over and what are you gonna do with the rest of your life? For Edward and Alex, the choice was obvious. They planned on playing music for the rest of their lives. David Roth was definitely down for it as well. It now appeared their lineup was set. Having just gotten the Gazzarri's gig, man, now was the time to start kicking some major ass, right? Unfortunately, for Mark Stone this was not the case.

Mark was a darn good bass player and had plenty of chemistry with the brothers. But while the brothers had known and wanted nothing more than to play music for the rest of their lives, Mark saw himself on a different path. He'd been a straight-A student in school and while he did enjoy playing, well, music just wasn't something he saw himself doing for the rest of his life. He knew it wasn't his calling and the brothers seemed to notice that as well. So the brothers called a band meeting and fired Mark. Damn, that *has* to suck. In a way, Mark Stone is basically the "Pete Best" of Van Halen. Leaving that band was not easy because anyone could see that Edward and Alex were gonna make it.

It was a difficult decision, cuz the brothers liked Mark, but they'd always been dead serious about their craft and they only wanted to be in bands with people who were in it for life. Mark Stone simply wasn't, so they let him go. Talk about bad timing. Mammoth was finally scoring gigs in clubs and then they suddenly find themselves without a bass player. Man, anyone who's been around music or in a band knows that finding a good bass player is not an easy task. Surprisingly, the answer came in the form of someone they had already run into on the local music scene, as well in some of those music courses over at Pasadena Community College.

Michael Anthony Sobolewski (a.k.a. Michael Anthony, Mike Anthony, Mikey, Mad Anthony, and Mr. Jack Daniels) was born in Chicago, Illinois on June 20, 1954. His family had moved from Chicago to California a couple times before they finally decided California was the place to be. And it was quite the family. There was Mike, his parents, his three brothers Steve, Robert, and Dennis, and his sister Nancy. Like the Van Halen brothers, his dad was also a musician. Walter Sobolewski was a professional trumpet player.

Mike's entry into the world of music began at the age of seven when, like his dad, he picked up the trumpet. By the time he hit his teens, he left the trumpet for the guitar. Noticing that everyone else was picking up either the guitar or drums, he simply figured he'd go for the bass instead. What's really cool is that Mike and the Van Halen brothers actually shared many of the same influences, from Cream to Led Zeppelin.

Being a bass player, of course, Mike was really into Jack Bruce and John Paul Jones. If you had to pick one, I believe John Paul Jones was his main man. Tim Bogert's playing on the *Beck, Bogert and Appice* album and Felix Pappalardi's playing on Mountain's *Nantucket Sleighride* album were a big influence, too. Harvey Brooks of Electric Flag is another player Mikey was into while he was growin' up. Finally, Dick Peterson of Blue Cheer was an early influence and inspiration as well. Later on, he got into and really came to admire the great Jaco Pastorius.

By 1974, the Van Halen brothers had already crossed paths with Mike several times. Being in different bands in the same music scene, it's just bound to happen. Plus, Mike was also taking courses over at Pasadena Community College at the same time as the brothers and David. In fact, Alex and Mike were in the same music theory class at PCC. Well, at this time, Mike had a band called Snake. Like Mammoth, Snake was a power trio, with Mike handling all the bass and lead vocal duties. The two bands ended up playing a gig together at Pasadena High School, with Snake opening for Mammoth.

Apparently, Mammoth's P.A. blew up, so they approached Mike about using his band's P.A. system. Mike, who to this day is known as one of the truly nice guys in rock, allowed them to use Snake's P.A. I also believe Mike did this because he also knew what bad-assed musicians the brothers were. Hell, Mike is so damn nice he probably woulda hooked 'em up even if they'd sucked. It's not like he was loaning it out to total strangers, either. Mike had already seen the brothers play before and was blown away. In fact, the very first time Mike saw Mammoth was when they played at his high school. Apparently, the school had a yearly carnival on their football field and Mammoth was there. Mike was stunned to see this band, made up of kids his age, doing note-for-note versions of songs from Grand Funk Railroad, Cream, Black Sabbath, and other big bands of that time. I believe they played material off the Who's *Live at Leeds* album on that day as well. Man, how in the world could you not be impressed? Mike had heard about the brothers and then he got to witness it firsthand with his own eyes and ears.

Well, the brothers got to see Snake perform that night at Pasadena High, and while they didn't much care for the rest of the band, they really liked Mike. The brothers could tell he was a damn solid bass player and they really dug his energy, too. But the real bonus was his voice.

Mike Anthony can sing his motherfuckin' ass off. I wish I could put it more eloquently than that, but I can't. This guy has an amazing set of pipes. He is also very natural on stage and pretty damn lively far as bass players went. Mike has tons of energy when he performs. On top of all that, of course, he is the nicest guy on the planet and had lent Mammoth his band's P.A. The brothers took note of all these qualities and felt this could be the man to replace Mark Stone.

Alex and Edward asked Mike to audition and he accepted their offer. The audition took place in a tiny garage in Pasadena. It was just Edward, Alex, and Mike. The brothers threw all kinds of crazy shit at Mike. From straight up four-on-the-floor type shit to stuff with odd time signatures, they just tore it up and listened to see if Mike could keep up with them, and he could. In fact, Mike held his own and kept up with them through the whole audition. Edward and Alex must have been impressed, because Mike was offered the bass chair in Mammoth *immediately* after his audition. It was as simple as, "Hey man, wanna join the band?" Of course, Mike said yes. Fact is, he felt honored they'd even asked him over to jam. When they offered him the gig right there on the spot, well, saying "yes" was a total no-brainer.

Man, you wanna talk about a smart decision. And when I say that, I mean a smart decision on all sides, the brothers and Mike. You know, it's funny how some people consider Mikey to be "the luckiest guy on the planet." For my money, I've always considered Van Halen to be "the luckiest band on the planet" for having a dude like Mikey in it. I mean that sincerely, too.

So there they are. Edward, Alex, David, and Mike. Sound familiar? This is the *classic lineup* the world would eventually come to know and love. It was born in 1974. Now they are set to conquer the world, right? Well, not quite. There was just one more issue to be dealt with and that was the name of their band. Apparently, they didn't know there was another band out there that had been using the name Mammoth before them, so they had no choice but to change their name. Well, since the brothers worshipped Black Sabbath, they wanted to rename the band Rat Salad, after a Black Sabbath tune. But of all people, it was actually David Roth who suggested the name Van Halen. He felt it had a certain ring and majesty to it. Well, the brothers absolutely hated it! They thought they would look conceited if they used their own name as the band name. It took quite a bit of discussion, along with some prodding from David, but they all finally agreed. From here on out, they would be known as Van Halen.

From 1974 to 1977, Van Halen attacked the Hollywood club scene with everything they had. This is the same legendary club scene that – after Van Halen got signed – would produce many other great bands over the course of the next decade. I'm talkin' about bands like Metallica, L.A. Guns, Mötley Crüe, Quiet Riot, Guns N' Roses, and Dokken, to name just a few.

By the early to mid-'80s, the Hollywood club scene had exploded. It was insane. Well, this era and new wave of American hard rock/metal all started with Van Halen, baby. And while most people associate Van Halen with the Sunset Strip and legendary clubs such as the Whisky, Gazzarri's, and the Starwood, the truth is that these guys played *everywhere*. From Hollywood and Pasadena to Norwalk and Rancho Cucamonga. Hell, they didn't even get to the Whisky until, like, the fall of 1976. Yeah, you could say these guys played anywhere and everywhere.

For example, they once played a gig at a place called Walter Mitty's Rock and Roll Emporium in Pomona. You know, a real high-class joint adorned with lots of boozers and bikers. Well, right in the middle of their set, as they were playing "You Really Got Me," two bikers got into an argument out in front of the stage. So, of course, they settled it like most of 'em did back in the day. By this I mean one biker pulled out a blade and stabbed the other. Yes, right in front of the stage as the band played! It's like VH had their very own personal Altamont, right there.

Apparently, the two bikers had been arguing over whose bike was faster or something. Well, ever the troopers, the band kept playing as the biker lay there in front of the stage with his guts on display for everyone to see. What's even wilder is Van Halen had to play another gig the following night as well. Rumors were flyin' around that payback was in order, cuz I believe the biker had died. So as to avoid being caught in the crossfire, the next night the band placed their amp cabinets a couple feet in front of the wall. This way if the shit hit the fan, they could simply bolt and hide behind their cabs!

While doing the "club thing," the band continued playing high school dances, backyard parties, weddings (yes, Van Halen actually played weddings), wet T-shirt contests, and Lord knows what else. I believe they even played over at the Pasadena Hilton Hotel a few times. But their main focus at this point was really the clubs. These guys were out there *nonstop*, and Gazzarri's was the first place to give 'em a shot. Well, they quickly went from being rookies to becoming the house band. Talk about payin' dues, Van Halen would play Gazzarri's about two or three weeks out of each month and do five forty-five-minute sets a night. Man, that's almost four hours of playing *every single night,* ok? Basically, they were playing their balls off. For their efforts, Bill Gazzarri would pay them a whopping $75 per gig. However, the funniest thing is when, every so often, Bill would slip David an extra $20 and say, "Nice job, Van." Poor Bill musta been gettin' up there in years, cuz he actually thought Dave's name was "Van!"

Man, this band went on to become so huge that, as is the case with many successful bands, some people tend to forget these guys used to lug their own gear to and from gigs in a crappy van while playing for beer money. Along with the fact that they had to be their own manager and PR team. In other words, they had to deal with the club owners and get gigs all on their own, just like everyone else had to, and they had to promote themselves by making flyers and then going around to all the local high schools and sticking those flyers in lockers and so forth.

I know they'd go to the parking lot of the L.A. Forum during concerts and flyer all the cars in the parking lot, as well. This is another way to promote yourself that many unsigned acts are quite familiar with. Yes, there once was a time Edward Van Halen and David Lee Roth were runnin' around stickin' flyers in lockers and under the windshield wipers of cars. Hard to imagine, but it's true. Mötley Crüe guitarist Mick Mars was part of the scene at Gazzarri's at the same time Van Halen was payin' their dues. Mick recalls the impression the boys made, especially Edward.

> **Mick Mars:** "I had a band called White Horse who played with Van Halen a few times at Gazzarri's. Ed was always great...my mouth would fall open."

Far as the music went, their sets at Gazzarri's basically consisted of covers. Back then, the only way you got hired was by playing covers. You see, most people go to clubs to drink, dance, and hear the latest music. So club owners would look for bands that could bring people in to dance and, of course, drink. Liquor equals money, baby. If you brought in big crowds, well, you got to charge 'em at the door and then charge 'em for the booze. So if you couldn't play covers – and by that I mean the latest Top 40 material – you simply did not get gigs. Despite the fact that VH had already written a good amount of original material, they played the game and learned covers.

However, what always set Van Halen apart is they played covers their own way. That's not to say they rendered 'em totally unrecognizable, either. Just go back and listen to bootlegs of VH during their club days (believe me, there are *plenty* in circulation) and you'll see what I mean. They learned those songs note-for-note, but in a way, you could say they "Van-Halenized" those songs. So go check 'em out cuz it's pretty interesting and fun to hear.

In fact, it wasn't long before the band had built up a repertoire of over 300 cover songs. Their arsenal of covers included everything from the music of their influences to the latest Top 40 material out there. So here is a group that could play tunes from the Beatles and the Kinks, then turn around and hit you upside the head with Cream, Sabbath, Zeppelin, Hendrix, the Who, Ten Years After, Deep Purple, and many more. Then, they could turn around again and hit you with all the latest Top 40 stuff, like the KC and the Sunshine Band classic "Get Down Tonight." Yes, Van Halen actually played "Get Down Tonight" by KC and the Sunshine Band! These guys could literally play *anything,* including material from the Isley Brothers and Stevie Wonder as well. I've heard bootlegs of VH playing the Stevie Wonder classic "Superstition," and it's a trip.

Of course, they were all over the big rock acts of this time as well. They covered Queen, Thin Lizzy, Kiss, ZZ Top, the James Gang, Grand Funk Railroad, Mountain, Johnny Winter, David Bowie, Foghat, Edgar Winter, Aerosmith, and so forth. They really had to have a deep repertoire of cover material. Edward and Alex also dug bands like Captain Beyond, Trapeze, and Cactus. These bands weren't as well known as some of the other bands they covered, but they were just as good. Hell, some might say even better. I guess they could have been considered more "underground" or "progressive," but they displayed tremendous musicianship and the VH brothers really got off on that. So they covered these groups as well.

Now, it takes a lot of hard work to learn all that material. I don't care how talented you are, learning other people's material and playing it correctly is not easy. Plus, you have to remember that most of that material had just hit the airwaves. It was all new music, so they had to learn it as quickly as possible, while making certain it sounded tight when performed live. This required total dedication, and so the band spent many hours practicing in the basement of Dave's parents' home. Dave's dad, Dr. Roth, was cool enough to let them practice down there. Of course, this is also where they would jam and write original songs as well. The basement was like their lab. It was about twelve feet in width, twenty-five feet in length. They would go down there and stay down there until the experiment was complete. Basically, they'd be learning all those covers while writing original material at the same time.

With beer cans, guitar picks, cigarette butts, and broken drumsticks all over the floor, I can't imagine how many thousands of hours they spent down there. Some of the greatest rock music the world would ever know was completed and perfected in the basement of Dr. Roth's home in Pasadena. Basically, a song didn't see the light of day until it was played, in its entirety, in that basement. They would usually emerge from there with plenty of killer original stuff to go along with all those covers they'd mastered. In fact, quite a bit of the material you'd eventually hear on those classic era Van Halen albums had already been written at this time.

So they would then go down to Gazzarri's and play sets consisting of covers. But after a couple sets, when the audience was really groovin' and all liquored up, they would slip in the occasional original. Of course, their originals sounded good, so most people didn't seem to mind. This became standard operating procedure until they would eventually play all original sets.

Man, it wasn't long before Van Halen had worked their way up to the top of the local music scene. If you wanted to go party and hear some killer music, all you had to do was find out where Van Halen was playing. The people of Southern California knew. Seems every gig would draw more people than the last. It's like Gazzarri's just wasn't big enough to contain that band. You have to remember that this is a band that would go on to pack arenas, even stadiums. It's pretty amazing the roof of that place didn't cave in when they played there. I mean, I don't know if you could really call Gazzarri's a *"dive,"* but I've heard you needed a police escort just to go to the bathroom in that place.

As their reputation spread, other clubs became interested. But Van Halen remained faithful to Bill Gazzarri. And while they would not play any other clubs, they did continue to play all their other gigs like weddings, backyard parties, school dances, hotels, and so forth. They also began playing gigs at a place called the Pasadena Civic Center. They'd save up the money they were earning from all their other gigs and rent the place out for a Friday or Saturday night. They'd post up flyers all over the damn place and charge two or three bucks a head at the door. Yes, there actually was a time when you could go and see Van Halen for just two or three bucks. People showed up in droves. They would pack the Pasadena Civic Center, and that place held well over 2,000 people. And Van Halen knew how to give people a show.

They combined their killer music and super energetic live show with a few cool surprises as well. For example, they used to build their own "flash pots" – which are basically tin cans filled with gunpowder – and fire 'em up during the show. Kids, *do not* try that at home. Sometimes they would simultaneously set off a few flash pots and the entire Civic Center would fill up with smoke! Their stage setup also consisted of different colored floodlights that Mike would operate with a foot pedal. Where did the lights come from? Well, let's just say there were hotels all over Pasadena that were missing outdoor floodlights...we'll leave it at that.

David Roth was already "Diamond Dave," even back then. Well, as far as the energy, the swagger, and the mouth. His look, on the other hand, owed a debt to Jim Dandy. Apparently, Dave went through a phase where he was basically a Jim Dandy clone. For those who may not know, Jim Dandy was the killer frontman for a terrific band called Black Oak Arkansas. For starters, David looked just like Jim Dandy. It's like they were separated at birth or something?

On top of that, David had gone to a Black Oak Arkansas concert in L.A. around this time and really dug what Jim Dandy was doing. I believe they even met and spoke at that show after someone informed Jim there was another Jim Dandy in the crowd. David loved what he was doing, so much so that he actually dressed like Jim and did all kinds of the same moves and poses. Eventually, David would get past that and do his own thing.

Meanwhile, Mike and Alex would provide a most solid and thundering rhythm section, as usual. They had *groove* to spare. As for Edward, well, it was already a common sight to see tons of local guitarists lined up at the front of the stage, on his side, watching his every move like a bunch of hawks. Alex began to notice all the players out there and felt they may have been watching his brother a little *too* closely. So Alex suggested to Edward that he begin turning his back to the crowd. This way all those players out there couldn't see what they hell he was doing and cop his chops. Just as Robert Johnson and even Eric Clapton had done before him, Edward Van Halen was now turning his back to the crowd so they wouldn't rip his technique. It was the smart move, because once he got his stuff down on tape, it was there for the world to learn and borrow.

In 1976, a cat named Rodney Bingenheimer took an interest in the band. Basically, in music circles, Rodney is a legend. He's introduced the world to many great bands through his work on the Hollywood club scene (which he helped create), along with decades of work as a disc jockey on L.A.'s legendary rock station, KROQ. I believe he still dj's there to this very day.

Man, Rodney was even dubbed "The Mayor of Sunset Strip" by none other than the late, great actor, Sal Mineo. The title was due in part to Rodney's insane knowledge of music, as well as his close relationship with many of the stars of the day. In fact, in 2003, director George Hickenlooper put together a very cool documentary on Rodney's life, which was titled, appropriately enough, *The Mayor of Sunset Strip*. Well, by early 1976, Rodney began to hear the rumblings about an explosive young band that was tearin' up the local club scene. He knew he had to go see this for himself.

Rodney Bingenheimer: "There weren't really very many local bands happening in 1976. I remember going to Gazzarri's to see Van Halen and the crowd was just incredible. A lot of girls; I always thought the bands who had a lot of girls going crazy were gonna make it big. They were already playing 'You Really Got Me' and 'Runnin' with the Devil.' Their fans used to park right in front—that's where they'd meet their girlfriends—and I'd say, 'You guys should be playing the Starwood—it's more happening.' Eddie would always say the same thing, 'No, we like it here. Bill [Gazzarri] treats us so well."

Rodney dug their cover material, but wanted to know if they had any original material. Edward told him to go to the Pasadena Civic Center on a Friday night and check out their show. He did, and was again blown away by the hordes of people, as well as by the band's killer original material and super-energetic live show. Rodney continued to pursue the band and soon after, his persistence paid off.

Rodney Bingenheimer: "Finally they agreed that it might be time to move on, so I spoke to the Starwood but the club owners were hesitant. They said, 'Well, I don't know, they're a Gazzarri's band.' Back then, if a band was labeled as a Gazzarri's band, they never played outside of Gazzarri's. But I said, 'Yeah, but these guys attract a lot of beer drinkers.' Bar owners always like that, so they gave the band a shot."

By 1976, the buzz surrounding this amazing and yet unsigned local band began to hit a fever pitch. The locals would talk about this wild, killer band with a bad-assed frontman, thunderous rhythm section, and an insane guitar player you had to see to believe. As 1976 began, Van Halen had already been the house band at Gazzarri's for about two years. Ironically enough, their big break would not come at Gazzarri's. In fact, it would be at the Starwood where Van Halen would catch their big break and be discovered.

Now, the Starwood was *way* different than Gazzarri's. For starters, the Starwood was probably *the* top club on the Sunset Strip for hard rock/metal. Unlike Gazzarri's, I don't believe they much cared for Top 40 material. Hell, they were probably one of the only clubs that didn't. You could also say that if Gazzarri's was a "dive," um, then the Starwood was like the freakin' cantina scene from *Star Wars*. The owner of this fine establishment was a gentleman named Eddie Nash (his real name was Adel Gharib Nasrallah). And if Bill Gazzarri was known as "The Godfather," well, Eddie Nash was on his way to actually *becoming* The Godfather. No bullshit. In other words, Bill Gazzarri dressed the part, but Eddie Nash *lived* it.

Yeah, Eddie Nash was an interesting man, to put it mildly. This cat was a total badass and had quite a reputation. You see, while he was known in many circles for being the owner of the Starwood, he was also known in many circles for being the patron saint of Peruvian marchin' powder. Yes sir, Eddie Nash was drug czar. He was wheelin' and dealin,' baby – sometimes, right out of his own club. However, what truly made him famous – or infamous – was his involvement in the legendary "Wonderland Murders" that took place up in the Hollywood Hills on July 1, 1981. Basically, Eddie Nash sent a few of his associates, along with "king-ding-a-ling" John Holmes (a.k.a. Johnny Wadd), over to 8763 Wonderland Avenue to, um, "handle some business," so to speak. Apparently, a group of people who lived there, known as the "Wonderland Gang," had done him wrong. Well, what ensued is one of the most brutal and gruesome murder scenes ever known to man, with porn king John Holmes stuck right in the middle of it (no pun intended).

The rest, as they say, is history. Man, it's a freakin' unbelievable story. If you wanna learn all 'bout it, just go out and get the cool 2003 film *Wonderland*, which stars Val Kilmer as John Holmes and Eric Bogosian as Eddie Nash. Also, the terrific 1997 film *Boogie Nights,* which is loosely based on the life of John Holmes, has characters based on Holmes and Nash. In this film, Mark Wahlberg plays a character named Dirk Diggler (based on Holmes) and Alfred Molina plays a character named Rahad Jackson (based on Nash). Oh, and go easy with the firecrackers, Cosmo.

So anyway, after much prodding from Rodney Bingenheimer, VH finally decides to play the Starwood. And wouldn't you know it, their big break happened in May of 1976 when they played a gig at Mr. Nash's Starwood club with another local band called the Boyz. In fact, the Boyz were the headliners on this night, with Van Halen opening for them. Apparently, the Boyz also had a lot of buzz surrounding them, and many people were there to see them play. They also had a pretty great guitar player by the name of George Lynch. If the name sounds familiar, it's cuz George would later go on to be the guitar player for the band Dokken.

Two of the people at the Starwood that night would end up playing a pivotal role in Van Halen being discovered. One was Rodney Bingenheimer. Not just cuz he had suggested to the band they should play the Starwood, but because on this night, he'd brought a friend along with him to see the show. That "friend" was none other than Kiss's fire-breathing bass player, Gene Simmons! Ironically, Rodney and Gene weren't there to see Van Halen. Unh uh, this was to be the Boyz's night. They were headlining and Gene was interested in them because he had just started up his own record label at the time – Man of a Thousand Faces – and was looking for some good new bands to sign. So they were there to check out the Boyz.

In fact, most of the people at the Starwood that night were friends and followers of the Boyz. It was their gig, with their people out there showing support. Plus, you had none other than the one and only Gene fuckin' Simmons in the house to check you out. Remember, it's 1976 and Kiss was probably the biggest American rock band out there at the time. I mean, they were *huge*. So all this adds up to what looks to be a very promising evening for the Boyz. Basically, it looked like they had it in the bag.

Well, you ever hear of a little thing called "Murphy's Law?" You know, whatever can go wrong *will* go wrong? Man, did it ever go wrong for the Boyz on that night. In fact, that might be putting it mildly. You see, George and the Boyz had never so much as even heard of Van Halen. Man, they couldn't even pronounce their name.

> **George Lynch:** "Van *Haleran?* Van *Quaglen?* Somebody told me they were born in Holland, but nobody could pronounce their name. Hey, like it mattered, right? I mean, it was *our* gig. All I cared about was that they didn't suck and drive people away before our set."

Well, um, they didn't suck. Not only did they not suck, on this night, Van Halen stepped out onto that stage at the Starwood and tore the roof off. They were just filthy out there and took to the stage as if that was *their* show. They weren't opening for the Boyz, the Boyz were following *them*. Dave swaggered as if he was playing to 20,000 people, Mike and Alex were totally locked in, and Edward's playing was ferocious. Hell, the motherfucker went out there and smoked. Basically, Van Halen's combination of sick musicianship-meets-insane energy was absolutely devastating. Man, you wanna talk about stealing the show? George Lynch and the Boyz knew they were in big trouble. Despite the can of whoop ass Van Halen opened on 'em, George knew instantly that he was witnessing something very special at the Starwood that night.

> **George Lynch:** "I was like, shit, what am I gonna do *now?* To see everything you thought you knew about guitar playing change right before your eyes, at your *very own show*. Talk about depressed. But I knew I had to learn from this guy. He was doing something new, and I had to get with the program if I ever stood a chance at competing."

Just like that, the Boyz became a footnote. Van Halen didn't steal the show, they flat out *owned* it. Period. What was supposed to have been a dream come true quickly turned into *Nightmare on Elm Street*, courtesy of a bunch of kids from Pasadena, baby. Remember how Gene Simmons was there to see them? Well, he never did.

> **Gene Simmons:** "Rodney [Bingenheimer] invited us to go see a band called the Boyz play at the Starwood. They were the headlining act, but I never got to see them because the first act was a group called Van Halen, which I thought was the dumbest name I'd ever

heard, and they knocked me out. Initially, I was also turned off by Dave, who I felt looked like Jim Dandy, the singer of a B-level band called Black Oak Arkansas. But within two numbers I thought, 'My fucking god, listen to these guys!'"

Soon as Van Halen finished their set, Gene headed straight to the backstage area at the Starwood and quickly introduced himself to the band. Of course, the band knew who he was. They all liked Kiss and were actually blown away to see Gene without his makeup.

Gene Simmons: "I was waiting for them in their dressing room and when they got back there, I pulled Eddie and David aside and said, 'Look, I'd like to help, because I think you guys can make it. I'm not stroking you, I'm not interested in doing anything for myself, but I love your band and I'd like to help you.'"

I believe the first question Gene asked them was, "Do you guys have a manager?" The answer was no. At this point, Gene's mouth probably started watering. How in the world could this amazing band, with that insane guitar player, not have a manager? But indeed that was the case. Ever the sharp businessman and knowing a real good opportunity when he sees one, Gene tells the band about his new record label and offers them a contract on the spot. This had to be mind-blowing. After all, they were just supposed to open for the Boyz at the Starwood. It was just gonna be another gig. Instead it turns out to be their big break. Man, could this get any more Hollywood? I mean, seriously, this is like something out of a movie.

The first thing Gene wanted was to get them into the studio. Well, by the next morning, that was accomplished. Apparently, Gene had given Edward his phone number at the Starwood that night, and Edward called him up soon as he got home. The very next morning they were in the studio and immediately got to work on a demo tape.

Gene Simmons: "I wanted a cassette of everything they had. They even played me things like 'Ice Cream Man,' which I was not crazy about. I then took them into a proper recording studio and they were signed to my company, Man of a Thousand Faces. We cut thirteen songs, I know I was talking their heads off, and I must have sounded like their father or something. If I had been them, I would have said, 'Would you shut up already?'

"What amazed me was when we got into the studio, Eddie recorded a lot of his effects direct. The usual practice is to add effects from the board, but he had everything so under control all you had to do basically was mic his amp. He really knew what he was doing.

After we recorded some of the demo, I flew them to New York and got them into Electric Ladyland Studios and finished off the tape. It cost about $6,500. I told them I'd try to get them a deal right away and if I couldn't, they'd be free to do whatever they wanted to. But before I could shop their tape, I had to do a three-week tour with Kiss. To make a long story short, I couldn't get any interest, so I tore up the contract. I told them they were free and told them to go get a deal."

There are bootlegs of the Gene Simmons VH demo floating around and it's a pretty cool listen. I believe all the songs on the demo were done with instruments from the studio. In other words, the band was not able to record with their own gear, but rather with gear provided for them. In fact, I think it may have been Kiss's gear they ended up using.

Also, you'll notice that Edward actually overdubs his solos on this demo. If you listen close, you'll hear a rhythm guitar playing underneath the solo, which is something that would later be absent on all those early Van Halen albums cuz Edward would cut his solos live at that point. Edward didn't like overdubbing *at all,* to put it mildly. To him, you lose *feel* when you overdub. He definitely preferred to be spontaneous and just let it fly live. But he went along with it cuz Gene suggested it and Edward wasn't gonna rock the boat, you know? In all honesty, it was pretty much standard operating procedure to cut your solos like that in those days. In fact, I believe that's how most bands had been doing it for years.

The fact that Gene was not able to get any interest in the band is mind-boggling. That demo contained some songs that would go on to become classics! It's funny to think of some cheesedick label guy sitting there listening to songs like "Runnin' with the Devil," "Somebody Get Me a Doctor" and "House of Pain" while going, "Um, sorry Gene, I just don't think we can do anything with this." Apparently, most labels said their music just didn't have enough "commercial potential." Yeah, so go figure this is a band that would go on to become a staple of rock radio, score a dozen consecutive multi-Platinum albums, and sell over 75 million albums worldwide.

Ironically, even Kiss's manager didn't care for the band. Gene Simmons played the demo for Kiss manager Bill Aucoin and he was not impressed. However, Bill actually took time to meet with the band. The story goes that Bill was getting his shoes shined while he met with the band and basically told them they had "no commercial potential." In fact, he actually passed on Van Halen to sign a band called Piper. Damn, Bill, you kind of blew it there, dude. Anyway, Gene and the band ended up being stuck with a nice $6,500 demo and that was it. Poor Gene. He discovered what would go on to become one of the greatest rock 'n' roll bands ever, with one of the greatest guitar players ever, and no one cared. Frustrating probably couldn't even begin to describe how that must have felt.

Regardless, it was a good learning experience for the band and it definitely played an important role in them eventually being discovered, again. Aside from all that, the fact is the band got along great with Gene, especially the brothers. Apparently, Gene really took a liking to Edward and Alex, so much so that he would even invite them down to the studio to work with Kiss! Well, to work with him and Paul Stanley, specifically. You know, Gene and Paul would go into the studio with the Van Halen brothers and jam. I believe they even cut some songs, too.

For example, have you ever heard the Kiss song "Christeen Sixteen?" Well, Gene has always stated that the guitar solo on that song was actually written by Edward Van Halen. They cut that in the studio and Gene liked it so much, he would later have Ace Frehley copy the solo pretty much note-for-note. But if you listen to it, you will clearly see that it was *not* a classic type of VH solo. Perhaps Edward didn't wanna give some of his own stuff away, but the solo is really nothing like most of his solos. It's funny, cuz the solo actually sounds like Edward doing an Ace type of guitar solo, and then Gene has Ace play it! It's very much a Kiss type of solo. Not surprising considering Edward was playing a Kiss song with half of Kiss in the studio.

Despite all the camaraderie and good times, the sad fact was the demo was pretty much dead in the water. However, it wouldn't be long before the word got out about Gene Simmons's discovery. Remember, this all went down in and around Los Angeles. The music industry is all over that damn city and it has ears, so it wasn't long after he cut them loose that other labels came looking for this unbelievable young band with the insane guitar player that Gene Simmons had discovered. The funny thing is that by the start of 1977 Van Halen had already graduated from Gazzarri's and finally gotten into the Whisky A Go-Go, along with the fact that by now they were playing all original sets. Now, the Whisky is legendary. In fact, it may just be the most famous and legendary club for live music in all of Hollywood, period. Hell, possibly in the entire country! It seems like everyone's heard of it. That's the jewel of the Sunset Strip, right there.

Unlike Gazzarri's (which I believe is now Billboard Live) and the Starwood (which closed after the "Wonderland" incident), the Whisky is still very much alive and kickin'. Not bad for a club that opened its doors back in 1964! Man, to this very day, people flock to it, both musicians and music fans alike. Back in the day, the Whisky was owned by a former Chicago policeman named Elmer Valentine, so basically, we are dealing with a different kinda cat here. Yeah, pretty different from Bill Gazzarri and Eddie

Nash, that's for sure. And I believe the club is managed by a gentleman named Mario Maglieri. Over the last four decades, everyone from the Doors to Van Halen has paid their dues at the Whisky. Not to mention that fact that everyone from Hendrix to Zeppelin played there as well.

However, the funny thing is, despite making it to the Whisky (which is basically the "promised land" for up and coming bands, far as clubs go), it would once again be at the Starwood where they'd get disco, well, re-discovered almost a year to the day Gene Simmons had found them. This all went down in May of 1977, when Van Halen was playing the Starwood on a miserable, rainy Monday night in front of like ten people. But out of those ten people at the show, two of them were scouting the band. They'd actually seen the band the night before and had come back again on Monday night. It was as if they just could not believe what they had seen and heard the first night, so they went home, slept on it, and came back again to make sure this was for real. These two people were none other than Mo Ostin and Ted Templeman.

Mo Ostin was the president of Warner Brothers Records. Ted Templeman was a very well-respected producer who'd already worked with great bands like Montrose and the Doobie Brothers. Apparently, a copy of the Gene Simmons demo ended up in the hands of a cat named Marshall Berle. He was blown away by it and so he took Mo and Ted to see VH at the Starwood. If the name rings a bell, it's probably cuz Marshall went on to become Van Halen's manager for a brief time before a gentleman named Noel Monk took the helm as their manager for the entire classic era.

Well, Mo and Ted were absolutely blown away by what they witnessed at the Starwood and knew they had to work with these guys. They offered Van Halen a contract on the spot. Damn, this is the kinda shit that only happens in movies, you know? So, of course, you'd think the boys would immediately jump at the offer, right? Amazingly, this was not the case. The band's response was to tell Mo and Ted that they'd think about it. Well, they thought about it for about twenty-four hours and signed the contract the next day! Van Halen was now officially signed to Warner Brothers. As Gene Simmons had done a year earlier, Ted Templeman wanted to get Van Halen into the studio *immediately.* He had really been blown away by the band – *especially* by Edward Van Halen's insane guitar playing.

Ted Templeman: "I've worked with such legendary guitar players as Allan Holdsworth, Ronnie Montrose, Eric Clapton, Lowell George and Steve Vai, but none of them come close to having Ed's fantastic combination of chops and musicianship. I rank him along with Charlie Parker and Art Tatum as one of the three greatest musicians of my lifetime. Unfortunately, I don't think Ed puts himself in that class."

Basically, Ted Templeman wanted to take the sound of Edward's guitar and blast it off all over the world. He immediately booked the band at Sunset Sound Studio in Los Angeles and began to work on a demo tape. They quickly cut a twenty-five-song demo for Warner Brothers. Then, of course, comes the process of figuring which of these songs would end up making up what would become Van Halen's debut album. And when I say quickly, I mean *quickly*. All the music on their debut album was recorded in just twenty-one days, ladies and gentlemen. Well, the music itself was actually cut in just six days, while the vocals took about fifteen days.

Finally, they would settle on nine songs off that demo (plus one song, "Jamie's Cryin," which they had written in the studio) and a little instrumental/solo piece called "Eruption." Ted had actually heard Edward messing around with this piece in the studio and had him cut it for the album. Overall, their debut album would contain eleven tracks.

Meanwhile, for the rest of 1977, the band would continue to play their original sets over at the Whisky A Go-Go. At the same time, Ted Templeman and the folks at Warner Brothers were preparing a plan as to when and how they wanted to release their debut album. Well, a release date would finally be set for February 10, 1978.

1978 Rookie of the Year

"I'd stopped playing, didn't even want any guitars around. But while I was in Milwaukee I went to see two shows. One was because Neal Schon [Journey] said to me, 'Leslie, you gotta check out this kid who's opening for us; he plays guitar like an organ, like a Bach organ fugue.' I was totally taken aback—it was Eddie Van Halen, and he impressed me the way Clapton impressed me."

— Leslie West

As 1978 began, the world had never heard of Van Halen. It's hard to imagine a time when that name wasn't out there, you know? The big music of this time was disco and punk. Although I must admit that there were a few great rock bands out there that were doing well, commercially speaking. But disco and punk were truly ruling all. Oh, and as far as breaking new ground in the world of rock music, there really wasn't a whole lotta that going on either, to put it mildly. The world of guitar was going through the same thing – *especially* the world of rock guitar. During an interview with *Guitar Player* magazine that would appear in their December 1977 issue, the great Les Paul was asked if he liked any of the currently popular guitarists. His response pretty much summed up the state of guitar at this time.

Les Paul: "Oh, sure. There are a lot of them I like for certain things. It seems to me that there's a number of guys that got a lot of things going for them, and I could understand what they're doing. And I can't say that any of them seems to have a corner on the market, I think everyone would agree: There is no one guy shining, no one guy who is king above all."

Oh boy, was that ever about to change. In fact, that change would come within just two months of Les Paul making that statement. I can give you a precise date, too. February 10, 1978. That is the day Van Halen's self-titled debut would hit record stores. Basically, that is the day *everything* changed, overnight. Suddenly, one guy was shining. Suddenly, one guy was king above all.

Van Halen is a classic, groundbreaking album. There are only a handful of bands and guitarists in the history of rock music who changed the face of rock and reinvented the guitar when they hit the scene. Edward Van Halen and his band managed to do both, all at once. Folks, I could probably sit here and give you that "Van Halen kicked rock 'n' roll in the ass!" cliché bullshit, but that would be so goddamn VH1 of me. Nah dude, Van Halen kicked rock 'n' roll in the *balls,* and when it was lying on the floor they stepped on its throat and went after its sister.

The mayhem actually began in January '78, when their cover of the Kinks' "You Really Got Me" began to get airplay on about thirty-five radio stations across the United States. By the end of January, it was being played on over 140 stations! The single exploded and was being requested from coast to coast. This helped build a nice buzz for the band, which is precisely what the folks at Warner Brothers had hoped for. The funny thing is, this was not part of some master plan. Fact is, it happened by accident.

Apparently, Edward had been hanging out with some of his buds from a band called Angel. This was before their debut album was to be released, ok? Well, the boys in Angel were bragging about some of the stuff they had recorded. In turn, Edward told them to check out what his band had been doing. So they all went to the house of Angel's drummer, Barry Brandt, kicked back, and listened to a copy of the yet-to-be-released *Van Halen* album.

Well, that was a big mistake. You see, the boys in Angel liked what they heard. I mean, they *really* liked what they heard, and Edward left there feeling pretty good cuz he could tell they really liked it. Well, the very next morning, Edward received a call from Ted Templeman. Ted wanted to know if Edward had played a copy of the *Van Halen* album for anyone. The funny thing is that not only had Edward played a copy of the album for the boys in Angel, he'd actually played it for many other people, too! When he told Ted what he'd done, well, to say Ted was pissed would be putting it mildly. You see, somehow Ted got word that Angel had rushed into the studio to cut their very own version of "You Really Got Me," which, of course, would then be released as a single. Basically, they were trying to release a single of "You Really Got Me" (which was, um, quite similar to VH's version) *before* Van Halen released their debut album!

44

Once Ted heard about it, a decision was made to immediately get the VH version out there first. So before their debut album hit stores, VH's cover of "You Really Got Me" was released as a single in January of 1978. Well, it ended up working out great for them. Although Edward was not really pleased with the fact that they had released a cover as their first single. He definitely would have preferred one of their original songs. But hey, it wasn't his call. In the end, I think it was the smart thing to do. I mean, the VH version of "You Really Got Me" is a true classic. They definitely made it their own. Besides, that was just a teaser of what was yet to come. If people were blown away by Van Halen's searing cover of that Kinks tune, well, they hadn't heard anything yet. When their debut finally hit stores on February 10, well, to quote a line from the classic film *Animal House,* "War's over, man...Wormer dropped the big one."

Upon the release of *Van Halen,* you could hear jaws collectively dropping worldwide. The music exploded out of your speakers with incredible power and energy. It was raw yet tight. Front to back, all killer, no filler. And what can you say about that guitar? I mean, is that a *guitar?* What the hell is *that?* Not since Jimi Hendrix had someone taken people's preconceived notions of what an electric guitar could do and so thoroughly pissed all over 'em. However, Edward Van Halen didn't break the rules. As far as he was concerned, there were no rules! What he did went *way* beyond that. Overall, it's an album that marries otherworldly guitar with great songwriting in a way rarely seen before or since. For a full track list and review, please turn to the VH Discography.

Believe me when I tell you that even to this very day, the impact of the first Van Halen album is still very much felt. As I mentioned before, at the time the album came out, rock music and guitar in general were simply not seeing any new ground being broken. While some rock bands were selling records, disco was really all the rage, and punk rock was exploding, too.

This album helped the electric guitar and guitar-driven rock/metal regain their proper place in the world, baby. Van Halen basically "crashed the party," so to speak. Without so much as an invitation, they just showed up and proceeded to crush everything in their path, from disco to you name it. Eddie and the boys simply stepped up and showed the entire world that hard rock/metal music and the electric guitar were not all used up or maxed out. Not even close.

Jimmy Page: "People always think the guitar is reaching its limits. They thought guitar music was stagnating in the late seventies, and then Eddie Van Halen comes in and changes everything. For my money, Eddie was the first significant new kid on the block.

Very dazzling. And I think he played a vital role in keeping kids interested, because they could look up to this cheeky little guy with the big smile. He flew the flag well, I think."

So part one of their mission was complete. Now that they were armed with an amazing album, it was time to take it to the people. The band would play their final club shows at the end of February 1978. They did a couple gigs over at the Pasadena Civic and what would be their last real club gig ever at the Whisky A Go-Go on February 25, 1978. Not even a week later, their first official tour began. The band was to hit the road in support of major rock acts of that time such as Journey and Montrose.

Later on into the tour they even opened shows for Edward and Alex's heroes, Black Sabbath! The tour began on March 3 at the Aragon Ballroom in Chicago, Illinois and continued all the way till the very first week of December! After payin' dues in clubs since 1974, Van Halen was now payin' dues as an opening act by playing about 140 shows on that first tour. It was grueling, but these guys were young and hungry. They toured America, Europe, and Japan. As an opening act, they would only get about a half hour to play, but they made the most of it every single night and just attacked each show.

Whereas many young bands might be intimidated, Van Halen simply weren't. They went out there every night and tore it up. No different than they'd done a million times before over at Gazzarri's, the Whisky, the Starwood, and so forth. You have to remember, it's 1978. There is no MTV, no Internet, or anything like that. You couldn't just make a video, throw it out there, and become known overnight. All you had back then was your music and your live show, that's it. Lucky for Van Halen, they were even better live than on record.

But it wasn't easy, you know, being the new kids on the block. The headliner doesn't always appreciate feeling the heat of some new unknown band that's there to warm up *their* crowd. Van Halen went out on a nightly basis and flat out *killed*. They were young and fiery and just tore it up every single night. Even Black Sabbath struggled to follow these youngbloods, and that's Black *motherfuckin'* Sabbath, ok? That is one of the greatest bands of all time, but by 1978 they just couldn't hang. Ozzy Osbourne knew it, too.

Ozzy Osbourne: "They blew us off the stage every night. It was so embarrassing. We didn't have the fire anymore. They kicked our asses, but it convinced me of two things: my days with Black Sabbath were over, and Van Halen was going to be a very successful band."

Right here we have the changing of the guard, with Black Sabbath basically passing the torch to Van Halen. But Sabbath weren't the only ones to feel VH's heat on this tour. The boys in Journey knew VH had the fire as well. Which is saying something, cuz Journey is a terrific band, led by great players like Neal Schon, Aynsley Dunbar, and Gregg Rolie. It's just not easy when you have a young, hungry band going out every single night trying to make a name for itself. Van Halen had that fire in their belly, man.

During that first tour, VH crossed paths with and opened for many great bands. Aside from Black Sabbath and Journey, they crossed paths with Boston, Foreigner, Ted Nugent, and Pat Travers. Remember, back in 1978, you had big festival shows. Legendary festivals like the California Jam, the Texxas Jam, and Bill Graham's Day on the Green in Oakland, California.

In fact, it was at the Day on the Green Festival in July 1978 that VH ran into another young up-and-coming band, AC/DC. Man, right here you got two of the greatest, most slammin' hard rock units of all time. And remember that back in 1978, AC/DC were being fronted by the legendary Bon Scott. Other acts on the bill were Pat Travers, Aerosmith, and Foreigner. Overall, it was definitely one of the biggest concerts of the '70s. There were about 60,000 people in attendance...one of which was a fifteen-year-old kid from San Francisco named Kirk.

> **Kirk Hammett:** "A gig I remember going to that had a huge impact on me was the 1978 Day on the Green festival in Oakland, California, when AC/DC, Van Halen, Pat Travers, and Aerosmith were all on the bill. There I was, a young kid, barely able to play a barre chord, and all these bad-assed guitarists were appearing together under one roof—Joe Perry, Brad Whitford, Angus Young, Pat Travers, and Eddie Van Halen. As you can imagine, it was one of the most awe-inspiring shows I've ever seen."

At this show, Van Halen actually went on after AC/DC played and they really had to work, cuz AC/DC absolutely ripped live. In fact, Bon Scott is actually Edward Van Halen's favorite rock 'n' roll singer of all time. Not to mention the fact that Edward has always professed tremendous respect for Angus and Malcom Young as well. You see, AC/DC are a "brother band," just like VH with Edward and Alex. I guess you can say that Edward really likes AC/DC. It was definitely a tall order for a young band on their very first tour to follow the boys from down under. Lucky for Van Halen, they went out there and were able to hold their own. AC/DC were young, but they had already been touring and releasing albums since the mid-'70s. These guys were definitely at the top of their game and well on their way to superstardom. Meanwhile, the boys in Aerosmith were already there!

Aerosmith was one of the top American rock bands at this time. There might have been some turmoil going on within the band, specifically between Steven Tyler and Joe Perry, but commercially speaking, they were at their absolute zenith. From 1975 to 1978, Aerosmith had scored one Gold album and three consecutive Platinum albums. Not to mention the fact that they were still very much a top concert draw, despite the occasional off night due to their wild partying. Didn't matter though, cuz Van Halen went out and just took it to 'em. The boys in Aerosmith became another band to feel VH's heat, big time. Lucky for them, they only crossed paths with Van Halen a couple times during 1978.

Black Sabbath, Aerosmith, and Journey are three monster bands. They are truly giants in their respective styles. But honestly, would *you* wanna follow Van Halen on stage, especially on their first tour? Dave was about twenty-three. Mike and Alex were about twenty-four. Edward had just turned twenty-three. "Young, dumb, and full of cum," ever hear that saying? There was a whole lotta fire and testosterone here, folks. I wouldn't wanna follow them on stage *today*. Imagine in 1978 when they were just kids going out there trying to prove themselves? Man, it was tough enough to just follow Edward! The kid went out on that first tour and introduced himself to the world by dropping bombs every single night. Van Halen was definitely one of the best and toughest opening acts, *ever*.

Sadly, this doesn't always go over well with the acts you are opening for. I've come across a 1982 interview with *Guitar Player* magazine where Edward tells the story about how he ran into Joe Perry backstage at one of those Festival shows in '78. Basically, Edward saw Joe backstage at one of those festivals they played together. Apparently, he walked up to Joe to shake his hand and tell him how much he liked Aerosmith. Well, Joe Perry just turned his back and walked away. Folks, you don't have to be a rocket scientist to figure out why this happened. But I don't believe it was anything personal, really. The thing is, well, would you like to get your ass handed to you by a guy who looks like he should have a curfew? Man, Edward was just a kid on his very first tour, but he was out there tearin' people a new one every single night! It was simply *impossible* to follow a phenom like that, even though Joe is a great player. Although I must admit these days Joe Perry has actually been quite complimentary of Edward during interviews, so I'm guessing there were never any hard feelings there. In fact, during an interview with the *Boston Globe*'s Steve Morse in 2004, Joe had nothing but praise for Edward.

Joe Perry: "No one can play guitar like Eddie. He took everything that went before him and said, 'I've heard all of that before.' And then introduced all the finger-tapping stuff that he does. And not only is he a great player, he's a great showman, and that's what it's all about."

Frankly, I think anyone would have lot a little sleep over having to follow Edward on stage. Hell, it didn't help that the rest of the band killed, as well. By this time Dave Roth had become "David Lee Roth," and it wasn't long before he became *the* frontman in rock. David was a "rock god" in every sense of the word. Call him a "rock god," "metal god" or whatever you like, but Dave was just the coolest guy on stage. He was *"the man."* Mike and Alex laid it down full-force and were rock solid, as always. Edward had basically reinvented the guitar, period.

In fact, Van Halen could even be given credit for lighting a fire under Aerosmith's ass when the boys from Beantown eventually found themselves struggling by the early '80s. During an interview with *SPIN* magazine in 1997, Steven Tyler described how seeing Classic Van Halen impacted him. Frankly, it reminds me of the epiphany Jake Blues had while he and his brother Elwood danced at the back of the Triple Rock Church in the classic film, *The Blues Brothers*. Only in this case, "the light" came from a television set.

Steven Tyler: "In the middle of my morphine haze, I was watching TV and I saw Eddie Van Halen and David Lee Roth jumping around and I thought, 'What the fuck is this?' They're a great band, but coming from an ego place with Aerosmith, I thought, 'We've got to get the fucking band back together.'"

Folks, when you can snap Steven Tyler out of a morphine haze and inspire him to reunite with Joe Perry, well, you know you are making quite a powerful impact. And just like Lord Tyler, the rest of the rock world was snapped out of its haze, as well, along with millions of people everywhere. All around the country, word began to spread like wildfire about this amazing young band. The rest of the planet wasn't far behind, either. Van Halen's energy and power was simply brutal. It was undeniable. The bar had been raised, big time. As had been the case during their backyard party and club days, it was through their killer live show and word of mouth that Van Halen began to get recognized and earn its reputation. As word of mouth spread, album sales soared. Within just three months of release, *Van Halen* went Gold. A Gold album in today's market is still a terrific achievement, but back in the late '70s, man, it basically meant you had made it.

Their debut album raced up the Billboard Album Chart, cracking the Top 20 and peaking at the number 19 spot. How impressive is that? Man, this is most impressive – *especially* for a debut album. By comparison, it had taken Aerosmith's classic debut album almost three years to achieve Gold status and, upon release, it had peaked at the number 166 spot on the Billboard Album Chart. By the end of the 1978 tour, *Van Halen* had sold almost 2 million copies in the U.S. alone. It would eventually go on to earn a Diamond Award for selling over 10 million copies in the U.S. alone. Basically, you could say Van Halen had arrived. They had begun their 1978 tour as complete unknowns. However, halfway through that tour, a whole lot of people were showing up to see them. They were all over radio and people were actually showing up to see an *opening act*. You know, most people use the time an opening act is on stage to go get beer and take a piss.

Well, this was not the case with Van Halen. Fact is, people began to actually show up to these concerts early just to see them. Many guitarists scrambled to get seats close to the stage so as to get a look at the young master's gear, technique, and so forth. The word was out, baby.

These kids from Pasadena were *no joke.* By the last leg of that first tour all the major rock magazines were descending upon the band to find out just who the hell these kids were.

What you are about to read is the introduction to an article about Van Halen that appeared in the September 1978 issue of *Hard Rock* magazine. Eileen Sperber, a writer for HRM, went to check out Van Halen during that first tour. In her article, titled "**Van Halen: Will They Be the Biggest Heavy Metal Monsters since Led Zeppelin?**" she wrote:

> **The long haired kid in the row up front turned around in his seat and spoke to me "Van Halen is going to be the next Led Zeppelin," and from the tone in his voice I knew he was speaking with personal sincerity. But, come on, the mighty Zep—now that's a band to beat. Certainly this relatively unknown West Coast-based group couldn't be in the same league as those great British rockers.**
>
> **By the time I left the theater that night I thought I must be dreaming. Van Halen is everything they promised to be—and more. They just happen to be one of the most exciting new bands around, and from the reaction audiences have been extending them, it won't be long before Van Halen is performing in large halls and outdoor stadiums just like the superstar groups they are out to compete with.**

Not a bad intro, huh? Could you imagine a young unknown band, on tour in support of their first album, actually being mentioned in the same breath as Led Zeppelin? Hell, could you imagine *any* band being mentioned in the same breath as Led Zeppelin? Well, fact is, Van Halen was – and on their very first tour, no less. During her article, Eileen also points out, "Every time Van Halen goes on stage they put themselves on the line and give the best they've got to offer. They literally work their balls off for the audience." The folks over at *Circus* magazine laid some serious praise on the boys as well. David Fricke was a writer for *Circus* back in 1978 and he did an article on VH that appeared in their August 3, 1978 issue. Here's a sampling of what he wrote in this article about Van Halen's debut album:

"From Raunch to Riches"

With a debut album already gone Gold and nudging Platinum, Van Halen, a fierce California foursome, snowballed their way to fame with a relentless rock & roll attack that even certified crowdpleasers like Aerosmith and Black Sabbath may find hard to beat ...Van Halen appear ready to take on all comers and the odds look impressive.

Folks, I wasn't kidding when I mentioned earlier that Aerosmith and Black Sabbath felt their heat, big time. Van Halen was dropping adrenaline-soaked performances every single night, and it seems everyone from the bands they were opening for to unsuspecting concertgoers were caught in the crossfire. Basically, they had people losing their minds. What was even wilder is the fact that many of the people in attendance who were losing their minds were women. As had been the case during their high school and club days, lots of women showed up to see them, too. Van Halen was one of those rare bands that managed to rock hard and kick ass while building a very healthy following of women. When that happens, well, you know you're definitely doing something right. Their concerts became Black Sabbath-meets-Tom Jones. Basically, dudes were throwin' up the horns while girls were throwin' up bras and panties.

Needless to say, the band quickly began to earn a reputation for being a rowdy bunch of motherfuckers onstage *and* offstage. For example, you know how some bands trash hotel rooms? Well, Van Halen trashed *entire floors.* I'm not joking, either. For example, during a tour stop in Madison, Wisconsin, the band stayed at the Sheraton Inn. Apparently, the seventh floor didn't survive their visit. Not bad for a buncha rookies. In fact, if you check the "Thanks to" in the liner notes for their second album, 1979's *Van Halen II,* you'll see the following:

Thanks to: All at Warner Bros., and WEA worldwide, the guiding influence of Premier Talent, The Road Company, the Sheraton Inn (seventh floor), Madison, Wisconsin, and all the hall managers who waded through the rubble of Van Halenized backstages around the world.

Susan Masino is a rock journalist and radio dj. Back in 1978, however, Susan was the associate editor for the *Emerald City Chronicle* in Madison. When Van Halen rolled into Madison to play the Shuffle Inn, back in March of 1978, Susan was able to attend the show and hang out with the band backstage. As mind-blowing as that was, things were about to get even wilder. Along with attending the concert, Susan was also able to go over to the Sheraton Hotel, hang out with the band, and bear witness to some of the madness.

> **Susan Masino:** "Some of their antics included tapping frozen fish to the ceiling of the hallway (to thaw for later, of course) and locking Eddie out of his room during one of the many times Madison's Finest were called to the scene. As the police questioned Eddie about the noise problem they were called for, Alex pretended to be asleep in his 'empty' room while ten or fifteen people snickered in the darkness. On the last night they were in town, Alex tried to throw a table out of his hotel window onto the parking lot seven floors below. Just mentioning the fact that it was definitely coming out of Alex's paycheck seemed to do the trick. On the fourth night, we all went to the Riverside Theater in Milwaukee to see them perform with Journey and Montrose. That night I met Leslie West, the legendary guitarist from Mountain, who had come out to see 'this Van Halen kid who everyone has been talking about.'
>
> "All in all, it was a week that shall live in infamy. We had all been Van Halenized, and would never be the same again. Whether they are at the Shuffle Inn, the Sheraton, or playing in sold out stadiums around the world, Van Halen is the definitive rock 'n' roll party band. In the first press kit that I received on them, there was a description that still holds up today, 'We celebrate the sex and rebellion on television, all of the rockin' on the radio, the movies, the cars and everything about being young or semi-young at heart. That's Van Halen.' I couldn't have said it better myself!"

In other words, the term "adrenaline-soaked performance" could now be used to describe what went down onstage, backstage, on the tour bus, and at the hotel, too. Hey, can you really blame them? Man, I just like to believe they reacted how most people would, given their situation. Look, if you're in your early twenties and getting to live out your dream, well, what the hell would you do? Light a sparkler, call for a group hug, and recite excerpts from a Tony Robbins self-help book? Hell no! Basically, Van Halen picked up where Led Zeppelin and the Who left off and just went ballistic. They did what any normal, red-blooded American kid would do in that situation. They basically went nuts, partied their ass off, and nailed everything that wasn't nailed down, so to speak. Do we really need details here? Let's just say they would partake in all the *excess* that comes with being a great rock 'n' roll band. Amen. In fact, it wasn't long before they had earned the title "America's Premier Party Band." You better believe that title was well-earned, baby.

Sadly, we live in a day and age where rock 'n' roll more resembles a therapy session than a party. Many bands actually seem bummed by their success. Others go on television and actually whine about having "partied too hard" or whatever. Even worse, you got some idiots runnin' around, struttin' and actin' like "rock stars," complete with tats and all, who simply are not "walkin' the walk," so to speak. Man, screw all the whiners and posers. Van Halen worked their ass off, paid their dues, and when they finally broke through, they truly enjoyed themselves.

After all, they are and always have been a "rock 'n' roll band." Sadly, most people out there don't even know the term "rock 'n' roll" equals "sex." You know, to "rock 'n' roll all night long, baby." This is *not* a term used to describe a procedure one performs during a fire drill, ok? Man, rock 'n' roll = sex. That is something I have always loved about this band. Van Halen made *no* apologies for enjoying their success and having a good time. I mean, if the Beatles, the Stones, Led Zeppelin, and the Who never apologized for having a good time, then why should Van Halen?

Basically, rock 'n' roll is wild party music. It came from the blues, which is wild party music, too. I mean, when's the last time you walked into a blues bar and saw a buncha people sittin' around, cryin' in their beer? When you walk into a blues bar, you'll see people partyin', drinkin', dancin', and gettin' it on, baby. Well, rock 'n' roll is the same way, just like its daddy, the blues. The apple does *not* fall far from the tree, ok? One of the coolest things about Van Halen is the fact that they took their craft *extremely* serious, but they never took *themselves* serious. It's rare to find that in a band, especially a very talented one.

By the end of 1978, it was clear who the new young band to watch was. Hell, just one look at any of the big music magazines at this time proved it. Remember, back in '78 there was no MTV and no Internet. If you wanted to learn all about a band, you only really had one option: magazines. Back in the day, magazines were like the Bible. And the fact is that just about all of 'em flocked to VH, immediately. From *Hard Rock* and *Circus* to *Guitar Player* and *Musician*.

However, as great a job as most of 'em did, I don't think any of 'em dedicated more covers and pages inside their magazine to VH than the legendary *Creem*. Basically, from 1978-1984, Van Halen appeared on the cover of *Creem* more times than any other artist out there. I mean, it wasn't even close. Man, the good folks at *Creem* even dedicated an entire issue to VH! Yup, an all Van Halen issue, baby. More than anyone else, *Creem* definitely had VH's back, big time.

So by the end of 1978, everyone knew. Well, almost everyone, anyway. Unlike the good folks over at *Creem, Hard Rock, Guitar Player,* and so forth, *Rolling Stone* magazine's Charles M. Young didn't much care for Van Halen, at all. In his review of Van Halen's debut album for *RS* back in 1978, among other things, Charles laid down these glowing words of wisdom:

"Mark my words: in three years, Van Halen is going to be fat and self-indulgent and disgusting, and they'll follow Deep Purple and Led Zeppelin right into the toilet."

So, Charles, tell me, how does crow taste? All kidding aside, the fact that they were so tough on VH was not surprising, really. After all, this is the magazine that spent the first half of the '70s slamming a little band from England called Led Zeppelin. Yeah, um, nice going. In fact, from 1978 to 1984, take a wild guess how many times Van Halen appeared on the cover of *Rolling Stone* magazine? Come on, just guess. You ready? Well, from 1978 to 1984, Van Halen appeared on the cover of *Rolling Stone* a grand total of... drum roll please...zero times. Yeah, you heard me right. *Zero,* baby. Here we have, what was during this period, the biggest and most successful American rock band on the planet. Hell, arguably the biggest rock band on the planet, period. With the baddest and most innovative rock guitarist since the great Jimi Hendrix. Apparently, in *Rolling Stone's* eyes, that doesn't merit a cover. Not one. Man, that's unbelievable to me. I mean, what the hell happened? Come on, y'all are better than that. Well, at least I like to believe so.

Nonetheless, Van Halen exploded onto the scene and rock music would never sound or look the same again. It was also clear that guitar would never be the same, either. Everything changed with their debut album. A new era of rock *and* guitar began in 1978. In fact, you could say the 1980s actually began in 1978. *Van Halen* can be described so many ways. It is one of the greatest debut albums, ever. It is one of the greatest guitar albums, ever. It is one of the greatest hard rock/metal albums, ever. It single-handedly ushered in the modern era of "shred" guitar. It is the most groundbreaking guitar album since Jimi Hendrix's *Are You Experienced* (1967).

Just like Jimi's debut, as well as *Led Zeppelin* (1969), *Appetite for Destruction* (1987), and *Nevermind* (1991), Van Halen's debut album clearly marks the beginning of a new era in rock music. It's a true classic and I have actually heard every single song on that album played on the radio.

Honestly, how many albums can you say that about? Can someone even begin to calculate how many copies of *Van Halen* were worn out by guitar players repeatedly dropping the needle on "Eruption," alone? Could you even be a true rocker or metalhead and not own this album? Could you possibly be a guitar player and not own this album? Again, while legendary bands like Led Zeppelin, Guns N' Roses, and Nirvana changed the face of rock, VH changed the face of rock *and* reinvented the guitar.

When it comes down to it, I don't care if you're into rock, metal, punk, alternative, nu-metal, pop, or whatever. Seriously, the style of music you may be into is completely irrelevant. When Edward Van Halen hit the scene, it was all eyes on him, baby. Man, the fact is most musicians have owned or heard this debut album at one point or another in their lives.

For example, Billy Corgan, Yngwie J. Malmsteen, Slash, and Jake E. Lee are four legendary musicians who consider *Van Halen* to be a monumental recording and grew up cuttin' their teeth on this album. Back when this album dropped in February '78, Billy was ten, Yngwie was fourteen, Slash was twelve, and Jake E. was twenty-one. So basically, they each experienced the explosive arrival of Van Halen and were absolutely blown away.

Billy Corgan: "*Van Halen* was the ultimate play along album, and I'd pick up a lick here and there. But it was more the feeling behind it. If you wanted to draw a parallel between my attack style of lead guitar and someone else, it's totally Van Halen. In his early days he was an *attack* guitar player. That guy had some fucking balls and that ability to translate gut feeling is what separated Eddie from everybody else."

Yngwie J. Malmsteen: "When I heard the first Van Halen album, I couldn't believe how great the guitar playing was—and I heard that album at a point when I didn't like any of the new guitar players. I mean, he totally changed the whole guitar field—and he's still as great now as he's ever been. I would love to jam with him."

Slash: "In junior high school *[original Guns N' Roses drummer]* Steven Adler and I would race our bikes and cut through the school fence so we could hang out, smoke pot and do chicks. One day he played 'Eruption/You Really Got Me' for me, and I couldn't believe the intensity of it. We listened to that first Van Halen album constantly. But I never picked up on that whole whammy-bar, tapping school of playing. But the last time I saw Eddie *[Van Halen]*, he really gave me some nice compliments on my solo in 'Paradise City.' Suddenly

I realized that even though I never tried to imitate him, I do have a knack for going for the same kind of fast, fluid passages he does—which I obviously picked up from listening to Van Halen records."

Jake E. Lee: "Eddie had an enormous influence on my playing. In the late '70s I was becoming bored with 'rock' guitar (other than Uli Roth) and I was in a couple of different bands, looking for a direction. Even auditioned for...ohhh...I forgot his name...he was the violinist in the original Mahavishnu Orchestra, wait...oh yeah, Jerry Goodman's band (didn't get it)...when all stakes were raised by Mr. Van Halen. I was so impressed with his playing, and fire, and innovativeness, that I got back into playing rock with a whole new outlook and vision of what I wanted to accomplish. And, of course, like everyone else, I tried desperately to get that 'brown sound' every time I plugged in! Finally settled for what I could get, but still use him as a reference point when I'm in the studio. Not since Jimi [Hendrix] has anyone turned the entire rock guitar scene upside-sideways-down-everywhichway and loose, like Eddie did."

So it was really no surprise that by the end of 1978, Edward Van Halen had been voted "Best New Talent" in *Guitar Player* magazine's Annual Readers Poll. What is really cool is the fact that this is voted on by the *people,* and they definitely knew who the new "young gun" was. And before the year was over, Edward had also given his very first official interview to *Guitar Player* magazine, as well. Legendary music journalist Jas Obrecht scored the first ever Edward Van Halen interview and it's a great read. You can actually locate it online at *Guitar Player's* official Web site in their "Archives" section, and over at *www.van-halen.com* as well.

Overall, it was about as good a debut as any band could ever hope for. They worked hard every single night and made it the old fashioned way: with their music and live show. Fact is, they are one of the last great bands that can claim that. Once MTV hit the airwaves in the fall of 1981, the game would change, forever. But in 1978, Van Halen went out there armed with nothing more than a killer album and live show. They did it how Led Zeppelin, the Who, Black Sabbath, Jimi Hendrix, and all the other greats did it: by taking their music to the people and playing everywhere. Basically, they *earned* everything they got, and that's how you do it, baby.

Soon as the first tour wrapped in early December, the band took a quick five-day vacation down in Mexico. They deserved it, cuz they'd just spent about nine straight months on the road playing night after night. After their little break, they immediately went back into the studio to work on what would become the follow-up to their debut album. Pressure had already begun to mount. Could they do it again? How do you follow up a monster debut like *Van Halen*? Would there be the dreaded "sophomore jinx?" Any doubts would soon be quickly extinguished. This was actually the beginning of what was to become one of the most impressive, influential, and successful eras any rock band has ever experienced.

Classic Van Halen '78 - '84

"No band flaunted the hard rock lifestyle of high times, hot women and general excess more flamboyantly than Van Halen...especially with its original frontman, David Lee Roth."

– Kurt Loder

The success Van Halen achieved during their classic era is absolutely staggering. I've heard people say that Aerosmith is America's Rolling Stones. If that is the case, then Classic VH is America's Led Zeppelin. I can't think of too many other bands in the history of rock music who possessed the kind of juice VH had during this period. They simply could do no wrong.

Van Halen exploded onto the scene in 1978 and basically became the hottest young band on the planet, along with Edward becoming known as the baddest motherfucker since Jimi, period. They had begun 1978 as total and complete unknowns. By the end of the year, people not only knew their name, they even knew how to spell it and pronounce it properly, too. The new era of rock was here and they were leading the way. Van Halen quickly became the band all other bands would be measured against, onstage *and* off. Dave became "the bar" for frontmen, and Edward "the bar" for guitarists.

As 1979 began, people were eagerly awaiting their second album. The boys didn't keep 'em waiting long. After their first tour ended and they took that quick vacation, the band went back into the studio and emerged just six days later with a new album. To say these guys worked fast is an understatement. I mean, an album of killer music in just six freakin' days? Um, I think it takes most bands six days just to tune their guitars.

Their second album was titled, appropriately enough, *Van Halen II*. It was released on March 23, 1979 and it did pretty well. That's if you consider "pretty well" to be another hit record! In fact, *Van Halen II* went Gold just one week after its release. About a month later, it had gone Platinum! The album raced up the Billboard Chart, cracking the Top 10 and peaking at the number 6 spot. From this point on, every single album Van Halen released throughout their career would make its home somewhere in the Top 10 on the Billboard Album Chart. That's just freakin' amazing. Their second album also contained what would become the band's very first Top 20 hit, "Dance the Night Away." So much for the 'ole "sophomore jinx," huh? For a full track list and review, please turn to the VH Discography.

Basically, their status was set and they were here to stay. Soon as the album was released, they embarked on another tour. This became standard operating procedure for Van Halen during their classic era. They would go into the studio, quickly pound out an album, and then tour for the rest of the year. As the song says, one foot out the door. The 1979 tour was known as the "World Vacation Tour." It kicked off on March 25 in Fresno, California. and continued till October. The band played about 120 shows on this tour. Again, it was grueling, but they persevered and continued to win over audiences everywhere they went with their superb musicianship and insane energy.

Brother Cane guitarist/frontman Damon Johnson was just fifteen years old back in 1979, when he and his buddies in Renegade (his first garage band) hooked up in Birmingham, Alabama to see VH in concert. Basically, you could say it was a life-changing experience.

Damon Johnson: "That show completely changed my whole life. I remember the four of us with our arms around each other, screaming the lyrics to 'Ain't Talkin' 'bout Love,' while David Lee Roth held the microphone out to us. And Eddie Van Halen was just...God, he just crushed me. The guitar playing, the volume, the lights...the whole experience just blew my face off. I am a musician to this very day because of that show."

It also was during their second tour that Alex Van Halen actually began lighting his drum kit on fire. Apparently, Big Al would pour some kind of tiki-torch fluid or lighter fluid on his drumheads and spark 'em up. He'd also dip the tip of his drumsticks into the fluid and play with them while they were on fire as well. The effect was truly mind-blowing. Unfortunately, Alex managed to spark himself up one time, too! Needless to say, um, the fire drums were removed from the show by the end of the tour. I believe the closest he'd ever come to that again would be when he'd light the big gong behind his drum kit on fire. You can see that cool effect during the end of the band's music video for "Unchained," taken from a live show in Oakland, California during their 1981 tour.

The really cool thing is that by 1979, the band was actually headlining many of their shows. They'd gone from being an unknown opening act to headliner status in one year. Not bad at all, boys. Edward continued to rack up praise and awards. In 1979, he was voted "Best Guitarist" in *Guitar Player* magazine's Annual Readers Poll. Once again, the people had spoken.

In fact, Edward would be voted "Best Guitarist" in 1979, 1980, 1981, 1982, and 1983. Five years in a row, baby. After 1983, he was actually retired from the poll altogether. You see, *Guitar Player* magazine only allows a player to be voted "Best Guitarist" five times in their entire life. Well, Edward won it the first five years he was eligible. So by the ripe old age of twenty-eight, he was retired from the poll. No more fruit cup for you, Mr. Van Halen.

As 1980 began, the band were now full-fledged headliners and easily the biggest American hard rock/metal around. Dave and Edward had already become *the* duo in rock 'n' roll, right up there with Mick and Keef, Plant and Page, and so forth. After their second tour ended, the band took another quick break, and then it was back to the lab to pound out another album. On March 26, 1980 they released their third album, *Women and Children First*. This album was recorded in just seventeen days! Within eight weeks of its release, the album went Gold *and* Platinum! It raced up the Billboard Album Chart, cracking the Top 10 and peaking at the number 6 spot. For a full track list and review, please turn to the VH Discography.

Meanwhile, the folks over at *Circus* magazine gave this album major props during a review in their May 13, 1980 issue, stating: "***Women and Children First*** delivers. A decibel-defying document even esteemed competitions like Aerosmith and Ted Nugent may find hard to beat."

Soon as the album hit the street, the band did as well. Actually, they hit the road a few days before the album had even been released. Their third tour was to be known as the "World Invasion Tour." It kicked off in Spokane, Washington on March 22, 1980 and continued all the way into November. The band played just over 100 shows on this tour. It was nine months straight on the road, taking their music to the people. In the end, their first headlining tour was a major success and the band was really packin' 'em in.

Billy Sheehan is a legendary virtuoso bass player. In fact, he is considered by many to be the "Eddie Van Halen of bass guitar." Back in 1980, his band, Talas, earned the opening slot on VH's World Invasion Tour. Billy recalls their amazing energy and devastating impact.

Billy Sheehan: "Every night they [Van Halen] were totally awesome. On their worst night they were incredible. Every night I went out front and watched. It was an incredible education on how you perform live. How you do an arena. I'd been a club player my whole life and I was pretty good at that if I do say so myself. I knew how to do the club thing. But I learned so much more about entertainment and how it works from watching that band play night after night. Just sitting and really studying what was goin' on; it was an incredible experience. Dare I say a lot of my success, I think, eventually came from some of the inspiration that I acquired right there."

In terms of energy, their killer live show and music was only matched by their backstage *and* offstage activities. By the start of 1980, Van Halen were now rock royalty. You know, when you achieve this kind of status your roadies are now pretty much walking around wearing T-shirts that read: "NO HEAD, NO PASS." Continuing a trend that began on their very first tour and would last throughout their career, Van Halen was drawing tons of guys *and* gals. At this point, it wasn't uncommon to find a couple hundred chicks standing outside the arena six hours before the show started, demanding to, um, "see the band." In fact, *Rolling Stone* magazine writer Mikal Gilmore went on the road with VH on this tour. Let's just say that 'ole Mikal got a crash course in what being "rock royalty" meant.

Mikal Gilmore: "During my stay with Van Halen, I've seen enough nude women and heard enough graphic, abasing, morning-after anecdotes to fuel an article on porn rock."

This was also the tour that saw the birth of the legendary M&M clause. Ok, lemme explain. When a band plays a show, they have what is known as a "contract rider." Most people simply refer to it as "the rider." The rider is basically a list of things you need for your band and crew. From food and booze to lighting, sound, etc. The rider is then sent over to the venue and it usually ends up in the hands of the promoter. It is then supposed to be followed to a tee. This way, when you get to the gig, you will have everything you need. Well, I guess the boys in the band wanted to see just how closely their rider was being followed, so they came up with the M&M clause. This way, you can tell who's reading and respecting your rider, and who isn't. Basically, strategically placed among all the other items on the rider is one simple item requesting big bowls of M&M candies backstage.

Now, I've actually come across copies of Van Halen's old riders. The clause could usually be found under "MUNCHIES," and here's what it basically looked like:

25 pounds M&M's (Regular, nut nut. NO BROWN ONES.)

It looks harmless enough, right? And this way you can see who is really paying attention to your needs. I mean, if the venue can't even follow a simple demand like removing all brown M&M's from a freakin' bowl, well, how can they be trusted to follow all the other demands? Unfortunately, the folks at the University of Colorado didn't properly follow the rider when VH played a gig at their campus during the 1980 tour. Apparently, they forgot to remove all the brown M&M's from the bowls backstage, and so the band responded by basically demolishing the entire backstage dressing room! I'm talking about thousands of dollars worth of damage, which the band eventually got the bill for. But it's small change considering what it ended up getting the band: *publicity*. Not that it was intended as a publicity stunt. No, that was not the case, at all. And Lord knows Van Halen were already *huge* at this point. The simple fact is that word of this incident got out. Well, the band – especially Diamond Dave – knew there was really no such thing as "bad publicity." So they did the smart thing and totally owned up to what they had done in the press.

Word spread rapidly about the clause and to this very day, you'll find young bands doing their own version of it! From the world of rock to hip-hop, I've heard some of today's biggest acts joke about having candy backstage with a certain color removed. Far as I can tell, it all began with Van Halen back on their 1980 World Invasion Tour.

Ironically enough, the M&M clause would play a part in Edward meeting his future wife. On August 29, 1980, VH played the Hirsh Memorial Arena in Shreveport, Louisiana. At this gig, actress Valerie Bertinelli and her brother Patrick would show up backstage to meet the band. For the people out there who may not know, Valerie was basically "America's Sweetheart." She was the beautiful, talented young star of the hit television show, *One Day at a Time*.

Apparently, Valerie knew all about the M&M clause, cuz she showed up with a bag of M&M's for each member of the band. However, the brown ones were included! Nice touch, Valerie. By all accounts, it was love at first sight between these two. Barely eight months after having met, they would get married. Very cool, indeed. Although, to many people, it was a pretty surprising union. I mean, "America's Sweetheart" marrying the resident "Guitar God" of what was, at that time, the wildest and most raucous band on the planet? Folks, to put that in perspective, um, the modern-day equivalent would be, like, Hilary Duff marrying Zakk Wylde. Well, as far as the whole "Guitar God-marries-America's Sweetheart" thing. Obviously Zakk and Hilary have a pretty good age gap there. When EVH and Valerie wed, Edward had just turned twenty-six and Valerie was days away from her twenty-first birthday.

Soon as the tour ended, the band would take a quick break. Then it was back to the lab to make another record. They would emerge from the studio in just twelve days with an amazing album titled *Fair Warning*. This album was released on April 29, 1981. Within nine weeks, it went Gold, and would later hit Platinum status by the fall. The album quickly raced up the Billboard Album Chart, cracking the Top 10 and peaking at the number 5 spot. It had been their first album to crack the Top 5! For a full track list and review, please turn to the VH Discography.

As had become standard operating procedure for Van Halen, they would quickly make an album, put it out, and tour their ass off in support of that album. The "Fair Warning Tour" would kick off in Nova Scotia on May 12, 1981, and ran till October. In fact, the final gig of this tour was a special gig where Van Halen got to open for none other than the Rolling Stones. The band played about eighty-eight shows on what was to be, up until this point, the largest continental tour in the history of rock music. The band earned a cool $10 million for this tour. Man, it's nice work if you can get it.

I should also point out this is the year where tension really began to brew within Van Halen. Well, between Dave and Edward, specifically. Many people seem to think the shit hit the fan in 1984. Fact is, it really started right here. Hell, there's always been tension between 'em, even going back to the club days. Anyhow, most people have no clue as to just how bad the situation was at this point. Wanna know how bad it had gotten? Edward almost quit Van Halen in 1981. Yeah, you heard me right. The man almost quit *his own band*. Lucky for all of us, Alex Van Halen was able to talk to Edward and convince him to stick it out. Major props go out to Big Al for diffusing a very tense and nearly catastrophic situation.

Once the tour wrapped up, well, you know what's next. The band took another quick break and then went back to the lab again. Van Halen would record their fifth studio album, titled *Diver Down*, in just twelve days. Talk about one foot out the door! I don't think any of their albums till this point had taken more than three weeks to complete. That's just too freakin' cool. *Diver Down* was released on April 14, 1982. Like all the previous VH albums, it would immediately go Gold, then Platinum. In fact, it was the first VH album to ever go Platinum *before* a tour began. The album quickly raced up the Billboard Album Chart, cracking the Top 10 and peaking at the number 3 spot! At this point, Van Halen had scored five consecutive Platinum albums, folks. The reason I bring this fact up is because this set a record for most consecutive Platinum albums in the history of Warner

Brothers Records. Nice job, boys. For a full track list and review, please turn to the VH Discography.

However, while the album did incredibly well, Edward hated it. Well, I dunno if "hate" is the right word, but let's just say that to this very day, he has pretty much apologized for making this album! The reason being that out of the twelve songs on the album, four were cover tunes. Well, four covers and an a cappella version of "Happy Trails" that closes the album. Apparently, Dave and producer Ted Templeman had the idea to do multiple covers. The rest of the band went along with it. And while the idea paid off, Edward simply did not want to succeed doing other people's material. The one good thing that came out of it is that Edward decided he was going to build a studio. Not just a place to rehearse or jam, a place where you could actually make records! His legendary 5150 studio would be built in 1983, just up the road from his home. After *Diver Down,* every single Van Halen album would be recorded at 5150. For those who may be wondering, "5150" is the Los Angeles Police code for the "criminally insane."

Now, I won't get too technical on y'all and break down every little aspect of 5150 Studio. However, after speaking with one of the privileged few who've been inside the hallowed walls of 5150, what truly set it apart was the board. This person agreed to speak about this "CLASSIFIED" information on the condition they remain anonymous. So let's just call them "X." (Sorry, "Deep Throat" was already taken.)

X: "What I remember most about 5150 was the Bushnell board. When they first put the room together, they bought an old Bushnell board (Eventually replaced by an API or Harrison, I don't remember which). VH was very secretive about that board because they were embarrased by it. They thought it wasn't up to snuff, but everybody in the know (Donn Landee) was telling them it was the shit!

"The Bushnells were made by a division of JBL in the late '60s and early '70s. The designers were aerospace guys from Rocketdyne in Chatsworth, doing it as a side job. It looked like it, too. That thing could have come out of mission control at NASA. It had big 'ole '50s Sci-fi Movie-looking knobs. I worked on the wiring under the hood a couple times. It was a work of art. All Mil Spec, gold sputtered. You couldn't buy a rig like that today. That board could go head to head with any vintage Neve. It was like a Flickinger console (which is what much of the first Boston album was tracked on). It had a sound that couldn't be matched. You'd have to verify this, but I'm fairly certain *1984* was tracked/mixed on that board. So was at least some of *5150,* too. It had headroom for days, which is why those records are so present and dynamic. The attack transients translate so well through the summing buss on a board like that. An SSL or in the box Protools production can't come close to it because all that precious metal in the circuits allows electron flow. It's like a true Class A hand-wired Dumble amp vs. a Line 6 amp."

Pretty killer, indeed. So at least some real good came outta the DD album. However, regardless how most of the band felt about *Diver Down,* well, they still had to do their best and support it. In other words, hit the road, baby. The tour in support of *Diver Down* would be known as the "Hide Your Sheep Tour" (please, don't ask...and again, feel free to do the Beavis and Butt-Head laugh now). It kicked off in Augusta, Georgia on July 14, 1982 and ran till February of 1983. The band would play just over 100 gigs on this tour and continued to really pack 'em in. In fact, this tour sold out all eighty of its U.S. concert dates! And once again, the band would earn another cool $10 million on this tour. Oh, by the way, did I mention there was an industrywide slump in concert ticket sales at this time? You sure could have fooled Van Halen! Everyone else might have been suffering, but VH were kickin' some serious ass.

Apparently, they were kickin' some serious ass offstage, too. By now their rowdy behavior had even drawn the attention of *Life* magazine. The November 1982 issue of *Life* contains a feature on Van Halen titled, "Rock's Rowdiest Rogues." It's a great read that covers life on the road with VH, along with a step-by-step guide on trashing your hotel room, courtesy of none other than Diamond Dave! In fact, the practice of trashing one's hotel room would become known as "Roth-ing your room" among musicians. I mean, Dave wouldn't just tear up a room or glue everything in the room to the ceiling in the precise order it had been in. Sure, he did all that. But this is a man who had the vision to hook a television set up to several very long extension cords before throwing it out a hotel window. Why? So the television set would remain on as it plummeted to a gruesome death, of course.

So 1982 was definitely another wild year for VH. From another highly successful tour to even receiving several mentions during the classic film *Fast Times at Ridgemont High.* In fact, director Cameron Crowe had wanted Edward and the boys to contribute some music to the film's soundtrack. Unfortunately, Edward didn't get word of it until it was too late. So instead, we simply hear Van Halen mentioned several times throughout the film. The biggest one, of course, comes towards the end of the film, when we find out that Jeff Spicolli saves Brooke Shields from drowning and then blows the reward money hiring Van Halen to play his birthday party!

While Top 10 albums and mentions in classic films are extremely cool, I believe the true highlight of 1982 was when Edward Van Halen received a phone call from none other than legendary producer, Quincy Jones. Seems

Q was producing an album for Michael Jackson and he needed some smokin' guitar on a rock song they had been working on. Hey, if it's smokin' guitar you need, Q, you've come to the right place! That "rock song" they had been working on was none other than "Beat It." The fact is this collaboration between Q, EVH, and MJ was very important. It's historic, really. For the full story, please turn to the FAQ.

As if we need any further proof as to how damn huge VH was at this point, check this out. The band was then asked to perform at the 1983 US Festival in San Bernadino, California. It was to be a three-day music festival, with Van Halen headlining "Heavy Metal Day" on May 29, 1983. The US Festival was the brainchild of Apple Computers wiz, Steve Wozniak. Apparently, Steve came up with the idea while driving around in his car one day. It would be a truly groundbreaking concert event that married killer music with technology.

Basically, next to Live Aid, the US Festival was the biggest concert of the '80s. So on Memorial Day of 1983, Van Halen would headline "Heavy Metal Day," along with other great acts of the time such as Judas Priest, Ozzy Osbourne, Mötley Crüe, the Scorpions, Triumph, and Quiet Riot. Man, those were truly some of the biggest bands alive. The fact that Van Halen was given the headliner spot clearly shows just were the boys stood in the hierarchy of the rock/metal world. I believe they earned a cool $1.5 million for this gig. Up until that point, it had been the highest amount ever paid to an act for a single show. Once again, nice work if you can get it.

Man, this gig was roller coaster. Apparently, the band – *especially* Dave – had a little too much fun backstage before the show. Needless to say, they were "feeling no pain" when showtime came. The band would take the stage and give an insane performance, led by the fact that Diamond Dave probably couldn't even feel the stage beneath his feet! I don't think the rest of the boys were far behind, either. Overall, it wasn't their tightest performance, but there were plenty of great moments. The bottom line is they were still able to go out there and win over most of the 300,000-plus people in attendance that day. Again, it's a testament to how popular VH was at this point. Simply put, the boys could do no wrong. At this point, they probably coulda gone on stage and played the phone book. It really wouldn't have mattered. VH had truly reached a level few artists ever achieve. What could have been a total disaster turned out to be a wild, legendary performance. Sure, some people mighta been pissed off, but I've seen the US Festival video and I didn't see anyone leaving, ok? I believe most of those out in the audience were "feeling no pain," too. So it was one big party, with VH providing the soundtrack and Diamond Dave as the toastmaster general.

There are a couple of cool moments I just can't pass over. One was when Dave was speaking to the audience in between songs. Some nimrod towards the front of the stage actually squirted water at Dave while he was speaking. Never one to be at a loss for words, Dave quickly responded with, "Hey man, don't you be squirtin' water at me...I'm gonna fuck your girlfriend, pal!" The 300,000-plus in attendance roared their approval! Oh, it gets better. At one point, Dave was toasting the crowd. So he's standing there, bottle of JD held high, and he fired off a verbal jab at none other than the Clash. You see, the Clash had performed at the US Festival the day before. Well, apparently, they had made some political comments and whatnot, even taking some shots at the U.S., too. Hey, it's the Clash, you know? It's who they are and what they do. But frankly, many of the people in the audience weren't there to be preached to. They just wanted to rock out and have a good time. I don't think it went over well, at all.

Well, I guess 'ole Dave heard about what had transpired and didn't really appreciate those boys comin' over here and bad-mouthing our country, especially on *his* home turf. So as Dave stood there toasting the crowd, he proudly proclaimed [complete with Lou Gehrig "Luckiest man on the face of the earth" speech-type reverb] "I just wanna say...this is *real* whiskey I have here...the only people...who drink iced tea...out of Jack Daniel's bottles...is the Clash, baby!" It wasn't anything too severe, but he made his point. I mean, how many people woulda had the *cojones* to do that, ok?

The band would survive the US Festival intact. It was a gig that definitely helped VH continue to elevate their profile. But while the band was enjoying a level of success no American hard rock/metal band in history had ever come close to, the situation within the band continued to sour. Well, I should say the situation between Dave and Edward, specifically. That tension that had been brewing for years just continued to mount. The US Festival didn't help much, either. I just don't think the rest of the band was too pleased with Dave's behavior at this gig.

Along with their strong dislike of the *Diver Down* album, well, this was a tough time for the band. Although I must say they always maintained as far as being out in public or at a gig. You hear stories about great bands like Aerosmith and how the tension between Steven and Joe was so bad that Steven would dance by Joe on stage and swing his mic stand about an inch from his head! That kind of stuff never happened here. Somehow, Van Halen were able to go out there and still put on kick-ass rock shows.

Man, I don't know how they did it. All the turmoil, tension, and wild partying going on in that band *never* affected them as it did others. The boys in Van Halen never embarrassed themselves, or most importantly, their music. In fact, in the midst of all this madness, they would end up recording one of the greatest rock albums of all time.

After spending the second half of 1983 locked up in 5150, day after day, working through the night, Van Halen's sixth studio album would be ready to go. Word was the band would be injecting keyboards into their sound. You can bet a whole lotta people were nervous, especially at the label. Hell, even within the band, there was some concern. But Edward Van Halen stood firm. It had been his idea and he truly believed he could make it work. I think most people out there were praying VH wasn't about to go "new wave" or whatever. Their new album would be titled *1984*. Appropriately enough, it was released on January 9, 1984. Simply put, it had been the second time in six years that Van Halen would kick rock in the balls.

I mean, all of their albums, with the exception of maybe *Diver Down*, were slammin' rock albums. But I'm talking about scene-changing, groundbreaking albums. Far as that criteria goes, VH accomplished that with their 1978 debut, and *1984*. This album became an instant classic. It is absolutely mind-boggling to think they recorded this brilliant album as the band was falling apart. Within just eight weeks of release, the album went Gold, then Platinum. In fact, you wanna know how big VH was at this time? By the end of the year, *1984* had sold five million copies in America. By comparison, Nirvana's classic *Nevermind* album sold four million copies in America during its first year out, ok? Hey, I'm not comparing albums. Obviously, both are classic albums and both went on to earn Diamond Awards. I'm simply pointing out how unbelievably huge VH were in their day.

1984 raced up the Billboard Album Chart, cracking the Top 10 and peaking at the number 2 spot! Man, this woulda been a number 1 album any other year. But take a wild guess as to who held the number 1 spot? Remember that phone call Edward received to contribute some killer guitar to a certain project? Well, that project was the *Thriller* album, and it held the number 1 spot at this time. Hell, the *Thriller* album held the number 1 spot for what seemed like 100 freakin' years. So Edward was actually on the number 1 and number 2 albums in the country at the same time. Pretty damn cool, dude! For a full track list and review, please turn to the VH Discography.

Along with this amazing album, Van Halen made three of the coolest music videos you've ever seen in your life. They were all over MTV in 1984. In fact, the first contest with a band that MTV ever had was the "Lost Weekend with Van Halen." Over one million entries were sent in, and the winner was a twenty-year-old cat named Kurt Jefferis from Phoenixville, Pennsylvania. 'Ole Kurt musta been doing backflips, while his mom was having a conniption fit. Apparently, Kurt had just had brain surgery not too long before the contest was announced. Obviously, I'm no doctor, but I don't believe part of your rehab for brain surgery requires you to go on the road with the wildest freakin' band on the planet. But of course, Kurt went.

So Kurt and his buddy got to meet up with VH in Detroit to hang out with 'em for an entire weekend. Of course, this included attending a VH concert. Meanwhile, MTV followed 'em around over the course of the entire weekend and filmed it all. The band was really cool to Kurt, even bringing him on stage during the concert and introducing him to the packed arena as "the winner of MTV's Lost Weekend with Van Halen!" The crowd cheered as Kurt was then ceremoniously doused with champagne and cake. Oh, but the fun wouldn't end there. No, apparently Diamond Dave decided to add a "bonus clause" to the Lost Weekend contest. Folks, I don't know how else to put this, but Dave, um, "loaned" Kurt one of his female companions. Hell, you could say he flat out gave her to Kurt! After the gig, Kurt found himself in a bathroom, backstage, with Dave's "friend." Now, um, no one really knows what went down in there, but the word is you could hear Kurt howling all the way to Toledo.

1984, the album *and* the year, was a level of success that no American hard rock/metal band had ever come close to achieving. Hell, I dunno if *any* American band had ever experienced anything like that, period. Not even the great Aerosmith had ever experienced anything like this. Same thing goes for other great American bands like Kiss, Cheap Trick, Ted Nugent, ZZ Top, Mountain, Journey, Lynyrd Skynyrd, and more. To this very day, few have matched it. In fact, you could say their entire classic era was a level of success no American band had ever come close to achieving. And again, to this very day, few have matched it. Overall, Van Halen had blown the doors off, taking hard rock and metal to a level of popularity and commercial success not seen since the heyday of Led Zep. Meanwhile, the shit had already hit the fan within the band. But they were able to maintain and give us one more tour.

The "1984 Tour" would kick off in Jacksonville, Florida on January 18, 1984 and run till September. Autograph earned the coveted opening slot on the legendary 1984 Tour. Van Halen would play 110 shows on this tour, selling out about 100 of them. Um, can you say "cha-ching," boys and girls? Van Halen was a bona fide phenomenon. The *1984* album, along with their MTV exposure, turned the boys into something they'd never been before: *pop stars*. I mean, the band was already huge by this point. They had five straight Platinum albums and five incredibly successful tours from '78 to '82, so you'd think they couldn't get any bigger? Oh, but they did.

Sadly, the 1984 Tour would turn out to be the last tour for the original lineup. On September 2, 1984 Van Halen would play their very last show with Diamond Dave at Zeppelinfield in Nuremberg, Germany. Jimmy Briscoe was one of Dave's mini-bodyguards on Van Halen's legendary 1984

Tour. The fact that he lived to talk about it is pretty damn miraculous. Jimmy was a part of one of the most legendary and insane tours in rock history and managed to survive. So when I contacted the man and asked him about the experience, he was able to sum it up quite eloquently.

> **Jimmy Briscoe:** "What can I say? It was fun! Whacked out a few brain cells, didn't catch anything. That's rock 'n' roll, dude."♪

September 2, 1984 would mark the end of an era. But man, what an era! During this era, Van Halen changed the face of rock, kicked rock in the balls (twice), and reinvented the electric guitar. A whole nation had been "Van-Halenized." Hell, most of the planet had been, for that matter. Far as where VH stood in the pantheon of American hard rock/metal, well, check this out. From 1978 to 1984, Van Halen released six studio albums. During this time, each album went Platinum upon release. In fact, at the time of Dave's departure, every single album, with the exception of *Fair Warning,* had already gone multi-Platinum. According to the R.I.A.A., by the end of 1985, Van Halen had achieved certified sales of 18 million albums in America.

You wanna know how sick that is? According to the R.I.A.A., by the end of 1985, the legendary Aerosmith had achieved certified sales of 6.5 million albums in America. Mind you, Aerosmith was already one of the most successful American rock bands of all time, so that's a pretty staggering fact. Frankly, it's a revelation. At the time Van Halen broke up, you could easily say they were the most successful American hard rock/metal band of all time. Man, it wasn't even close. Van Halen had pretty much outsold and outdrawn every other American hard rock/metal band in history. The numbers don't lie, baby.

In fact, I believe at this point Van Halen may have been the most successful American rock band in history, period. Aerosmith had been around twice as long (and with four more albums in their catalog). Nonetheless, here at home, Van Halen had sold about three times the amount of albums Aerosmith had. Man, that's insane. Plus, Van Halen's catalog was *entirely* Platinum. Hell, with the exception of one album, *entirely* multi-Platinum! And Van Halen's albums had all enjoyed much better (higher) chart success than the albums of any other American hard rock/metal band in history. Again, it wasn't even close.

However, the boys from Beantown would regroup. In the process, they would become bigger than ever. Aerosmith's "comeback," which began with 1985's *Done With Mirrors,* would eventually lead to them selling a staggering 59 million albums in America from 1985 till present! Yes, you heard me right. They have sold almost 60 million albums in America since 1985! All their new albums were going multi-Platinum and their entire classic catalog began to go multi-Platinum as well. Basically, their new strategy of working with MTV and outside songwriters paid off insanely well. Although a lot of that is owed to the great John Kalodner, who steered 'em back on the right track. Regardless, when Diamond Dave split in 1985, Van Halen was number one, baby. In fact, Van Halen would actually remain the number one-selling American hard rock/metal band here at home until Aerosmith finally surpassed them...more than a decade later.

Man, when you can mention a band's success in the same breath as that of an Aerosmith, well, you know you have reached a level most people can only dream of. Fact is, at the time Diamond Dave split in 1985, VH stood head and shoulders above all of 'em. And when you change the face of rock *and* reinvent the guitar with your debut album, which is something no other American band has ever done, well, you know you are dealing with a truly special band. For my money, if Classic Aerosmith was *"the shit,"* I believe that would make Classic Van Halen *"the shiznit."*

Basically, I'd put the Classic Van Halen era up against *anybody,* with the exception of the Beatles and Led Zeppelin, of course. Hey, I'm crazy but I ain't stupid, ok? In terms of talent, impact, influence, songs, popularity, live show, album sales, and overall success, Classic Van Halen is pound-for-pound one of the greatest to ever come down the pike. They were easily the greatest, most important and influential hard rock/metal band of this respective era, just as Edward Van Halen was easily the greatest, most important and influential guitarist of this respective era as well. And without a doubt, Van Halen was, by far, the most successful and popular American hard rock/metal band of all time when Diamond Dave split.

You know, some people like to believe this era is called "classic" cuz it was their original lineup. Well, I beg to differ. For my money, this era is called "classic" cuz the original lineup was so damn brilliant, influential, and successful. Hell, they didn't have to hang around for thirty years to be considered "classic," you know what I mean? It's like that joke about hookers and old buildings. You know, if they hang around long enough, they start to get respect! Well, the fact is Classic VH became "classic" while it was still active. And that, my friends, is pretty rare indeed.

Sayonara, Dave

"David Lee Roth was a great frontman. And I think that pair (Dave and Edward) was the thing. I was sorry when that didn't continue."
– Jeff Beck

So as 1985 began, Van Halen was sitting atop the pyramid as the most successful American hard rock/metal band in history. At the same time, their empire was crumbling. Man, as far as hard rock/metal goes, only the great Led Zeppelin had been bigger. In fact, Zep is still the big dog to this day. Man, ain't nobody gonna catch those brilliant bastards!

Dave seemed to really be enjoying his time after the 1984 tour ended, even going out and recording a solo album, *Crazy from the Heat.* He also made a couple of classic, hilarious videos for two songs off this album: "California Girls" and "Just a Gigolo." Unfortunately, the situation between Edward and Dave was beyond repair at this point. What happened next has been debated to this very day. However, I must say the truth has always been pretty clear to me, anyway.

In the spring of 1985, Dave and Edward would meet up at Dave's mansion in Pasadena. Apparently, Edward didn't dig Dave's solo album. Or should I say, the fact that he'd gone out and done a solo album. He also didn't much care for the fact that Dave had a movie in the works. Yes, Dave had been working on the script for a film and apparently CBS pictures was gonna back him on it. The film was to star Dave, of course, and he wanted Van Halen to do the soundtrack. Again, Edward didn't care for this at all. Far as he was concerned, he would rather go back into the studio and work on the follow-up to *1984.* Meanwhile, Dave wanted to go off and really take on Hollywood. Now, that's not to imply that Dave left VH to go be an actor, ok? Some folks seem to believe that to be the case, while others don't. All

I know is that he apparently had a film in the works and there's no doubt he wanted to explore that avenue. Far as his leaving the band, I believe the tension that had been brewing between Dave and Edward for years probably made his decision easier.

The bottom line is that Diamond Dave quit Van Halen. There's no mystery here, folks. If you go back and look up interviews he did when all of this went down, you'll clearly see that he told everyone, from *Creem* magazine to MTV, that he bailed. I believe that was precisely how he put it: "I bailed." The story goes that Dave and Edward met up at Dave's crib, discussed what they each wanted to do, shed a few tears, and it was over. When Edward left Dave's crib that day, it would be the last time those two men would speak to each other for many years.

April 1, 1985...a day that would live in rock 'n' roll infamy. Ok, nobody died or anything like that, but this flat-out sucked. A nation mourned and stoners wept! Ok, maybe only the second part was true. But again, this freakin' sucked. Of all days, Diamond Dave would announce his departure from VH on April Fools Day. Man, now who's gonna provide the soundtrack for our lives? I may have been a little kid at the time, but I knew this shit sucked. Man, I just didn't know this was possible. The mighty Van Halen seemed indestructible. Fact is, they weren't. History has proven that no band is. Some of the greatest bands ever, including the Beatles, have broken up. Well, VH seemed poised to join all of 'em. If this was the end, well, we couldn't be too sad, really. Shit, they'd left us with all that killer music! On top of that, they'd touched an entire generation. Basically, if you coulda gone around to all the schools in America during 1984 and confiscated notebooks from the kids, I guaran-damn-tee you the majority of 'em woulda had the VH logo scribbled on the cover.

Of course, many will blame the breakup on "ego." But really, who doesn't have an ego? Everyone from the Beatles to Guns N' Roses had ego. Hey, I'm not knocking it either. In fact, I believe you gotta have some kind of an ego to go out on stage and perform music in front of people. I look at the beef between Dave and Edward as a something that goes on in almost every single band on the planet. I don't care who you are, there's always gonna be some kind of beef, ego, friction, or whatever the hell you wanna call it. Believe me, this crap didn't begin with Van Halen, ok? You think Lennon and McCartney got along perfectly? If you do, well, you are delusional. In fact, their beef continued even after the Beatles broke up!

Many of the greatest bands ever are famous for having tension between members. From Led Zep to Metallica, from Guns N' Roses to the Who, from Nirvana to Black Sabbath, from the Beatles to the Stones, they all had it. For example, while they were all together in Cream, the tension between Eric Clapton, Jack Bruce, and Ginger Baker was legendary. Hell, it was insane! Honestly, I think that had a lot to do with their music being so damn powerful and explosive. Unfortunately, that also had a lot to do with the fact that Cream only lasted just over two years.

However, that seems like an eternity compared to the next band Eric Clapton was in. As soon as Cream disbanded, Clapton and Baker actually hooked up and the great Steve Winwood – who had just recently departed from the band Traffic – to form another supergroup, Blind Faith. Bassist Rick Grech rounded out the lineup. Well, Blind Faith did one album and one tour in about six months, then broke up. Yup, this amazing unit lasted just six months. Hell, the great Jimi Hendrix went through this, too. For example, the Jimi Hendrix Experience released their debut album in 1967. Well, in 1969 Jimi disbanded the Experience and formed the Band of Gypsys. Like Cream, the Experience lasted just over two years.

So that's just a fact of life, man. Most great bands have tension. In fact, the tension in Van Halen wasn't just between Dave and Edward, either. Lord knows Edward and Alex butt heads as well. It's that brother thing where you argue, kick each other's ass, then hug and have a beer after. There is plenty of to and fro between the brothers. Some would say they even argue about agreeing on things! In the end, I just view it as par for the course, really. You can even look at sports and see it. Do you honestly believe every member of the Yankees loves each other? You think Michael Jordan loved and got along with every single member of the Bulls? Again, if you believe that, you are delusional. Hell, MJ had friction with everyone from his teammates to the freakin' team owner! But hey, the Yankees have been to six of the last nine World Series, winning four of 'em. And the Bulls won six championships with Jordan at the helm. The point being, you don't have to get along, or even really like each other, to achieve success. Those teams are proof of that. And I even won't get into the whole Shaq and Kobe thing! We now know those two were never really close, to put it mildly, but they still managed to kick ass and win three consecutive NBA championships.

I mean, look at our everyday lives. Do you get along with and like everyone at your job? How about with everyone in your own family? Yeah, I didn't think so. But you still have a job to do, right? A band is just like a family, a team, or even a job. So while Dave and Edward were never really tight, that tension is precisely what made this band and this era so damn explosive. They were able to ride that from 1974 till the end of 1984. Many people forget these guys were together for over a decade! And the years between 1978 and 1984 were spent in the bright light of the music biz. Unfortunately, a band is also like a marriage, too. And I think we all know that more than 50 percent of marriages end in divorce.

Regardless, the fact is that Edward Van Halen, Alex Van Halen, Michael Anthony, and David Lee Roth own that piece of time from 1978 to 1984. You can't take that away, *ever*. History shows it and the numbers prove it. The music, well, it speaks for itself. As does Edward's guitar. Basically, Van Halen could have ended right here and they still would have been one of the most important, successful, and influential bands of all time. Along with the fact that Edward would still have been one of the greatest ever. Fact is Edward Van Halen coulda quit music in 1985 and taken up chess for the rest of his life. It really wouldn't have mattered, cuz by this time, his legacy was secure. Hell, some would say his legacy was secure with his debut album back in 1978.

Overall, the material Edward put out from 1978-1984 is some of the most revolutionary, incendiary, and influential guitar playing the world will ever know. Not to mention, some of the greatest freakin' hard rock music the world will ever know, too. In a way, this period actually mirrors the early period Edward's main guitar hero had back in the day. From joining the Yardbirds in October 1963, to his amazing collaboration with John Mayall's Bluesbreakers in 1965, to his explosive formation and detonation of Cream from 1966 to 1968, to the incredible material he recorded as Derek and the Dominos during 1970's *Layla* sessions, Eric Clapton had about a six-year run that was simply insane. Other than Jimi Hendrix, no one was more important or breaking more ground at this time. And to many people, Clapton was, is, and forever will be "GOD."

Since the 1970 *Layla* sessions, well, you can say the man has released solid material for about three and a half decades. However, in my humble opinion, that run he had from 1964 to 1970 was revolutionary and incredibly influential. I'm sure many people would agree. During this period, Eric was a member of the Yardbirds, John Mayall's Bluesbreakers, Cream, Blind Faith, Delaney and Bonnie, and finally, Derek and the Dominos (not to mention the fact that he also found time to lay down a sweet guitar solo on the Beatles classic, "While My Guitar Gently Weeps").

Man, I honestly don't know if anything he's done since can even come close to touching what he accomplished during this period of time. Basically, anything that Eric Clapton has done since then will always and forever be held up against what he accomplished during this period. Well, I view what Edward Van Halen accomplished between 1978 and 1984 in the same light. You know, without going through all those different bands, of course. Since 1984, Edward has released solid material for over two decades. And, you know, there is still plenty of great music and guitar playing there. However, in my humble opinion, that six-year run Edward had from 1978 to 1984 is untouchable. It's truly insane. As I have mentioned before, most great artists reach a point in their career where they are no longer compared to other artists. Rather, they are compared to themselves.

Basically, to this very day, Edward's groundbreaking work during the Classic Van Halen era is still very much recognized. Former Korn guitarist Brian "Head" Welch, who grew up during the '80s, can pretty much sum up Edward's nuclear impact during this time.

Head: "I'm sure he's on everybody's [Top 5 players of all time] list, but back when I was little, he was just doing amazing stuff, so different from any other guitar player."

So for the rest of his life, whether fair or unfair, everything Edward Van Halen will ever do, write, or play will forever be held up against what he accomplished during this period of time. Just as an aging Michael Jordan was compared to a younger Michael Jordan, Edward has had to go through that as well. Same thing goes for Eric Clapton, too. Meanwhile, Jimi Hendrix got spared of having to go through this cuz he tragically passed away in his prime. Basically, Edward and Eric have had to compete against their own astonishing legacy and reputation for decades now. And they will continue to do so until the cows come home. No doubt about it.

Sadly, I think some people today have absolutely no clue as to how devastating these two cats were. You know, cuz both Clapton and Edward have released solid, radio-friendly material for decades now. And, of course, they're both a bit older, too. Many people out there simply have no idea that, in their respective primes, these two cats, along with Jimi, were the scariest and most incendiary freakin' rock guitarists on the planet when they held a guitar in their hands.

Seriously, you just couldn't touch 'em (remember, Jimi hit the scene *after* Eric). It's just that both Eric and Edward kinda moved on from that and went off in a different direction. You know, after a while, I don't believe either one wanted any part of that whole "Guitar god" thing, really. Hell, they never really signed up for that, anyway. Man, it has to be so intense to have every cat in the Western Hemisphere gunning for you. When you're at the top, people are comin' for your head from every direction, baby. It ain't easy being the big dog and having to live up to your own reputation, day in, day out, for the rest of your life.

In the end, it always comes down to the simple fact that Edward and his band owned that period of time from 1978 to 1984. So while many in the press have a field day, to this day, mulling over the fact that VH made a lead singer change and going on about which singer is better, perhaps they should just focus on the incredible music, guitar playing, success, impact, and influence this band achieved. Then again, that doesn't sell papers, does it? Why focus on the positive when you can focus on the "drama," right? Yeah, never mind the fact that Van Halen was, by far, the most successful American hard rock/metal band of all time when Dave split. Maybe some of those media folks will get it, one day. It would be pretty goddamn sad if this band's legacy is for being a band that made lead singer changes. Man, it's pretty funny how no one ever cracks on Eric Clapton for all the different groups he was in, you know? Hell, if Van Halen couldn't keep a lead singer, Eric Clapton couldn't keep a band!

All kidding aside, you can probably count on one hand the number of bands that have changed the face of rock music. Same thing goes for guitarists who reinvented the instrument. Van Halen managed to do *both* of these things with their debut album. For that alone, these four men should own some prime real estate in a certain building over in Cleveland, *comprende?* Perhaps one day, the good folks who run that establishment will realize this fact. Oh, and while you're at it, um, could you please let Black Sabbath in, too? For crissake, that's *long* overdue. Hell, just make it a joint induction! Could you imagine VH and Sabbath getting into the RNRHOF, *together?* Man, somebody punch me in the mouth. Please. Cuz I dunno if I or anyone else on this planet could freakin' handle that. That would be amazing, and well earned.

Anyhow, after Diamond Dave split, Van Halen was basically doomed. All that incredible success didn't seem to mean anything now. Again, when a frontman leaves, it's a "breakup." And this wasn't just "a frontman" leaving. Nah dude, this was *the* frontman leaving. That's a big difference there, folks. It's hard enough to replace any frontman, you know? When it happens to be arguably the biggest rock star on the planet and the man against whom all others were measured, well, the situation appears quite bleak. I can think of only one band in the history of hard rock/metal, up until that point, that had successfully survived a lead singer change. Especially surviving a lead singer change while managing to keep your band name and not just by going off and forming an entirely new project. The boys in AC/DC pulled it off after the great Bon Scott passed away on February 19, 1980. They went out, found the amazing Brian Johnson and were able to forge on. Far as hard rock/metal goes, that's about the only one I know up until that point. And in all honestly, at the time that went down, AC/DC was nowhere near as high-profile was VH in '84. Not even close.

So as you can see, the future for Edward, Alex and Mike didn't look too promising. 99.9 percent of the time, when a frontman splits, a band crumbles. But the boys knew what they had to do. First off, quitting was never an option. All these guys know, and all they want to know, is music. There is no way in hell the brothers could ever stop making music. That would be like asking them to stop breathing, ok? Same thing goes for Mikey. It was quickly decided they would find another singer and move forward. Again, this is a tall order, especially when you have to follow up a classic album like *1984*. Another major issue was their band name. There are many who felt they should no longer use the name Van Halen. In the end, this was never an option, either. It's one thing if your band name is a word or set of words you just picked out or something. In this case, the band held the name of its founding members and nucleus, Edward and Alex Van Halen. Far as they were concerned, if they are still in the band, then it's fuckin' Van Halen, period. It was *their* band. They formed it, they made up the nucleus, and they wrote all the music. Case closed, folks.

So the search for a frontman begins. As you could imagine, quite a few names were thrown around. In fact, their first idea was to make an album with different singers on it! I guess it woulda been like Santana's *Supernatural* album. You know, a different singer on each track. Edward really appreciates great singers, so he had people like Joe Cocker and Phil Collins in mind. Apparently, he'd already written the future hit, "Right Now." The song actually had kind of a Joe Cocker "Feelin' Alright" kind of vibe to it. So, not surprisingly, Edward had envisioned the great Joe Cocker singing "Right Now." In the end, the project never came to be. Basically, it would have been a total logistical nightmare. On top of that, Alex pointed out that it would only be a one-off type of deal. There is simply no way this could have been permanent. Therefore, the idea was scrapped. I believe at this time Edward had also been in contact with one of his heroes, the great Pete Townshend of the Who. But again, it never panned out. Scheduling conflicts would not allow the project to get underway for years. The brothers knew they had to bring in a permanent frontman.

As the search continued, none other than Patty Smyth came into the mix. Patty was the singer for the band Scandal. She's very cool and has a terrific voice. While Patty loved the band and was honored, she respectfully declined. I think she realized that a woman singing VH tunes would not go over well, especially with the hardcore fans. So in the end, she respectfully declined and that was that. Meanwhile, another name to come up was Eric Martin, the future frontman for the band, Mr. Big. Apparently, Edward had come across a tape of Eric's band at that time. While he didn't much care for the music, he really liked Eric's voice. Edward was able to locate Eric, call him up, and summon him down to 5150. Meanwhile, Eric was stunned! I believe he was like twenty years old at the time, and the thought of his young, skinny ass replacing a "rock god" like Diamond Dave was enough to make him lose sleep. Poor Eric Martin must have been excited and terrified, all at once.

Well, he finally showed up at 5150, did the audition and that was that. Needless to say, Eric didn't get the gig. Again, it wasn't a question of talent, cuz this dude can sing his dick off. It's just, well, the mere thought of trying to fill those shoes (and you know whose shoes I'm talkin' about) could be nightmare inducing for anybody – *especially* for a twenty-year old kid.

Around this time, I believe Edward got a hold of a tape by a cat named Jimmy Barnes, a great vocalist who actually hails from Australia. While Edward recognized that the man had a great voice, he simply felt that – for whatever reason – Jimmy wasn't a good fit for Van Halen.

The search continued. Man, this was not an easy task. There were plenty of singers who wanted the gig, but again, they knew what shoes they had to fill. I believe most of 'em knew they would forever be compared to Diamond Dave, and so they chose to stay away from 5150 and any audition that may come their way. The funny thing is, Edward would actually find the answer to his lead singer problem at, of all places, an auto shop.

Enter Sam-man

"What Van Halen did was just move on and get another great singer in Sammy. They just played all the new material and didn't rely so much on the older material."

– Neal Schon

During the fall of 1985, Edward Van Halen stopped by the auto shop of his pal, Claudio Zampolli. Edward is a big car freak, so he would swing by the shop every now and again to shoot the shit with Claudio. You know, two dudes just lettin' it hang, talkin' cars. Well, one day he shows up and Claudio notices Edward looks really bummed out. Edward explains that he hasn't found a lead singer yet and how he is still bummed over the fact that Dave split. Claudio simply responds with, "Why don't you give Sammy a call?"

The "Sammy" that Claudio was referring to was none other than Sammy Hagar. Like Edward, Sammy was also a customer of Claudio's. In fact, he'd just left one of his cars at Claudio's shop to have some work done. Since he had Sammy's number, Claudio passed it along to Edward and told him to give the man a call. Needless to say, Edward called him. In fact, I believe he called him right there from Claudio's. Within a couple of days, Sammy was over at 5150 auditioning for the band. Nice work, Claudio.

During his audition, the band jammed unfinished versions of "Summer Nights" and "Good Enough." As the band jammed, Sammy would improvise lyrics. The chemistry was immediate. So much so that I believe it only took about a half hour before they boys asked Sammy to join the band! Of course, Sammy accepted. It was the right move to bring this man in. I don't give a damn what anyone tells me. Sure, I'll always love Classic VH. It was, after all, *the shitznit*. But I truly believe Sammy was the right man at the right time. And this wasn't some rookie, either. Sammy had been payin' his dues for years.

Sammy Hagar was born in Monterey, California on October 13, 1947. He was the youngest of four children born to Gladys and Robert Hagar. His dad was a pro boxer. Apparently, 'ole Robert was a bruising southpaw who actually won the bantamweight championship back in the 1940s. This love of boxing was passed on to Sammy, who actually took up the sweet science as a teenager. Not long after, he would discover rock 'n' roll and quit boxing. Hey, the boxing world's loss was rock 'n' roll's gain. Sammy grew up on Elvis, the Beatles, and the Stones. He was also heavy into Cream and the Who. These were two of Edward Van Halen's biggest influences, too, so you could begin to see common ground right here.

In fact, Sammy picked up a guitar at age sixteen after hearing Eric Clapton and Cream. He'd go through several bands in high school, of course. Finally, in 1968, he moved to San Fancisco, where he would gig in clubs for several years. In 1972, he caught his break when Ronnie Montrose formed the band, Montrose. Ronnie had just left Edward Winter's group and was looking for a singer. Sammy auditioned and got the gig. Montrose's self-titled debut, *Montrose,* was released in 1973. Oh, take a wild guess as to who produced it? It was none other than future Van Halen producer, Ted Templeman. Oh, by the way, *Montrose* is a freakin' brilliant album.

Well, Montrose would release just one more album before their situation turned sour. Sammy appreciated the fact that this gig got him into the music biz, but he honestly wanted to have more control over his music. In 1975, he split Montrose and went solo. Funny thing is that all the members of Montrose, except for Ronnie, of course, would end up joining Sammy! His solo career was solid. His early years were bigger overseas than here at home. Throughout the late '70s, he'd continue to release albums and was always known as a great live act. In fact, he also played a couple of those festival shows in the late '70s with Van Halen! I believe Edward and Sammy met around this time, but it was really nothing more than two guys shootin' the shit backstage. You know, Edward tellin' Sammy how he really liked that *Montrose* album, and so forth.

The funny thing is, the folks at Warner Brothers seemed to have had Sammy on their mind when they signed Van Halen. Word is that Ted Templeman and others wanted to bring Sammy in to replace Dave when they signed the band in 1977! Again, this is just what I've heard over the years, ok? Doesn't seem that far-fetched when you think about it, either. Montrose had been signed to Warner Brothers and Ted Templeman had been their producer, so all the signs were there, you know?

Anyway, by the early '80s Sammy's fortunes had reversed. While still appreciated overseas, his popularity here at home began to soar! He had several big albums and hits in the early '80s, and was still known as a fine live act. So as I said before, this cat was no rookie. And while I agree with the choice, hey, I'll be there first to admit that at the time it seemed like an odd choice. It's just, well, the differences between Sammy and Dave are enormous. You'd truly be hard pressed to find two more different and opposite individuals than these two! When a band loses a frontman, they will usually try to replace them with someone similar. You know, try to maintain the image and get someone who is similar vocally as well. In this case, Van Halen went the complete opposite direction.

For starters, Sammy was older than Dave. You gotta remember that Dave had just turned thirty years old a few months before quitting Van Halen. Damn, that' pretty sick when you think about it. You know, to have that kind of a legacy under your belt at just thirty years of age? Man, that ain't fair! Anyhow, Sammy had just turned thirty-eight when he joined VH. On top of that, their look was totally different, too. Dave was a "rock god." Hell, he looked like a freakin' movie star. Meanwhile, Sammy had that "everyman" type of thing going on. As Diamond Dave has always been fond of saying, "The difference between Sammy and I is that Sammy throws a party, while I *am* the party."

Dave was also one of the greatest interviews around, while Sammy, well, wasn't. Then again, *no one* could compete with Diamond Dave when it came to interviews. He possessed amazing verbal skills and basically turned interviews into a freakin' art form. Plus, Dave had always been a "star," while Sammy had always been the "blue-collar rocker." On the other hand, Sammy is a freakin' singer. Hey, I have always loved Dave's voice. He had that cool, sleazy "used car salesman-meets-lounge lizard" type of thing going on. You know, a certain whiskey and cigarettes vocal quality that was very cool. Meanwhile, Sammy just goes out there and blows the freakin' P.A. to all bloody hell. He truly is a fantastic singer. So what you may have lost in terms of looks and swagger, you more than made up for in terms of vocal ability.

Add to that the fact that Sammy is a musician. Dave was a musical guy who could play some guitar, and even a bit of harmonica, too. But Sammy is a freakin' guitar player, ok? It's like the difference between, say, a Kid Rock and a Zakk Wylde. You know, Kid Rock can go out there and kinda strum the guitar a bit, perhaps even play a few licks. Meanwhile, Zakk Wylde is a fuckin' *guitar player*, ok? He is someone who dedicated *his entire life* to the craft. I mean, the dude could already play the entire Ozzy and Randy/Black Sabbath catalog by the time he was outta high school, for crissake. Basically, Zakk's a total ass-whompin' shredasaurus who will knock you off the stage with a single lick! Amen, brother. So while Dave could play guitar, Sammy is a *guitar player*. This just added to the mix and I believe it made Sammy's communication with Edward that much easier. You could also point out the fact that Sammy is a songwriter. Obviously, Edward is a songwriter, too. So again, more common ground between these two guys. Dave wrote lyrics, but he wasn't really a songwriter.

Overall, they are two very different guys. Very talented, but *very* different. I've always joked that you could ask Sammy and Dave to dial a phone number for you and each would find a way to dial the same number, differently. So it was pretty shocking to see them choose Sammy and not just go out there, bring in some really young Dave-clone and live off those six albums from their classic era. Because folks, at this point, Van Halen would no longer play any of their classic material! Well, they would shut the door on 99.9 percent of it, anyway. From here on out, if you saw VH with Sammy in concert, you'd be lucky to hear two or three songs from the Classic VH era. The boys figured if they were gonna start new, well, they were really gonna start new! It was to be all about the new material they had been writing. They even decided not to make any videos for MTV in support of their debut with Sammy. The band preferred to let people experience their new lineup in concert, rather than on television. So as the boys went into 5150 in November 1985, I think it's safe to say that most people thought they'd lost their minds!

It simply appeared that VH was doing everything you were not supposed to do. They made a lead singer change, which right away spells impending doom. They refused to change their band name. They brought in a guy who was older and the complete opposite of their first guy. They continued to inject keyboards into their sound. They would no longer perform 99.9 percent of their classic material, in concert. They would make no videos for their next album. Um, fellas, are you outta your freakin' minds?

Well, what happened next was truly mind-boggling. Let's just say Van Halen would never get to have their very own VH1 *Behind the Music*. You know, where that narrator with the serious voice goes on and on about how the band broke up (cue the somber music) and how their career would now plunge into a downward spiral of misery and substance abuse. Followed by, of course, their fans abandoning them, the loss of all their money, and finally, a band member: a) dies, b) overdoses but doesn't die, or c) loses a limb.

Which leads us, of course, to our grand finale, where the band gloriously reunites as it's raining skittles and all that giddy bullshit. Um, that wasn't happening here, ok? Save the drama and stop the press, cuz the fact is Van Halen isn't goin' anywhere...

Van Halen '85 - '96

"They did something no one else could ever do. They made a lead singer change and still continued on with big success. I've never seen anybody really pull that off in that way."

– Rob Thomas

Van Halen went into 5150 Studio in November of 1985 and emerged a few months later with a new album. Appropriately enough, their first album with Sammy Hagar would be titled *5150*. Any doubts as to whether this band was gonna survive would be crushed right out the gate.

5150 was released on March 26, 1986. Within eight weeks of release, this album would go Gold, Platinum, and then double Platinum. The album quickly raced up the Billboard Album Chart, cracking the Top 10 and peaking at…drumroll please…the number 1 spot. Yes, Van Halen finally scored their first number 1 album! In fact, it was to be Sammy's first number 1 of his career, too!

Folks, can you name me a single other band in the history of music that made a lead singer change *and* scored a number 1 album? Anyone? Bueller? Ola? Screw it, I'll just sit here and listen to the crickets chirping. For a full track list and review, please turn to the VH Discography.

Regardless what you think, man, you gotta tip your cap. What these guys pulled off is insane. Not just for the whole frontman thing, but to have to follow up an album like *1984*! Man, I truly don't know how they did it. It's a testament to the amazing talent and hard work of this band. Sure, some people weren't satisfied. Many out there were still waiting to see the live show. That was to be the true indicator as to whether VH still had it. Again, all doubts would be immediately crushed. The "5150 Tour" would kick off in Shreveport, Louisiana on March 27, 1986 and run till November. The band would play about 110 shows on this tour. Anyone who saw this tour knew the band hadn't lost a step. Van Halen sounded as tight as ever, and the chemistry with Sammy was obvious. If you want proof, simply pick up *Van Halen: Live Without a Net* (1986). This is the first official concert video the band ever released, and it's terrific.

So not only did VH succeed on the recording side of things, but they would continue to pack arenas, too. And while they had basically shut the door on all the music of their classic era, there were some cool new twists to their live show. The fact that Sammy was a guitar player gave us a chance to see Edward and Sam team up on several songs, like the raucous "There's Only One Way to Rock." The guitar play between Edward and Sam on this number was enough to leave you drooling! There would also be several song were Edward would handle the keyboard duties, while Sammy played guitar. These are definitely things we'd never seen before from VH in concert. Overall, the lead singer change was a success and they retained their status as one of the top concert draws around.

I'd be tempted to say this year was absolutely perfect, but sadly, this was the year that Edward and Alex would lose their best friend and biggest inspiration. In December of 1986, Jan Van Halen would pass away at sixty-six years of age. Hell, devastating isn't the word. This man had been their biggest influence and inspiration, musically, as well as personally, of course. He was their biggest supporter and fan from day one. Jan knew his sons had "it," and he always encouraged them. You hear stories about Jan going to see his boys in concert and just breaking down in tears watching them play. Often Edward would see his dad crying from the stage and lose it, too. This would happen back in their home when they were growing up, too. The story goes that Edward would be jamming a song, or right in the middle of a solo, when Jan would just break down in tears listening to him. It wouldn't be long before Edward would start crying, too. Right in the middle of the song, Edward would break down with his old man. When Van Halen got signed and their debut album broke through, the first thing Edward ever did with his money was retire his dad. He bought his old man a boat and retired him.

On the day their dad passed away, Edward and Alex went into 5150 and jammed for ten hours straight. Man, the music swirling around the studio on that day must have been so beyond words. It says a whole lot about these two men when you think about it. What did they do to cope with the passing of their dad? They turned to music. Yes, music helped them get through it. Folks, if that don't tell you everything you need to know about the brothers, well, then you just ain't been listening.

I would imagine they spent 1987 recovering and then gearing up for another album. After a few months in the studio, the next album would be ready to go. Their second album with Sammy, and eighth overall, would be titled *OU812*. You know, it's like sayin' "Oh, you ate one too? (Again, please feel free to do the Beavis and Butt-Head laugh now.) It was released on May 24, 1988. Within eight weeks of its release, the album went Gold, Platinum, and then double Platinum! The album quickly raced up the Billboard Album Chart, cracking the Top 10 and peaking at the number 1 spot! It had been their second straight number 1 album! At this point I gotta believe that a whole lotta people – including Diamond Dave – were absolutely stunned. I should mention that this would be the first VH album to ever be dedicated to someone, and that someone was their dad, Jan Van Halen. Nice touch, boys. For a full track list and review, please turn to the VH Discography.

Of course, soon as the album dropped, the band was ready to hit the road. Only this time, the tour would be a bit different. Apparently, none other than Sharon Osbourne had come up with the idea for a massive outdoor-only, stadium tour (sound familiar?), and named it the "Monsters of Rock." It was to be the first traveling festival of its kind in the U.S., and would include the top hard rock/metal acts of the time. (Again, sound familiar?) Before the amazing Ozzfest, Sharon cut her teeth on this tour, right here. I believe she took all the pros *and* cons from this tour and would later use that in forming the now legendary Ozzfest. The Monsters of Rock consisted of the following acts, in order: Kingdom Come would open, followed by Metallica, Dokken, the Scorpions, and finally the headliner, Van Halen. Each gig was a ten-hour affair, running from daytime into nighttime. The tour did well and managed to be the second highest grossing tour of 1988, earning a cool $26.7 million. The only tour to top it was by the amazing Pink Floyd, which grossed $27.6 million.

The really cool thing was that all the bands got along well. I think a lot of that had to do with the mutual respect among bands. I know VH and Metallica got along quite well. In fact, several members of Metallica have even gone done to Sammy's Cabo Wabo Cantina in Mexico to hang out and jam with him. Kingdom Come did a solid job opening, and Dokken was a good live act, too. The Scorpions are a legendary band and they always deliver live. And holy shit, Metallica! This is when they were still in black and seething.

I was a little scrub when I attended this Monsters of Rock tour, and I have to admit that Metallica stole the show. Van Halen headlined and did a great job, as usual. But in all honesty, well, the music they were doing at this time was not the best fit for a tour like this. Hey, I dig a lot of their material with

Sammy, ok? It's just that, well, most of these bands were full-on hard rock/ metal, while VH was leaning much more towards the "pop" end of things, at this point. I mean, their music always had pop edges to it, but this went beyond the edges and more into the whole picture. If this had been Classic VH, hey, it would have made much more sense; or at the very least, the new VH lineup performing more of their classic material. I believe Edward Van Halen didn't feel this tour was right for them at this time, either. Especially due to the fact that they only had one album under their belt with Sammy at the time. I believe they'd just released their second album with Sammy the very same week the tour began.

Nonetheless, it shows how much respect there was for Van Halen. The fact that these men had been given the headliner spot over some of those other great and legendary bands shows in what high regard Van Halen was held. Just as Sabbath had passed the torch to VH back in 1978, I believe VH passed the torch to Metallica on this tour. In fact, after the Monsters of Rock, Sammy Hagar himself said Metallica would become the biggest band on the planet. Man, did he ever call it. Just a year later, they would release the classic, *And Justice for All.* Then, in 1991, they would release the monstrous "black album." Metallica were now, officially, the biggest American metal band on the planet. Hell, they were the biggest metal band around, end of story. I believe the Monsters of Rock was one of the last times Metallica would ever open for anyone.

Overall, it was great to see five of the biggest hard rock/metal bands in the world come together and put on a great show for the kids. In the end, I believe everyone involved—from the fans to the bands—had fun. Well, Van Halen still knew how to have fun, that's for sure. Apparently, the boys in VH had an item in their contract rider that called for a fluffer to be present backstage at each gig on the Monsters of Rock. For those who many not know, a "fluffer" is a chick who hangs around the set of a porn movie while it is being filmed. Her sole purpose, or "job," is to keep the male actors', um, "spirits up." You know, in between takes and whatnot.

As the tour ended, VH took another break and basically chilled during 1989. However, there were a couple of things that went down during that year, despite the fact that the band didn't release any new music. For starters, *MTV Unplugged* had just started up around this time. Yes, I believe 1989 was when the first *Unplugged* show was recorded. Anyway, from what I understand, Van Halen was actually one of the first bands MTV really wanted when they started their *Unplugged* series. You know, they put together a list of different artists they wanted and no doubt Van Halen was definitely high on their list. So the folks over at MTV pursued VH and truly wanted to do a Van Halen *Unplugged*. Well, the band respectfully declined. Rather, I should say that

Edward Van Halen didn't really care to do it. In several interviews he's done over the years, Edward has been asked about the whole *MTV Unplugged* thing. His response has always been the same. Basically, he's always stated that he was *not* going to butcher his music just so he could be the flavor of the week. In other words, the majority of Van Halen music is obviously written and performed on electric guitar, and he simply didn't want to perform it any other way. You know, if he'd intended for his music to be acoustic, well, he woulda written it that way in the first place!

For all the fun and cool this man exudes, inside there is a serious artist who simply did not want to compromise his music. I totally respect the fact that he stuck to his guns, but damn, I can't lie, a VH *Unplugged* woulda been killer! You know, cuz Edward can do all his shit on acoustic, no problemo. On top of that, he even coulda shown his killer piano chops as well. And Sammy coulda picked up his axe and kicked some serious ass, too. No doubt a Van Halen *Unplugged* woulda been a monster success, as well as a *huge-*selling album. But Edward said no, so that was that, baby. 1989 would also be the year Van Halen and the world of hip-hop would meet up in a really big way. Apparently, there were two Van Halen songs sampled by hip-hop artists during this time. The first was "Ain't Talkin' 'bout Love," whose classic riff was sampled by the godfathers of nasty, Miami's one and only 2 Live Crew. You'll find this sample on the song, "Fuck Shop," off their classic (and controversial) album, *As Nasty as They Wanna Be.*

The second was "Jamie's Cryin'," which was sampled by Los Angeles-based rapper, Tone Loc. You'll find this sample on the hit song, "Wild Thing," off his classic album, *Loc-ed After Dark.* Basically, it's a sample of Edward's guitar and Alex's drums. Apparently, when Tone first heard "Jamie's Cryin'," he thought Edward's guitar sounded like it was saying the words "wild thing," hence the title of the song.

2 Live Crew's *As Nasty as They Wanna Be* is a classic hip-hop album. While "Fuck Shop" was cool, I don't believe it was ever released as a single. It was really their song "Me So Horny" (built around a sample of a Vietnamese hooker saying "me so horny," which was taken from Stanley Kubrick's classic film, *Full Metal Jacket*) that was released as a single and enjoyed major chart success. Hey, everyone's heard that song, right? *As Nasty as They Wanna Be* would eventually sell a couple million copies, a lot of which was due to the attention it received for its wild lyrical content. Basically, this was the first album ever deemed "obscene" by the powers that be. Uncle Luke and the boys really pushed some buttons, to put it mildly.

Meanwhile, Tone Loc's *Loc-ed After Dark* is also a classic hip-hop album, only this one crossed over in a *huge* way, and without any controversy. In fact, it was only the second hip-hop album in history to reach the number 1 spot on the Billboard Chart, and the first by a black artist to do so. The first hip-hop album to reach the number 1 spot was the Beastie Boys classic, *License to Ill*, released in 1986. Obviously, a whole lotta the success of *Loc-ed After Dark* was due to its first single, "Wild Thing." This classic hip-hop anthem, which was built around that "Jamie's Cryin'" sample, became a monster hit. In turn, this propelled the album to the top of the charts and Platinum status, baby. "Wild Thing" was actually written by Tone Loc and Marvin Young, a.k.a. Young MC.

The trippy thing is that back in 1989, there were absolutely no laws against sampling, whatsoever. In other words, you could sample whomever the hell you liked and get paid off that sample, without needing any kind of permission from the artist you sampled, and without having to pay them any kind of royalties or anything like that. Sampling laws would come into effect some years later, but back then, it was the Wild West, baby.

In 1990, the time had come to head back into 5150 and fire up the next VH record. Well, the band found itself without any new material or even a producer. After some deliberation, two men were brought in to produce their next album. The fantastic Andy Johns, a legendary producer who had worked with many greats, including none other than Led Zeppelin, and their old pal, Ted Templeman. The band would quickly begin the writing process. In fact, they wrote so damn much they had enough material for a double album. This is part of the reason they brought Ted in. After looking over the situation, he told the boys to just pick enough material for one album and get it out there. In the end, that is precisely what they did. The whole album took about a year to make, from recording to mastering. By far, it was the longest amount of time any VH album had ever taken to record. Oh, and on a personal note, 1991 would be the year Edward and Valerie welcomed their first child into this world. On March 16, 1991 Wolfgang Van Halen was born. For those people out there who may be wondering, he was named after Edward's favorite composer, Wolfgang Amadeus Mozart – *not* after the chef, ok?

Finally, on June 17, 1991 their third album with Sammy (ninth overall) was released. The album, titled *For Unlawful Carnal Knowledge,* was to be their third smash in a row! Within eight weeks of its release, the album went Gold, and then Platinum. A couple months after that, it went double Platinum. The album quickly raced up the Billboard Album Chart, cracking the Top 10 and peaking at the number 1 spot. Man, that would make three consecutive number 1 studio albums. And yes, if you take the first four letters of each word in the album's title (again, please feel free to do the Beavis and Butt-Head laugh now) it spells out "fuck." Apparently, Sammy's pal, legendary boxer Ray "Boom Boom" Mancini, had informed him that the word "fuck" was actually an acronym for "for unlawful carnal knowledge."

Sammy and the band liked it so much they used that as the title of the album. For a full track list and review, please turn to the VH Discography.

The "For Unlawful Carnal Knowledge Tour" would kick off in Atlanta, Georgia on August 16, 1991 and run till May of 1992. The band would play about 110 shows on this tour, and continued to be a top concert draw. Simply put, Van Halen continued to pack arenas with the greatest of ease. The opening act for much of this tour was none other than the amazing Alice in Chains! The boys in AIC and VH got along great. I saw this tour as well. Definitely one of the greatest rock concerts I've ever seen in my life. I hear that Edward spent as much time in Alice in Chains's dressing room as his own! The great thing about Edward and Van Halen is that they were always very cool to their opening acts. Edward never forgot how as an opening act back in 1978, Van Halen would be given very few luxuries and short soundchecks. Hell, sometimes they wouldn't get a soundcheck at all! So when it came time to headline, Edward never forgot that. Man, I hear that at the end of this tour, Edward personally gave Jerry Cantrell one of his own guitars and 5150 amps. That's total class, right there.

While on the subject, here's a cool story that I came across in an issue of *Guitar Player* magazine (Sept. 1998). One night, Alice in Chains was on stage doing their thing. I believe they had just kicked into their classic hit, "Man in the Box," when Jerry Cantrell noticed his guitar didn't sound right. It didn't sound bad, it's just something didn't sound *right*. There appeared to be a very slight delay on his guitar, but Jerry was not using a delay pedal during this song. He looked over to the side of the stage at his guitar tech, but the dude just kind of looked back and shrugged. Jerry kept looking around to see if he could figure out what the hell was up when suddenly, something down in the pit caught his eye. He quickly slid on over there to see what it was. Well, what Jerry saw next almost made the dude piss himself! Down in the pit, guitar in hand and grinnin' like a rat bastard, was none other than Edward Van Halen. Apparently, he was all plugged in and playing "Man in the Box" right along with Jerry, *live*, note-for-note.

Overall, it was another insanely successful album and tour for VH. On top of that, this album would earn the band their first Grammy! Van Halen took home the "Best Hard Rock Performance with Vocal" at the 1992 Grammy Awards. The *F.U.C.K.* album also won "Best Rock Album" at the Billboard Music Awards in December of 1991. Chalk up another great year for the boys. If you don't mind, I'd like to take a minute to explain why 1991-1992 was so special. When you understand the musical climate at this time, you will hopefully understand just how freakin' amazing their success truly was.

Just twelve weeks after Van Halen released *For Unlawful Carnal Knowledge,* Nirvana would hit the scene and drop their classic debut album, *Nevermind.* Needless to say, by the end of 1991, "grunge" would be ruling the world. Man, I hate that term. Most of that music was simply great guitar-driven hard rock. A lot of it was downright metallic! But that is was that era is known as, so I have to use that term. Anyway, grunge exploded, led by Nirvana and other great bands like Pearl Jam, Alice in Chains, Soundgarden, and so forth. Sadly, this terrific era only lasted from 1991 to 1994. However, a decade later, the media and press love to make it appear as rock 'n' roll was completely dead at the time this scene exploded. They make it appear as if these bands were the only bands out there doing well, while all other bands that were not from this genre or scene fell by the wayside. Specifically, any and all bands that had been around in the '80s, you know?

I gotta tell you that is total bullshit. I was a teenager when grunge exploded and hey, like many people, I freakin' loved it. Yeah, I cranked it up and thrashed around to that shit till I was seeing double. And I ain't complaining, either!

But the reality is Van Halen didn't feel grunge, at all. In fact, they sailed right through it unscathed and lookin' lovely. While grunge was ruling the world, VH continued to score number 1, multi-Platinum albums. Most impressive, they continued to be a top concert draw and packed arenas everywhere they went. In fact, Van Halen won the "Video of the Year" award at the 1992 MTV Video Music Awards for the groundbreaking video of their hit, "Right Now." Mind you, Nirvana's "Teen Spirit" video was up for that award as well.

Now, I am not stupid. I know that at this time Nirvana's "Teen Spirit" video was *the* video, ok? Yes, that is the video that set the world ablaze and ushered in a new era of rock. However, the fact that Van Halen won the 1992 "Video of the Year" award right in the middle of the incredible grunge explosion is somehow conveniently overlooked by music historians. On top of that, VH was still all over rock radio. Several songs off the *F.U.C.K.* album were hits, so they were getting a whole lot of airplay. Add to that their very first Grammy award and the "Album of the Year" award from Billboard, too. Oh, and if you check the guitar magazines, well, you'll clearly see EVH was still getting major respect.

For example, in *Guitar World* magazine's 1992 Reader's Poll, Edward Van Halen was voted "Best Rock Guitarist" and overall "MVP" as well. Along with the fact that *For Unlawful Carnal Knowledge* was voted "Best Rock Album." Meanwhile, the classic *Nevermind* was voted "Best Alternative Album" and the equally classic *Metallica* (a.k.a., "the black album") was voted "Best Metal Album." Basically, *GW* readers knew what the hell they were talkin' about.

To go along with all this amazing success, Van Halen showed how cool and open they were when they took a "grunge band," the amazing Alice in Chains, on the road with them as an opening act. Well, the boys in AIC were more than happy to oblige! It seems the band, especially guitarist Jerry Cantrell, really looked up to VH. Edward had always been one of Jerry's heroes, so to be able to go on tour with VH was like a dream come true for the boys in AIC.

Like many, I totally embraced "grunge." For my money, it separated the men from the boys. By that, I mean it allowed the truly great bands from the '80s to continue into the '90s with major success. At the same time, all hacks, posers, and most "hair bands" from the '80s were cast to the bargain bin, forever. Notice how I said "most" hair bands, and not "all," ok? Some of those guys wrote cool tunes and were good musicians, so I can't bag on all of 'em. To this very day, I'll proudly crank my Mötley Crüe albums and I don't give a damn who knows it, *comprende?* Believe me when I tell you that eventually there would be as many crappy wannabe "grunge bands" out on the scene as there had been "hair bands," ok? Sadly, this happens to every scene. I think my point is this: don't believe the hype.

At the time grunge exploded, Van Halen was kickin' some serious ass. So were Metallica, the Red Hot Chili Peppers, R.E.M., and U2. Just look at some of the albums that were released in 1991 by these amazing bands: *Metallica* (a.k.a, the black album)*, Sex Blood Sugar Magik, Automatic for the People,* and *Achtung Baby.* I can go on and name killer records by the Smashing Pumpkins, Jane's Addiction, Faith No More, and My Bloody Valentine, too. There were plenty of amazing albums released at this time. And yes, many of them even topped the charts! So this idea that rock was dead, or that the charts were littered with nothing more than pop acts and hair bands, is absolutely false. Did rock need a kick in the ass? Absolutely. You always need a new band to come out on the scene and shake things up. But there was still plenty of great music out there. Anyway, the idea that Van Halen and lots of other great bands of the '80s somehow fell off the face of the earth in 1991 is absolutely preposterous. Nothing could be further from the truth.

When the *F.U.C.K.* Tour ended in May of 1992, the band would take a break. However, it wouldn't be long before they would take their music to the people. In fact, on January 23, 1993, the boys would release their first live album, ever! *Live: Right Here, Right Now* was a double album of live material. The majority of the material on this album was recorded on May 14 and 15 of 1992, during their *F.U.C.K.* Tour. Within twelve weeks of its release, the album went Gold, then Platinum. About four months later, it would go double Platinum. The album quickly raced up the Billboard Album Chart, cracking the Top 10 and peaking at the number 4 spot! It was a most impressive showing for a live album, especially a double live album mainly consisting of material they'd done with Sammy Hagar.

So of course, the band would go on tour in support of this album as well. However, just before the tour kicked off, the band would play a secret gig at the Whisky A Go-Go to celebrate their fifteenth anniversary of being in the music biz! Yes folks, Van Halen had now spent fifteen years in the bright light, managing to survive all trends and a lead singer change to remain right atop the rock pyramid. They were still one of the biggest, baddest, and most successful bands on the planet. So on March 3, 1993, the band would go back to one of the places where they had paid their dues! The fact that an act of this stature would go back to one of their old clubs on the Sunset Strip and put on a show for their fans is just too cool. Tickets for the show were only like twenty bucks, which made it even cooler!

Well, the gig didn't remain a "secret" for long. Once the news began to spread, through radio stations and word of mouth, thousands of people descended upon the Whisky by that afternoon. Extra police officers had to be called in to get a handle on the situation, cuz it had pretty much escalated into a mini riot! One of the songs on their set list that day was "Dreams," and the band ended up making a music video for this song. The video included plenty of footage of the wild scene outside the Whisky on that day.

On March 30, 1993 the "Right Here, Right Now Tour" kicked off in Munchen, Germany. I believe this tour would be their first U.K. appearance with Sammy at the helm. The tour ran 'till August, and the band would play about sixty shows. It would be another highly successful tour for the boys. By the beginning of 1994, the boys were itching to make another album. I'm tellin' ya, these guys were on a roll and they didn't wanna stop. Grunge may have been ruling the world, but it was still very much business as usual in the VH camp. So in May of 1994, the band would go back into 5150 and began work on their next album. I believe in 1994 the folks from Woodstock came calling, too. Seems they were gonna put on another festival to celebrate the twenty-fifth anniversary of the original Woodstock. This one would simply be titled "Woodstock II." It would again be a three-day festival and apparently they wanted Van Halen to headline the festival. After some thought, the band would respectfully turn them down. It seems the band preferred to focus on and complete their new album, rather than have to halt everything to go play this type of gig. In the end, I believe Aerosmith was brought in to headline and the boys from Beantown did a fine job, as usual.

Van Halen continued working on their new album. They'd brought in the great Bruce Fairbairn to produce it, and he definitely kept the band in check. This album, titled *Balance,* was completed in just about twelve weeks. It would finally be released on January 24, 1995. This would definitely be a different album for VH, lyrically as well as musically. No matter, though, cuz within just eight weeks, the album would go Gold, Platinum, and then double Platinum! The album quickly raced up the Billboard Album Chart, cracking the Top 10 and peaking at the number 1 spot! In fact, I believe it debuted at the number 1 spot. Um, grunge who?

Folks, the fact that VH continued to pull off this kind of success is simply mind-boggling. It had been their fourth consecutive number 1 studio album. Basically, every studio album with Sammy went multi-Platinum and hit the number 1 spot. Again, say what you want, but I think we should give credit were credit is due. That's freakin' amazing. For a full track list and review, please turn to the VH Discography.

Of course, the band would hit the road in support of the album. The "Balance Tour" would kick off in Pensacola, Florida on March 11, 1995, and ran till November. The band would play almost 140 shows on this tour. The amazing Skid Row opened many dates on this tour, as did two other cool bands: Brother Cane and Collective Soul. I was lucky enough to see this tour as well. Man, the boys still sounded tight. Musically, VH was a well-oiled machine at this point. And Edward's playing on this tour was absolutely top-notch. No doubt, at forty years of age, the man was still a major force to be reckoned with. And I believe this had been their biggest tour with Sammy, too. Not just in the sense that they played 140 gigs, but the fact that the band earned a cool $32.7 million for this tour! Once again, VH remained one of the top grossing acts on the planet.

Unfortunately, not everything was peachy keen at this time. Apparently, a bit of tension had begun to mount within the band, specifically between Edward and Sammy. Man, why is it always the frontman and the guitarist? We should bring in a team of scientists to study this strange phenomenon. I mean, when are we gonna see the bass player and drummer go at it?

Anyway, aside from the tension brewing, the brothers began to have health issues during the Balance tour, too. Edward began to experience severe pain in his hip during the early part of this tour. Turns out that "pain" was actually a condition known avascular necrosis. Basically, it's a degenerative hip condition. Being the warrior that he is, however, he still went out there and played almost 140 dates on this tour. Sometimes the condition was so bad it would ground him. In other words, he wouldn't move much during a show. Other times it was better and he still managed to fly around a bit. Overall, I must say it didn't affect his playing one bit. I caught the boys on this tour and own plenty of bootlegs of this tour as well. Man, Edward was still in top form. Alex Van Halen had his own issues to deal with, too. I believe his neck was giving him some trouble, and it wasn't uncommon to see him playing an entire show in a neck brace. Overall, it didn't affect his playing either. I don't know how these two guys did it, but they went out there and still managed to consistently kick ass. Freakin' warriors, man.

On a happier note, this would also be the year the band received a special award from their label, Warner Brothers Records. When their *Balance* album went double platinum, Van Halen had now sold in excess of 60 million albums throughout their career. The label celebrated this by presenting the band with a special plaque at the Museum of Flying in Santa Monica, California on April 3, 1995. Man, 60 million albums in about seventeen years. Nice work, boys. In fact, at this point, Van Halen had a dozen consecutive multi-Platinum albums under their belt. No other American hard rock/metal band was even close. In fact, as far as hard rock and metal goes, I believe only Led Zeppelin had more multi-Platinum albums than VH at this point. This shows just how insane Van Halen's success was and how incredibly consistent they were, despite a lead singer change and all of the turmoil/issues that are commonplace within a rock band. Somehow, all the tension, hard living, and even a dreaded lead singer change *never* affected their music or status in a negative way. And while I give the boys credit, I think a whole lotta credit should go to the late, great Ed Leffler, too. This gentleman managed VH from when Sam joined the band all the way up to this point, and he did a helluva job. Truly fuckin' amazing. R.I.P., Ed Leffler.

So by the end of 1995, you have a band that is as successful as anyone could ever dream of being, but who internally is beginning to show signs that all is not well. What would go down the following year will probably be debated, forever.

In 1996, the boys were kickin' back and recuperating from their last tour, when they received a phone call asking if they'd like to contribute some music for the soundtrack to the film *Twister*. Edward and Alex seemed cool with the idea, and I believe Mikey was, too. Apparently, Sammy did not dig the idea at all. Since the band was only to contribute one song, Sammy felt it was a ripoff to make the fans buy an entire album for just one VH track. You know, the rest of the album was comprised of different songs from a bunch of different artists, none of which even resembled the kind of music VH played. Despite the fact that their song would be the title track, Sammy just didn't much care for the *Twister* soundtrack. After some deliberation, he somewhat reluctantly agreed and began to work on the song for the movie. One day, *Twister* director Jan De Bont swung by 5150 to see how the song was coming along, when he happened to walk in as the brothers were playing an instrumental that Alex had written. Jan was so blown away by what he was hearing that he immediately requested the piece for his film!

So in the end, Van Halen would have two songs on the *Twister* soundtrack. The first would be the song, "Humans Being." The other was the instrumental Alex had written, which would be called "Respect the Wind." What's really cool is the instrumental features Alex on keyboards! Edward adds some of his most fiery guitar playing over Alex's keys, and it sounds amazing. "Humans Being" would be played during the film, while "Respect the Wind" would play over the film's closing credits.

Overall, the songs sounded great. Unfortunately, it just elevated the tension within the band, especially between Edward and Sammy, to an all time high. Soon after the music for *Twister* had been completed, the shit hit the fan. Ironically enough, as had been the case back in 1985, a movie was in the middle of it! Remember that back in 1985, Diamond Dave wanted to go off and do a film. This time, it was about a soundtrack to a film. Word of advice: boys, please try to stay away from any and all film work. All kidding aside, the situation fell apart in June of 1996.

Some will say Sammy was frustrated, not just with the soundtrack, but along with the fact that he wanted to do some solo projects and such. Others will say this was simply not the case. Whatever the deal was, Van Halen was about to break up, *again*. After an amazing eleven-year run with Sammy that had produced four consecutive number 1 multi-Platinum studio albums, eleven number 1 hits on the Rock Mainstream Chart (world record), and five top-grossing tours, it was over.

On June 25, 1996, radio stations all over the country begin to announce the breakup. Again, when a frontman walks out, yeah, it's a "breakup." The next day, SRO Management released an official statement confirming that Sammy was out of the band and that the original lineup was in the studio, recording some new material. I believe Sammy sent out his own press release on this day, which simply cited "creative differences" as the reason for the breakup.

Yeah, I know what you are thinking: "Hey, back up for a minute…the original lineup is in the studio?" Yes, the VH press release stated that Sammy was out and that the "original lineup" was in the studio recording some new material. Could this be? Was David Lee Roth back in the mix? The answer to that would be yes and no, really.

Welcome Back?

"We need Classic VH back to kick everyone's ass and set everything straight."
– Billy Corgan, at the 1996 MTV Video Music Awards

In June of 1996, music fans would receive the shocking news that after eleven amazing years, Sammy Hagar and Van Halen had parted ways. Immediately after, however, they received even more shocking news when word began to spread that none other than Diamond Dave was back at 5150 for the first time since 1984!

Almost a decade later, there still appears to be a whole lotta confusion about what went down in 1996. I'll try my best to simplify it and make it clear as possible for you. Ok, at the time Sammy split, the band had been gearing up to release their very first greatest hits album. Apparently, Sammy wasn't a big fan of that idea, either. He didn't much care for the *Twister* soundtrack and he didn't much care for a greatest hits album. I believe his line of thinking was, "Hey, we are not done yet, so why release a greatest hits?" I guess he believed this is something you do when your career is over. On the other hand, the rest of the band felt it was cool. Frankly, I think they felt it was long overdue. This band had been around for eighteen years at this point, and they had so many damn hits! I think Edward, Alex, and Mike felt it was about time and that it would be cool for the fans, many of whom had been demanding a greatest hits for years. Whatever the case, the idea for the greatest hits was on the table when Sammy and VH split up.

Now, it is standard operating procedure for all band members past and present to be involved in the making of a greatest hits package. By that I mean that all members have to agree upon what songs are selected, the album cover, and so forth. This means they had to reopen all lines of communication with David Lee Roth. You know, he absolutely had to be informed about it and was entitled to have input on all matters relative to the project. This all went down around the same time Sammy split. So the folks over at Warner Brothers called up Dave to inform hit of the Van Halen greatest hits package.

Since leaving VH in April of 1985, Dave had a pretty darn good solo career for the rest of the '80s. He put together the DLR Band, featuring the amazing Steve Vai, Billy Sheehan, and Greg Bissonette. This lineup would release two very cool albums. The first being 1986's *Eat 'Em and Smile,* and the second was 1988's *Skyscraper.* Both albums went Platinum and this lineup took their music on the road for two wild and successful tours. Sadly, the DLR Band broke up after the *Skyscraper* album. As the '90s hit, Dave's career began to wane a bit. He'd hooked up with an amazing talent named Jason Becker to record the follow-up to *Skyscraper.* Jason is a virtuoso guitarist who'd been part of the band Cacophony with future Megadeth guitarist Marty Friedman.

During the sessions for Dave's new album, Jason began experiencing pain in his lower leg. Well, it turns out this "pain" was actually Lou Gehrig's Disease. Jason did the best he could to finish up the album before his condition progressed any further, but eventually he was not able to play at all. Tragic can't even begin to describe it, man. Being the warrior that he is, Jason is still with us today. About fourteen years after being diagnosed and basically being given three to five years to live, the man is still with us, battling every single day. Eventually, Dave would release *A Little Ain't Enough,* but how happy can you be after what happened to Jason? He would then follow this up with 1994's *Your Filthy Little Mouth.* It was a fun album, but in all honesty, it didn't have much of an impact. So by the mid '90s, Dave was really out of the limelight. Meanwhile, VH was still one of the most successful and popular bands around. Dave would then actually have a stint in Las Vegas in 1996. He put together a cool new band, David Lee Roth and the Mambo Slammers. Well, it was right after his Vegas trip that Dave would receive the call from Warner Brothers informing him about the Van Halen greatest hits package.

After getting the news from WB, Dave personally called Edward. Apparently, the call went surprisingly well. These two men spoke and actually hit it off in a very cool way. There was a lot of water under the bridge, so to speak. The conversation was to have been strictly about the greatest hits package. Turns out they spoke for almost an hour, even apologizing for a lot of the bullshit and mudslinging that had gone down in the past. Everything seemed cool and they agreed to a meeting soon after. When they saw each other in person, again, everything went very well. The story goes that they kicked back at Dave's house for a few hours, smoking some cigars and having a very cool time. The following week, there was a meeting for the greatest hits package, and Edward brought up the fact that he wanted to do something new. You know, add some new music to the greatest hits to really make it special. He informed Alex and Mike that Dave wanted to be involved, and the boys had no problem with that. Edward got back to Dave and asked him if he'd be cool with doing a new song. Dave agreed, and that was that.

Ok, so up till this point, things are pretty damn clear. What would happen after, sadly, isn't. I mean, the boys went into the studio and began working on their one new song. Eventually, they would end up doing two new songs. The tracks were produced by the terrific Glen Ballard and they sounded great. At the same time, the word has gotten out that Dave is back at 5150 working with the band. I even remember seeing Kurt Loder report it on MTV. They did the whole "Sammy is out, Dave is in" type of thing. It was reported that Sammy and the band had split, and that the band was working on some new material with Dave. Well, Kurt and MTV didn't really do anything wrong here. Fact is, Dave was back at 5150.

The problem was the majority of people heard that and immediately thought, "Hey, Dave's back in the band!" The reality was that Dave was back, but *only* to do a couple of new tracks for their first greatest hits package. Unfortunately, I believe most people simply heard the "Dave is back" part and skipped the rest. It didn't help that MTV began to run ads that actually welcomed Dave back. The ads showed video clips of Dave from the past, put to the theme song of the classic hit television show *Welcome Back, Kotter*. Again, this didn't help much, cuz I believe most people who saw this immediately assumed that Dave was back in the band. I can totally see how people were confused. The ads were cool, but a bit misleading. Man, and what would happen next really screwed everything up, big time. The folks at MTV wanted the original lineup to come to the 1996 MTV Video Music Awards and present the award for "Best Male Video." Man, they should have said no *immediately*. There were already plenty of mixed signals being cast out there, and a walk-on at the Video Awards would not help this at all.

To walk out on stage together at the world's biggest music awards show, man, you could imagine what people are gonna think, right? It would be like confirming all the rumors and reports, for sure! Edward, Alex, and Mike walking out there with Dave is like pretty much signaling a reunion. It's just how people will take it, period. Well, the boys went along with it. MTV wanted it and the folks at Warner Brothers obviously wanted it, too. What better way to get the word out about your first greatest hits package, you know? Millions upon millions of people would be watching that show, so it made total sense, from a business standpoint, to do it. Sadly, music and business don't always mix well. Again, these four men walking out there, *together,* was certain to get a big reaction. Not just from the fans and so forth, but obviously from the media as well. Sure enough, that night at Radio City Music Hall in the fall of 1996 would basically turn into a total and complete cluster-fuck.

The host of the show was the always cool comedian, Dennis Miller. When it came time for the "Best Male Video" award, he introduced Van Halen as the presenters. Immediately, "Runnin' with the Devil" begins blasting throughout Radio City Music Hall. I remember sitting there watching and thinking, "Holy shit, VH is here tonight? Wow, cool surprise! I wonder if it's Edward and Alex, or Edward, Alex, and Mikey?" Never in a million years did I expect to see what happened next. I knew Sammy was out and Dave was at 5150 working on new tunes for a greatest hits package. But man, I never thought I'd see the original lineup appearing *anywhere.* Shit, especially not at an MTV awards show.

"Runnin' with the Devil" began to play and then the band hit the stage. First came Edward, Alex, and Mike. Then, finally, out walked Dave. At that very moment, the shit hit the fan, big time. The place erupted! The sight of those four men, *together,* is enough to give anyone a conniption fit. Basically, everybody from Billy Corgan to Chris Rock was up on their feet cheering. Not surprising, since Billy and Chris are major VH fans. Man, Chris Rock looked like he had seen a ghost! You can tell this walk-on was totally unexpected by the look of surprise on the faces of all those in attendance. The original lineup had sent the place into a total frenzy and earned them a standing ovation. I gotta admit, it was mind-blowing to see them together on stage.

Problem is, again, they are *not* "officially" reunited. But at this point most people have lost their minds and couldn't give a shit. I believe many didn't know, and those who did just didn't care. Then again, Edward, Alex, Mike, and Dave, *together,* on stage, could only mean one thing: they're back! You just can't blame people for thinking that was the case. Hell, for a moment there, I believed that, too. Anyhow, the band proceeds with the award presentation. Dave goes off, ad-libbing and saying some wild shit, complete with f-bomb and all!

Dave would also point out it was the first time they'd all been on stage together in over a decade. Then he turned and hugged Edward. It seemed like a really cool moment. As if it even mattered at this point, the winner of the "Best Male Video" award was the great Beck. Poor Beck, he looked totally shell-shocked as well! I know he is a fan of Classic Van Halen, too. So it must have seemed surreal to be receiving an award from the original VH lineup. After the show, he was asked if he felt he'd been upstaged. Beck's response was no. Apparently, he didn't feel it was "upstaging"; rather, he felt happy to have just been part of this "miraculous thing" that has occurred. Even after the show, he still looked dazed. It was hilarious! Unfortunately, the band didn't find Dave's behavior to be hilarious. They didn't appreciate some of the wild shit he said and they didn't seem to appreciate him shakin' his booty behind Beck as he was giving his acceptance speech. What went down backstage after the presentation didn't help much, either. By then, the media was ready to descend upon the band with a vengeance. Shit, the original VH lineup had just walked out on stage at the biggest music awards show on the planet. Folks, you just knew a shit storm was comin'. Boy, did it ever.

Backstage at the MTV Awards, there is a press area where artists go after winning awards and so forth. The boys in VH hit the press area and the media just came after 'em. Edward, Alex, and Mike did the best they could to defuse this situation, but to no avail. Edward Van Halen actually stepped up to the mic (something he's never really been comfortable doing) and explained that the original lineup had only reconvened specifically for the sake of the greatest hits package. You know, to add those two new songs as a bonus for the fans. Along with this, Edward also began to mention his hip condition and how he was in need of a hip replacement in the very near future. Some will say Dave didn't care for Edward's hip condition, cuz he felt the night was about him being back in the mix. Others will say Edward shoulda kept the mood light and not brought up his hip condition at all. But I guess you can't really blame the dude for being honest and tellin' people what the deal was.

Whatever the reality may be, the fact is that Dave and Edward, not so surprisingly, would not see eye to eye. In the end, the reunion that never really was, was over. Their appearance at the 1996 MTV Awards could easily be called the biggest mistake this band ever made. Not only cuz it appeared as if the band had reunited, but cuz of all the "he said, she said" bullshit that came out after. Actually, it was all the "he said, he said" bullshit, really. It didn't help that Sammy got in on the action, too. You had a verbal ménage-a-trois going down between Edward, Dave, and Sammy. Lots of mudslinging and bullshit, none of which is even necessary to print here. The bottom line is that their appearance at the 1996 MTV Music Video Awards totally blew up in their face. It sucks cuz the fact that the band and Diamond Dave had reopened all lines of communication may have actually led to some more new material down the road. Instead, the shit hit the fan and they would never work together again.

The funny thing is that in the middle of this whole mess, the greatest hits package was released! *Best Of, Volume 1* dropped on October 22, 1996. This was about seven weeks after the MTV Video Awards madness. The album did very well by going Gold, Platinum, and then double Platinum within about six months. It also raced up the Billboard Album Chart, cracking the Top 10 and peaking at the number 1 spot! It was Van Halen's fifth number 1 album of their career. For a full track list and review, please turn to the VH Discography.

Sadly, there would be no videos to go along with the two new songs the band had recorded with Dave. Oh, there were supposed to be, but after what went down at the MTV Awards, well, there would be no videos made. On top of that, many people were still confused about what had gone down.

I'm sure the events of 1996 will be hotly contested forever. In the end, people are gonna believe whatever they want to believe. I simply feel that what seemed like a cool idea ended up blowing up in their face. To bring in Dave and do those two new tracks was a very cool thing. It also would have left the door open for more material with Dave in the future. Sadly, their appearance at the MTV Awards backfired. If you could change one thing about that year, I would guess that woulda been it. But hey, you can't go back and change things. What's done is done, baby. Fact is that in the fall of 1996, Van Halen still didn't have a lead singer! So while the media frenzy continued, the band actually had to begin auditioning singers. Just like in 1984 when Dave split, there was no way the band was gonna end here. The only realistic option was to go out there and find someone to replace Sammy.

Once again, Van Halen would forge on…

Van Halen '96 - '99

The search for a frontman really began after the MTV Awards. Within a couple of weeks, the band came across someone they felt could be right for the job. This person was none other than former Extreme frontman, Gary Cherone. Apparently, Gary's name had been brought up by then Van Halen manager, Ray Daniels.

Gary Cherone was born in Malden, Massachusetts on July 26, 1961. Basically, he grew up about seven miles north of Boston. His mom was a phys-ed teacher, while his dad served as a master sergeant in the U.S. Army. Overall, it was one big, happy family, with Gary being the third of five brothers. Growing up, Gary was into bands like the Who, Queen, and Aerosmith, of course. So obviously, some of his biggest influences were Roger Daltrey, Freddy Mercury, and Steven Tyler. Not surprisingly, he was also a huge fan of Classic Van Halen, too.

By the early '80s, he was in a band known as the Dream. In the summer of 1985, Gary and another member of the Dream, Paul Geary, hooked up with guitarist Nuno Bettencourt and bassist Pat Badger to form Extreme. After payin' dues on the local Boston music scene, Extreme would finally be discovered.

In November of 1987, A&M Records offered the band a record contract. This would lead to their debut album, *Extreme,* which was released in 1988. The follow-up to their debut would be the album where they band truly broke through. 1990's *Extreme II: Pornographitti* was a bona fide smash. Led by the hit ballad, "More than Words," this album broke them into the mainstream in a huge way. The video for "More than Words" was as big as the song! After the album exploded, the band would embark on a twenty-five-country tour, during which they would even open shows for none other than David

Lee Roth! By the mid-'90s they'd released two more albums, while Gary also branched out by performing in the Boston Rock Opera's production of *Jesus Christ, Superstar*. In 1996, Extreme decided to split up and go off to do separate projects. The timing of the split came right around the time of the whole Van Halen Sammy/Dave saga.

So in October of 1996, VH manager Ray Daniels suggests they give Gary a shot. The boys agree, and Edward sends Gary a tape of some music for him to audition on. Well, when Edward got the demo back, um, let's just say he and the boys weren't too impressed. Now, Gary is a fantastic singer, so I dunno what musta happened on that demo. Whatever the case may be, his voice on that demo didn't do much for anyone. However, along with the demo audition, Gary had been promised an in-person audition. The band agreed. Hey, if the guy shows up and can't cut it, he'd be sent packing. It was that simple. The day Gary arrived at 5150, he didn't sing the material on the demo. Instead, he sang Van Halen songs from both eras of the band. Suddenly, the band began wondering who the dude on the demo was. In person, Gary was flat out wailing. After nailing songs from both VH eras, the band began to jam on some new material while Gary sang over it. In fact, the very first thing they jammed on ended up being a full song that would appear on the next VH album. The song, by the way, would be called "Without You."

Aside from the fact that they were impressed with his voice, Gary's persona was definitely way different from that of Dave and Sammy. Gary was just more, well, quiet. Sure, the dude can sing his dick off, but overall he is just kind of quiet and down to earth. Edward, Alex and Mike sensed Gary was a real team player, and that is something they really dug, too. As had been the case with Sammy, the band pretty much hired Gary right after his audition at 5150. Soon after he got the gig, Gary actually moved into Edward's guest house. This enabled Gary to work with Edward and the band at any and all times. From practice to actual recording, Gary could be at Edward's 5150 Studio in a second.

Now when word got out about Gary gettin' the gig, well, there were mixed reviews. You see, Extreme is probably one of the most talented and yet misunderstood bands ever. The masses seemed to only know them for "More than Words." Mind you, that song was the exception, really. Extreme was a freakin' hard rock band. They could rock their ass off, injecting everything from rippin' guitar to funk in their sound. Sadly, most people didn't know this. Many people began to wonder what Mr. "More than Words" was doing in Van Halen? I guess these people just didn't really know Gary or Extreme. Perhaps they never heard their entire albums. And they probably never saw how Extreme stole the show at the 1992 Freddy Mercury Tribute concert by performing a searing twenty-minute medley of Queen classics. In fact, Gary was one of the few singers on that day whose band didn't have to tune *down,* ok? Regardless, most people had no idea and only saw this amazing singer as Mr. "More than Words." I imagine that song had to be a blessing and a curse for Gary and Extreme, all at once.

On top of that, many people were still fuming about the whole MTV Awards debacle. Hell, many had still believed Dave was back in the band! So when all this went down and Gary got the gig, you could basically say he started out with three strikes. Say what you want, but I'll tip my cap to Gary Cherone. How many people woulda had the *cojones* to step up in that situation and take on that gig? A lot of singers run around blabbing about how they would *love* to sing in Van Halen, but when there was an opening, man, most of 'em went into the witness protection program. Man, it was an *extremely* tall order for Sammy to replace Dave. Now Gary had to replace both Sammy *and* Dave! In the end, I simply believe it was too much to ask of anyone, you know? Nonetheless, Gary approached the situation with total respect of both eras of Van Halen. Unlike during the Sammy era, where the band basically shut the door on 99.9 percent of their classic material, Gary told the band he was open to singing *anything.* Whether it be Sammy era tunes or Dave era tunes, Gary was cool with singing it. This was another major reason he got the gig.

By the start of 1997, the band was locked up in 5150, working on a new album. The media were goin' mad and they wanted answers. For the most part, the band, especially Gary, steered clear of the media and just focused on the task at hand. I hear there was quite a bit of to and fro between the band and Warner Brothers on this album. Frankly, I just don't think the label dug it much. Nonetheless, Edward Van Halen stood his ground and really believed in this album. Unfortunately, the fans would not. Their first album with Gary Cherone would be titled *Van Halen III.* You know, like signaling the "third era" or "third incarnation" of the band. It was released on March 17, 1998 and can basically be called Van Halen's first and only commercial failure. Then again, a "failure" by Van Halen's insane standards means the album "only" went Gold and "only" peaked at the number 5 spot on the Billboard Album Chart.

Also, the first single from the album, "Without You," set a record by being the first single to debut number 1 on the Billboard Mainstream Rock Chart. Again, Van Halen's standards were so insanely high that despite the fact that they had accomplished all this with a third singer, most cried out "failure!" After a dozen consecutive multi-Platinum albums, the streak was officially over. For a full track list and review, please turn to the VH Discography.

The "Van Halen III Tour" kicked of in Wellington, New Zealand on April 10, 1998 and ran till November. The boys played about eighty dates on this tour. A terrific young guitar-slinger named Kenny Wayne Shepherd open many of the shows. I know Creed opened two shows for them at Madison Square Garden as well. However, the band was actually scheduled to play more shows, but about a dozen shows had to be cancelled. The reason? During a soundcheck for a show at the Docks in Hamburg, Germany, Alex Van Halen was struck by a chunk of ceiling! I guess the venue wasn't in the best of shape, so while Big Al was drumming away at soundcheck, a chunk of ceiling came hurtling down and landed on his arm. When you think about it, he's lucky to be alive. Alex ended up wearing a soft cast and the following dozen dates had to be cancelled. Meanwhile, the venue was immediately condemned the very next day.

Overall, you could say it was a wild tour. This would be the first time since 1984 that Van Halen would break out many of their classic tunes. Gary was cool with singing anything, and so he sang songs from both eras of VH, along with some of their new material, of course. The band, as usual, sounded tight. I know, cuz of course, I saw 'em on this tour as well. Edward Van Halen was still runnin', jumpin', and flyin' across the stage despite the fact that he still had not received that hip replacement. Alex would often still be playing in a neck brace, too. However, it never seemed to affect their musicianship. Unfortunately, the tour didn't produce the monster numbers of previous VH tours. Obviously, there was a bias against this new lineup that had been brewing before they ever even released an album. So when they hit the road, it seems that bias continued.

In the end, the simple fact is that Gary wasn't a good fit for Van Halen. It certainly wasn't a matter of talent, cuz again, the guy can sing his dick off. By all accounts, he is also a very decent man and quite an energetic frontman. Most people would never guess that on stage, Mr. "More than Words" could actually run circles around most frontmen. Some will say that on the *VH III* album, he was kind of trying to push his vocals to sound like Sammy Hagar. Well, whatever the case may be, Gary was only singing how the band wanted him to sing. Basically, he stepped up to the mic and did what he was asked to do. He was the new guy, so he certainly was *not* gonna be telling Edward, Alex, and Mikey what to do, you know? Gary did everything that was asked of him, gave it all he had on stage, and treated each era of VH with proper respect. For that alone, I tip my cap to the dude. You simply couldn't ask for anything more.

When the tour wrapped in November of 1998, the band would take a break. In August of 1999, the boys were all set to begin work on their next album. Apparently, Danny "Kootch" Kortchmar was brought in to produce. Well, just two months later, everything came to a screeching halt. In November of 1999, Van Halen issued a press release stating that Gary Cherone was leaving the band. According to the press release, the split was amicable. After just three years and one album, the third incarnation of Van Halen was over. Basically, this is where the Van Halen story ends. Or so it seemed, anyway…

Don't Call It a Comeback

"I never saw Eddie playing live with Van Halen until the very end of Van Halen with Sammy Hagar, so I never saw the original but I heard the records, and he was just awesome, he was great. I hope his health is doing better, I don't know what's going on with that, but he rewrote the book, kind of like Hendrix and Clapton. He was the next guy to actually turn it all around."

– Eric Johnson

Since the release of 1998's *Van Halen III*, the band has not released any new material. Although I will say Edward Van Halen took part in a pretty cool collaboration around this time. In 1999, legendary filmmaker Ennio Moriccone released the film *Legend of 1900*. Ennio was in charge of the soundtrack too, of course. The amazing Roger Waters came on board to pen the film's title song. For the three people out there who may not know who he is, Roger was an original member of the legendary rock group, Pink Floyd. So Roger penned the very cool song, "Lost Boys Calling." The bonus? None other than Edward Van Halen contributed some sweet guitar to this track. Many people out there are simply not aware of this very cool collaboration, so if you have a chance, please check out this track, cuz it's definitely worth a listen.

Anyway, after Gary Cherone and the band had parted ways in November of 1999, you could say a whole lot has gone down in Edward Van Halen's life. Sorry folks, but I honestly believe the man's personal life and struggles are nobody's business. In other words, I've honestly made absolutely no effort to look into that side of things. However, to be fair, I can relay to you what Edward himself told *Guitar World* magazine in 2004. After maintaining complete and total silence since 1999, Edward Van Halen finally opened up to the boys of *GW* in their August 2004 issue. Seems that period of his life, 1998 to 2003, had been quite a roller coaster ride.

For starters, in 1998, VH released an album that could be considered their first and only commercial failure. On November 5, 1999, Van Halen issued a press release stating that they've parted ways with Gary Cherone. On November 16, 1999, Edward Van Halen finally had hip replacement surgery. Surprisingly, it was only a one-hour procedure and Edward was totally conscious during the whole thing! For kicks, I believe he even made an audio recording of the procedure. Everything went amazingly well and Edward was on his feet again within just two days. I believe the procedure is the same one the great Bo Jackson had done back when he suffered a career-ending hip injury playing football.

In another shocking turn of events, somewhere around the year 2000, Edward was diagnosed with cancer. I believe it was a form of tongue cancer. Well, it seems the cancer was no match for Edward, cuz he kicked its fuckin' ass. I have to say it's refreshing that someone would keep something like this private while they were dealing with it. We live in a day and age where most celebrities so much as stub a toe and they're on *Oprah,* whining about it the very next day. Edward Van Halen decided to go through his battle in private, and so I feel he's the only one who can truly talk about that. I will say that aside from being a musical inspiration to millions worldwide, the fact that he battled cancer and kicked its ass is as inspiring as his music, perhaps even more. Sadly, the high of beating that dreaded disease was met with the low of his twenty-year marriage to Valerie Bertinelli ending. I also believe that around this time, Van Halen parted ways with Warner Brothers Records. The band had been on that label for about twenty-five years, but now that relationship would end, too.

So as you can see, the six years from 1998 to 2004 were a very emotionally and physically trying time for Edward Van Halen. I believe there were times during this period were he didn't even play guitar or write music. Then again, when you are fighting for your life, hey, it's totally understandable. Fortunately, he had the support of his family, friends, and fans to help him along the way.

By early 2004, rumors began to circulate that Van Halen was going to reunite with one of their former singers. The question, of course, was who? Obviously, it had to be Dave or Sammy. Both of 'em appeared to be in fightin' shape after their surprising *Sam and Dave* tour during the summer of 2002. Well, in the spring of 2004, a press release was issued which confirmed that

Van Halen had hooked up with Sammy Hagar and was going to hit the road in June 2004.

Apparently, Sam and Alex had spoken over the phone in early 2004, which led to Sam and Edward speaking over the phone. The phone conversations seemed to go very well, and the boys buried the hatchet, so to speak. Man, it had been six years since Van Halen had last toured. You could say it had been six *very* long years. I believe the longest amount of time Van Halen had ever gone without touring had been about two or three years. So six years is like a goddamn eternity.

Of course, many fans were pissed off that the band hadn't hooked up with Diamond Dave again. Hey, I totally understand. Many people would love to see the Classic VH lineup have one more go at it. In the end, for reasons I'm sure only they know, the band decided Sammy was the man for the job. What was really different about this tour is that it would be the first VH tour ever that would not be done in support of a new album. Instead, the tour was in support of their second greatest hits album, *The Best of Both Worlds*, which was released in July 2004.

This two-disc set is really what their first greatest hits should have been. In fact, it's what the band had originally wanted to do back in 1996 before settling on just one disc. As a bonus, the band would go into 5150 and record three new songs with Sammy. "It's About Time," "Up for Breakfast," and "Learning to See" would be the three new tracks added to their new greatest hits package. The album did pretty well, especially for being their second greatest hits package. It actually peaked at the number 3 spot on the Billboard Album Chart and has gone Platinum. For a full track list and review, please turn to the VH Discography.

Now as you can imagine, the critics had a field day. I mean, the majority of critics have never been kind to VH to begin with, but now the majority of 'em were screaming out "MONEY TOUR!" Folks, I'm gonna let you in on a little secret. Um, every single freakin' tour is a "MONEY TOUR," ok? I hate to burst anyone's bubble, but a band's very first tour is as much a "money-making tour" as their third tour, fifth tour or twelfth tour. Sure they love and live to take their music to the people and play live. But the reality is that touring is how these men earn a living, therefore every tour, by definition, is a "money maker." I just don't think anyone in their right mind ever tours to end up broke, ok?

At the same time many cried out "COMEBACK!" Well, how do you "come back" from a dozen consecutive multi-Platinum albums and over 75 million albums sold worldwide? How do you "come back" after having changed the face of rock and reinvented the guitar? Yeah, it had been six very long years since VH last toured at all, and nine very long years since they had last toured with Sammy. But I just don't see it as a "comeback." Damn, that just sounds so cliché to me, you know? If anything it could be classified as a "comeback" for Edward Van Halen on a very personal level. That period from 1998 to 2003 was simply brutal. The fact that this man was able to survive that period and come back to play for us again is very cool. You know, I believe Edward has *earned* the right. Just as Jordan *earned* the right to try his hand at baseball, or to come back to basketball a couple of times, Edward has *earned* the right to get up on that stage for another go around. Unfortunately, some people just don't see it that way. You could say Van Halen's 2004 tour was by far their most controversial, ever.

Van Halen's "Best of Both Worlds Tour" kicked of in Greensboro, North Carolina on June 11, 2004 and ran till November. The band would play eighty dates on this tour. Silvertide, a young, talented and rockin' new group, opened many dates of this tour. Toward the final leg, the equally cool Laidlaw handled the opening duties. Now, there's been all kinds of talk about this tour, and the Internet certainly doesn't help any. Man, sometimes you have people who attended the same show giving different versions of that very same show! Whispers abound as to whether the boys still had it. Or, specifically, does Edward still have it? As if Edward and his band have anything to prove at this point, you know?

Well, I caught the boys on this tour (my fifth time seeing them live). The night I saw 'em, they played for two and a half hours without a hitch (well, other than Edward's guitar strap malfunction during the middle of "Panama," which was quickly corrected, and the invisible keyboard player hittin' a couple of bum notes during the "When It's Love" intro). I was even lucky enough to score a video bootleg of the show (sweet).

Man, to see Edward Van Halen up on stage, after all he's gone through, was very moving. But to see him run around that stage nonstop for two and a half hours was freakin' mind-blowing. The 'ole hip replacement didn't slow him down at all. Then again, he had a brand new hip put in, so it makes sense that he hasn't slowed down. It's not like they replaced his bum hip with a hip from some recently deceased 106-year-old former field goal kicker, you know? Edward and the band were absolutely indefatigable on the night I saw them. To begin with, Edward is ripped. Somebody musta slipped our boy a Pilates tape, cuz man, no one should look that physically fit just a few months shy of their fiftieth birthday.

During the show, he was in constant motion, performing many of his classic "Flying Eddies" and even sliding across the front of the stage on his knees during the intro to "Panama." I just could not believe this was an almost fity-year-old guy with a hip replacement who had just finished battling cancer a couple of years before. His playing was on point throughout the whole show. From "Dreams" to "Somebody Get Me a Doctor," the boys were tearin' it up. Sure, there would be a little flub here or there. But hey, *everyone* has that. Overall, I just gotta say that Edward was, well, Edward! Put it to you this way: the concert opened with "Jump" and he flat out *nailed* the solo. Any questions?

Sammy also displayed lots of energy and his vocals were absolutely top notch. Mikey held down the low end while providing his classic background vocals and plenty of onstage energy, too. And then there's Alex Van Halen. Man, what can you say about Big Al? Flat out, one of the most underrated drummers in the history of rock. I know that sounds crazy, but I truly think he gets overlooked. Obviously, his little brother gets a whole lot of attention, and it's well- deserved. But man, without Alex Van Halen, this band would not be. If you saw him on this tour, then you know precisely what I mean.

Strangely, the most controversial aspect of the 2004 Van Halen Tour seemed to be, of all things, Edward Van Halen's solo guitar spot. For whatever reason, a whole lot of folks, including the majority of music critics, seem to be a bit puzzled by Edward's solo spot on this tour. To be honest, Edward did change things up a bit on this tour. But hey, the man actually told us he would! I can only speak about the one show I attended, but here's what went down. Oh, and before I begin, lemme say that I have *never* attended a concert for a "solo spot." Yes, that even includes Edward's solo spots, which have always been bloody brilliant. I do enjoy the solo spot and look at it as a nice bonus, but I don't go to concerts to hear a solo spot. Hell, I don't even go to concerts to hear guitar solos. I go to concerts to hear the *music*. It just so happens Van Halen's killer rock music happens to contain a lot of sick-ass guitar! Anyway, here's a blow-by-blow of Edward's spot from the 2004 concert I attended.

The solo spot kicks off with Edward jammin' the main riff from the Who's smokin' cover of "Young Man Blues." Right off the bat, this is something completely different from what he's done in the past. Edward has *never* started his solo spot like this. So he tears into the main riff and is simply playing the hell out of it. He then walks towards Alex, who joins in for just a few bars but then stops. Shit, they're teasing us! Edward then walks towards the front of the stage and jams that main riff some more. He then walks back towards Alex, counts off "one, two, three, four!" and then they both tear into "Young Man Blues." I imagine this was the equivalent of being transported back to the Van Halen family home in Pasadena during the late '60s and early '70s. How many times did these two cats jam on this song back when they were growing up? Edward was facing Alex the whole time and absolutely wailing. He then began to play his own variations on the "Young Man Blues" riff, and even managed to throw in a little soloing, too. As Edward went off, Alex held down the rhythm. Man, they were *totally* locked in.

Folks, this is how Van Halen was created, and they were showing it to us. This is *precisely* how Edward and Alex wrote music when they were growing up and how they have continued to write music throughout their entire life. It was the two of them, *together,* jamming. As I watched, I almost felt like an intruder. It just seemed so damn personal, you know, watching them jam. After precisely two minutes, their jam ended and the crowd roared their approval.

Edward then walked up to the mic and said, "If I go on too long, throw something at me! 'Cause I tend to get wrapped up in this shit. I don't know what the fuck we're doing...we're just jamming." And there you have it. The dude is actually letting us know and yet some people just don't get it? I know for a fact my show was not the only one he did this at. In fact, I believe he did this at every single show on this tour! Edward has *never* done this before. He's basically telling the audience that he doesn't know what the hell he is gonna do and that he is just gonna jam. Obviously, he more or less knows the things he can and can't play. What he didn't know was in what order. You know, he improvised quite a bit. For the first time ever, he went out there and did a solo spot without really having a regimented plan as to what he was gonna do.

Right after he says this he unleashes some absolutely searing blues licks, with plenty of tasty string bending, too. He then throws in an assortment of his trademark fast, fluid passages, dive bombs, pull-offs and two-hand tapping. After about a minute, this leads into him jamming some chords. I never heard what he was playing before, so perhaps it's a jam/song he's been working on. After about a minute of jammin' those chords, he throws in some more two-hand tapping licks. These are some of the more classical-sounding tapping licks he's always been known for. I've heard them before and they still sound wicked to this day. He also throws in some very cool tapped harmonics as well.

After about thirty seconds, this leads to the intro for the classic VH song, "Women in Love." Edward merrily taps his way through it with ease as he palms his pick in his right hand. When he finishes playing the intro to "Women in Love," Edward actually throws the pick away and begins to play some cool licks with a combination of finger-picking/pull-offs. You know, finger-picking with the right hand and pull-offs with the left hand. This leads into more nasty blues licks and furious trilling on the high E string above the twelfth fret. Mind you, he's not using a pick. Edward was going off with nothing but his fingers, á la Jeff Beck, and it sounded fantastic. He signals the conclusion of this section by slamming an E chord and letting that bitch ring.

As that wonderful, bright red E chord was ringing, Edward strolled over to his amps. Apparently, he had a box of smokes placed right next to them, while a cigarette lighter dangled on a string in front of one of his amp cabinets. Edward grabbed a smoke and lit up. He also grabbed another guitar pick, too. Edward then laid down right in front of that monster stack of amp cabinets and began to work some feedback into a single, glorious ringing note. Now the uninitiated will sit there and go, "Huh, what the hell?" You know, some people would be totally clueless as to what the man is doing, while others may think, "Oh, cool, he's just working some feedback and ringing a note." I tend to look a bit deeper. Go back to the beginning of this book and see what I wrote about Edward's earliest memory of music. Remember?

Edward Van Halen's earliest memory of music is of his dad, sitting in his practice room in their home, holding a note on his clarinet for as long as he could. His dad would play long, sustained notes, dripping with *tone*. While Edward laid on the stage in front of that monster wall of cabinets, eyes shut, cigarette dangling from his lips, holding that one glorious note, he was doing *precisely* what his old man had done for years. Edward was going after it, letting that single note wash over him and the entire arena. No different than what his old man used to do in his little practice room in their home. It seemed that Edward lay there ringing that single glorious note for an eternity. In actuality, it was for just about thirty seconds.

After that, he got back up to his knees, threw in a few wicked dive bombs, rose up to his feet, and strolled back to the front of the stage. Once there, he took another slow drag from his cigarette, placed it in the headstock of his guitar (a signature EVH move he's been doing forever) and began to play the intro to another VH song, "Little Guitars." Man, it sounded sweet! Those familiar with this piece know the intro consists of some very cool flamenco-flavored passages. So to hear this one live is always a treat. Edward freakin' nailed it, complete with furious trilling on the high E and all. After this he did a bit of jammin', throwing in some different chords and whatnot. This leads into a cool and slightly different version of the classic VH instrumental, "Cathedral." By that I mean he actually threw in a bit of a new variation on the opening chords, as well as some wah pedal during the piece, too.

At the start of "Cathedral," he really drew some cool sounds out of his axe. Since he uses a delay pedal on this piece, it makes all those sounds even wilder. Overall, it was cool, although he did tend to go on a bit too long on this. The studio version of "Cathedral" is just one minute and twenty seconds. Edward carried "Cathedral" to about three minutes on this night. It sounded fine, but I could see how some people may think it went on for about a minute or so too long. On a positive note, nobody threw anything at him! When "Cathedral" concluded, he then proceeded to play one of the many classic searing passages from the immortal "Eruption." For those familiar with the piece, it's the passage he plays just after that pause in the middle of the track. You know, after the pause and just before he breaks into the tapping section. Edward played the hell out of it, and threw in some more filthy blues licks, too. Man, Edward can play those Eric Clapton Cream-era licks with the best of 'em.

While he did this, he dicked around a bit with what I'm guessing to be a volume pedal. It was a trip, cuz he's just rippin' some blues and suddenly the volume drops to a whisper! It almost sounds like he is playing underwater, and then slowly he'd bring the volume all the way back up. I've never seen him do this before, either. But it really came off sounding cool. He then throws in another dive bomb, to boot. After this, he immediately goes back into that smokin' passage from "Eruption," and this leads to the insane intro of another VH classic, "Mean Street."

Man, Edward was just pounding the neck into submission and played the living shit out of the "Mean Street" intro. He didn't do the whole thing, but he did enough to where you knew *precisely* what he was playing and that it was spot on. He also threw in some more two-hand tapping and jammed some blues as well. This leads back to that passage from "Eruption," only now he continues right on into the closing section of "Eruption." You know, that classical-sounding two-hand tapping section that closes the piece. Edward pulled this off fluidly and gracefully. As he got above the twelfth fret on his axe, he threw in some cool variations on the closing section with even more wicked, classical-sounding tapping licks. Without missing a beat Edward segues right back into the closing of "Eruption." As he strolls to the right of the stage, the cheers of the crowd grow louder. Edward acknowledges them by bowing his head and mouthing "thank you." By this point, the crowd is going apeshit, of course.

He then goes back to his side of the stage and stands right on the very lip of the stage. This is where he finishes off the final section of "Eruption." There he stood, head back, eyes shut, tapping furiously. Eventually, his head bowing down, eyes still shut, nodding in perfect unison with the piece. As is commonplace during his solo spot, Edward appears to be off in his own world. Man, it's a world most of us mere mortals will never be lucky enough to even visit. Meanwhile, it seems like Edward owns beachfront property there.

Finally, Edward concludes the last section of "Eruption," smacks that one freakin' harmonic on the low E string at the twelfth fret, and dive bombs to all bloody hell. He then whips his guitar around and heads back towards Alex, who has now jumped in to signal the end of Edward's solo spot by madly thrashing away on his drums. Oh, but he's not finished. Edward spins around, strolls back to the front of the stage, and proceeds to empty his clip. He fires off a few more searing blues licks and even throws in the classic "hummingbird" picking section from "Eruption," to boot! And yes, he played it seamlessly.

At this point, I don't think the arena can get any louder. Even the security guys at the front of the stage were peeking back at Edward during his solo spot! (You know who you are, Mr. "Concert Security" guy. Don't even try to deny it dude cuz I have the videotape to prove it.) Anyway, by now the entire place has officially gone mad. Edward begins thrashing about at the front of the stage like a kid who just ingested too much Kool-Aid. He then unleashes five, count 'em, freakin' *five* of his classic "Flying Eddies" in a row! As if that wasn't cool enough, what's even more insane is they were each in perfect unison with Alex's drumming. Talk about being in sync, but this was ridiculous. After this came a bit more of his "Little Johnny's had too much Kool-Aid" type of thrashing about. Edward was then able to somehow regain control of his body and walk back towards Alex, who was still pounding away. The solo spot officially ended the same way it began, with Edward standing in front of Alex's kit. The two brothers, facing each other, *together,* jammin' the closing section from the Who's cover of "Young Man Blues."

Soon as they hit the final note, the entire arena is already chanting "Eddie! Eddie! Eddie!" at the top of their lungs. You know, I've been to many rock concerts in my life, but I have *never* seen this happen at a single other show. The entire arena doesn't chant "Kirk! Kirk! Kirk!" at Metallica concerts or "Joe! Joe! Joe!" at Aerosmith concerts. Even Clapton and Hendrix never had an entire arena full of people chanting "Eric! Eric! Eric!" or "Jimi! Jimi! Jimi!" Why do they do that at Van Halen concerts? In fact, it's not uncommon to hear the entire arena chanting "Eddie! Eddie! Eddie!" *before* the freakin' concert even begins. You wanna know why that is? *Respect.* It all comes down to good 'ole fashioned respect. You see, the people who attend a Van Halen concert know they aren't just seeing a "good" guitar player, or even a "great" guitar player. No, they are fully aware they are seeing *"the"* guitar player. And when you are in the presence of *"the"* guitar player, you pay your respects. Frankly, it reminds me of the 1975 film *King Kong.* You know, the scene where the natives all line up in front of that huge wall and summon that monster by chanting "Kong! Kong! Kong!" It's the same thing, really.

At this point Edward is clearly moved. He strolls up to the mic, throws his arms up in the air and says, "Sometimes it works and sometimes it doesn't! I had fun and I hope you did, too. Love y'all." The crowd kept going, "Eddie! Eddie! Eddie!" He stood at the front of the stage, saluted the crowd, closed his eyes, and pounded his chest several times. Then he flexed his arm, as if to say, "Yeah, I'm *still* here!" There is one indisputable fact, ladies and gentlemen, and that is this: When Edward Van Halen is on his game, man, he can still tear the freakin' roof off an arena with an ease that can be both inspiring and frightening, all at once. Man, I don't know if it's even fair for one man to have that kind of power. Unbelievable.

As the cheers continued, Edward strolled back to the mic and said, "Thank you. Man, you're gonna make me lose it here! Thank you." Hey, go on and lose it Edward. I know there were some people standing around me who'd already lost it. Knock yourself out and let it out. After six very long, brutal years, Edward Van Halen was right back were he's always belonged. It had been too long since this cat had been on stage, and he was obviously quite moved by the reception the crowd was giving him. I don't wanna get all Oprah on you, so let's just say a few tears were shed and move on.

Man, what more could you want? I really wanted to give you the full blow-by-blow account, cuz I think a lot of people out there have a totally wrong idea about what a "solo spot" is truly like. As if hearing over two hours of some of the greatest hard rock music ever written isn't enough, we got treated to about seventeen minutes of Edward Van Halen going ballistic on his own. Well, the first couple of minutes (and the final minute) were Edward *and* Alex going ballistic, really. Talk about a bonus! I say this because traditionally Edward's solo spot has always been anywhere from six to ten minutes in length. Even during "major" concert events like 1983's US Festival or the shows from their 1992 tour that eventually became their double live album, his solo spot was just about ten or eleven minutes in length. On this night, Edward Van Halen gave me and everyone else there a few extra minutes of madness, and it was terrific. Of course, many critics will bitch about the solo spot being "excessive." Frankly, these cats just don't get it.

For starters, Edward didn't invent the solo spot. Tons of fantastic musicians have been doing solo spots in concert for hundreds of years. If you really look at it, what Edward does is really no different than the "extended jamming" legends like Hendrix, Clapton, Led Zeppelin, or even the Grateful Dead did. Well, except Edward does it during his solo spot, while the others would usually do it during actual songs. The term "extended jamming" is just a nice way of saying, "Um, excuse me while I go off and solo for a long while during this song."

If Hendrix and Clapton had the right to do fifteen-minute (or even longer) versions of their songs, with minute after minute of soloing, then Edward has earned his right to do his thing, too. If Led Zeppelin earned the right to give us half-hour versions of "Dazed and Confused," then Edward has earned his right to do his thing, too. Hell, I believe some Grateful Dead "jams" are *still* going on today! All kidding aside, if the Dead earned the right to do that, then Edward has, too. Man, you can even look outside the world of rock. The legendary John Coltrane was known to solo for a half an hour or more. Same thing goes for the legendary Duane Allman, too. So are they "excessive?" Whether you solo during a song with the rest of the band or solo by yourself during a "solo spot," hey, a solo is a solo. Actually, you could say what Edward does is a bit different in that he doesn't mess with his songs. Van Halen has never been a group to go off whipping out fifteen-, twenty-, or even thirty-minute versions of their songs. Plus, Edward's solos during songs are actually pretty damn short. I like the fact that in concert he will basically give us the music the way we've always heard it, and then throw in that solo spot as a nice bonus. Traditionally his solo spot has always ranged from about six to ten minutes, so to get some extra minutes during the 2004 Tour was very cool.

In fact, during Van Halen's club days, as well as on their first tour in 1978, Edward's solo spot was "Eruption." That was it. But as the years go on and you get more and more music under your belt, obviously you are gonna have more ideas to add to the solo spot. In turn, the length of the spot grows. Considering all the amazing music and ideas this man had during his twenty-six- year career, I think it's actually quite impressive he keeps his solo spot so concise and entertaining. In the end, his solo spot really is a nice bonus. It's like going to a baseball game early so you can catch batting practice *and* the game, you know?

In concert you get to hear Edward and his band's music for a couple of hours and then you get to see a bit of how he comes up with that music and how he can further flesh out some of his ideas during his solo spot. Another major bonus is that during the solo spot he gets to play passages and intros from many different Van Halen songs. You know, from songs that he will not be performing in their entirety during the concert. Man, that's *definitely* a sweet bonus.

Frankly, complaining that Edward Van Halen's solo spot is "excessive" would be like complaining that your girlfriend gives you "too much head." Man, gimme a break. Of course, in the end, it's all in the eye (and ear) of the beholder. So I am not gonna say that it's right or wrong. I may not attend concerts specifically for solos, but hey, I've always enjoyed Edward's solo spot very much. In the end, what I am simply saying is that he's *earned* the right to do whatever the hell he wants during his solo spot. After twenty-six years in the bright light, hey, do your thing, dude. His solo spot is just that, *his* solo spot. If Edward wants to go out there and kick his guitar around the stage for ten minutes while wearing nothing but a cup and singing "I'm a Little Teapot," hey, knock yourself out, bro. My point being that as an artist, it is his right.

For my money, as long as he gives me those two hours of killer music and plays the hell out of it, I'm cool. The solo spot, to me, is a bonus. Besides,

I simply can't think of too many people on this planet who can go out on stage *alone,* armed with nothing more than a damn guitar, and keep an entire arena full of people absolutely mesmerized.

The true irony lies in the fact is that for well over twenty years now, Edward Van Halen has wanted to drop the solo spot from his concert altogether. He has mentioned this fact many times during countless interviews over the years. Since even before David Lee Roth split the band, Edward has wanted to scrap his solo spot. Well, everyone from his bandmates to people at the record label would probably dropkick him if he did. And Edward himself knows there is that faction of fans out there who actually show up specifically to see that solo spot. For some people, it is the highlight of their night! So in the end, to try and please the fans, Edward kept the solo spot. But if he had his way, man, he woulda dropped the solo spot, like, back around 1982.

That's not to say he still doesn't enjoy it. I'm sure he does. But like anyone else, from Hendrix and Page to Clapton and Stevie Ray, Edward has his good days and bad days. He's human. But that's not to say he still doesn't get off doing it. Man, he had that shit-eating grin on his face throughout much of the night when I saw him, including during the solo spot. For those who know EVH, well, you know this is a good sign. The man still puts himself into it. You know, the *commitment* is still there. Don't take my word for it; just listen to what Silvertide's talented young guitarist Nick Perri had to say about Edward during an interview in February 2005, just a few months after touring with VH.

Nick Perri: "Eddie Van Halen has this room that he calls his 'tuning room.' It's really another dressing room – bigger than some gigs we've played – and it's completely empty except for one amplifier and his guitar. He'll go in and play for hours and hours before a show."

One man, one amp, one guitar, baby. It always seems to come down to that, doesn't it? How many summers has Edward been doing this for now? About twenty-seven of 'em, right? This man has absolutely zero to prove. Not a damn thing. Yet there he is, before a show, playing for hours and hours. It's that *commitment* to the craft that made Edward who he is.

To this very day, the man simply loves to play. I mean, this is a guy who does interviews while playing his freakin' guitar. No bullshit. He'll sit there and do interviews while playing an unplugged electric guitar. It's like he can't stop!

In fact, I've heard stories that Edward actually moves his fingers in his sleep. You know, he lies there, fast asleep, and moves his fingers as if he's playing the guitar. Could you imagine?

Over the years, Edward's always made it very clear that either he was gonna make it playing music or end up pumping gas. However, he's always added that if he had ended up pumping gas for a living, he'd still gig at night and on the weekends. In other words, he'd still find a way to get out there and play his music. He's in it for life, baby. Frankly, I don't think Edward could *not* play music, you know? And as if that isn't cool enough, on the 2004 tour, he still continued his tradition of being very cool to his opening acts. Hell, he even took time to jam with Nick before shows.

Nick Perri: "When I became buds with him, he invited me in to the tuning room, and we were doing forty-five minutes to an hour every night for a month. He would play a riff and I would play off it and we'd jam, and it was an amazing opportunity."

Could you imagine? That's like Michael Jordan inviting you to into his private gym every night, for a month, to shoot some hoop. What a mind-blowing experience. Most people would give their left nut just to meet EVH, never mind to even jam with him once. Nick got to jam with the master every night for a month. Well done, kid.

Overall, 2004 was another wild year in VH history. Will they come back and do it again? Who knows? Frankly, Edward and the band have had absolutely zero to prove at this point. In fact, they haven't had a damn thing to prove for decades now. Regardless what their future plans might be, rest assured their legacy is intact. I just hope the boys stay in good health and continue to be passionate about their music and their musicianship...

Discography...

Van Halen (1978)

1) Runnin' With the Devil
2) Eruption
3) Your Really Got Me
4) Ain't Talkin' 'bout Love
5) I'm the One
6) Jamie's Cryin'
7) Atomic Punk
8) Feel Your Love Tonight
9) Little Dreamer
10) Ice Cream Man
11) On Fire

Simply put, the most groundbreaking guitar album since Jimi Hendrix's legendary *Are You Experienced?* (1967). As cliché as it may sound, this is the *motherlode*. A truly seamless masterpiece that can also be chalked up as one of the most devastating debut albums, ever. I'm tellin' ya, even your grandmother would throw up the horns listening to this shit.

The album opens with a backwards car horn, as if signaling the arrival of a new era. This leads into Michael Anthony playing eight simple bass notes on the low E string. The next sound you hear is Edward raking his pick behind the bridge of his Gibson Les Paul, which to me is the sonic equivalent of someone striking a match right before setting off a freakin' powderkeg of explosives. This leads into the super chunky riff from the album's opening track, "Runnin' With the Devil." Folks, the world would never be the same. For the next thirty-five minutes, this band proceeds to hit you upside the head with great song after great song. You know, most bands are lucky to write a single anthem in their entire career. Van Halen managed to do that with the opening track of their debut album, alone. Next up comes "Eruption." Man, this piece is so freakin' classic, it deserves its own section. So basically, I gave it one. Please turn to the FAQ for the story of the immortal "Eruption."

The third track is a cover of The Kinks classic, "You Really Got Me." VH took this song and "Van Halenized" it, baby. It is one of the greatest covers you will ever hear in your life. They totally made it their own while respecting the integrity of the original. The fourth track is another anthem, "Ain't Talkin' 'bout Love." Edward unleashes one of the greatest riffs of all time on this song, making a simple A-minor chord sound like the end of the freakin' world. Again, most bands are lucky to write a single anthem in their entire career. Van Halen wrote two on their first album, alone. Actually, three if you count their cover of "You Really Got Me." Lord knows that's an anthem, too. But it is a cover, and I'm talking more about their originals, dig? The fifth track is the searing "I'm the One." I believe this to be the earliest example of what would go on to become known as the "Van Halen boogie," or "VH boogie." Basically, it's Van Halen's take on a Texas-style boogie rhythm by way of California. For those of you out there who play guitar, um, you could make your bones playing this song. The absolute insanity, intensity, and swing of this track are simply ridiculous. The entire debut album is a clinic, but damn, this song is a true gem. The two short guitar solos on this track are among the best on this album, and that's saying something, ok?

The sixth track is the classic, "Jamie's Cryin'" Here is a terrific example of the boys showing their versatility. Coming off the madness of "I'm the One," they hit us with a cool, danceable song like "Jamie's Cryin'." The seventh track is the smokin' "Atomic Punk." To open this song, Edward rubs his hands across the strings while engaging his MXR Phase pedal. This gives us some really chewy sounding scratching before the rest of the band kicks in. Plenty of great riffing and another nasty guitar solo, too.

The eighth track is another cool, danceable track titled "Feel Your Love Tonight." Man, Van Halen is one of those rare bands, like Led Zeppelin or AC/DC, that could totally kick your ass but then turn around and write something everyone can shake their ass to. This song also happens to contain another sick guitar solo. The ninth track is "Little Dreamer." I guess you can say this was Van Halen's first attempt at a ballad. Well, kind of, anyway. The song has a slow, grinding rhythm to it. The tenth track is their raucous cover of the John Brim blues song, "Ice Cream Man." For starters, the song opens with Dave singing over some cool blues played on an acoustic guitar. What many people don't know is that is was Dave playing the guitar! Yes folks, it was indeed Dave, not Edward, who plays the acoustic intro to this song. When the intro ends, Dave summons the boys and the whole song explodes! On an album just brimming with insane guitar, the solo on "Ice Cream Man" would get many people's vote for the sickest solo. Well, excluding the immortal "Eruption," of course.

The eleventh and final track of *Van Halen* is "On Fire." Definitely an appropriate title cuz the boys go mad on this one. After pounding a few power chords, Edward gives us some rude, almost mechanical-sounding riffing to open this song by slamming a couple of harmonics at the fifth fret. The solo on this song is about ten seconds of "what the hell?" The story goes that Edward wasn't too sure of what he wanted to play during the solo, so the rest of the band told him to just play like John McLaughlin. So he did! Edward's solo during "On Fire" is basically a tip of the cap to the legendary guitarist, John McLaughlin.

Overall, this album gets five stars. It is about as perfect as an album can get. As I mentioned earlier in the book, I've even heard every single track from this album played on the radio. The fact that the album was recorded live with minimal overdubs is a big part of the reason it explodes out of your speakers and still sounds fresh to this very day. Remember, the music was cut in just six days. The band would usually do just two or three takes of each song and then move on. The vocals took about two weeks. This album, like most Classic VH albums, was done on a shoestring budget. I'm talkin' peanuts. It's amazing how much they were able to do with so little money and time. Truly amazing. So, as is the case with just about any album, it had its flaws, the most obvious being the mix. Basically, the mix is certainly uneven in the sense that Edward's guitar was waaay up front, while Al's drums and Mikey's bass were definitely a distant second. Not to mention the fact that if you pan your speakers hard left, you'll notice EVH's guitar is basically comin' outta one speaker. That wasn't by accident, either. That was by design, and I don't believe Edward was ever truly happy about that. But hey, it is what it is, you know?

Van Halen also signaled the beginning of an era of new rock, as well as the beginning of the '80s, too. Lord knows this album became a blueprint for a whole lotta people. You know, big anthemic rock/metal with pop edges, catchy hooks, big sing-along choruses, soaring background vocals, searing solos, and mad energy. A lot of people got rich off the formula VH helped create and perfect. Far as I know, *Van Halen* is one of the few albums in the history of music to change the face of rock *and* reinvent the guitar. Definitely a must-own and a true classic in every sense of the word. Oh, and please turn this shit up *loud,* ok? Music like this deserves to be heard *and* felt. It's the only way to get the full experience, really. Thank you.

Van Halen II (1979)

1) You're No Good
2) Dance the Night Away
3) Somebody Get Me a Doctor
4) Bottoms Up!
5) Outta Love Again
6) Light Up the Sky
7) Spanish Fly
8) D.O.A.
9) Women in Love
10) Beautiful Girls

"Some of the things about the second album I like the best. The vibe. It just seemed like it was just them jamming. It didn't seem like it was even a record, it sounded just like a tape of them playing. It seemed so live. And like songs like 'Outta Love' and the solo he does in 'You're No Good,' I just thought that stuff was over the top in feeling and what I call 'lava.' His playing is phenomenal. It's visionary."

– Trey Azagthoth

Van Halen II is a very strong follow-up to a debut album that seamed impossible to follow up. Man, most bands would crumble under the pressure of following up a debut album like *Van Halen,* but the boys managed to pull it off.

The music on *Van Halen II* was recorded in just six days (that includes vocals). Highlights from this album include the smokin' "Somebody Get Me a Doctor," the swingin' "Beautiful Girls," the insane "Light Up the Sky"(complete with sick solo), and the band's first Top 20 hit, the classic "Dance The Night Away."

For my money, there are a couple of gems on this album, too. "Outta Love Again" is a rippin' track that is definitely a favorite among hardcore VH fans. The same could be said about "D.O.A." too (the riff alone is priceless). "Bottoms Up!" shows us more of that killer VH boogie, and "Women in Love" has a very cool tapped intro and groove as well. Their cover of "You're No Good" is solid. I honestly believe this album contains some of the greatest riffs Edward Van Halen has ever crafted. Not to mention the fact that Alex Van Halen really shines on this album as well. You know, the first Van Halen album really showcases Edward's guitar. On *Van Halen II*, I believe there was a more conscious effort to bring Big Al to the forefront.

Last, but certainly not least, is the flamenco-flavored instrumental piece, "Spanish Fly." Man, I think even Andrés Segovia himself would have exclaimed, "Ay caramba!" if he'd heard this. Basically, "Spanish Fly" is Edward Van Halen picking up a nylon-string acoustic guitar and showing the world he can play all that sick shit of his on an acoustic, no problem. The track is pretty short, only about fifty-five seconds. Then again, that's all the time Edward needed to make his point. If for even a second, anyone out there doubts Edward Van Halen's chops, um, listen to "Spanish Fly." The reason being cuz there is absolutely nothing to hide behind when you are playing an acoustic guitar, folks. Edward proves that even on an acoustic guitar, his shit is still absolutely mind-boggling. From those insanely fast and fluid runs to his two-hand tapping, it still sounds just as tasty and majestic on an acoustic. Man, Edward Van Halen proved that he didn't need to be plugged in for his playing to be "electric," you feel me?

The funny thing is that just like "Eruption," this piece wasn't planned for the album, either. On December 31, 1978, Edward was hanging at a New Year's Eve party being thrown at the home of his producer, Ted Templeman. Apparently, he came upon an acoustic guitar, picked it up, and began jamming. Ted was absolutely stunned to see that Edward could play all of his insane shit on an acoustic guitar *precisely* as he did on an electric guitar. He told Edward to go home and come up with an acoustic piece for the next album, and that is how we ended up with "Spanish Fly," ladies and germs.

Overall, this album gets four stars. It is a fine sophomore effort and proved the boys were here to stay.

Women and Children First (1980)

1) And the Cradle Will Rock…
2) Everybody Wants Some
3) Fools
4) Romeo Delight
5) Tora! Tora!
6) Loss of Control
7) Take Your Whiskey Home
8) Could This Be Magic?
9) In a Simple Rhyme

On Van Halen's third studio album, the band continued to expand their horizons and try things they had never done before. For starters, this is the first Van Halen album to contain keys! Most people seem to believe their *1984* album was the first to contain any kind of piano or keyboards. Fact is 1980's *Women and Children First* had 'em before *1984* did. On the opening hit anthem, "And the Cradle Will Rock…" Edward plays the main riff on an old Wurlitzer electric piano. The sound was then run through an MXR Flanger and then into a fully cranked Marshall stack. So I could see how some people may not even notice that it's a damn piano, but it was.

Edward also brings back the acoustic guitar on this album for some really tasty blues on "Take Your Whiskey Home." Well, the intro was done acoustically before they crank it back up on the electric side of things. On "Could This Be Magic?" Edward breaks out a slide for the very first time! Apparently, Edward had *never* played slide before in his life. Well, he didn't let that stop him. The guy picked up that acoustic guitar again, grabbed that slide, and just had fun with it. It's definitely one of the gems on this album, a very cool tune that comes complete with the sound of rain. On the day the band recorded this song, it was raining outside, so they just opened the windows of the studio to capture some "outside sound." Oh, and if you listen close, you'll hear the late singer Nicolette Larson lending some cool background vocals on this tune as well.

"Everybody Wants Some" is another anthem. Well, an anthem for those who want some bootay! You know, the title is pretty self-explanatory. Although, damn, I keep seeing dancing hamburgers when I hear this song? Yeah, hardcore VH fans know what I'm talkin' about (for those who don't know, check out the wild 1985 John Cusack film, *Better Off Dead*). That rumbling you hear at the beginning of the song is Edward actually rubbing his low E string against the pickup of his guitar.

"Romeo Delight" is absolutely insane, complete with another classic solo. "Fools" contains more bluesy type riffing and a filthy groove. "Tora!

Tora!" is a cool instrumental that serves as the intro to "Loss of Control." It's an appropriate title, cuz the band sounds wild on this song. Like another classic VH hit, "Ain't Talkin' 'bout Love," this song pokes a little fun at the whole punk scene. In fact, both of these songs were written around the same time, but "Loss of Control" wouldn't see the light of day until this album. The album closes with the super rockin' "In a Simple Rhyme." For the first time ever, Edward breaks out a twelve-string Rickenbacker electric to record this song. It's definitely a cool album closer.

Overall, this album gets four stars. It's a killer album that kept the Mighty VH rollin'.

Fair Warning (1981)

1) Mean Street
2) Dirty Movies
3) Sinner's Swing
4) Hear about It Later
5) Unchained
6) Push Comes to Shove
7) So This Is Love?
8) Sunday Afternoon in the Park
9) One Foot Out the Door

*"**Fair Warning** is riff heaven from beginning to end. I just hear testosterone, an attitude of confidence. The best soloing I've ever heard in my life is on **Fair Warning**. Ed's playing on that album is non-stop melody. He's not just ripping, he's totally tasteful on every song."*
– Stephen Carpenter

Van Halen's fourth studio album, *Fair Warning,* is considered by many to be one of the most underrated rock albums of all time. I must say the people who believe this may have a good case. Then again, if you know your rock and guitar, well, you better damn well know this album. Not only cuz of the killer music, but man, this album contains some of Edward Van Halen's filthiest, bluesiest, most insane playing ever. And his tone, while always killer, is grimy, dirty, and thick as molasses on this puppy.

The album opens with Edward's insane, percussive "slap bass" style tapping, which serves as an intro to another classic anthem, "Mean Street." Basically, the intro to "Mean Street" sounds like Edward turned his guitar into conga drums or something. You gotta hear it to believe it, really. "Mean Street" is definitely another favorite among the hardcore VH fans. In fact, if you polled most of the hardcore VH fans, I guaran-damn-tee you a whole lotta them would pick this album as their favorite. Anyway, "Mean Street" is Classic Van Halen at its best. It has a classic riff, monster groove, and lots of attitude. And then there's that solo! While it only lasts about eighteen seconds, Edward manages to unleash a solo that will make your entire life flash before your eyes. It is fiery and yet quite lyrical, too. What a way to open an album. Remember how I mentioned that most bands are lucky to write one anthem in their entire career? Well, three out of the first four albums this band ever released open with an anthem. Not bad, boys…

The second track is "Dirty Movies," a cool song about a prom queen turned porn queen! The third track is "Sinner's Swing." Here we have more manic riffing and licks. The fourth track is "Hear about It Later." Yes, another fave with the hardcore VH fans. This is really a great song that was actually written on a keyboard before Edward transferred it to the guitar.

The fifth track on this album is the classic "Unchained." This song is considered by many people, hardcore fans and fans in general, to be one of the greatest, if not *the* greatest Van Halen song ever written. Basically, this song is quintessential Van Halen. Hell, I've actually come across several magazine articles and interviews over the years where none other than Edward Van Halen himself has said that "Unchained" is one of the few times in his entire career where he can listen back to his own playing and get goose bumps. For starters, the riff alone is worth the price of admission. This riff is given extra chunk and heaviness in part due to the fact that Edward had his guitar in Drop-d tuning for this song. In fact, about half of the songs on the *Fair Warning* album are played in Drop-d. The Drop-d tuning would go on to become very popular during the early '90s, obviously due to the fact that many grunge bands used this tuning. Well, Edward Van Halen was all over the Drop-d tuning way back in 1981, a full decade before the grunge scene even existed.

This song also contains the famous line "Come on Dave, gimme a break..." during the breakdown section in the middle of the song. So just who was that telling Dave to give him a break? That would be none other than Van Halen producer, Ted Templeman. Apparently, while they were doing the vocals for this song, Dave kept fooling around during the breakdown section and giving Ted a bit of a hard time. Finally, Ted punched right into the song and told Dave to give him a break. I guess when they played the song back, they liked it so much they decided to use it! Oh, by the way, the solo is pretty goddamn sweet, too.

There also happens to be a really cool music video for "Unchained" as well. During their 1981 tour, VH played a gig in Oakland and their live performance of "Unchained" from this show ended up being turned into a music video. In fact, I believe this may have been the very first music video VH ever did. I mean, it's concert footage, but nonetheless, I believe it was the first video VH ever made for MTV. And man, if you've seen it, well, you can clearly see how absolutely devastating Classic Van Halen was. The great Billy Corgan can recall the power and impact of the mighty Van Halen at this time, too.

Billy Corgan: "If you've ever seen the 'Unchained' video, you've seen a band at its public epiphany. Beautiful and free, Van Halen ruled the world with a wink and a smirk. The rockers dressed like them and the girls all wanted to fuck them—the ultimate forms of teen tribute."

The sixth track is a true gem titled "Push Comes to Shove." The reason I say it's a gem is for several reasons. For starters, it is the first and only Van Halen song the band ever wrote that could be classified as, well, "reggae." In fact, I heard the boys were influenced by the Rolling Stones song "Miss You," and so they wrote this little number. But hey, that's just what I've heard, ok? Others would say it was influenced by Led Zeppelin's tongue-in-cheek reggae tune, "D'yer Maker." Whatever the case, the band shows their versatility by pulling it off. However, the real bonus here is the guitar solo. Man, even by Edward's standards, it is quite sick! I believe the amazing Steve Vai has even said that the "Push Comes to Shove" guitar solo is his favorite Van Halen solo. On an album that is chock full of otherworldly guitar playing, um, that's saying something, ok? I can't even begin to describe it here, so please go listen to it. Believe me, you'll thank me.

"So This Is Love?" is the seventh track on the album. Another cool sing-along type of anthem, sweet solo included. The eighth track is the creepy, synthesizer-driven "Sunday Afternoon in the Park." Once again we have keys on an album way before *1984*. I believe Edward used a cheap Electro-Harmonix Micro-Synthesizer on this track. The ninth and final track on the album is the smokin' "One Foot Out the Door." I believe producer Ted Templeman came up with the song's title, which was inspired by the rapid pace at which Van Halen albums were being made.

Overall, this album gets four and a half stars. From front to back, this album is another clinic. In my opinion, it is one of the best albums the band has ever done. There is an aggressive, dark edge throughout most of the album, a lot of which had to do with the tension between Dave and Edward at the time they recorded it. Along with the fact that the band were superstars by this time and very much indulging in all the, um, "perks" that come with being a rock star.

You know, plenty of people consider *1984* to be the last "true" Van Halen album. However, I know plenty of others who'll tell you that *Fair Warning*, not *1984*, is actually the last "true" VH album. Many will tell you it's their last true hard rock album. It's all subjective, but that may just be the case.

Ironically, *Fair Warning* is the least-selling album of the Classic Van Halen era! This despite the fact that it was the band's first album to crack the Top 5 on the Billboard Album Chart. In my opinion, this album is kinda like their *Powerage*.

My favorite AC/DC album of all time is *Powerage* (1978). Yes, I even like it more than the brilliant *Highway to Hell* (1979) and the classic *Back in Black* (1980). Man, talk about a killer album. The nine tracks on *Powerage* are insane. Songs like the killer opener, "Rock 'n' Roll Damnation," the smokin'

"Downpayment Blues," and the classic "Sin City" are just mind-blowing. The band goes bananas on this album, and Bon Scott's voice is simply amazing. Cheers to Bon, always.

The funny thing is that this album is the least selling of AC/DC's classic era, too! For whatever reason, just like *Fair Warning,* the album didn't put up monster numbers. I believe it went Platinum and just stayed there ever since. Its sales absolutely pale in comparison to most of their other albums – especially classics like *Highway to Hell* and *Back in Black.* That's why I tend to compare these two. If you speak with hardcore fans of both these bands, plenty of 'em will tell you that *Powerage* and *Fair Warning* are their favorite albums.

Finally, I should point out the overall production/sound/mix of *Fair Warning* was killer. I truly believe this was the first VH album of the classic era to have a decent budget. It shows, too. If you have a good ear, you can totally tell. Listen to the first album, then listen to this one. Huge difference, man. The fact that Edward began to have a lot more input at this time probably had something to do with it, too. Plus, I believe that after seeing them score three consecutive Platinum albums in three years, Warner Brothers actually realized the band was the real deal and opened up their wallets. So while this album was still done quickly, the production/sound/mix on this album is probably the best of any of their albums, up until this point. Overall, it's still one of their best produced/sounding/mixed albums, even to this very day.

Diver Down (1982)

1) Where Have All the Good Times Gone?
2) Hang 'em High
3) Cathedral
4) Secrets
5) Intruder
6) (Oh) Pretty Woman
7) Dancing in the Streets
8) Little Guitars (Intro)
9) Little Guitars
10) Big Bad Bill (Is Sweet William Now)
11) The Full Bug
12) Happy Trails

Basically, *Diver Down* is the first and only mistake of the Classic Van Halen era. Then again, the band was so huge at this time, the album still managed to go multi-Platinum. It also charted higher than any of their previous albums, peaking at number 3 on the Billboard Album Chart. Don't ask me to explain how this happened, cuz I don't know?

Over the years, the band – specifically Edward Van Halen – has pretty much apologized for making this album! Edward really tried to put himself into it, but hated making it. The reason being that of the twelve songs on the album, four of them are covers. Well, four covers plus the 'a cappella version of "Happy Trails" that closes out the album. Apparently, David Lee Roth and producer Ted Templeman wanted to go this route. The rest of the band went along with the idea, although none of them really liked it.

Now, Lord knows plenty of bands in the history of music have done multiple covers on an album. I mean, each of the Beatles' first three albums contains about four or five cover songs. Everyone from Clapton to Hendrix has done many covers. Hell, look at Nirvana's classic *Unplugged* album – it's, like, half covers. But hey, it's Van Halen, so you know critics had a field day with this album. The sad part is the original songs on the album are pretty cool. Along with the fact that their cover of the classic "(Oh) Pretty Woman" sounded terrific. Man, the intro to "Pretty Woman," which is titled "Intruder," is killer, too. Edward does everything from wrestle insane feedback to actually draw wild sounds outta his guitar by rubbing, of all things, a Schlitz Malt Tall beer can over the strings! So, overall, there are still some cool spots on this album.

For starters, the third track is the instrumental "Cathedral." This piece shows Edward using volume-swells in a very cool manner. Using a combination of echo and chorus effects, Edward hammers notes on the fretboard with his left hand while simultaneously rolling the volume knob on and off with his right hand. The fourth track is "Secrets." It's a rockin' song, and I believe it's the first song Edward ever recorded with a doubleneck guitar. He used a Gibson twelve-string/six-string doubleneck to record this track.

The eighth and ninth tracks are "Little Guitars (Intro)" and "Little Guitars." The intro is a cool, flamenco-flavored piece that I believe was inspired by Edward listening to some Montoya. Like "Spanish Fly," this piece was also played on a nylon-string guitar. If you listen close, the final section of the intro actually sounds like two people playing. The way Edward pulled this off was really quite clever. He tremolo picks the high E, B, and D strings (open) while performing hammer-ons and pull-offs on the low E string with his left hand!

For my money, the true gem of this album may just be "Big Bad Bill (Is Sweet William Now)." Despite the fact that this is a cover song, I say this for several reasons. For starters, the band shows incredible versatility in pulling this little number off. Edward uses a Gibson hollow-body on this track, while Michael Anthony used a large acoustic bass and Alex played the drums with brushes. It is unlike anything the band has done before or since.

The real bonus is that Edward and Alex coaxed their dad out of retirement to come play on this song! Yes, Jan Van Halen dusted off his trusty 'ole clarinet and contributed some very cool playing on "Big Bad Bill..." The funny thing is, their old man hadn't played for years. On top of that, he had actually lost a part of one of his fingers due to an accident he had while doing work around the house. And as if this didn't give him enough reason to be apprehensive, I've heard he was also worried that his dentures were gonna fly out while he played!

In the end, the boys convinced him to have a go at it and Jan did a fine job. He plays clarinet throughout the entire track, even rippin' out a cool solo, too! The album closes with the band doing an a cappella version of "Happy Trails." To me, this is quite reminiscent of how Cream closed out their *Disraeli Gears* album with the raucous sing-along, "Mothers Lament." The boys of VH were just having some fun here, although the track proves they probably could have made a living as a barbershop quartet if the rock 'n' roll thing hadn't worked out!

Overall, this album gets two stars. Most of the original tracks are cool, and their cover of "(Oh) Pretty Woman" is terrific, but I just can't give it a higher rating due to the covers and lack of any real anthems, either. The really cool thing is that this album really lit a fire under Edward Van Halen's ass. He's always been a man who would rather bomb doing his own music than succeed doing other people's music. Edward knew he could write great rock songs and wanted to get back to that.

So, thanks in big part to *Diver Down,* Edward decided he was going to build his own studio. Not just a rehearsal space, but rather a place where the band could actually make records. After this album, Edward went to work and built his legendary 5150 studio. So, if nothing else, at least some good came out of this album. I mean, just look at what they followed this up with for crissake.

1984 (1984)

1) 1984
2) Jump
3) Panama
4) Top Jimmy
5) Drop Dead Legs
6) Hot for Teacher
7) I'll Wait
8) Girl Gone Bad
9) House of Pain

*"This might sound cheesy, but ever since I was a kid I've always pictured myself driving down Hollywood Boulevard with huge speakers in my car blasting 'House of Pain.' Everything about that era of Van Halen is the very definition of '**cool**.' You had rock combined with heavy metal and David Lee Roth's show-biz routine. Some Van Halen fans don't like 1984 because of the synths on 'Jump,' but I think that it's a great record. Eddie Van Halen's playing is out there, especially on songs like 'House of Pain,' 'Top Jimmy,' 'Drop Dead Legs' and 'Panama.' Still my favorite Van Halen album."*

– Daron Malakian

For the second time in a six-year period, Classic Van Halen kicked rock 'n' roll in the balls when they released *1984*. Like their debut album, *1984* would go on to earn a Diamond Award for selling over 10 million copies in America alone. Artistically and commercially, *1984* was an album *and* a year the likes of which no other American hard rock/metal band had ever seen up until that point. Man, it's not even close. Even to this day, few have matched it.

This album also signaled the beginning of Edward stepping up and really taking control, which is something he started to edge into during the *Fair Warning* sessions, but unfortunately quickly relinquished during the *Diver Down* sessions. Not just control of the music, but more on the production side of things as well. He also had to deal with the fact that many people, including certain other band members, didn't much care for him playing keyboards. Apparently, they felt that a "guitar hero" shouldn't be playing keyboards! Edward paid this no mind, stuck to his guns, and did his thing anyway. In fact, you could say *1984* is the closest thing you'll ever get to an Edward Van Halen solo project. Basically, the entire album was put together by Edward and his trusted "extra ear," engineer Donn Landee.

Edward and Donn holed themselves up in 5150 Studio night and day, only bringing in the rest of the band once the music was all set and ready to record. The band had *never* recorded like this before. Alex Van Halen had some input, too, of course. But really the band was split into two camps during the making of this album. Edward, Alex, and Donn Landee were on one side, while David and producer Ted Templeman were on the other. I believe Mikey was pretty much neutral here. You know, Mikey never really had beef with anyone, least from what I've heard. Although I definitely think he was closer to the VH brothers than to Dave. So things were pretty divided at this point, not to mention the tension between Edward and Dave, specifically, had reached a boiling point. Nonetheless, the boys were able to give us this amazing, classic album. This would turn out to be their swan song, the last album of their classic era. But man, what a way to go out, huh? Talk about goin' out with a bang!

The album opens with an instrumental keyboard track, "1984." This cool little intro segues nicely into what would be the bands very first number 1 single of their career, "Jump." What can you really say about this song? First off, it would be the fourth time during their classic era that one of their albums would open with an anthem. "Jump" would now join "Runnin' With the Devil," "And the Cradle Will Rock..." and "Mean Street" in that department, although this song ended up being bigger than all of 'em! Edward had played keyboards on previous albums, but in all honesty, this is the first song where he really put them right up front. It was a risky move that paid off royally for the band.

"Jump's" instantly recognizable synthesizer-hook is truly classic. Not to mention the insane fifteen-second guitar solo, which is just bloody brilliant. It is definitely one of the greatest Van Halen songs *and* solos, ever. Oh, and there's also a very cool thirty-second keyboard solo by Edward, too! Lyrically speaking, "Jump" is really about an attitude. When David Lee Roth tells us to "jump," it's not meant physically, but rather, you know, as a way of saying, "go for it!"

The funny thing is, *1984* was being touted as "the keyboard album." In the end, there were only three tracks on the album that contained keyboards: the instrumental "1984," the synthesizer-driven number 1 hit "Jump," and the seventh track on the album, the very cool "I'll Wait." And though "Jump" and "I'll Wait" were indeed synthesizer-driven, both songs had very cool guitar solos, too. Fact is this album actually contains some of the sickest guitar playing Edward's ever laid to tape. So please don't be fooled into believing that on this album Van Halen went "New Wave" or something! Man, it's no surprise musicians like Steve Vai have often referred to *1984* as "a milestone for guitar playing."

The third track is yet another anthem and hit, "Panama." Here's what Classic VH was all 'bout. Big hooks, mad energy, terrific sing-along chorus, rippin' guitar, a short but sweet solo, and a very sexy breakdown section in the middle of the song, to boot. During interviews he's done over the years, Edward has always stated that "Panama" was AC/DC influenced. It makes sense, too. Aside from the fact that Edward and Alex are huge AC/DC fans, if you listen close, you'll notice a kinda "If You Want Blood (You Got It)" type of groove and riff goin' down.

The fourth track is "Top Jimmy," a nod to the late-great Top Jimmy, a musician who used to play the same club scene as Van Halen. While songs like "Jump" and "Panama" obviously got major attention, and it was well-deserved, a song like "Top Jimmy" is another one of those gems I've talked about. It may not have gotten a whole lot of radio play or whatever, and it may never have been a hit, but man, it's a really cool song. It kicks off with a very tasty intro built from natural harmonics. It has a killer rock groove and a nasty solo, complete with tapping and full-on whammy-bar molestation.

"Top Jimmy" is also the first time Edward ever used a Ripley Stereo Guitar to record a song. In fact, I think he might be the first to *ever* use the Ripley on a record! Basically, the guitar has an individual pan pot for each string, which in turn allows you to designate where each note you're playing will come out in the stereo spectrum. "Top Jimmy" is also played in an open D7 tuning, which, um, is a pretty unusual tuning, to put it mildly. The fifth track is another gem, "Drop Dead Legs." Another song that puts Van Halen's amazing and punishing rhythmic abilities on display, along with a rippin' outro solo, too.

The sixth track on the album is another classic hit and anthem, "Hot for Teacher." Man, this song is another clinic unto itself. Here we have the classic VH boogie in full effect. Basically, "Hot for Teacher" is what ZZ Top would sound like after two six-packs, a bottle of Jack, and an eightball. From the wild intro featuring Alex Van Halen's insane drum solo (which Big Al accomplished in just one-take...after downin' a few brews!) to the song's crushing boogie rhythm to Edward's kamikaze solo, man, you can make your bones on this song.

Definitely a favorite among the hardcore fans, you could say this song just flat-out rocks in a way most people can only dream of. Another really cool thing is that like the song "Drop Dead Legs," "Hot for Teacher" is also a staple of strip clubs all across America! Amen, brother.

The seventh track is "I'll Wait." This would be the third and final track on *1984* to contain keyboards. I guess some would describe this song as kind of a ballad, but it's really just a matter of opinion. This song contains a terrific groove, which is actually mellower than the hyperactive and crushing grooves of most other tracks on this album. Like "Jump," this song is synthesizer-driven and contains a very cool, lyrical guitar solo. The eighth track is the scorching "Girl Gone Bad." Yet another gem, baby. Actually, there are quite a few amazing songs on this album that weren't released as singles, but man, the songs themselves and the musicianship that went into them is mind-blowing. Well, "Girl Gone Bad" is a prime example of that. The song has a terrific, Zeppelin-esque, "Song Remains the Same" type of energy and vibe. It opens with some very cool tapped harmonics and contains another sick solo, too. In fact, you could say the solo in this song is Edward's tip of the cap to the legendary Allan Holdsworth. Not surprising, really, when you consider that Edward and Allan had met and struck up a friendship back in 1982, which was just a year before Edward began writing and recording the *1984* album. Edward and Allan had been hanging out and jamming, so I think a little bit of that experience shows up on this track during several spots in the solo. By the way, if you wanna know which guitar player Edward considers to be the best in the business, well, it's none other than Allan Holdsworth.

The ninth and final track of the album is "House of Pain." This song was actually written way back during their club days of the mid '70s! None other than Alex Van Halen insisted on having this song on the record. Nice job, Alex. I guess since he relented and let his little brother have a few keyboard tracks, Alex felt the band needed to have a slammin' metal track, too. And so we get "House of Pain," which sounds like something Black Sabbath woulda written if they had been a bunch of wild and horny skate punks raised in California. From the big riffs and monster groove to yet another smokin' solo and sexy breakdown, man, it's safe to say this is another favorite of the hardcore VH fans.

Like their debut album, *1984* is seamless. Front to back, all killer, no filler. It's a true classic, baby. *1984* is one of the greatest rock and guitar albums of all time. In fact, none other than *Guitar World* magazine named *1984* the "number 1 album of the 1980s" (along with *GW* naming Edward the "Player of the Decade" for the '80s as well). Man, when you kick back and begin to consider just how many great albums and guitar players the 1980s contained, well, you realize that's a tremendous honor. For example, here are five albums from the '80s that *1984* managed to beat out: *Blizzard of Ozz* (1980), *Master of Puppets* (1986), *Back in Black* (1980), *Pyromania* (1983), and *Appetite for Destruction* (1987). Aside from the fact that these are all classic albums, think of all the amazing guitar players who appear on these albums. Randy Rhoads, James Hetfield, Kirk Hammett, Phil Collen, Steve Clark, Angus and Malcolm Young, Slash, and Izzy Stradlin. Holy shit! Then you can get into even more albums from that decade by Steve Vai, Joe Satriani, Stevie Ray Vaughan, U2 (The Edge, of course), Ozzy Osbourne with Zakk Wylde, Yngwie J. Malmsteen, Megadeth, Slayer, and so forth. But out of all these amazing players and bands, *Guitar World* named *1984* the "number 1 album of the '80s." Man, that's unbelievable. Again, it's quite an honor.

As I mentioned earlier, *1984* was a level of success, artistically *and* commercially, that no other American hard rock/metal band in history had ever come close to. In fact, I don't think any American rock band ever came close to this level, period. Even over the last twenty years since this album came out, you could probably count on one hand the number of rock bands – foreign *and* domestic – who've experienced and matched this level of success.

Another thing that made this album so cool was that the band made three killer videos in support of this album. Sadly, 1984 would be the only year Classic Van Halen would be on MTV. Yeah, the band made a video in support of their cover of "(Oh) Pretty Woman" back in 1982, but the video was banned by MTV! So the fact is that Classic Van Halen only got to enjoy the fruits of MTV for just one year, really. But what a year, huh?

The three videos the band made in support of this album are all considered classics. To this very day, the video for "Jump" is considered one of the greatest music videos ever made. What's really cool is the video was totally low budget. Basically, it's the band, set up in a warehouse somewhere, playing live. Then again, that's all they really needed! The video for "Panama" was very cool, too. It contained plenty of live footage from a concert during their 1984 Tour, along with other footage of the band goofing around onstage, backstage, and even of Diamond Dave riding his Harley through the streets of Los Angeles. Like most people, I love both of these videos. However, my favorite just might be their "Hot for Teacher" video. This video is another candidate for one of the greatest videos of all time. From the little kid Van Halen band to Diamond Dave as the bus driver to the, um, "teacher" in the video who strips off her dress and dances on the desk, this video is *"the shit."* Plus, you can't forget the band all dressed up in maroon wedding-style tuxedos, pulling off what is arguably some of the worst and most hysterical choreography this side of TRL. Well, Dave could shake his ass. Meanwhile, um, the rest of the boys had a little bit of trouble keeping up, to put it mildly.

Tom Morello: "The highlight of the 'Hot for Teacher' video is when they're doing the dances...which, like, *clearly* Dave has choreographed and the other guys just can't learn to save their lives [*laughs*]. Yet, they gotta film it sooner or later!"

Basically, tons of kids wanted to form a rock band after watching this video. You could also say tons of kids probably went through puberty watching this video, too. Man, to this very day I swear that I sprouted a five o'clock shadow and a couple of chest hairs when the, um, "teacher" climbed on top of the desk, ripped her dress off, and began shimmying all over the damn place. And, of course, we can't forget the poor nerd, Waldo. I believe none other than the late, great Phil Hartman provided the voice for Waldo. Another other cool fact is that this video totally pissed off the PMRC. You know, the Parents Music Resource Center, which was led by none other than Tipper Gore, wife of former vice president Al Gore. The band and this song get major bonus points just for this alone.

Overall, this album gets five stars...and the band shoulda gotten a national holiday, too.

5150 (1986)

1) Good Enough
2) Why Can't This Be Love?
3) Get Up
4) Dreams
5) Summer Nights
6) Best of Both Worlds
7) Love Walks In
8) "5150"
9) Inside

This would be the band's first album with Sammy Hagar. It would also end up being the first number 1 album of their career. To this day, I simply can't think of a single other act in the history of music to make a lead singer change *and* score a number 1 album. Once again, unbelievable.

The album opens with Sammy giving us the 'ole Big Bopper "Hellooooo Baaaaaby!" before launching into "Good Enough." Aside from Sammy's powerful vocal chops, you quickly realize the band is no longer tuning down a half step to E flat. With Sammy at the helm, the majority of their material from here on in would be in standard tuning. It's a solid opener with another cool sing-along chorus. The second track would be yet another hit anthem for the band, the classic "Why Can't This Be Love?" I believe it was also the first single the band ever released with Sammy. I don't give a damn what anyone says, this is a great fuckin' song, period. Once again Edward breaks out the keys on this little number. In fact, this album would actually have more synthesizer-driven songs than *1984*! On *1984,* there was the little opening instrumental and two full songs. On *5150,* there would be four full synthesizer-driven songs. I mean, maybe *5150* should have been hyped as the "keyboard album" or whatever.

The third track is "Get Up," which is precisely what this makes you do. Alex Van Halen really shines on this track, and the vocal interplay between Sammy and Mikey during the closing section of this song is unreal. You quickly realize their voices blend amazingly well together. Edward breaks out a Steinberger GL-2T guitar and matches Alex's fire on this track, too. The fourth track is "Dreams." Yes, I know, another hit anthem for the boys. In fact, it's another hit anthem driven by keys. On this song, Edward plays a 1912 Steinway seven-foot baby grand piano MIDI-ed to an Oberheim OB-8. It also contains a sweet guitar solo, too. I truly believe "Dreams" is one of the best songs Edward and the boys have ever written. Very inspired stuff.

The fifth track is "Summer Nights." Yes, another terrific anthem you could sing along with, complete with a wild solo and all. The sixth track is

"Best of Both Worlds." Definitely a fan favorite and concert favorite, too. I've always thought the song had a bit of an AC/DC flavor to it. Sure enough, if you dick around with the main riff on the guitar, you'll quickly notice the "BOBW" riff is basically the "Highway to Hell" riff played backwards. Hey, I'm not claiming this was Edward's intention or whatever, just pointing out it's the exact same chord progression played backwards. This is a great song and has a monster groove.

The seventh track is "Love Walks In." How boring, yet another classic hit for the boys! This song is what many could and probably would consider the band's first official "power ballad." I have to say the boys pull it off rather well and without a bunch of that high-pitched squealing that seems to turn up on most power ballads. Again, the band is showing their versatility. Not to mention Edward's solo just sings. I mean, the dude's guitar is basically singing during the solo. Talk about matching the melody and vocals, man, it's spot on.

In the end, some fans loved this song and some didn't. Hey, that's life. Oh, and this one was synthesizer-driven as well. The eighth track bears the same name as the album, "5150." To me, this is another gem. Man, Edward's playing on this song is fantastic throughout, with the main riff containing enough double-stops to leave most mere mortals cross-eyed. More of that classic VH groove on display here, too. The ninth and final track is "Inside," a bluesy number during which Sammy and the boys let you know what is goin' down "on the inside," far as the band's situation and so forth.

Overall, this album gets four and a half stars. The material on here is really strong. I believe most people consider the band's first album with Sammy to be the best of the four studio albums they would record together. Indeed, that may just be the case. Man, that would really be saying something when you consider all four albums with Sammy contain solid material. To this day, this is the highest-selling album of the Sammy era, clocking in at over 6 million copies in the U.S. alone.

OU812 (1988)

1) Mine All Mine
2) When It's Love
3) A.F.U. (Naturally Wired)
4) Cabo Wabo
5) Source of Infection
6) Feels So Good
7) Finish What Ya Started
8) Black and Blue
9) Sucker in a 3 Piece
10) A Apolitical Blues

OU812 would be their second consecutive number 1 album. Man, two albums with Sammy, two number 1's. Not bad, boys. The band also continued to employ keys in a very successful manner.

Highlights on this album include the groovin' "Black and Blue" (groove-wise, think AC/DC's "Rock 'n' Roll Ain't Noise Pollution"), the drivin' "Mine All Mine," the danceable "Feels So Good," and yet another hit, "Finish What Ya Started."

On "FWYS," Edward merrily fingerpicks his way through the entire song, including the cool chickin' pickin' style solo. I believe this is the first time he'd ever recorded an entire song without using a pick. It's a classic hit that was inspired by an argument Edward had just had with his wife Valerie. Apparently, right after the argument Edward went to hang out with Sammy, who'd actually bought a house right next door to him after joining the band. While they were hanging out, Edward and Sammy began to jam. Well, this cool little number came out of that.

For my money, "Source of Infection" is the gem on this album. Man, the band was on fire during this song. From the wild tapping intro to the incredible groove, the band flexes their muscle on this track. The interplay between Edward and Alex here is insane, and once again the vocal interplay between Sammy and Mikey is mind-blowing. Not to mention Edward unleashes a few short but fiery guitar solos as well.

Oh, and the hit synthesizer-driven power ballad "When It's Love" was huge for the band, as well. Just as on "Love Walks In," Edward unleashes another short, beautiful solo that absolutely sings. I mean it, too. His guitar is literally singing during the solo and it sounds perfect. It's definitely a "Clapton-esque" type of solo.

Overall, this album gets three stars. A solid effort lodged in between what could arguably be the top two albums of their tenure with Sammy at the helm. Obviously, *5150* came before, and that is a very tough album to follow. When you see what album they released next, well, you'll see what I meant about this album being stuck in between…

For Unlawful Carnal Knowledge (1991)

1) Poundcake
2) Judgment Day
3) Spanked
4) Runaround
5) Pleasure Dome
6) In n' Out
7) Man on a Mission
8) The Dream Is Over
9) Right Now
10) 316
11) Top of the World

This would be their third consecutive number 1 album with Sammy at the helm. I believe this is the album many fans, including the hardcore fans, were waiting for. I mean that in the sense that the band pretty much put away the keys on this entire album with the exception of just one song, the hit anthem "Right Now." I'm man enough to admit I dig most of their keys-driven material, but I know that as a fan I was waiting for them to get back to some really slammin', guitar-driven anthems. Folks, this album is just brimming with sick-ass guitar playing and great rock songs.

The first track is the rockin' hit anthem, "Poundcake." Now we're talkin'! *F.U.C.K.* is yet another VH album to open with an anthem. Man, this song has all the elements VH became known for. You know, a killer riff, monster groove, great harmonies and a nasty solo. However, the very first sound you hear on the album, of all things, is the sound of a cordless Makita power drill! Apparently, one day at 5150 Edward's guitar tech, Matt Bruck, left the drill on the recording console after replacing the tubes in Edward's Soldano amp. While Matt was away on his break, Edward stumbled across the drill and began to dick around with it. He was able to determine the proper pitch by setting it at sixty cycles and then proceed to crank it up as he ran it smoothly over the strings of his axe, just above the pickups, of course. The end result is one of the wildest sounds you'll ever hear. What could easily have turned into a "gimmick" in the hands of most musicians ends up being employed tastefully *and* musically in the hands of the master. Not only did Edward use the drill during the intro of the song, he also used it a bit during the insane solo, too.

The second track is "Judgment Day," which is another slammin' tune that comes complete with a wild solo that opens with a two-hand tapping passage you have to see to believe.

Basically, Edward positions both hands *over* the neck of the guitar to perform the passage. It's very cool. The third track is "Spanked," a cool funk-sounding tune. On this song Edward plays a Danelectro six-string bass through a Marshall stack, along with a custom built Fender Esquire, too. He also breaks out his wah pedal for a very tasty solo. Edward doesn't use the wah very often, so it's a treat when he does. I have to say he is one of the few guitarists I have ever heard who is able to use a wah pedal without it sounding like a '70s porn film. The fourth track is another hit tune, "Runaround." This song has another terrific groove and chorus. Once again Edward breaks out his Danelectro six-string bass and Fender Esquire custom. This song became a fan favorite at VH shows, and the accompanying video they made for MTV was very cool as well.

The fifth track is "Pleasure Dome." For my money, it's the gem of the album. Man, the band was really cooking on the track. It's one of those times you just can't believe four individuals can be that tight. The interplay between Edward and Alex *alone* is absurd. I also believe this song contains the best damn solo on the album, which is saying something, considering how much killer guitar this album has. The solo begins right around 4:10, and at about 4:24, Edward switches to the neck pickup and unleashes one of the sickest runs I've ever heard him play on record. If you have a chance, please check it out, cuz it's nasty. The entire song was built from three different riffs Edward had come up with. However, the man responsible for arranging those pieces together was none other than Alex Van Halen. For only the second time on record, Edward would also break out some chickin' pickin' just before the song closes out. "Pleasure Dome" is definitely another clinic.

The sixth and seventh tracks are "In n' Out" and "Man on a Mission." These are two kick-ass rock songs that really show more of VH's amazing rhythmic slam. It seems these boys are just not capable of running out of groove. The eighth track is "The Dream Is Over." In my opinion, it's one of the most overlooked Van Halen songs ever. Definitely worth a listen, cuz this one rocks. The ninth track is "Right Now." How many hit anthems does this band have now? Well, add one more to the list. On an album chock full of great songs, this was probably *the* song. The funny thing is it was the only song on the *F.U.C.K.* album to contain keys. On this song, Edward used an acoustic Steinway piano and a Hammond organ. Once again the boys display incredible versatility on a track like this. Oh, it also contains a pretty sweet guitar solo, too. "Right Now" was easily one of the biggest songs of 1991. The accompanying video was actually named a "Groundbreaking Video" by MTV. Not surprisingly, the video took home "Video of the Year" honors at the 1992 MTV Video Music Awards (even beating out Nirvana's classic "Teen Spirit" video for crissake).

"Right Now" also shows that this band could go off in a lyrical direction most wouldn't expect from 'em. Actually, the entire Sammy era displayed a lyrical direction and style that simply was not present in their classic era. You could say that is what many fans loved about this era. Then again, you could turn around and say this is precisely what many fans *didn't* love about this era! In the end, and as usual, it's all in the ear of the beholder. Regardless, "Right Now" is one of the biggest and best songs this band has ever written. Oh, and here's some cool trivia. Edward had actually written this song way back in the early '80s. He'd always envisioned the great Joe Cocker singing on this tune, but alas, I guess it just wasn't meant to be. In the end, Sammy sang the shit out of it, so hey, it's cool.

The tenth track is the instrumental, "316." Basically, it's a cool little piece Edward wrote and the title is derived from his son's birthday (March 16). It's really a lullaby for his son. While Valerie was pregnant Edward used to lie next to her stomach and play this piece. Apparently, it had quite a soothing effect on his then-unborn son. When it came time to record "316" for the album, Edward used a Chet Atkins steel-string acoustic solid-body guitar and an Eventide H3000 Harmonizer. The eleventh and final track is yet another hit anthem, "Top of the World." The intro riff to this song is actually the outro riff of their classic hit, "Jump." This is a really great sing-along rock tune that closes out the album in fine fashion.

Overall, this album gets three and a half stars. With this album, the band proved they could still rock their ass off. It also proved that Edward still had plenty of ammo left, you know, as far as riffs, licks, solos, and so forth. Not to mention the album is chock full of great songs and anthems. There's plenty of strong material here. I also believe, and I'm sure many would agree, that the *F.U.C.K.* album is probably the first Van Halen album to fully capture the sound of their rhythm section the way it truly sounds live. A lot of that is owed to the amazing producer, Andy Johns. After all, this dude worked with Led Zeppelin, for crissake. Andy came in to produce this album and really got Alex's drum sound on point. Along with that, Andy also managed to dial up a great bass sound for Mikey, too. Man, the sound of Alex's drums on this album are just insane. And we *finally* get to properly hear Michael Anthony! For years, it seems Mikey got lost in the mix, literally. My hats off to Andy Johns and the band for getting it all squared away on this album. The end result is a killer rock record that definitely ranks as one of the best the boys have ever done.

Live: Right Here, Right Now (1993)

DISC ONE:

1) Poundcake, 2) Judgment Day, 3) When It's Love, 4) Spanked, 5) Ain't Talkin' 'bout Love, 6) In 'n' Out, 7) Dreams, 8) Man on a Mission, 9) Ultra Bass (Mikey's solo spot), 10) Pleasure Dome/Drum Solo (Big Al's solo spot), 11) Panama, 12) Love Walks In, 13) Runaround

DISC TWO:

1) Right Now, 2) One Way to Rock, 3) Why Can't This Be Love?, 4) Give to Live (Sammy solo), 5) Finish What Ya Started, 6) Best of Both Worlds, 7) 316 (Edward's solo spot), 8) You Really Got Me/Cabo Wabo, 9) Won't Get Fooled Again, 10) Jump, 11) Top of the World

After fifteen long years in the music business, one of the greatest live bands ever finally released their very first live album! It is a two-disc set, and the majority of the music on this album was recorded on May 14 and May 15 of 1992 at Selland Arena in Fresno, California. Once again, the great Andy Johns was brought in to mix this album.

The album mainly consists of material from the 1991 *F.U.C.K.* album, along with other songs the band wrote with Sammy on their previous two albums together. There are also three songs from their classic era as well. The gem on this album is their rippin' cover of the Who's classic, "Won't Get Fooled Again." VH really pulled off a stellar tribute to one of their heroes and biggest influences, complete with Edward replicating the song's keyboard intro by finger-picking it on his guitar, note-for-note.

I guess you could say fans were split on this album (shocker). Some really loved it, while others didn't much care for what they perceived to be an "over-polished" sound. Reportedly there were different mixes done, with fans forever debating which one should have been released. In the end, as usual, it's all in the ear of the beholder. I will say the band sounded tight as hell during these shows. They were definitely running on all cylinders in Fresno.

Overall this album gets three stars. I find it to be a pretty solid representation of the band with Sammy at the helm. Sadly, we have yet to see an official live album from their classic era.

Balance (1995)

1) Seventh Seal
2) Can't Stop Lovin' You
3) Don't Tell Me (What Love Can Do)
4) Amsterdam
5) Big Fat Money
6) Strung Out
7) Not Enough
8) Aftershock
9) Doin' Time
10) Baluchitherium
11) Take Me Back (Déjà vu)
12) Feelin'

What can I say, other than it's their fourth consecutive number 1 studio album with Sammy? Musically speaking, it's definitely a bit different, but still interesting. Man, the way this album opens up immediately lets you know this one is gonna be a different trip altogether. I mean, you know you aren't in Kansas anymore when you hear a VH album that opens with chanting monks. Hell, their last album opened with a damn power drill!

Anyway, this album opens with full-on Buddhist harmonic chanting, courtesy of the Monks of Gyoto Tantric University by way of Gyoto Wheel of Dharma Monastery. The intro was actually taken from their album *The Gyoto Monks Tibetan Tantric Choir* (Wyndham Hill, 1987). Apparently, these were a pretty rockin' group of monks, cuz they'd already appeared in concert with none other than the Grateful Dead. After all, the Dead's Mickey Hart produced the monks' 1987 album I just mentioned above. The cool monk chanting opens the album and kicks off the first track, "Seventh Seal." The chanting also appears during the song, as well. The fact that the band still sounds powerful here is no surprise, really. What is a surprise were Sammy's lyrics, which were pretty religious in the sense that he basically threw a lot of "fire and brimstone," Armageddon-type of material into this song. It's definitely different, but it worked. The second track is "Can't Stop Lovin' You," yet another hit for the band. It's not a power-ballad, but definitely a "ballady" type of song. Nonetheless, it has a great groove and continued to show this band's versatility. And again, the lyrical treatment stems from the fact that Sammy was going through a divorce at this time.

The third track is "Don't Tell Me (What Love Can Do)," a powerful song that was inspired by the death of Kurt Cobain. Basically, it's about how Kurt's death affected Sammy. Like most people, Sammy was disappointed that Kurt had decided to go out the way he did. During a 1995 interview with *Guitar*

World magazine, Edward Van Halen also expressed his disappointment about it. (Both Sammy and Edward were fans of Kurt and Nirvana.) The song is really driven by Edward's simple, yet heavy-sounding riff. In my opinion, the "Don't Tell Me…" riff kinda sounds like a simpler but heavier take on Kurt's cool "Come As You Are" riff. In fact, both of these songs are played in the Drop-d tuning. And if you listen to Sammy's words, you'll clearly begin to see how it was about Kurt. The song also contains some fiery solo work by Edward as well.

The fourth track is "Amsterdam," a rockin' anthem that serves as a tip of the cap to the land the brothers came from. Well, kind of. The music was done as such, but Sammy's lyrical treatment apparently didn't go over too well with the brothers. The lyrics Sammy came up with are basically an ode to marijuana. Meanwhile, I think the brothers were hoping for a much different lyrical treatment. The fifth track is the swingin' "Big Fat Money." It's a cool song, and the solo sounds like jazz from hell or something. Edward broke out a Gibson ES-335 (which happens to be a guitar used by several of Edward's influences, like Eric Clapton and Alvin Lee) and proceeded to fire off a wild, first-take solo.

The sixth track is "Strung Out." Ah, pure madness! This wild instrumental was actually recorded way back during the spring/summer of 1983. You see, back at that time, Edward had been renting a beach house in Malibu, California that belonged to none other than Marvin Hamlish. Apparently 'ole Marvin had a lovely white Yamaha grand piano at his beach house, too. How can I put this? Basically, um, Edward went ballistic one night and began to trash the damn thing! He threw everything at that piano but the kitchen sink. On top of that, he raked many different items across the piano's strings. From D-cell batteries and ping-pong balls to silverware. While this massacre was goin' down, Edward rolled tape and recorded it all. From that we get "Strung Out," which is only about a minute and a half, but actually comes from *hours* of tape Edward made while destroying the damn piano.

The seventh track is "Not Enough." Another cool, piano-driven VH tune. Again, I dunno if you could call this a "ballad" or whatever, but it's great to hear the opening part where there is nothing but Sammy's voice over Edward's piano. It really sounds good.

The eighth track is "Aftershock." For me, this is the gem on the album. Here we get back to more of their classic sound. Monster riffs and rhythm, big vocals and choruses and the two solos on this track absolutely smoke. Basically, Edward went apeshit and unleashed everything from pull-offs to furious trilling to tapping on this one, baby. I would say his playing *and* solo on this track are the best on the album. Well, there is another solo that deserves consideration, but we'll get to that shortly. Flat out, "Aftershock" is truly a kick-ass rock song.

The ninth track is "Doin' Time." This is a cool instrumental performed by Alex Van Halen. The tenth track is "Take Me Back (Déjà Vu)." On this song, Edward breaks out the 'ole acoustic guitar, and even plays a bit of slide, too. The eleventh and final track is "Feelin'." Here's another song where the boys get serious, musically *and* lyrically. The song builds slowly and then just explodes. And then comes the solo. Man, I'm runnin' out of adjectives to describe this cat's playing! Let's just say Edward's solo on this track is "intense," ok? There's just something about it, damn, cuz the dude was all over his axe on this one. Next to his playing on "Aftershock" and "Don't Tell Me (What Love Can Do)," the "Feelin'" solo is a total mind-blower, even by his standards. The song is a keeper and one of the highlights of the album.

Overall, this album gets three stars. It's pretty serious stuff and shows a very different side of these men, but in the end it's still a solid, rockin' album.

Best Of Volume 1 (1996)

1) Eruption
2) Ain't Talkin' 'bout Love
3) Runnin' with the Devil
4) Dance the Night Away
5) And the Cradle Will Rock…
6) Unchained
7) Jump
8) Panama
9) Why Can't This Be Love?
10) Dreams
11) When It's Love
12) Poundcake
13) Right Now
14) Can't Stop Lovin' You
15) Humans Being
16) Can't Get This Stuff No More
17) Me Wise Magic

This would be the band's very first greatest hits album of their career. It would also be released right smack in the middle of all the mayhem the band was experiencing during the fall of 1996 when they appeared at the MTV Video Music Awards with Diamond Dave. Remember, that the last two tracks on this album, "Can't Get This Stuff No More" and "Me Wise Magic," are bonus tracks. These are the two new songs the band did with Diamond Dave in 1996 as a bonus for this album. Sonically, these new songs sounded terrific. I believe a lot of that had to do with a combination of the band's playing and Glenn Ballard's fine production.

As you can clearly see, the first eight tracks on the album are from their classic era. Tracks nine through fifteen are from their next era with Sammy. Oh, and track fifteen is none other than "Humans Being," a cool song that would unfortunately be at the center of the band splitting up with Sammy. Remember, this is the song that ended up on the *Twister* soundtrack.

Anyhow, the *Best Of* did well. This album actually hit number 1 on the Billboard Album Chart, which is pretty damn insane for a greatest hits album. At first I was pretty surprised this one didn't sell like ten million copies or something. But when you think about it, Van Halen is a band that sold tons of their studio albums throughout their career. In the end, I just think most people already owned their damn albums! I also believe the fact that they decided to make it just one album, instead of a double album, turned some people off. I'd say this album is a fair representation of the band, but man, there are so many songs missing here, to be honest. I totally understand cuz you had to fit in the music of both eras, so everything from "Jamie's Cryin'" and "Mean Street" to "Best of Best Worlds" ended up being left off. I guess you could say Van Halen simply had too many great songs to choose from! But that's a pretty damn good problem, you know?

Overall, this album gets three stars. It contains hits from both eras, but it leaves off way too many of them as well. My rating is really based on what's *missing*, not what's on here! I must also say the bonus tracks with Dave were a nice touch and sounded cool. And the remastering of all these songs for this album was a nice touch, too.

Van Halen III (1998)

1) Neworld
2) Without You
3) One I Want
4) From Afar
5) Dirty Water Dog
6) Once
7) Fire in the Hole
8) Josephina
9) Year to the Day
10) Primary
11) Ballot or the Bullet
12) How Many Say I

This would be their first, last, and only album with Gary Cherone at the helm. *Van Halen III* can be described as the first and only commercial failure of their twenty-six-year career. However, I must once again point out that a "commercial failure" for Van Halen means a Gold album that charts at the number 5 spot on the Billboard Album Chart. Hell, most people would take Van Halen's "failure" in a second. Anyway, as is the case one most albums, there are still some cool moments to be enjoyed here.

For starters, most people would agree that Edward's guitar playing on this album is still top notch. In fact, *Guitar World* magazine's J.D. Considine reviewed this album in their March 1998 issue and called Edward's playing "astonishing, even by Van Halen standards." So if Edward could still rip, um, what was the problem? Well, the problem, if you can even call it that, was a couple of things. First, I believe there was a major bias against this lineup before they'd even recorded so much as a single note. The whole 1996 MTV award show appearance simply left a bitter taste in the mouths of many. There was also a major bias against Gary Cherone. This guy is a terrific frontman and can sing his dick off, but hey, most people just wondered what Mr. "More than Words" was doing in VH. Sadly, it seems most only knew him from that one song. So in all honesty, I believe this lineup was hexed before they even began.

Another thing would be that this is basically the closest thing Edward Van Halen has ever done to a solo album. Sure, *1984* was pretty much Edward's baby, but he had his trusted "extra ear," the amazing Donn Landee, at his side back then. Not to mention that was their classic era and he was very much still writing with that classic sound in mind. So that was a completely different time and scenario. And frankly, Gary doesn't really sound like Gary on a lot of the songs? On this album, Gary's voice kinda sounds a bit Sammyish, to be honest. But Gary was only doing what he was asked to do. Frankly, and this is just my opinion, as far as hits and anthems go, shit, there really isn't a single one on here. Then again, I don't think that was the intent of this album, either. It appears Edward wanted to go off in a completely different direction that was nothing like either of the band's previous eras.

Apparently, he had this material in him and wanted to let it out, opinions be damned. This is a band that has hits and anthems on pretty much every single one of their albums. The material on this album is a total departure from anything the boys had ever done. Lyrically *and* musically speaking, worlds removed from both previous eras of the band. Other than the songs "Without You" and maybe "Fire in the Hole," nothing else on here even remotely sounds like VH. It was a gutsy move that simply didn't pay off.

Hey, I tip my cap to Edward for trying this, because in the end, this album was really *his* album. I also give him credit for owning up to it and standing by it. Say what you want, but it was a totally honest attempt on his part. Whereas other artists may just go out there and follow whatever the "new sound" is, or even bring in a bunch of song doctors, Edward went in the complete opposite direction and released an album chock full of material that, simply put, doesn't really sound like Van Halen in any way, shape, or form. Man, if someone didn't tell you this album was a Van Halen album, you may not even know it was them. All of this proves a major point, and that is the following: anyone who thought this band sold tons of albums with Sammy simply cuz of their band name is 100 percent *wrong.*

Sorry, folks, but if nothing else, this album proves that no one survives on their name alone. If that was the case then *Van Halen III* would have gone multi-Platinum like their previous twelve albums had all gone. Yes, this is the album that broke their streak of a dozen consecutive multi-Platinum albums. It also proves that killer guitar playing alone does not sell albums. In the end, it's all about the songs. Always has been, always will be. All their previous albums had 'em, and the material on this one simply didn't live up to their previous work.

I'm certainly not saying it's good or bad, just saying it doesn't live up to their previous material. Then again, how in the hell do you compete with those other two eras of Van Halen? Hey, that's a tall order for anyone. And as I mentioned earlier in this book, great artists like Van Halen reach a point where they are no longer so much compared to other artists as they are compared to *themselves.* So again, how do you compete with those two monster eras? Simply put, you can't. But every album has cool moments, and this one does have a few.

Right off the bat, the track "Year to the Day" comes to mind. For me, it's the gem on the album. Edward's playing on this one is brilliant. This ballad has a bluesy "Zeppelin-esque" vibe to it, especially during the intro, where

Edward unleashes some very tasty fingerpicking. Gary's vocals on here sound great, too. And Edward's solo is pretty sultry sounding for a dude who's known to most people for burning it up. He burns on this track, but it's a different kind of burn. It's really a *slow burn,* but it proves to be just as lethal. I believe this was another one of his classic first-take solos, too. Another cool track is "Fire in the Hole." This is one of two songs on the album that actually sounds like VH to me. It has some major power-chord riffage, strong groove, and a wicked solo. Oh, and a big 'ole sing-along chorus, too! The other track on the album that sounds like VH to me is "Without You." It's a cool, energetic boogie with terrific vocals and a great chorus. Other than these two tracks, everything else on here sounds way different from anything the boys have ever done.

For example, the track "Once" is reminiscent of something Peter Gabriel might have done during his "Biko" period (not surprising, since Edward is actually a big fan of Peter Gabriel). It's a total departure for the band, but I have to admit that it's worth a listen. They've always been extremely versatile and managed to pull this one off nicely. Another example of this would be the track "From Afar." This is out there, but I liked it! I believe Edward broke out his 'ole Ripley guitar on this track. That is the type of guitar he used on the song "Top Jimmy" back on the classic *1984* album. This song is definitely worth a listen because there are so many wild sounds here. For starters, the Ripley guitar allows Edward to pan each string individually, so you hear notes comin' at you from all over the damn place. The solo on this song is some cool, backwards sounding Hendrix-type of shit that is really wild. Well, that's to my ears, anyway. I've never heard Edward pull off anything like this before, and I have to admit the song *and* solo sounds cool.

"Dirty Water Dog" is another track I would like to point out. The riff of this song was actually from another song called "Stompin' 8H," which was a jam Edward played with G.E. Smith and the Saturday Night Live Band during an appearance on *SNL.* Other interesting tracks on this album are "One I Want" (great rhythm, smokin' solo), "Ballot or the Bullet," and "Josephina." Oh, and if you wanna hear Edward take the mic, check out his piano-driven ballad, "How Many Say I." This is the last track on the album and again, unlike any they've ever done. It comes complete with Edward on lead vocals and piano, accompanied by a string section and other instruments.

Overall, this album gets two stars. While it contains hardly any Van Halen-sounding material, there are still some interesting things going down here, musically speaking. Once again, at the very least, I tip my cap to Edward Van Halen for sticking to his guns and believing in this album. It's an honest album, so I can totally respect that.

Best of Both Worlds (2004)

DISC ONE:

1) Eruption, 2) It's About Time (new track w/Sammy), 3) Up for Breakfast (new track w/Sammy), 4) Learning to See (new track w/Sammy), 5) Ain't Talkin' 'bout Love, 6) Finish What Ya Started, 7) You Really Got Me, 8) Dreams, 9) Hot for Teacher, 10) Poundcake, 11) And the Cradle Will Rock, 12) Black and Blue, 13) Jump, 14) Top of the World, 15) (Oh) Pretty Woman, 16) Love Walks In, 17) Beautiful Girls, 18) Can't Stop Lovin' You, 19) Unchained

DISC TWO

1) Panama, 2) Best of Both Worlds, 3) Jamie's Cryin', 4) Runaround, 5) I'll Wait, 6) Why Can't This Be Love?, 7) Runnin' with the Devil, 8) When It's Love, 9) Dancing in the Street, 10) Not Enough, 11) Feels So Good, 12) Right Now, 13) Everybody Wants Some, 14) Dance the Night Away, 15) Ain't Talkin' 'bout Love (live w/Sammy), 16) Panama (live w/Sammy), 17) Jump (live w/Sammy)

In many ways, this greatest hits album is everything their first greatest hits album should have been. Then again, in some ways, it isn't. What can I say other than most of us VH fans are picky bastards! For starters, the fact that this was a double album is killer! However, the fact that the track list wasn't in chronological order is *not*. Hey, that's just my opinion. I mean, I totally understand what the boys tried to do here. Basically, the tracks are all mixed up to show us this is *all* Van Halen music. And yes, it is all VH music. But I'll admit that it was pretty damn stunning to hear "Eruption" not being followed by "You Really Got Me." Or to hear "Black and Blue" followed by "Jump."

Basically, the track order totally threw me off at first. The three new tracks with Sammy are a nice touch. I like all three, and "Learning to See" is my personal favorite. Wow, what a cool, moving song. However, the three live tracks on this album are all of Sammy performing songs from the Classic VH era! Sam does a fine job, but as a fan, once again, I'm a bit disappointed no live material has been included of the original lineup performing their material. I totally understand it's not easy to put something like this together. This band has so much great material from both eras, but I would just like to see some live material from their classic era. I'd also like to have seen more pictures from their classic era in the CD booklet, too. I know…picky, picky, picky!

Overall, this album gets four stars. Regardless of the flip-flop track list and other small issues, this is a collection of some of the greatest hard rock music and guitar playing ever, period. You could arrange the songs in alphabetical order and in the end, they would still kick ass. This album also contains many of those songs I was bitching about earlier that had been left off their first greatest hits album back in 1996. In the end, if you handed this album to someone who didn't know the band, it will definitely provide that person with a pretty strong representation of both major eras. You can never truly please everyone and it's impossible to get it perfect, but in the end, they did a pretty good job. The remastering of all this material was a nice touch, too.

FAQ...

The Elements of a Great Guitar Player

*"I do like Eddie Van Halen as a player. He gets it **right** quite often."*
— Paul McCartney

What makes a great guitar player? While it sounds like a simple enough question, you'd be amazed how many people can't even begin to answer that. Quite often you'll get nothing in return other than the very cliché, "Well, so-and-so is *'the shit!'*" or "Man, (fill in the name of any musician) is a legend!" Sadly, many people out there can't even begin to understand or explain what the hell makes a musician truly great.

Now, I could get a bit technical on you here. You know, break out all that crazy musician jargon and begin discussing everything from pinched harmonics to inverted triads. But let's face it, folks, most people out there probably think an "inverted triad" is some freaky three-way position you'd read about in a *Penthouse* "Letter of the Month."

So rather than go off on some grandiose and highbrow explanation involving words you'll only find people using at some GIT kegger, I'll keep this as simple as possible, ok?

For my money, there are a few specific elements that make a great guitar player. You know, aside from the obvious answer, like chops. Hell, you could say these elements apply to just about any type of musician, period. It doesn't matter if we are talking Edward Van Halen or Nicolò Paganini. Sure, there are some intangibles and whatnot, but in the end I can pretty much narrow 'em down to these few elements. Man, I don't care if you play guitar, drums, or a damn tuba! I honestly believe these are the elements that make a musician truly great, and they are as follows: songs, rhythm, tone,

163

innovativeness and originality, stage presence, solos, and speed. We'll look at each of these elements, in order, beginning with songs.

SONGS

> *"You know who has balls? Someone I didn't always respect: Eddie Van Halen. That guy does a lot of cool stuff, and he isn't always Mr. Flash. He's matured, he's sold records, and he knows how to write a song and do a solo without blowing his wad."*

> **– Kim Thayil**

It's all 'bout the song. Always has been, always will be. Man, if you don't have the songs, I don't give a goddamn how well you can play an instrument. In the end, you'll probably just end up selling your music online or in the back pages of some music magazine. That's the cold, hard truth. Music begins and ends with the song. For me, that is the single most important thing, and I'm sure many others will agree. As the great Zakk Wylde told me, "Solos are like the icing on the cake. But you gotta have a cake, you know?" In other words, you need that *foundation,* which is the song. No one is just gonna eat a jar of icing, right Zakk?

For example, just a couple years ago, I was watching MTV's *20 Years of Rock.* During this show, they talked about Van Halen. One of the big things they do during these types of shows is they ask musicians, past and present, to comment on other musicians and bands. When it came time to talk about Van Halen, the great John Cougar Mellencamp simply stated the following: "Man, even their *bad* songs were good." I'd say 'ole John knows a thing or two 'bout songwriting and good songs, wouldn't you?

Well, the fact is, Van Halen wrote some of the greatest hard rock music of all time, baby. The man responsible for this music was none other than Edward Van Halen. I think one of the biggest musical injustices of our time is the fact that to this very day, Edward has never truly received the credit he deserves as a songwriter. First and foremost, Edward Van Halen is a *songwriter.* That's what he's all about. This man came up with all that killer music his band has released. Of course, his brother Alex played a role in this as well. You know, cuz many songs came to be from just Edward and Alex jamming together. But Edward Van Halen was, is, and always will be the chief songwriter in his band, period.

It's all about the song and I know this from firsthand experience. For several years, I worked at one of the largest record stores on the planet. Now, take a wild guess how many times someone walked in to the store and asked for a record with great guitar solos? Not once. Take a wild guess how many times someone walked in and asked for a record with fast guitar playing or with tapping? Not once. In my opinion, *no one* buys albums for guitar solos, fast guitar playing, or tapping. Sorry, that just isn't the case. Now, take a wild guess how many times someone walked in to the store and asked for an album of great music? Or specifically for an album of great rock music, pop music, blues, and so forth? Man, there are too many times to remember. Fact is, that happened just about every single day. I mean, if guitar solos, fast guitar playing, and tapping equaled record sales, man, a whole lot of guitar virtuosos out there would be super rich and famous, living in mansions, and driving Ferraris. Unfortunately, that is not the case.

So why were Edward and his band able to sell over 56 million albums in America? Why were they able to score a dozen consecutive multi-Platinum albums? Why were they able to kick rock in the balls, change the face of rock, and become one of the most successful, influential, and important hard rock/metal bands of all time? Um, because they had great songs, baby.

In fact, along with their album sales from overseas, this band sold a combined total of over 75 million albums during their career. I honestly doubt that even a single one of those 75 million albums was bought because of solos, tapping, blazing licks, or whatever. It's the song, the song, the song... Why is Van Halen a staple of rock radio all over the world? The songs! Why did Van Halen play to consistently jam-packed arenas throughout their career? The songs! Why do you hear VH everywhere from sporting events to bars to strip joints? The songs! Seriously, the music of Van Halen is at home at an NFL football game just as it is at your local strip club. Now how many artists can claim that? Aside from all the amazing things Edward has accomplished, here's one more: Edward Van Halen is probably one of the only, if not *the only* shredder I've ever heard in my life whose music was played in a strip club. Chalk another one up for the King for passing the "stripper test."

All kidding aside, the fact is a lot of women in general love Van Halen. It's never really surprised me this band had a major following of women throughout their entire career, because they had the songs, man. Sure, their looks didn't hurt, either. But I've always believed that while looks may get some chicks in the door, your music and musicianship is what keeps 'em there. I can't recall ever poppin' a VH tape/CD in my car and having a chick tell me to "turn that shit off," know what I mean? In fact, Van Halen is terrific driving music, which is usually another sign of great music.

Basically, Edward and his band got love from everyone. Men, women, boys, girls, young, old, musicians, athletes, stoners, and you name it. Hell, former President Clinton used to blast Classic VH during many of his rallies and speeches. Current President G.W. Bush has done the same. Why? The songs, baby. Man, that's why big league ballplayers like David Wells and Mike Piazza love this band and crank up their music before a game. Do they do this because a certain tapping-lick gets their mojo workin'? Hell no! It's because the music kicks their ass and gets 'em pumped up. Many pro athletes, from Tiger Woods to Stone Cold Steve Austin, are VH heads.

Man, their music simply kicks major ass. Let's not get technical here. Bottom line, if you can't enjoy and get pumped up listening to VH, well, then you don't have a pulse. Their music is pure sonic adrenaline. I honestly believe that is why Van Halen's music has been covered by so many different artists – *especially* live in concert, where "Runnin' with the Devil" *alone* has been covered by everyone from Pearl Jam to Phish. On record, everyone from the Mighty Mighty Bosstones to the Minutemen has covered Van Halen songs. And don't even get me started on all the movies that have used Van Halen's music. Man, you can write a book on all the soundtracks VH has been on. Not only that, but how many freakin' Van Halen references have been made in movies and televsion shows!

From *Bill and Ted's Excellent Adventure, Back to the Future,* and *Fast Times at Ridgemont High* to *The Wedding Singer, Wayne's World,* and *The Simpsons,* it's impossible to count. I mean, at this point, it's not a question of how many Adam Sandler films alone contain a VH reference, but rather how many actually don't? The Sandman is *definitely* a major VH head.

However, I believe the true testament to the power of Van Halen's music can best be seen by the events that took place during the U.S invasion of Panama some fifteen years ago. Back in 1990, the United States basically went down there to remove General Manuel Noriega from power. Wanna know one of the methods they used to accomplish this mission? Well, as 'ole pineapple face was cowering and quivering inside of his compound, our PsyOps teams blasted the music of Van Halen at him via loudspeaker, day and night, baby (no word as to whether the classic VH song "Panama" was one of the many tunes used, but it seems like an obvious choice, really). Yes sir, Van Halen played a role in toppling a foreign government. Nice job, boys.

Folks, all of this is owed to their killer music. Hell, even Edward and Alex Van Halen themselves have said this many times during countless interviews throughout their career. These two men live for writing great rock songs and truly touching people with those songs. Which really makes you love them even more. They could have chosen just about any musical medium to work in, you know? They could have been a super-serious technical band and released albums that like only 1 percent of society would have comprehended. You know, stuff that only other musicians could comprehend. When it came time to decide, they chose rock 'n' roll as the medium they wanted to express themselves in.

Rock 'n' roll is the people's music. Always has been, always will be. Van Halen's music is the same: for the people. Edward and Alex have always said the world is full of people, *not* musicians. In other words, they make music for the people. The kicker is that they were able to earn the respect and admiration of their peers as well. It's just kick-ass music, very powerful and moving, *definitely* high energy. Like most great rock music, it's got a dash of blues and pop edges. No matter how wild they played, their songs were always framed in pop edges. All the greats had that, from the Beatles and Led Zeppelin to Nirvana. And like most of the greats, during their classic era, Van Halen truly mastered the art of the three-minute rock song

Sadly, there are those – the critics – who truly love to rip the music of Van Halen. Well, specifically their lyrics. You know, the snobs who are always supposedly searching for "deep meaning" in an artist's lyrics? VH have never been "critical darlings" to begin with, but critics love to slam 'em. Who knows, maybe VH aren't "political" enough or something. Then again, that's just fine by me. Frankly, I've always believed that gettin' your politics from a rock band is the equivalent of gettin' your legal advice from a fuckin' plumber. You know, very few artists are able to be political, without being preachy or annoying, and still make great music. Very few.

So VH appears to have a big target on their back, especially concerning lyrics. But the sad thing is that for many of these people, i.e critics, "deep meaning" apparently only equals lyrics about pain and misery and all that shit. Yeah, as if being honest about lovin' life is not "deep"? I guess Van Halen wasn't depressing or whiny enough for 'em. Yeah, excuse them for actually enjoying themselves while they lived the dream, played to packed arenas, and got more 'tang than an astronaut. Jeesh. Those critics are precisely the kind of people who are totally baffled when they hear some old bluesman sing, "She just *loves* my long black Cadillac in tha mornin'." (Twenty bucks says they actually believe he's singin' about his freakin' car.)

In the end, I find Van Halen to be way more real, honest, and "deep" than a lot of the posers who ran around pissin' and moanin' about how their lives "supposedly" sucked. Besides, searching for "deep meaning" in Van Halen's lyrics is like trying to read Shakespeare during sex.

RHYTHM

"Eddie's one of the few guitarists who's a tremendous rhythm player and an exceptional lead player who is always very creative in both areas."
– Dweezil Zappa

I guess this ties into the songwriting thing, cuz it's such a crucial element. Overall, the next most important thing is the rhythm. This means the rhythm of the band, along with Edward Van Halen's rhythm playing. Van Halen is a band that has always had monster groove. If you look at all the greats, from Led Zeppelin to Pantera, they all had a strong rhythmic foundation. In other words, they had groove to spare.

When it comes to Van Halen, there are a couple of big misconceptions concerning this element of their music. First off, it seems that for decades now, Edward Van Halen has often been referred to as a "lead guitarist." Folks, that is not correct. First and foremost, he is a songwriter. Next up, he is a monster rhythm guitar player. In fact, he is one of the best rhythm guitarists to ever come down the pike. It's no surprise that musicians like Steve Vai have often said Edward's killer rhythm playing tends to get overlooked. Sadly, that seems to be the case.

Look at songs like "I'm the One" and "Hot for Teacher." Yes, they contain killer solos, but damn, the entire song is a clinic! Seriously, I challenge anyone to sit down and learn those two songs front to back. Try to match the overall swing, fire, and intensity of them. Those two songs contain some of the sickest and most insane rhythm guitar playing you will ever hear in your life. Man, there are so many examples from both of Van Halen's two monster eras. Songs like "Light Up the Sky," "Mean Street," "Atomic Punk," "Dance the Night Away," "Romeo Delight," and "Jamie's Cryin'" come to mind, as well. Or how about "5150," "Finish What Ya Started," "Best of Both Worlds," and "Pleasure Dome"? I could go on and on naming songs from this band that display some absolutely brilliant rhythm guitar work.

Folks, Edward Van Halen is all 'bout the rhythm. The funny thing is, he's been saying that for years during interviews, but for whatever reason, some people still don't get it. Whenever I hear players like Edward, Randy Rhoads, and Steve Vai referred to as "lead guitarist," it makes me physically ill. They are freakin' *guitar players,* ok? They do it *all.*

For my money, Edward is like the Keith Richards of shredders. I say that because when it comes to his rhythm playing, Edward always seems to be playing slightly *behind* the beat or just slightly *ahead* of the beat. He's always loose and slinky, yet very much in the pocket. This man is so much more of a rhythm guitarist than he is a lead guitarist, even though his leads are pretty insane, too. Hell, just listen to his music! The proof is right there, clear as day. I mean, 99 percent of the time, what is this man doing during a song? He's playing *rhythm*. Unless Michael Anthony's had a guitar magically hidden up his ass for the last twenty-seven years, um, all that killer rhythm guitar playing is coming from Edward Van Halen. And I must say, a lot of that comes from a lifetime of jamming with his brother Alex. When they started out, obviously, it was just Edward and Alex alone, jamming. So this became the rhythm section of Van Halen!

Many people seem to think a band's rhythm section is the bass player and the drummer. And oftentimes, it is. But in Van Halen's case, the rhythm section is really Edward and Alex. Back when it was just the two of them growing up and jamming together, Edward had to cover *everything*, rhythmically speaking. This band started with and has always been about the interplay between the guitar and the drums, period, end of story. Which is why I give Michael Anthony so much credit. Talk about a team player, this guy knew his role. He did his job, held it down, and allowed Edward to go ballistic throughout their entire career. Mikey is the man.

So when it comes down to it, I just don't believe in "rhythm guitar players" and "lead guitar players," really. For my money, you have to do it *all*. I don't care what anyone says. Just look at all the great players throughout history. From Hendrix to Wylde, they do it all.

Well, Edward Van Halen does it all, too. From writing great songs to crafting killer riffs. And yes, he plays both rhythm *and* lead exceptionally well. But between the two, if you absolutely *had* to choose, I must say that Edward Van Halen is a rhythm guitar player. I actually listened to each Van Halen album and timed his solos. I then turned around and compared that to the overall length of each album. Why? To determine what percentage of time he spent soloing and what percentage of time he spent playing rhythm. (I always knew all that math bullshit would come in handy one day.)

For example, look at the band's legendary self-titled 1978 debut album, *Van Halen*. The length of this album is thirty-five minutes and thirty-six seconds. The total amount of time Edward spends soloing on this album is just over five and a half minutes (yes, that's including "Eruption"). This means that about 15 percent of his time on this album was spent soloing. Guess what else that means? It means he spent the other 85 percent of his time on this album playing rhythm.

In fact, the same thing goes for every other Van Halen album. The guitar soloing on any given VH album always accounts for about (or less than) 20 percent of the overall playing. In other words, at the very least, he consistently spends about 80 percent of his time playing rhythm on every single album. So, um, when the amount of time Edward spends soloing surpasses the amount of time he spends playing rhythm, call me, ok? Until then, if you absolutely had to pick between the two of 'em, well, Edward Van Halen is a *rhythm guitar player.* Case closed.

TONE

"From the moment I heard Edward Van Halen's tone, I knew I had to play guitar. I became obsessed. I listened to Van Halen about a bizillion times. I really liked his rhythmic ideas and his phrasing. He was and still is a monster riff composer. His tone made everything he played sound aggressive, which in turn made his monster riffs sound even cooler. I religiously purchased every newly released Van Halen record after I wore out the first one."

– Dweezil Zappa

I've heard some great guitar tones throughout my life. Stevie Ray Vaughan had a monstrous, phenomenal tone. Allan Holdsworth has major tone, too. Eric Clapton's classic *"woman tone"* from his early days (the Cream-era, especially) was fantastic. Jimmy Page during his Zeppelin days, wow, amazing tone! But for my money, Edward Van Halen might just own the best damn tone I've ever heard in my entire life.

Sadly, the biggest misconception concerning Edward's legendary tone is that you can simply go out and buy all the gear he uses and sound just like him. Um, wrong. It's *not* in the gear. Sure, a person has their preferences and leans towards using whatever they feel comfortable using. In the end, a guitar player's tone is in his *hands.* You know, in his *fingers.* It's not in some pedal or anything like that. Hell, Edward only used a few pedals, anyway. He is a total minimalist. Basically, it's all in the *touch,* ladies and gentlemen. If playing like Edward came in a certain amp, pedal, or guitar, well, we'd all play like that! The simple fact is that *no one* does.

Man, no one on this planet touches the strings like Edward Van Halen.

A person's tone is as unique as his fingerprint. You may come close to sounding like them, but you'll *never* get it exactly like them. I've heard plenty of stories of countless musicians who've passed through the doors of Edward's 5150 Studio. Quite often, Edward will be cool enough to let these people play through his rig. Nuno Bettencourt is one of the many great guitar players to pass through the doors of 5150 to have had this experience. And as you'll see, he quickly learned where Edward's tone came from.

Nuno Bettencourt: "I got a chance to go to a Van Halen rehearsal. I walk in and hear Eddie and I go, 'Jesus, there's that tone he has.' I was thinking to myself, 'I would love to play his stuff. I would love to see if it sounds like that.' They stopped for a second and he goes,

'You've got to try my stuff out.' I sit down and grab his guitar and start playing and unfortunately it sounded like me. I was like, 'Oh man, it is in the guy's fingers.'"

Fact is, Edward Van Halen could pick up just about anybody's guitar and manage to sound like himself. Then you get the guitar back and you are back to sounding like you. I know, what a bummer. But those are the facts. And Edward Van Halen has a legendary monster tone that is known around most circles as the "Brown Sound." Basically, the "Brown Sound" is a term Edward uses to describe his tone. The term is supposed to mean, like, an earthy, wood-like tone. Hence the word "brown." Edward has often described his tone as the difference between an AM radio and a nice, warm home stereo. However, in all honesty, it was Alex Van Halen who actually coined the phrase "Brown Sound." Alex used this term to describe his distinct snare drum sound. In the end, I believe a lot of Edward's guitar tone came from him trying to match his brother's amazing drum sound – *specifically* Alex's snare drum.

If you wanna have some fun, just go online and do a keyword search on "Brown Sound." You'll find there are many Web sites entirely dedicated to all the aspects of Edward's legendary sound! It's insane, man. Entire Web sites with blueprints about the "Brown Sound" so detailed, the freakin' C.I.A. would be proud. In the end, I believe many people would agree that as far as tone goes, Edward truly possesses one of the greatest, if not *the* greatest guitar tone the world will ever know.

INNOVATIVESS/ORIGINALITY

"I do think Van Halen reinvented the guitar...he's an excellent musician, a shrewd guitarist, and as a person he is wonderful."
– Ritchie Blackmore

Edward Van Halen is one of the most original, innovative musicians to ever come down the pike. He truly created a style and sound all his own. You can hear just one note and know it's EVH, period. Many people often wonder if Edward invented a lot of the things he does. Well, no, he didn't. He didn't invent those things he does, per se, but he did invent his *own* way of doing them. In the end, that's the real deal. Folks, that's what is called "innovation."

To begin with, the *Merriam-Webster Dictionary* defines the word *innovate* as "to introduce as or as if new." That is precisely what Edward did, folks. The man *innovated*. He took shredding, tapping, harmonics, whammy-bar molestation, toggle switching, rhythm and lead playing, and feedback, and turned them all on their ass by doing 'em *his* way. He didn't "invent" these techniques and ideas, he innovated all of them. You know, he reinvented 'em. Besides, how can we ever truly pinpoint the first time a musician invented a certain sound or technique? Yeah, good luck with that one. There really is no way in determining that. You can, however, pinpoint when a musician introduced certain ideas or techniques to the masses.

For example, take the great Jimi Hendrix. Fact is, Jimi didn't invent all those techniques and ideas he used, either. Contrary to popular belief, Jimi didn't invent feedback, guitar smashing, playing behind the back, with his teeth, and so forth. Players had been doing those things years before Jimi did. Hell, Buddy Guy was doin' a whole lot of things *before* Jimi that Jimi would eventually learn and borrow from him. You could say the same thing about Pete Townshend, who Jimi learned and borrowed quite a bit from, too. In the end, it doesn't matter cuz Jimi was able to fuse all those techniques and ideas players were using before him into his own thing. You know, into his very own amazing signature style and sound.

Man, Edward Van Halen did the very same thing. Yes, there were people shredding before him, tapping before him, and so forth. Edward's genius, like that of Jimi, lies in the fact that he was able to take all these techniques and seamlessly fuse them into a devastating signature style and sound all his own. That's why a lot of people give him credit for inventing a lot of the things he does, cuz he was the one who introduced all those things to the masses. Hell, he introduced a lot of that into the world of pop, rock, and metal, which had never really seen the likes of him, *ever*. You may have heard or come across some of those things he did in the worlds of jazz/fusion, but as far as rock and other worlds, um, you rarely if ever saw that.

When Van Halen came out at the start of 1978, man, no one had ever seen or heard anything like it. It's hard to imagine a world *before* VH hit the scene. A lot of bands and musicians get respect and become legends by hanging around for a long time. You know, it's like that saying about old buildings and hookers? If they hang around long enough, they begin to get respect. Meanwhile, musicians like Edward Van Halen hit the scene and change *everything*, overnight. In turn, they earn their place in history right out the gate. When someone as brilliant as the late, great Frank Zappa coined the phrase, "Edward Van Halen reinvented the electric guitar," um, you know this kid was special. Again, the main reason being *not* because he invented those things he did, but because he invented his *own* way of doing them and was then able to introduce all of that cool shit to the masses. As Frank said, Edward "reinvented" the electric guitar. Of course, a lot of that goes back to his songwriting. If you don't have the songs, the fact is, the masses will probably never be exposed to what you do. Sure, he still would have been important and he still would have been known as a monster player, but the fact that Van Halen was also a great band and had killer songs put Edward on a level most musicians can only dream of reaching.

When he hit the scene in '78, everything about him was so different. From his style and sound to his guitars, man, it's like the guy wasn't from this planet. It's hard to put down on paper just how devastating and mind-boggling this guy's debut really was. Edward's impact was nuclear, and the fallout is still felt to this very single day. A lot of that had to do with the fact that he took all these amazing techniques and ideas and seamlessly fused 'em together. Again, *that* is where his genius lies. The fact that he was able to master many different techniques and then put them all into his own signature style and sound. In turn, by introducing all of these things into the mainstream, he became known as one of the most innovative and unique musicians of all time. Basically, if you look up the word "iconoclast" in the dictionary, you'll see Edward's picture next to it.

For my money, I truly believe Edward Van Halen is the first, last, and only guitar player I've ever heard in my entire life who was able to seamlessly fuse virtuosity, innovativeness, and sheer shreddery with great songwriting, melody, and pop sensibilities. I mean, honestly, can you name me a single other one?

STAGE PRESENCE

> *"When people saw Jimi Hendrix come on stage and start eating the guitar, they were going, 'What the hell is that?' That was the first time I was just blown away by somebody. The only person to do that to me later on was Eddie Van Halen."*
>
> **– Mick Jones**

All of the elements I mentioned before are important, but if you can't fuse 'em together and take your music to the people in a live setting, well, you are basically screwed. I don't give a damn how much ass you kick in your parents' basement or in your bedroom. The true test of a musician's worth is on the stage, folks. Fact is that on stage, Edward Van Halen is one of the baddest and most natural musicians to ever come down the pike. I don't just mean far as guitar players go, either. I'm talking about musicians in general, period. Edward is so at home on a stage, it's kind of surprising to find out this man is actually a pretty shy, quiet dude who has never fully felt all that comfortable in the spotlight. Man, he sure coulda fooled me, cuz on stage, the guy is a monster.

On his albums, you can hear a man that is at one with his instrument, but on stage, you can hear it *and* see it. This cat is nonstop motion on stage throughout the whole show. I have honestly never seen a VH show in my life where I was disappointed. The band always sounds tight and Edward is just relentless. The best thing is that he can play everything he plays on record in a live setting. That's how you know someone is the *real deal,* when you see them live and they are playing all of their shit with incredible ease. You know, the great ones *always* make it look easy.

I find that many of the greats had incredible stage presence. I guess many people will often refer to this as "showmanship," too. It's been going on for hundreds of years, really. Some will say the legendary violin virtuoso Nicolò Paganini was the world's first rock star! As virtuoso violinist Mark Wood told me, Paganini was quite a flamboyant character. Not only in the way he played, but also in the way he dressed and wore his hair, too. On top of that, Paganini used to actually cut the strings on his violin. The reason? So as he would play a fiery passage, the string would actually snap, therefore giving the audience the impression his playing was so fiery, he was actually breaking strings! That Nicolo was a clever one.

Throughout the years, you can look at everyone from Little Richard to Jimi Hendrix as master showmen. Edward is one, too, but I think he comes more from the mold of say, a Pete Townshend. Like Pete, Edward displays incredible nonstop energy and exuberance on stage. It was never in some rehearsed kind of way, either. Edward doesn't have a "schtick," so to speak. Hell, his one and only signature move is his patented "Flyin' Eddie." You know, where he jumps straight up into the air, right off the stage or from the drum riser, and does a scissor kick. Otherwise, he's just goin' apeshit up there. The guy just goes wherever the music takes him. You can tell by his body language on stage that this is a man who totally gets *inside* his music, so to speak. Not surprising, cuz the music is inside of him, too.

Edward is just the coolest dude on stage. Hell, from what I've heard, he's a cool all-around dude, period. The type of cool Edward has is not some phony, image-driven type of bullshit. It doesn't depend or rely on tattoos or hats or any of that stuff. It's more of a Steve McQueen type of cool, you know? Edward Van Halen just *is* cool, period. When you see the man on stage rockin' out and then he lights up a cigarette, takes a drag, and places it in the headstock of his guitar, damn, it's just too cool! It's obvious the dude is just being himself. He's just being Ed, and that's why it all comes across very natural. He just wants to play his music and have a good time doing so. After all, he is and always has been a rock 'n' roller. A lot of other players simply aren't. They can play rock 'n' roll, but they aren't *really* rock 'n' rollers.

On stage, Edward looks like a happy kid. Yeah, there are plenty of pictures of him with a crazed look on his face, too. You know, those intense, classic guitar-god pictures of him with his head back, eyes shut, jammin' away. Like most of the greats, Edward often "goes blind" when he plays. But most of the pictures you see are of Edward smilin' his ass off and lookin' like he's having the time of his life. Well, that's probably cuz he is. I mean, why wouldn't he be?

Man, if you got to live out your dreams and make a living doing the only thing you've ever truly loved and cared about, damn, wouldn't you be happy? All Edward Van Halen has ever wanted to do was play music. It is painfully obvious to me this man lives for those two hours he gets to go on stage and perform his music for the people. He is doing precisely what he loves and what he was put on this Earth to do. Over the years, Edward has often been referred to as the baddest motherfucker to tear up a stage since Jimi Hendrix. Yeah, I'll agree with that...

SOLOS

"Eddie Van Halen is great, a brilliant player. Some of his own stuff and on the Michael Jackson piece are short, concise, brilliantly crafted solos. They're not just about speed. He can do a bit of something that just blows you away because of the sheer pace of it for a second. And then he goes back to something else. There are moments when I would like to be able to do that, but, as I said, you get what you're given."

– David Gilmour

Jimi Hendrix, Eric Clapton, Chuck Berry, B.B. King, Stevie Ray Vaughan, Brian May, Dimebag Darrell, Zakk Wylde, Randy Rhoads, Tom Morello, Slash, Wes Montgomery, Django Reinhardt, Jimmy Page, John McLaughlin, Andrés Segovia, Paco De Lucia, Duane Allman, Pat Metheny, Kirk Hammett, Brian May, David Gilmour, John Petrucci, and Allan Holdsworth.

See all those legendary names? Well, those are just a few of the many great musicians in history who could solo their ass off. You can go beyond the guitar, too. Look at the amazing and legendary John Coltrane. That cat is one of the greatest soloists of all time, period. So was the Bird, Charlie Parker. And what about the insane piano shredding of Art Tatum? That dude was unreal and could solo his ass off, too. We can even look at the legendary violin virtuoso Nicolò Paganini. There's another monster soloist. You can even pick up a Ravi Shankar album and hear that cat go wild soloing on a sitar. Basically, you can find monster soloists on every instrument, from Yo-Yo Ma and Dizzy Gillespie to Jaco Pastorius and Earl Scruggs.

Now, in all honesty, you don't necessarily have to play solos to be a great player. However, you will find that most of the great ones did play solos! In the end, well, why wouldn't you wanna be a *complete* musician, you know? Well, Edward Van Halen is a complete musician, and his soloing is truly inspiring. Edward is a monster soloist, and his leads are like these wild little roller coaster rides in the middle of his songs. Many would say they are like little compositions within the song itself.

The fact that his solos are so damn tasty has to do with a little thing known as *"phrasing."* Many people would refer to it as "note choice" as well. Edward's phrasing is just so damn tasty, and I think a lot of that has to do with the fact that he loves the blues and grew up jammin' the blues. Even though he would later turn that into a wilder and more aggressive thing, his note choice/phrasing during solos is just absurd. Which again, stems from him always wanting to incorporate that "blues feel" into his playing. For my money, it's all 'bout the phrasing, and Edward has some truly tasty phrasing, baby. It's extremely tasteful and always melodic.

Basically, I believe that all ties into "feel." That's the keyword, right there. In the end, whether a solo is spontaneous or melodic, if it has no *feel,* well, what's the point? In fact, during his first big cover story – *Guitar Player* magazine, April 1980 issue – one of the many questions Edward was asked was, "What do you look for in a solo?" He responded with one simple word: "Feeling." He didn't say speed. He didn't say notes or how many notes you can play. He didn't say scales. He didn't say flash. He didn't say tapping. No, he said everything he needed to say with one simple word: "Feeling." 'Nuff said.

Far as playing guitar solos, well, when you really think about it, is it all that surprising Edward plays solos? Look at his influences! Guys like Clapton, Hendrix, Page, Beck, Blackmore, and so forth. All of them played solos and were pretty damn famous for doing so, too. They are truly some of the greatest soloist of all time. So Edward playing solos doesn't surprise me. However, what does surprise me is the fact that his solos are so damn short. Well, perhaps concise would be a better word. Yeah, his leads are *concise.* Basically, Edward Van Halen solos in the same manner a Navy SEAL team approaches their mission: Get in, get it done, get out, and leave no one behind. In fact, his music proves it.

For example, look at the Classic Van Halen era. You know, the six albums released between 1978 and 1984. This is where Edward is generally considered to be at his most gunslinger. Well, excluding "Eruption," "Spanish Fly," and

"Cathedral," which are all individual solo pieces, the average Van Halen solo during an actual song is just twenty-six seconds.

No, that's *not* a typo. You heard me right. During the Classic VH era, the average guitar solo was just twenty-six seconds, baby. Edward Van Halen basically proved that you don't need to take up a lot of time and sacrifice the song to play kick-ass solos. So while there are plenty of morons out there who, to this very day, accuse him of being Mr. "Overindulgent five-minute guitar solo man," the fact is, Edward's solos are insanely concise. Frankly, it makes you wonder if the, um, "geniuses" who accused Edward of playing really long, overindulgent guitar solos have ever even heard a freakin' Van Halen album. In fact, Edward Van Halen himself has always stated that he doesn't like long solos. He doesn't like playin' 'em and he doesn't even really like hearing 'em. For example, during an interview with *Guitar Player* magazine that appears in their January 1981 issue, Edward states: "I haven't heard anyone do an interesting long guitar solo outside of early Clapton." And back on his very first tour in 1978, Edward did an interview with Japan's *Young Guitar* magazine. Of course, one of the many questions they asked him was about his soloing. Edward's response was straight and to the point: "I don't like long guitar solos."

Edward has always consistently stated that, and his music proves it, cuz Van Halen songs contain really concise solos. The only lengthy solo Edward ever really plays is his "solo spot," in concert. Far as his songs go, the solos are short. So again, in no way, shape, or form did Edward Van Halen extend the length of guitar solos and play really long solos. Not one bit. In fact, if anything, Edward actually *shortened* the length of guitar solos!

For example, remember how during my look at "Rhythm," I pointed out that Edward spends, at the very least, 80 percent of his time on all Van Halen albums playing rhythm? Which, of course, means he spends about 20 percent of his time soloing. When you break that down, in terms of the length of the album vs. the length of the soloing, all Van Halen albums contain just about six minutes of soloing or less. Do you realize how freakin' little that is? Put it to you this way: Jimi Hendrix's classic masterpiece "Machine Gun" (*Band Of Gypsys,* Capitol, 1970) contains about six minutes of soloing. Folks, that's just one song, ok? The amount of time Jimi spends soloing on that one amazing song is about the same amount of time Van Halen spends soloing on an *entire* Van Halen album. And again, Edward often spends even less time than that.

Basically, Edward's solos are really concise. You know, really short. Not that I'm knocking long solos. If they are done right and serve the song, hey, go for it. Certainly Jimi's six minutes of soloing on "Machine Gun" are breathtaking. There are plenty of players who play long solos and do so amazingly well. For example, Stevie Ray solos for about five minutes on his classic instrumental, "Riviera Paradise," and the results are brilliant. Same thing goes for Ed King's killer four-minute solo on the classic Lynyrd Skynyrd anthem, "Freebird."

However, as amazing as they all are, when you realize that's about the same amount of time Van Halen solos on an entire album, well, it really drives home just how concise his solos really are. Overall, many of the most legendary musicians of all time, from Jimi Hendrix to John Coltrane, spent more time soloing on their respective albums than Edward Van Halen ever did on any of his. Hell, Nicolò Paganini's 24 Caprices are basically over one hour's worth of killer solos! And when it comes to individual songs, the same theory applies. For example, the solo in "Jump" is just fifteen seconds. The solo in "Mean Street" is eighteen seconds. The solo in "Hot for Teacher" is thirty-two seconds. "Runnin' with the Devil" contains two solos, each one a whopping nine seconds! The solo in "Unchained" is eleven seconds. The solo in "Beautiful Girls" is seven seconds. The solo in "Panama" is twelve seconds. The solo in "Feel Your Love Tonight" is twenty-five seconds.

Oh, and there are plenty more examples. "Ain't Talkin' 'bout Love" contains two solos, each one a whopping twelve seconds! The solo in "On Fire" is ten seconds. The solo in "So This Is Love?" is twenty-three seconds. The solo in "Light Up the Sky" is nineteen seconds. The solo in "Outta Love Again" is twenty seconds. The solo in "Ice Cream Man" is thirty-six seconds. The solo in "Beat It" is thirty seconds.

Folks, can you honestly name me a single other guitar player who can say so much, musically speaking, in such short, explosive bursts? That's really the point I'm trying to make here. I'd love for the "geniuses" who accused Edward of being Mr. "Overindulgent five-minute guitar solo man" to name me all the other players who can say so much in so little time. I mean, even when you look at "Eruption," which is by far his longest guitar solo (one minute and forty-two seconds), it is still shorter than the killer soloing of many other legendary players.

For example, Jimi Hendrix solos for over two minutes during classic songs like "Voodoo Child," "Come On Pt. 1," and "All Along the Watchtower." Eric Clapton's soloing on the classic "Crossroads" lasts one minute and forty-seven seconds. And that's actually pretty damn short compared to all the lengthy soloing Eric unleashed during his live jams with Cream. Even the great B.B. King solos, quite tastefully, for almost three minutes on his classic, "Sweet Sixteen." In the end, I can name you many great players, from Duane Allman to Jimmy Page, who pulled off long guitar solos that were done amazingly well, and with incredible taste.

Basically, it really does come down to the individual. Musically speaking, someone like Edward Van Halen can say more during the fifteen-second

"Jump" guitar solo than most could say in a lifetime. However, there are those who can solo for minute after minute and keep you absolutely enthralled. It truly does come down to the individual.

In the end, everyone can benefit from listening to all styles of soloing. Lord knows there's a major lack of soloing in today's scene. I believe a lot of that has to do with the "grunge explosion" of the early '90s. The funny thing is that music was guitar-driven. Not to mention the fact that everyone from Pearl Jam to Nirvana played solos! If you look at some of their biggest hits, they contained guitar solos. Regardless, I think there was a backlash against solos that is still felt to this very single day. However, I think someone like Edward Van Halen proves you can play kick-ass guitar solos that don't take up a lot of time. You know, you can play solos without having to sacrifice a song in any way, shape, or form. I hope some of the kids out there realize that.

If you look at Edward and all those other great players I mentioned, you'll clearly see that many of the all-time greats played solos and played 'em well. So you should *never* apologize for playing solos, *comprende?* If anyone cracks on you for soloing, please inform them of all the players who did. Hey, as long as you do it right and it serves the song, solos can be great. Edward Van Halen is proof of that.

The way I see it, solos are really just a great bonus. Like Zakk Wylde told me, "Solos are the icing on the cake." A great solo will usually take a song to another place/level. However, you absolutely need to have a great song. It always comes back to the song, doesn't it? Hey, I don't believe anyone on this planet would actually sit through a shitty song just to hear a guitar solo, regardless of how great that solo may be. For example, check out *Guitar World's* "100 Greatest Solos of All-Time" issue (September 1998). If you flip through that issue, you'll notice just about all the solos people voted for happen to be in great songs. Coincidence? I think not. There's a reason people voted for the solos in "Comfortably Numb," "All Along the Watchtower," "Freebird," "Stairway to Heaven," "Crazy Train," "Cemetery Gates," "No More Tears," "Bohemian Rhapsody," "One," "Hotel California," "Mean Street," "Smells Like Teen Spirit," "Crossroads," "November Rain," "The Thrill Is Gone," and so forth.

Do these songs contain great solos? Absolutely! Are the guitar solos in these songs performed by great players? Absolutely! But the fact of the matter is the *songs* are great, too. In my opinion, most people, whether consciously or subconsciously, end up voting as much for the song as for the solo. I honestly believe that to be the case.

In the end, Edward Van Halen had the tastiest cake and some really sweet icing to go with it. His solos are amazingly concise. Not surprising, really. Musically speaking, Edward's like a Ferrari, and I think we know it doesn't take a Ferrari long to get where it's going, you know? Possessing an astonishing amount of fluidity, Edward is able to transfer the sounds he hears in his head onto his instrument with frightening ease. An even scarier fact may be that most of his solos, including many of his classic ones, are actually spontaneous first-take fits of brilliance. Many times he'd go in to record a song and have absolutely no idea what he was gonna play. It was this sense of adventure that truly made his solos great and exciting.

Edward Van Halen was always willing to take risks. It's the whole "falling down the stairs and landing on your feet" mentality. In fact, you could sum up his entire career, along with his overall approach to music, with that mentality. This man would actually go in, play a song, and when it came time to solo, he'd just let it fly. More often than not, the first take would be the keeper. I mean, even if all his solos had been meticulously worked out prior to recording, man, they would still be absolutely amazing, you know? But the fact that many of his classic and most memorable solos happen to be spontaneous first-takes makes them all the more insane.

So again, to any kids out there who may be reading this, *never* apologize for playing solos, ever. As long as it's done tastefully and serves the song, it's cool. It doesn't matter if they are long or short, fast or slow, so long as it serves the song. If not, don't do it. And if anyone ever cracks on you for playing solos, just remember that many of the greatest musicians in history played solos, ok? Also, please remember what I mentioned during "Rhythm." First and foremost, Edward is a songwriter. This is followed by the fact that he spends more than 80 percent of his time on all Van Halen albums playing *rhythm*. That is a stone-cold fact. Edward Van Halen is *not* a lead guitarist. He is a fantastic guitarist that excels at both rhythm *and* lead. In other words, he is the *total package* as a musician.

SPEED

> *"Well, speed is impressive. There was a time when I thought, who was the fastest? I mean, Jeff Beck seemed to me as fast as you wanted to be. Clapton never made a point of playing fast. Django Reinhardt is probably the best, fastest guitar player in the world, even to this day. Then look at what Eddie Van Halen has done."*
>
> **– Rory Gallagher**

Nicolò Paganini, John Coltrane, Charlie Parker, Sergei Rachmaninoff, Art Tatum, Dizzy Gillespie, Jimi Hendrix, Django Reinhardt, Itzhak Perlman, Paco De Lucia, Neal Peart, Jaco Pastorius, Steve Vai, Randy Rhoads, Stevie Ray Vaughan, Earl Scruggs, Allan Holdsworth, Kirk Hammett, Jason Becker, Andrés Segovia, Al Di Meola, Shawn Lane, John Petrucci, Dimebag Darrell, and Zakk Wylde.

See all those legendary names? Well, those are just a few of the many great musicians in history who are amazingly fluid on their respective instrument. Ironically, they all happen to be phenomenal soloists, too. Hey, they are *complete* musicians.

As is the case with solos, you don't necessarily have to play fast to be a great player. However, once again, many of the greatest players of all time possessed the ability to play fast. Well, I prefer the world *fluidly*. That's all speed in music is, really. It's how *fluid* you are on your respective instrument. For example, in your car, speed is how fast you are driving. It's a simple measurement. In music, it's simply how fluidly you can transfer the sounds you hear in your head out through your instrument. That's just how I see it, anyway.

The funny thing is that there are people out there who will actually knock someone for playing fast. Could you imagine? Knocking a musician for being able to transfer what they hear inside their head onto their respective instrument with precision? Man, what's next, knocking athletes, too? Could you imagine knocking Muhammad Ali, Tiger Woods, or Michael Jordan for being too fast and fluid? Let's get into martial arts and knock Bruce Lee for having been too damn fluid. Oh, and that damn Lance Armstrong is too fast and fluid, too.

All kidding aside, anyone, and I mean *anyone,* who knocks a musician for being "too fast" is a complete moron, period. To me, Edward Van Halen and those other cats I named are the musical equivalent of a Ferrari. And, you know, who the hell puts down a Ferrari? If we were to castigate musicians for being fast and fluid, then everyone from Paganini to Coltrane would have to be tied to the whippin' post. For example, Niccolò Paganini played so damn fast that people actually believed he'd cut a deal with the devil! That is a true story. Mind you, this was well over a hundred years *before* the great Robert Johnson supposedly went down to the crossroads, ok?

For my money, it is quite easy to differentiate between someone who's laying down some *serious* shit with astonishing fluidity and someone who is just firing off a bunch of notes and ends up sounding more like an exercise than anything else. As the great Joe Satriani told *Guitar World* magazine back in November of 1993, "Whether it's John Coltrane or Edward Van Halen doing it, you can tell when the real shredding is going down." Damn straight, Joe. In fact, I believe all the musicians I've named and talked about so far are shredders. In their respective style and on their respective instrument they are, without a doubt, *shredders.*

The sad truth is that some people tend to knock what they don't have or can't do. In other words, anyone who looks at a musician and knocks them for being fluid is probably a jealous wienie who knows deep down inside that they'd love to be able to have that type of command over their instrument. You know, these are the type of people who come up with clever sayings like, "Faster's not better!" And you know, well, maybe faster is not better. But guess what? Slower is not better, either! The fact is it all comes down to how you *use it.* There are musicians who can play fast who are brilliant. Sadly, there are musicians who can play fast who aren't. Just like there are musicians who play slow who are brilliant. Sadly, there are also musicians who play slow who just aren't. In the end, it all comes down to how you use it. Hell, many of the great ones can play both fast *and* slow. Sometimes they even do it within the same damn song! Many of the great ones can change gears, and the results are just as cool.

Speed can be a wonderful thing. Well, in the right hands, anyway. To use a sports analogy, it's the difference between a great Major League pitcher and the prospect who spends his career in the minors cuz he can't throw strikes! You know, what good is it to be able to throw 95 miles an hour if you can't hit the side of freakin' barn? In other words, throw strikes. You *have* to be able to display control and throw strikes. You *have* to show command of all your pitches. No matter how hard you throw, you *have* to create a repertoire of pitches – fastball, changeup, slider, curveball, splitter, and so forth. You know, you have to be able to change speeds and mix it up!

Fact is that no matter how hard you throw, if you only throw fastballs, well, professional hitters will rip you. In music and guitar playing, it's no different. What good is that speed if you just can't use it wisely, properly, and tastefully? You have to be able to change pace and mix it up. That's why Edward Van Halen is like Roger Clemens, while a whole lot of other guitar players are more like Charlie Sheen's legendary Rick "Wild Thing" Vaughan character from the hilarious film *Major League*. Well, before he got his glasses, anyway.

What makes Edward or any other fluid musician great is *not* their speed. No, it's really the fact that they know *how* to use that speed and *when* to use that speed. Most important of all, it's the fact that they know when *not* to use that speed! That right there is what truly makes them great. Fact is speed/fluidity can be found in many of the greatest musicians in history, from the world of rock and jazz to classical.

When Edward Van Halen hit the scene in 1978, he was the "fastest gun," so to speak. Since then, there are plenty of great players who came down the pike who continued to push the envelope and who are faster than Edward. I mean, even by today's standards, Edward is still more fluid than any human being has a right to be, you know? But just as in sports and how athletes get bigger and faster, musicians go through the same thing, too. Basically, there were fast musicians *before* Edward and there were faster musicians *after* him. He blew the doors off and made jaws drop when he debuted in 1978. Hell, many people believed he was speeding up his recordings! But Edward has always managed to show incredible taste and melody, no matter how fast or slow he was playing. Edward is not a great player because he plays fast. He is a great player who has speed in his arsenal. And in the end, without the songs, who really cares?

The Classic VH Sound

"My first impression of Van Halen was that David Lee Roth was a God, and that so was Eddie."

– Dave Mustaine

Alex Van Halen's signature drum sound/style

Alex is the backbone of this band, period. He is to Van Halen what Cliff Burton was to Metallica. By that I mean that Alex is the heart, soul, balls, and leader of this band. Along with the fact that, pound for pound, he may actually be the band's hardest partier. That's really saying something when you consider just how wild this crew is. The man is one-part virtuoso, one-part "Animal" from *The Muppet Show*. He's *sooo* underrated, probably cuz he's always been more than happy to let his little brother shine. His distinct snare sound, which he coined "Brown Sound," ended up influencing Edward's overall sound. Far as gear goes, I believe he is a Ludwig man through and through. Alex Van Halen's powerful rhythmic slam is the foundation upon which this kingdom was built. Without Big Al behind the drum kit, fuhggedabout it...

EVH's signature guitar sound/style

Far as their classic sound, Edward's massive "Brown Sound" is an integral part of that. For the majority of guitar heads out there, the "Brown Sound" is most often associated with the Classic VH era. Over the years, Edward has always described it as the difference between an AM radio and a nice, warm home stereo. Anyhow, Edward's classic rig consisted of the following:

A guitar (homemade strats, Charvels, Les Pauls, and Ibanez Destroyers) equipped with an overwound, potted humbucker pickup in the bridge position, a stock 1959 model Marshall 100-Watt Plexi Super Lead amplifier (circa 1966-1967) run through an assortment of cabinets (too many to mention) hooked up to a Variac (starving the amp at 92 volts), and a pedal board consisting of a few pedals duct taped to a piece of plywood! These pedals were the MXR Flanger, MXR 6-band EQ, and the MXR Phase 90.

He also had two Echoplexes and a Univox Tape Echo. However, only the controls for the Echoplexes and the Univox were part of his pedal board. Edward kept the actual units housed in an old World War II bomb that he picked up at a junkyard in San Bernadino. (Yes, there was a World War II bomb on stage during Van Halen club gigs. Hell, it even found its way onto their first tour as well.) The Echoplex was a *major* part of his sound, whereas the Univox was only used at the end of "Eruption," after the very last note. Other than that, it wasn't really used at all.

Oh, and this fact may shock you, but Edward Van Halen *never* used any kind of distortion pedal or boost, ever. Also, please remember that he achieved that monstrous tone *before* "high gain" amplifiers ever even existed, ok? Basically, any and all distortion you hear is coming straight from his stock Marshall amp. Of course, in the end, Edward's amazing tone is really in his hands. Finally, as far as strings go, I believe Edward uses a set of .009's. However, he is known to boil his strings! Apparently, Edward believes that old, used strings give you a warmer sound, and I guess boiling a new pack of strings for about twenty minutes helps give 'em that used, warm sound. I've also heard that boiling 'em helps stretch the strings out, too.

Michael Anthony

A major part of their classic sound, and overall career for that matter, has always been Van Halen's amazing background vocals/harmonies. Many people don't realize these guys were a hard rock/metal band pulling off three-part harmonies! The reason they sound so good has a whole lot to do with their bass player, Michael Anthony. Rock-solid bass playing aside and killer stage presence aside, it was his golden voice that really took their sound to another level. In fact, his voice is so damn powerful that back in the day, when the band used to record their vocals, Mike would have to stand several feet *behind* Edward and Dave. You see, the three of 'em would all sing into the same mic, and Mike literally had to stand way behind his band mates so he wouldn't drown 'em out. Hey, Mikey didn't earn the nickname "Cannonmouth" for nothing, ok?

Diamond Dave

Yes, I know, Dave is not the greatest singer. Hey, he'll tell you that himself, ok? But this is rock 'n' roll, baby, *not* opera. And in rock 'n' roll, a "cool voice" can be just as powerful as a "great voice." Well, Dave had a really cool voice. I dig it and I know millions of others did, too. He just has that certain whiskey and cigarettes vocals quality I like. Sure, you can find lots of terrific singers who can hit all the high notes and do all those loopy vocal gymnastics and whatnot. But, to me, Dave's voice swaggers! There's a certain attitude present in his voice that comes across in their songs and the combination was perfect. In the end, his voice complements the music quite well. And as a frontman, well, he is simply one of the greatest of all time.

Ted Templeman and Donn Landee

I'm sure these two men would hate me writing about them, cuz they have never sought out the spotlight. Sorry, boys, but you were important to VH achieving their classic sound. Not so much for what these gentlemen did, but for what they *didn't* do. Producer Ted Templeman was smart enough to let the band do their thing. He'd set 'em up in the studio and basically let 'em play as if they were playing a live show. Edward, Alex, and Mike, *together,* jumping around, having fun, feeding off each other and playing their asses off.

That's why the music of Van Halen still explodes out of your speaker today, cuz it was recorded live, baby. And if he let the band go nuts, well, that went double for Edward. Ted basically threw a mic in front of Edward's cabinet, pressed "RECORD" and got the hell outta the way. He trusted the kid cuz he could hear that Edward knew what he was doing.

The same can be said for engineer Donn Landee. That's truly Edward's partner in crime, right there. Apparently, Edward and Donn bonded during the recording of that first VH album. Their relationship would remain strong through the entire classic era. Donn was basically Edward's "extra ear," and he was really able to relate to Edward and understand what he was looking for on a musical level. There was incredible trust and respect between these two men. In turn, I truly believe this helped make the Classic VH era what it was.

Richard McKernan worked as an engineer on Van Halen's debut album and can vividly recall the experience, as well as the magic between Edward and Donn.

Richard McKernan: "I worked as second engineer on Van Halen's first album at Sunset Sound in Los Angeles. Their musicianship was incredible and they were the greatest guys. It's a band that loved their music and it showed. Those guys came in and started playing and I started rolling tape. Of all the big-name groups I've worked with, they were quickest and easiest to record. I think that's what actually made them a step above everybody. They cut what they felt, and if it felt right, they put it out.

"Donn Landee was the first engineer, and he was a real quiet, shy type of guy—a real perfectionist and an incredible engineer. It explained why Eddie liked him so much—the superiority Eddie had on the guitar, Donn had in the studio."

This band, along with the team of Ted and Donn, would work together to produce some of the greatest hard rock music ever known to man. The really insane thing is that just about all of those Classic Van Halen albums were completed in a matter of two or three weeks! When it would come time to record a song, the band would usually do just two or three takes, and that was it. Hey, if you can't nail it in the first couple of takes, why even bother? Meanwhile, the music itself would always be complete in a matter of days, usually less than a week. So, believe it or not, there are mistakes on Van Halen albums! Of course, the public is not even aware of it cuz, you know, they didn't write and perform those songs. So, you know, most people will have *no idea* as to which songs contain mistakes.

However, during plenty of interviews throughout their career, both Edward and Alex have admitted that there are mistakes on all of their albums. Yes sir, everything from bum notes to speeding up the tempo, and so forth. However, if the overall *feel* and *vibe* of a song was really cookin', well, then that's the take they would keep and use – mistakes be damned. Besides, a Van Halen "mistake" is usually still better than most people's best.

Far as vocals went, well, the vocals had to be done separately, of course, and would usually take about a week or two. Ted Templeman was really vital in getting Dave sounding tight, as well. I believe the two of them really worked hard and were able to get Dave's vocals on point.

The Story of "Eruption"

*"Like a lot of guitar players, I couldn't believe what I was hearing when I heard 'Eruption' for the first time. The incredible playing, the warm, deep, smooth, comforting guitar tone, and those almost classical-sounding hammer-ons—I heard all that and thought, 'My God what **is** that?' This song probably made some people give up playing the guitar, while it really inspired others to practice even harder. I totally hopped on the bandwagon: I had to be able to do that."*

– Mike Mushok

Throughout the course of history, there have been a few important, groundbreaking pieces of music that change the way an isntrument is heard and played, forever. Basically, it completely reinvents it. For example, John Coltrane wrote a piece called "Giant Steps." While he obviously wrote many amazing and influential pieces, man, in just over four and a half minutes, "Giant Steps" took everything human beings thought they knew about the saxophone and crushed it.

Another cool example is Nicolò Paganini and his 24 Caprices. With an hour's worth of violin instrumentals – most of 'em ranging from about two to four minutes in length – Nicolò sent 'em all back to the woodshed. Or, like, Jaco Pastorius and his classic piece, "Donna Lee." In less than three minutes, Jaco made every bassist on the planet wanna take up the french horn or something. Other classic pieces ranging from Django Reinhardt's "Nuages" to Jimi Hendrix's version of "The Star Spangled Banner" – both clocking in at the three-to-four-minute range – did the same.

However, in less time than it takes to microwave a freakin' burrito, Edward Van Halen managed to compose a piece of music that changed how an instrument is perceived and played, *forever*. No bullshit. With everything

188

from vibrant soundscapes and searing passages to kamikaze whammy-bar dives, monster tone, and ear-boggling, classical-sounding two-hand tapping, the impact of "Eruption" was immediate and literally changed everything, overnight.

Again, the really sick part is that the damn thing is just over a minute and a half in length. Folks, that's all the time Edward Van Halen needed to take what at that point had been over twenty years of rock guitar history, and absolutely crush it. I mean, he freakin' decimated it. Sure, the entire first Van Halen album is a freakin' clinic, but "Eruption" *alone* was more than enough.

Basically, this instrumental/solo is one of the most devastating musical statements ever made. The really funny thing is that it almost wasn't even recorded! Sure, now everyone hears that first Van Halen album and sees "Eruption" on there and doesn't even think twice about it. But the fact is that during the sessions for that first VH album back in '77, this piece was in no way, shape, or form supposed to be on the album. So how in the hell did it end up on there? More importantly, how in the hell did it almost *not* end up on there? Well, Lord knows I've heard so many different versions of this story. In fact, some people even seem to believe "Eruption" was a warm-up exercise Edward used to do! Folks, I've done my homework and I know the story by heart. So here's the deal.

One day, during the sessions for that first Van Halen album back in 1977, Edward showed up to the studio early. While he was chillin' there, he remembered that he had a gig coming up that weekend. So rather than just sit around, he decided to practice his solo guitar spot. You know, to keep his chops up for the gig that weekend. Maybe this is why a lot of people think "Eruption" was a so-called "warm-up exercise" or something? Anyway, as he is practicing his solo spot, none other than producer Ted Templeman happens to walk in. Apparently, Ted had a conniption fit and immediately demanded to know what the hell he was playing. Edward explained that it was just his solo guitar spot he performed during gigs. Well, um, after Ted regained consciousness (just kidding), he demanded they put it on the record!

And there you have it. It's that simple. Basically, it happened by accident! Edward didn't walk into the studio and go, "Ok, I have this bitchin' little solo I wanna put on the album" or anything like that. His producer simply stumbled upon him playing it and then demanded he lay it down on tape. So, of course, Edward simply nodded his head and did just that. What's even sicker is the fact that they ended up puttin' it as the number 2 track on their debut album! Man, you gotta have some major *cojones* to put an instrumental/solo piece on your album just after the freakin' opening track. Seriously, man, whoever made that decision (I imagine it was Ted and Donn) has major *cojones*. It was a risk that paid off, big time. So to whoever the hell made that decision, nice call, dude.

Now, um, some of you may want to cover your ears right about now, cuz this next bit of information might hurt, too. Edward Van Halen did precisely two takes of "Eruption." Yes, I said just *two takes*. He did two takes, back to back, and they decided to go with the one that flowed best, which I believe was actually the first take. Pretty sick, huh? On top of that, I've read plenty of interviews where Edward has always claimed he could have played it better cuz there is actually a mistake at the top end. If you listen close, you might just realize what it is.

So "Eruption" was actually Edward Van Halen's solo spot during the club days. In fact, I actually own bootlegs of Van Halen club gigs from as early as 1975 where he is playing "Eruption." What's even wilder – and again, you may want to cover your ears – is that I believe he actually toned it down for the album! I'm serious, too. I've owned and heard plenty of bootlegs from their club gigs during the mid '70s where the versions of "Eruption" he was performing were actually a bit longer and wilder than the version he laid to tape on that first album. Most of the versions of "Eruption" he played in clubs would usually range anywhere from two to three minutes in length. You know, cuz it was his solo spot. The version of "Eruption" he played on the first Van Halen album is just over a minute and a half. Well, one minute and forty-two seconds, to be exact. I swear, there is a version of "Eruption" on a VH bootleg called "Golden West Ballroom 1976" that is just about three minutes in length and wilder than the one on the first album! It's just absolutely devastating.

Oh, and you may want to cover your ears again now. Guess how old Edward was when he came up with "Eruption"? Well, he was just twenty-two years old when he recorded it, which in and of itself is a truly staggering fact. However, he actually came up with it when he was about sixteen years old. Of course, the piece evolved over the years. I'm sure the first version he came up with back then was not the one we hear on the album. No doubt he experimented with it over the years and finally worked it into to a two-to-three-minute solo spot. For the album, he trimmed it down, and so it clocks in at just over a minute and a half. Basically, Edward Van Halen began playing guitar at age twelve, and by sixteen he'd composed "Eruption." Not bad, kid.

In fact, therein lies the major difference between Edward and everyone else on this planet. Sure, there are people out there who can play some if not all of "Eruption." I'm sure there are even some teenage kids who can play some if not all of it, too. I've never heard anyone get it exact, but there are those who get it in the ballpark, pretty damn close. You may be able to learn all the notes, but as far as the overall intensity and tone of that piece, well, good luck. Also, you'll obviously *never* be able to recreate the impact of it. You simply can't go back to 1978 and recreate the monstrous, jaw-dropping impact that piece had on everyone back then. Sorry, but you can't find that in a tab book, ok?

However, there are those who can play "Eruption" and play it pretty well. These are the people who went out and bought the album, played the song over and over, bought the music or tab, and maybe even bought a concert video, as well. It's become one of those pieces that, if you play guitar, you've probably had a go at. You know, one of those pieces of music that, when your friends learn you play guitar, they ask you if you can play it. And yes, after much time and practice, some people are able to play it. And that's cool. However, the major difference, my friends, is that those people *copied* "Eruption," while Edward Van Halen *wrote* "Eruption." And that, ladies and germs, is a universe of difference, baby. There are billions of people on this planet. Out of those billions, millions are musicians. Out of all those people, only one man can ever claim he wrote "Eruption," and his name is Edward Van Halen.

In the end, you just can't blame people for having a go at it. I mean, from the moment the first Van Halen album came out through the entire 1980s, "Eruption" was basically *the* musical Pandora's Box of that decade. If you played guitar, man, you pretty much had to know this piece. Billy Corgan can sum up what it was like for most guitarists growin' up during that time.

Billy Corgan: "When people found out that I played guitar, the question I heard most often was, 'Can you play "Eruption"?' Such was the suburban world, circa 1981."

So let people cut their teeth on it and copy it. Hey, after someone lays a blueprint for something, *anyone* can come along and learn it. Well, with a certain amount of talent and dedication, anyway. It's no different than the little kids I see who can play Beethoven and Paganini note-for-note. Or like some art school kid comin' along and copying a painting by Picasso or any other legendary artist. I'm sure they could paint you a damn good rendering of it, but in the end, that don't make 'em Picasso, *comprende?* No, Edward composed that piece of music. Basically, there was no "Eruption" for Edward to copy when he was growing up.

As if that is not humbling enough, throw in the fact that when it came time to record it for their debut album, he played it live and in just two takes. On top of that, throw in the fact that he played "Eruption" on his legendary "Frankenstrat" guitar. You know, his famous black-and-white-striped homemade guitar that he cobbled together from second-hand guitar parts? Yes, Edward Van Halen managed to record one of the most devastating musical statements ever known to mankind with a cheap, homemade guitar he built himself and painted with Schwinn bicycle paint! Add to that the fact that "Eruption" is pretty much effects-free, too. Other than a touch of MXR Phase 90 during a couple of sections, man, it's really all in his hands. The entire piece was pretty much effects-free. It was basically his "Frankenstrat" played through his legendary Marshall 100-Watt Plexi Super Lead amp. Although there was some tasty plate reverb added on to the track in the studio by Donn Landee.

The significance of this piece of music simply can't be overstated. When many people first heard "Eruption" back in 1978, they thought it was studio tricks. You know, lots of overdubbing and so forth. There were those who actually thought it was two guitar players. While others actually believed the tape had been sped up. Meanwhile, the final section of this piece is where Edward truly introduced his trademark two-hand tapping technique to the world. You know, it's those classical-sounding hammer-ons he does. At the time many people thought that was actually a freakin' synthesizer! Man, to this day I'll play "Eruption" for people and when it gets to the last section, many of them will be like, "Damn, is that a keyboard or something? That's not a *guitar,* right?"

Simply put, I think it's safe to say most people on this planet had never heard a guitar sound like that in their entire life. If some fifty-year-old dude would have played this, man, it still woulda been totally mind-boggling. The fact that it was written and played by a fresh-faced twenty-two-year-old kid (who still looked like he could be in high school) is as stunning as the piece itself. I mean, I dunno if anyone ever truly "masters" an instrument, but I know many people considered Edward a "master" of his instrument as soon as they heard this single piece. Man, to this very day, "Eruption" is still brutal and completely electrifying. Not to mention legendary.

In fact, I'd like to share a quick, funny story with you. About three years ago, I was chillin' with some friends at our favorite bar. Well, aside from having a vast and tasty selection of alcohol, this place has a killer jukebox. I'm talkin' tons of classic rock, along with a li'l bit of "newer" material, for lack of a better word. Yup, everything from Led Zep, Guns, and the Stones to VH, Metallica, Nirvana, Stevie Ray Vaughan, Audioslave, Skynyrd, and so forth.

So we're sittin' there downin' some brews when suddenly, "Eruption" comes roarin' outta the speakers. A smirk came across my face, and all I could think to myself is, "Thank you" to whoever the unknown person was who decided to shove a buck or two into the 'ole jukebox and make such a fine selection. As it came on, you could actually hear a few people in the bar go "Yeah!" or "Whooo!" out loud.

Well, then something totally and completely unexpected happened. Almost tragic, really. Not long after the piece came roarin' outta the speakers, the volume went down! And I mean it went down considerably, ok? Apparently, some damn waitress – a rookie, no doubt – made the mistake of goin' behind the bar, reaching under the bar to where the controls are, and turning the volume down. Oh man, *big mistake*. Immediately, a voice comes flyin' outta nowhere, "Hey, turn that shit back up!" A couple seconds later, another voice barks, "Yo, what the fuck, man? Turn it up!" Then another voice, "Hey! What the hell? *Turn that goddamn fuckin' shit up!*"

The people had spoken and, man, I can't lie...the smirk on my face instantly grew into a huge shit-eating grin as I sat there and thought to myself, "Man, I simply can't think of another freakin' guitar solo that could elicit such a swift and insane response." You know, especially when you consider that at this point the damn thing was almost twenty-five freakin' years old! Well, just as I was thinkin' that, some dude sittin' next to me at the bar turns to me and, with a look of total disgust pasted across his face, grunts, "Fuck, man, that's the only time in my entire fuckin' life that I've ever heard someone turn fuckin' 'Eruption' *down!*" I simply nodded in agreement and, with a huge shit-eating grin across my face, took another swig of my brew.

Oh, and in case you're wondering about that poor waitress, well, she survived. However, after her horrible mistake, the manager of the bar literally came sprinting outta the back room, pounced behind the bar, turned the volume all the way back up, and then proceeded to take that rookie waitress out from behind the bar and escort her into the back. I'd like to think he then explained to her that you *never* touch the volume on the damn system – *especially* when Classic Van Halen is playing. Well, ok, maybe he only told her not to touch the volume.

So as you can clearly see, even to this day, this piece is still very much respected. In fact, in *Guitar World* magazine's "Top 100 Solos of All Time" issue (September 1998), "Eruption" clocked in as the number 2 greatest solo of all time, behind only Jimmy Page's amazing solo from the classic Zep tune, "Stairway to Heaven." The fact that this was voted on by the readers of *GW* means all that much more. You know, cuz it's the fans speaking. What's even more amazing is that this poll was conducted twenty years *after* "Eruption" debuted. So, you know, many of the people who voted for "Eruption" hadn't even been born when it came out in 1978!

Finally, for any and all musicians out there who are interested, *Guitar World* magazine had the best breakdown of "Eruption" I've ever seen in my life. It's not just the tab/music, but also a full five-page breakdown of the piece, explaining everything from the gear Edward used and so forth. I mean, they even point out the fact that the super-blazin' hummingbird-picking section you hear at about thirty seconds into "Eruption" is actually a phrase Edward borrowed from Caprice Study #2 for Violin by Rodolphe Kreutzer! *GW* did their homework, baby. So here are the issues:

*Guitar World March 2003 issue (Zakk Wylde and Dimebag Darrell on the cover).

*Guitar World's GUITAR LEGENDS Special Collector's Issue (All Van Halen Issue w/Edward on the cover) Summer 2004.

Tapping

"Eddie brought tapping to the forefront, and I still think he was one of the tastiest players doing it."

– Jeff Beck

Let's get right down to it. Did Edward Van Halen invent tapping? In one word: NO. This goes back to what I said about innovation. He didn't invent tapping, but he did use it in his own way. Along with the fact that he introduced it into the mainstream in a way that had never been done before. The funny thing is Edward Van Halen has *never* claimed he invented tapping. No, it appears the music press and many of us fans in general are the ones who claimed it for him.

However, before I begin, please allow me to first point something out. What many people often refer to as tapping is, technically speaking, *not* tapping. What you hear during the final section of "Eruption" and "Spanish Fly" is actually *not* tapping. Tapping is when you literally "tap" on the neck of the guitar, on the fret, approximately one octave up, so as to produce a chime-like effect. If you want to hear tapping, check out what Edward does during the interlude of "Dance the Night Away." Or what he does during the intro to "Spanish Fly." *That's* tapping! The intro to "Women in Love" is another prime example of tapping. Folks, what Edward Van Halen performs during the closing section of "Eruption" and "Spanish Fly," where he literally hammers on the neck of the guitar with his right hand, is actually known as "hammer-ons," or "right-hand hammer-ons." But eventually people just started calling it tapping, or "two-hand tapping." So for the purpose of keeping it simple, I'll just call it tapping, too.

Now, this may shock some people but, frankly, I believe too damn much was made of the whole tapping thing. Honestly, tapping is like number 1,248 on the list of amazing and important accomplishments Edward has achieved in his career. Regardless whether Edward Van Halen had ever tapped or not, he still would have been one of the most amazing, innovative, and influential guitar players of all time. And Van Halen still would have been one of the most successful and influential bands of all time as well. It's pretty hysterical to think that Edward became so well known for a technique he rarely uses! I mean, I own all his albums and all the VH guitar tab books, too. After doin' my homework, I discovered that Edward rarely taps during his songs. Some people seem to think every single Van Halen song and guitar solo is some kind of happy tapfest or something. Well, nothing could be further from the truth. Folks, Edward does *not* tap during every solo.

In fact, Edward rarely taps during his solos. For proof, I went right to the source and whipped out my Classic Van Halen guitar tab books. This is the period when Edward was really known to be at his most "guitar slinger" or whatever you wanna call it. As I flipped through the pages, I came to realize just how little this man actually taps – *especially* during his solos. Over the course of those six classic era albums, I believe Edward only tapped during the soloing of about a dozen songs, total. That's it. Again, that is over the course of six freakin' albums, ok?

For example, let's take a look at the band's classic debut album, *Van Halen*. Aside from "Eruption," there are thirteen guitar solos on this album. Well, out of those thirteen solos, Edward Van Halen only taps during three of 'em, and they are: the solo in "You Really Got Me," the one solo in "I'm The One," and the solo in "Ice Cream Man."

Oh, and the amount of time he spends tapping during each solo is a whopping one to two seconds, tops. That's all, folks. Hell, if you blink, you'll miss it! Aside from the closing section of "Eruption," that's just a few seconds of tapping on the *entire album*. Man, the amount of restraint and taste Edward Van Halen displays is truly insane.

Basically, the twenty-six-second closing section of "Eruption" is where Edward really put his tapping style on display. He also displays it on his second album, *Van Halen II*, during the classic flamenco-flavored instrumental piece, "Spanish Fly." Honestly, "Eruption" and "Spanish Fly" are the only pieces of music in Van Halen's entire freakin' career that would have sounded any different without the tapping. You know, cuz both of these pieces rely on a closing section consisting of Edward's majestic classical-sounding two-hand tapping. I honestly don't believe a single other Van Halen song or solo would have sounded any different, better or worse without tapping. In fact, some of Van Halen's most popular songs/solos contain absolutely *no* tapping.

For example, Classic VH era tunes like "Runnin' with the Devil," "Ain't Talkin' 'bout Love," "Atomic Punk," "On Fire," "Somebody Get Me a Doctor," "Outta Love Again," "Light Up the Sky," "Romeo Delight," "Mean Street," "Feel Your Love Tonight," "I'll Wait," and "Hot for Teacher" have brilliant solos – none of which contain so much as an ounce of tapping.

Sometimes, Edward will actually use tapping to play intros. For example, check out the insane intro to "Mean Street," where Edward busts out with some wild percussive "slap bass" style of tapping. The intro to "Romeo Delight" shows Edward tapping as well. The intro to "Source of Infection" is also another great example, too. While other times he would simply use tapping to play fills during a song as well. And as I mentioned earlier, he employs tapping to chime out harmonics, too. Again, check out the intro to the song "Women in Love" to hear a perfect example of this idea. It appears Edward Van Halen explored just about every possible way to use this technique, constantly experimenting to come up with new and improved ways to do it. And while tapping itself is really not that difficult, knowing how to use it is. It's like a blues scale. Everyone and their sister can play a blues scale, but how many people can make you cry with it?

I believe the late, great Frank Zappa once said that Edward was the first musician he ever heard who was able to use this technique without having it sound like a technique. That, my friends, is the key. In the hands of most, tapping could easily become an annoying gimmick that is overused to the point it gets nauseating. In the hands of a master like Edward, well, let's just say he always knew how to use it, when to use it, and most important of all, when *not* to use it. And on those rare occasions he did use it, you better believe it was always done tastefully and never at the expense of the song. So, while it was a cool idea and all, I just don't understand why some people would reduce this man to one small aspect of his playing, you know?

To me, that would be like reducing Michael Jordan to one small aspect of his game: dunking. Imagine for a minute if the all encompassing achievement of MJ's career had been the fact that he was a monster at dunking? I mean, he was, but imagine overlooking *everything* else for just that one thing! Imagine overlooking the fact that he transcended the game, won six NBA titles, won a bunch of scoring titles, earned the highest ppg average ever, five MVP awards, played ferocious defense, was a great shooter, great ball handler, team leader, hard worker, twelve-time all star, etc... and just focus on that one little aspect of his game. Pretty stupid when you think about it, right? Well, why do the same thing to Edward? I dunno why, but some people do. Anyway, the stone-cold fact is Edward Van Halen didn't invent tapping. He "innovated" it and popularized it. When Van Halen hit in 1978 and that first album exploded, it seems the music world jumped all over his two-hand tapping style. Edward was really the first player to make a monster statement with tapping – "Eruption" – so that's why Edward is often credited for having invented this technique, cuz he unleashed it in a monster way into the mainstream, and the mainstream had never really seen that before. After hearing "Eruption," well, it seems everyone wanted to learn how to tap. Oh man, and after he threw a bit of two-hand tapping into his sick cameo solo on the Michael Jackson hit "Beat It" in 1982, well, even more people began to take notice of it.

So the question remains, if Edward Van Halen didn't invent tapping, then who the hell did? Well, the truth is, tapping has been around for centuries! Man, trying to locate the very first guitarist who tapped is like trying to locate the very first guitarist to use a freakin' pick! However, after doing my homework, I was able to locate the first book ever written about tapping, "Illustrated Touch System," which was written by Jimmy Webster in 1952. Apparently, tapping used to be known as "touch-style guitar" back then, and it's still known as such by many people today. Along with Jimmy Webster, the legendary Merle Travis was tapping around this time, as well.

Players like Dave Bunker continued to use and evolve the technique during the 1950s. Dave actually began to build his own instruments, specifically designed for the touch-style method. By the late 1960s Emmett Chapman hit the scene with his amazing creation, the Chapman Stick. This took two-hand tapping to the next level. Hell, it took it up several levels! Eventually, most of the guitar players who tapped were usually found in the world of jazz or jazz/fusion. However, there were guitarists from the world of rock who tapped *before* Edward Van Halen hit the scene in 1978. During the mid 1970s, you had cats like Billy Gibbons of ZZ Top, Brian May of Queen, and even Ace Frehley of Kiss, who actually tapped with his pick.

However, when these players tapped, they would literally just "tap" a single note here or there, so frankly, most people didn't even take notice. The way EVH tapped was more noticeable and frankly, much more mind-blowing. It was this super-fluid, almost saxophone-sounding type of tapping. Some may liken it to a rolling yodel or something, while sometimes it could be described as classical-sounding, like on "Eruption" and "Spanish Fly." And while Edward's own wild system of tapping is the one the majority of guitar players would eventually turn to as the blueprint, I must point out that there were a few players who laid that style of tapping to tape *before* Edward did.

The first is Steve Hackett, a phenomenal guitarist who has been in the music biz for over thirty-five years and is still kickin' ass today. He actually got his start doing session work in the late 1960s. Then he became a member of a band called Quiet World, and they released an album in 1970. Soon after, Steve put an ad in *Melody Maker,* and none other than Peter Gabriel (yes, *that* Peter Gabriel) answered it. At the time, Peter had a little band called Genesis, and he was searching for a replacement for one of their original members, Anthony Phillips.

Needless to say, by early 1971 Steve Hackett was out of Quiet World and now a full-time member of Genesis. This leads to us to the very first Genesis album Steve played on, *Nursery Cryme* (1971, Atlantic), which contains one of the earliest examples of two-hand tapping ever laid to tape. So I went directly to the source and asked him about this album and how he came up with the technique.

> **Steve Hackett:** "The technique I pioneered on Genesis' *Nursery Cryme* album started way back in '71 when I was trying to play Bach on an electric guitar for the first time. It enabled stretches that were way beyond the normal capabilities of guitarists and gave many a keyboard player a healthy shock! By the way, I love Eddie's playing and I'm thrilled he took tapping on to such dizzying heights!" ♪

Basically, Steve Hackett laid two-hand tapping down on tape way back in 1971. That's actually seven years *before* the first Van Halen album was released. However, along with Steve, the other player I absolutely have to mention is Harvey "The Snake" Mandel.

Harvey "The Snake" Mandel is a legend in music circles. The man is a virtuoso who's been in the music biz since releasing his 1968 debut album, *Cristo Redentor* (Mercury Records). He's truly paid his dues and, as he told me, "I even got to meet, jam and smoke a fatty with Jimi Hendrix." In fact, Harvey Mandel is still around today and kickin' much ass, not only as a player, but as a terrific producer as well.

After doing my homework, I discovered that Harvey Mandel's *Shangrenade* (1973, Janus Records) contains one of the earliest examples of two-hand tapping ever laid to tape. Whereas Steve Hackett's *Nursery Cryme* album has a couple of songs with tapping, every single one of the eight songs on *Shangrenade* contains tapping! This amazing album was released five years *before* Van Halen's debut album was released. Again, tapping has been around forever, so I'm strictly talking about that wild, super-fluid, two-hand style that Edward Van Halen put on the map and became known for. Well, the fact is Harvey Mandel laid that down on tape five years before the first Van Halen album was released.

Once again, I went directly to the source and asked Harvey Mandel about this album and how he came up with the technique. So, ladies and germs, I give you The Snake.

Harvey Mandel: "The way I got it is that I was playing at the Whisky [A Go-Go] when I first started doing the tapping thing, and I heard everyone from Hendrix to Van Halen happened to stop in and see me doing it. Eventually, Van Halen came out with their first hit records and stuff and he started doing the tapping in his own way.

"I was playing with Pure Food and Drug Act, and Randy Resnick was the other guitarist in the band. Randy was the first guitarist I ever saw tap, and he had his own little way of doing it. Then I took it off in my own direction. Then, of course, Van Halen saw me do it and he took it off in his own direction. So I kind of equate it to playing with a pick [laughs]. Like every guitar player uses a pick, everyone taps. Eventually, everyone taps in their own way or will come up with their own licks and stuff.

"After I saw Randy Resnick doing it, I got on it. I started playing it all over and people who saw me doing it were freakin' out 'cause most guitarists didn't have any idea in hell what was going on. And then Van Halen saw it and, of course, he's a really good guitarist just normally, without the tapping. So he was smart enough to figure out what was going on and took it off into his own world. Lucky for him he was with a hit pop band. As opposed to myself, who was doing underground instrumentals/albums at the time. You know, very few people got to see me or Randy or anyone like that doing that stuff.

"Eddie is definitely the one who made it popular. And, you know, when you're on a video and millions of people are seeing you do it, they all think he was the inventor. Truth is, none of us invented it! It's probably gone on for a million years. It's just that I made it popular in the rock/blues thing and then he took over in the pop world. I know he really impacted the hard rock and metal world with it, too.

"So yeah, after Randy and I started doing it, that's when the world started doing it. Nobody in the pop/blues/rock world at that time was doing it. I believe I was the first guy out there playing a bunch of jobs [gigs] where people were seeing me do it all the time. After that it spread like wildfire. I remember the reaction. At the end of a show I'd have twenty guys standing there going, 'What were you doing with your right hand?!' [laughs]

"There were guys touching the frets way before any of us, but they just didn't get the flowing, saxophone kind of style. You know, the way that me and Van Halen and other guys do it. Back in the day, those guys would hit a note here or there. You know, they'd be working up a scale and then hitting a note. Far as I know, I started it up in the rock world, Van Halen took it to another level, and now Jennifer Batten and millions of other people are doing all kinds of incredible tapping. Stanley Jordan comes to mind as well. His style is a whole other trip. Stanley's not only tapping, he's using all his fingers. And I believe he's got his guitar tuned like a violin, sort of. He has a completely different way of tuning and tapping, to be able to form the chords and the licks he does. I do some of that stuff myself, but in a standard tuning.

"In 1973, I released Shangrenade [Janus Records]. This album was all tapping. Every song contained tapping. Back then, they thought I was just some outer space jazz player. Truth is, if you know what you're doing, you could realize I was truly tapping! From melodies to you name it, everything was built off the tapping technique. And while I did tap on every song, I did it in a melodic fashion, so you can't always tell. I actually began tapping about two or three years before I released Shangrenade, but that was the first time I ever put it on record. Man, sometimes I think I shoulda put a patent on it or something. I coulda been rich! [*laughs*]" ♪

So there you have it, straight from the source. However, when Harvey Mandel mentioned to me that he got the idea from Randy "Rare" Resnick, well, I totally didn't see that coming! Once again, I knew I had to go directly to the source. After some research, I was finally able to locate Randy, who now resides in France. Randy Rare is a fantastic guitar player who's been in the music biz since he hooked up with the Sugarcane Harris Band in 1969. The late Don "Sugarcane" Harris was an amazing violinist who recorded with everyone from John Mayall to Frank Zappa. In 1970, Sugarcane changed the name of his band to Pure Food and Drug Act. Soon after, Harvey Mandel came onboard, as well. When I asked Randy Rare how he discovered tapping, his answer was quite a revelation.

Randy "Rare" Resnick: "I'll tell you exactly how I discovered this technique. I was listening to African chants and the bottle/whistle stuff, the kind that Herbie Hancock later used on his funk version of 'Watermelon Man.' I also listened to Coltrane and his 'sheets of sound,' like in 'My Favorite Things.' All of this music required a legato (as opposed to staccato) attack, but the guitar is a percussion instrument and very staccato by nature. Somehow, while trying to imitate the African bottle stuff by tapping say, an open E on the high E string at the ninth fret and letting go [pull-off], I got an extra finger in the way. I hear three, not two notes. Then I tried to use all four fingers of the left hand and I found what sort of sounded like Coltrane's thing that I envied so much. I'm studying sax now, by the way.

"I was actually turned on to that African music and John Coltrane by Paul Lagos. I think we started playing together in 1969-1970 and for a while, Victor Conte and I crashed in Paul's basement in L.A. I would guess the tapping thing happened in '70 or '71. At the Whisky [A Go-Go] gig in 1974 with the Richard Greene Group, tapping was the whole basis of my style. The Sugarcane Harris album *Cup Full of Dreams* was recorded in 1973 and has examples of tapping solos. I think *Shangrenade* was recorded the same year. By the way, I also played some tapping stuff on John Mayall's *The Latest Edition* [1975, Polydor]. See 'Deep Down Feelings' and 'Troubled Times.' Red Holloway and I wrote the hook of 'Troubled Times' based on my tapped riff in it in F#."♪

Shangrenade (Janus Records) and *Cup Full of Dreams* (BASF) were both recorded in 1973. Fact is, each album contains some of the earliest examples of that super-fluid two-hand tapping style Edward Van Halen would eventually bring to the mainstream and popularize some five years later. Which makes you wonder, just how in the hell did Edward Van Halen discover tapping, right? Well, there are several different stories/theories as to how Edward discovered tapping. But in all honesty, there is simply no way to prove or disprove any of 'em!

Apparently, Harvey Mandel has heard that Edward saw him tapping at the Whisky A Go-Go in Los Angeles back in the early-to-mid-'70s. It really wouldn't surprise me, cuz Van Halen was a part of that very same L.A. club scene at that very same time. Other people believe Edward may have heard the *Nursery Cryme* album and picked it up from Steve Hackett. Ironically, one of the many band names the brothers used before settling on Van Halen was the name Genesis. A few believe he may even have picked it up from Randy Rare. However, once again, how the hell can we verify any of those theories?

Over the years, I believe the most consistent story I've heard is that Edward actually came up with the idea for tapping while attending a Led Zeppelin concert way back in 1971, when he was just sixteen years old. Apparently, during the classic unaccompanied solo break in the middle of "Heartbreaker," Edward saw Jimmy Page doing open-hand pull-offs, and a light bulb suddenly went off in his head. At that moment, he figured that instead of pulling off to an open string, he would instead anchor one of the fingers on his fretting hand, kinda like a capo, and then just pull-off all over the damn place.

All these stories and theories are cool and I truly enjoy hearing 'em all. But as I said, there is simply no way to confirm any of 'em. I'm sure people will continue to wonder and speculate over how he discovered tapping, forever. However, I am a betting man. And in all honesty, if I had to bet on on any of these theories, I'd place my chips on Harvey Mandel. Not only cuz of the fact that he played the same club scene at the same time VH did, but also due to the fact that Edward and Alex Van Halen always kept their ear to the rail, so to speak, when it came to progressive music. It wouldn't surprise me to find out that Edward and Alex got their hands on *Shangrenade* back when it came out and just picked it up from that album. Or perhaps they even caught one of Harvey's gigs at the Whisky as well.

But whatever the case may be, the simple fact remains that Edward Van Halen is the man who brought tapping to the forefront. That's indisputable. However, in the end, I believe Steve Hackett, Randy "Rare" Resnick, Harvey "The Snake" Mandel, and Edward Van Halen *all* deserve credit for being pioneers and innovators.

Throughout the years, some of the greatest guitar players of all time added two-hand tapping to their arsenal. Players such as Steve Vai, Randy Rhoads, Joe Satriani, Zakk Wylde, Dimebag Darrell, Kirk Hammett, Buckethead, Yngwie J. Malmsteen, John Petrucci, Allan Holdsworth, Shawn Lane, Michael Hedges, Jason Becker, and many more. And I guarantee you a whole lot of other players practiced and learned how to tap, but for whatever reason they just never actually used it on their recordings. For example, amazing players like Slash and Dave Navarro actually messed around with tapping, but in the end, they decided against using it in their respective styles because they simply felt it was Edward's thing. Then you have a dude like the great Stanley Jordan, who Harvey Mandel mentioned. Stanley Jordan can tap out *entire* songs on his guitar! You also have players who mastered the Chapman Stick, like its creator Emmett Chapman, and the amazing Trey Gunn. They innovated the tapping technique as well.

Plus, you have to remember that, over the years, there were guitar players out there tapping who simply hadn't been discovered yet. You know, they just hadn't been signed and hadn't laid there shit down on tape yet. No doubt there were guys sittin' at home, in their bedroom or on their couch, merrily tapping away in complete and totally anonymity. Eventually, some of these cats would get discovered while, of course, some wouldn't. But at the time, I'll bet you that many of 'em believe they were the only ones tapping! You know, that they were the only ones who'd stumbled upon that technique.

Finally, you can also find tapping in the arsenal of legendary bass players such as Jaco Pastorius, Billy Sheehan, Victor Wooten, and Michael Manring. Yes, you can tap on a bass guitar, electric guitar, acoustic guitar, and so forth. Tapping is used on several different string instruments, really. I'm sure somewhere in this world, a banjo player is tapping out the classic "Dueling Banjos" as we speak (just kidding).

Too Many Notes

"My dear Mozart, your work is ingenious. It's quality work. There are simply too many notes, that's all. Just cut a few and it will be perfect."
— **Emperor Joseph II**

"Which few did you have in mind, Majesty?"
— **Wolfgang Amadeus Mozart**

Anyone remember that scene from the classic 1984 film *Amadeus*? Well, that actually happened in real life. No bullshit. That scene was not made up for dramatic purpose or whatever. After performing one of his compositions, the Emperor actually told Wolfgang Amadeus Mozart he played "too many notes." It's a fact.

Sadly, the "too many notes theory" has been around since the days of Mozart. I guess we can thank that airheaded emperor for that little nugget right there. Man, that went down back during the 1780s. Since then, over the course of the last two hundred plus years, many people have adopted that line of thinking. Slowly but surely, it found its way out of the classical world and into all forms of music. And just as Mozart and many other great artists throughout history have had to contend with that crap, well, so to has Edward Van Halen.

However, before I get into disproving this whole mess, I must admit that this is a pretty controversial aspect of Edward's guitar playing. Hell, you could say it's a pretty controversial aspect concerning just about every virtuoso/shredder who's ever come down the pike, really.

Yeah, most musicians and hardcore guitar heads will know *precisely* what I'm talking about here. Frankly, I would be surprised if anyone else cared or even remotely comprehended what this is all about. For the average person, I imagine this discussion may be like walking into the middle of a conversation between two people you don't know...who speak Chinese.

Anyway, one of the biggest criticisms, if not *the* biggest criticism of Van Halen's entire career is that he is an overindulgent wanker who plays too many notes – *specifically* during his soloing. Basically, that criticism has been laid on just about every shredder who's ever come down the pike – *especially* guitar players from the '80s. In the eyes of many, including plenty of music critics, they are truly Satan's spawn. However, it's not just some critics or fans who seem to adhere to this line of thinking. In fact, some of the world's greatest musicians seem to believe in the "too many notes theory," too. For example, I was flipping through some of my old issues of *Guitar Player* magazine and came across these very interesting quotes from two of the world's greatest guitar players, Joe Walsh and Neil Young. I just happened upon their comments, purely by accident. You know, I'm a fan of both these amazing players, so anytime I come across one of their interviews, I'm always down to read through it and see what these two bad-asses have to say. Well, their comments totally caught me by surprise.

> **Joe Walsh:** "I've found that, in general less is more. For example, Albert King can blow Eddie Van Halen off the stage with his amp on standby, even though technically Eddie Van Halen is probably the most overwhelming guitar player alive. You know, Eddie Van Halen can pretty much play circles around *anybody* existing. But Albert King can blow him away with two notes. I have nothing but respect for Eddie; I can't even comprehend what he does. But why would anybody want to play like that?"

> **Neil Young:** "I mean, Satriani and Eddie Van Halen are genius guitar players. They're unbelievable musicians of the highest caliber. But I can't relate to it. One note is enough."

Here we have two of the greatest players of all time letting their feelings be known about this controversial subject. Simply put, you have to respect their opinion. Although I believe both of these gentlemen – *especially* Neil Young – are Jimi Hendrix fans, so it's pretty damn surprising they would say, "One note is enough." In a moment, you'll see why.

Anyhow, the question remains, are they right? Honestly, I don't know if there is a right or wrong on this matter. However, after doing some research, I know for a fact that most great musicians, regardless of how they deliver 'em, actually play a healthy amount of notes. I'd love to sit here and tell you I came to this conclusion after years of research and with the aid of a stellar team of scientists sporting fancy clipboards, white lab coats, and goggles. The reality is this all came about by accident and over the course of a single afternoon.

One day, I'm sitting around – as I'm sure many have – with a copy of my Jimi Hendrix *Electric Ladyland* guitar tab book. You know, jammin' on my guitar and trying to figure out some parts of "Voodoo Child" and other classics. Then, suddenly, it hit me. Precisely as I was looking over the soloing in "Voodoo Child," I realized, "Damn, there sure are a lot of notes flying around this page right here? Hmmm, I wonder if anyone's ever actually counted all these notes." The more I looked at it, the more tempted I got (don't ask me what I was on).

Man, I have no idea where I got the urge and I've never had it before or since. I mean, it's a pretty silly, simple idea, when you think about it? Then again, no sillier than the people who continually bash Edward and many other brilliant musicians for playing "too many notes." In all honesty, I have heard of musicians – *especially* shredders – being timed so as to determine how many notes they can play per second. However, up until now, I've never seen anyone actually count up all those freakin' notes. To me, *that's* the more interesting and important stat.

So I quickly went over to my Van Halen tab books and began to thumb through them as well. The more I looked through them the more shocked I became. Not only at how short Edward's solos actually were, but the fact that on paper, it did not appear Edward played more notes than Jimi. Could this be? I mean, isn't Edward Van Halen supposed to be the guy who unleashes millions of notes per minute? Hell, don't *all* shredders do that? Although my ears have always told me different, my brain seems to get in the way. Probably cuz over the years Edward and just about every single other shredder on the planet has been repeatedly castigated and branded by most music critics (and some music fans, in general) as being wankers who play millions of notes at a million miles per hour. I've been hearing this since I was a little kid in the '80s, so frankly I just came to accept it as truth. I *never* questioned it. Frankly, I don't know if anyone has? Well, that is, until now…

So I figured what the hell, it couldn't hurt anyone to just count up the notes from some solos and compare. I mean, the music is not gonna lie, right? The notes are just sitting there on the paper, so there is *no way* the actual music is gonna lie. Besides, how hard can it be to count a buncha black dots? A freakin' chimp could do it (which would probably explain why I was able to).

All kidding aside, it seemed pretty damn easy. Even if I don't get the count precisely 100 percent accurate, hey, 99 percent accurate will be more than enough to give everyone a clear picture of what the real deal is. Hell, if human beings can put a man on the moon, um, then I believe we are capable of counting a few notes, ok? And in all honesty, well, the work had already been done! Without even knowing it, all the fine people who create sheet music and guitar tablature have laid the answer down for us, on paper, in a clear and easy to read format. You know, everything had already been transcribed. Basically, all I had to do was sit there and count. So I gathered up all my different tab/music books and sat down for an afternoon of note counting. The idea of being able to prove all the critics and naysayers wrong – *especially* over the course of just one afternoon – was simply too damn tempting to pass up.

Well, lemme tell you, man, one afternoon was more than enough for me, thank you very much. Weeks later, I was still seeing notes in my sleep! The reason being I didn't count the tab numbers. No, I actually counted the damn notes. You know, the black dots. I wanted my count to be as accurate as possible, you know? In return, I have been seeing black dots flyin' past my head ever since and I believe someone should call a priest now, please. All kidding aside, I think you will find the results of my little study quite shocking.

The first solo I tackled was obviously "Eruption," of course. Surprisingly, it didn't take long at all. You'd think it would take someone forever to count all those notes, right? Well, the fact of the matter is that it took me just about three or four minutes. The total amount of notes played during "Eruption" is just over 850 notes. Not millions of notes and not thousands of notes. Man, not even 1,000 notes. Just over 850 notes. Guess what? I then counted Jimi Hendrix's "Voodoo Child" soloing and it contained over 1,000 notes. At this point, I began to scratch my head and wonder what the hell? According to many of the critics and plenty of so-called "music experts," Edward is an overindulgent wanker who plays millions of notes. Definitely more than everyone else, you know? However, "Eruption" is his longest solo ever and that doesn't even contain a thousand notes? How in the world could the soloing during a Hendrix song contain more notes than "Eruption?"

After all, "Eruption" is considered by many to be the holy grail of guitar solos. You know, the mother of all solos. And yet here's a Hendrix track whose soloing contains more notes? So, of course, I counted 'em again. After just a few minutes, I was done, and had the same results staring me right in the face. Jimi Hendrix's soloing during the classic "Voodoo Child" contains more notes than Edward Van Halen's "Eruption." Basically, I was stunned.

You have to understand that I thought it wouldn't even be close. Even though my ears have always told me that Edward plays no more than anyone else, well, again, being bombarded with the "too many notes" line of thinking for years and years makes you question and doubt what you are hearing.

So, of course, I was absolutely certain there was no way in hell the note count during Hendrix's soloing could ever come anywhere near that of a Van Halen's soloing. For years, I like many have been beaten down with the belief that most of my favorite guitar players were overindulgent wanks. As a child of the '80s, man, the '90s was no cakewalk, far as my musical taste went. The millennium hasn't been much easier, either.

It seems that in a post-Nirvana world anyone who could solo was a wanker. Never mind (no pun intended) the fact that many classic Nirvana songs contained solos. It doesn't matter. For whatever reason, it seems Edward Van Halen, Steve Vai, Randy Rhoads, and many other brilliant guitar players were branded and dismissed by many music critics and naysayers as being "overindulgent wankers." Basically, if you were a "shredder," you were a "wanker" and you played "too many notes." Meanwhile, a select few of my favorite players like Jimi Hendrix, Eric Clapton, and Jimmy Page never appeared to receive such criticism.

I began to wonder if this was a fluke. So I decided to look at other songs. Again, since "Eruption" is by far the longest Van Halen solo, one could easily assume it would contain more notes than any other solo during his entire career. However, I had to make sure. So I dug in and looked over all his other solos, *especially* all his most classic ones. It turns out "Eruption" does contain the highest amount of notes of any VH solo, by far. I then turned my attention to another one of my favorite Hendrix songs, "Come On Pt. 1." This song is a clinic and contains some of Jimi's most fiery soloing ever laid to tape. Guess what? The soloing in "Come On Pt. 1" contains more notes than "Eruption," too.

As the note count of Jimi's soloing during "Come On Pt. 1" passed 1,000 notes, I simply stopped counting. Basically, the point had already been made. Again, how is this possible? Isn't Jimi Hendrix supposed to be one of those "one-note" guitar players I've always heard about? You know, the kind of guy who supposedly can say more with just one note than most players could with 100 or 1,000 notes! I think we've all heard the "single note theory," right? No, *not* the "single bullet theory" that's about John F. Kennedy, ok? The "single note theory" is something I've heard time and again throughout the years. Basically, it represents the belief that a single note can say more than several or even many notes. For years, brilliant and legendary players like Hendrix, Gilmour, and Clapton have been passed off to us as "one note players." You know, as musicians who simply do not play a lot of notes, and certainly nowhere near the amount of notes people like Edward Van Halen play, right? Well, according to my research, that is absolutely, positively, and completely 100 percent *false.*

Yes, a great musician can be recognized by just one note. You know, it's like you turn on the radio, hear a song, and *immediately* know who that player or band is by just hearing one note or a couple of notes. That is absolutely correct. But the fact is, most of 'em play a healthy amount of notes, *especially* during their soloing.

Frankly, I have always offended by this "one note" line of thinking. The fact is all of these brilliant musicians work their asses off and play a healthy amount of notes. So what may appear to some people to be the ultimate compliment, personally, I found the "single note theory" to be a slap in the face to all musicians. Why on earth would you reduce brilliant musicians to just one single note? Man, are you kidding me? Whenever someone mentions the "one note" thing to me, I always remember a scene from the great 1988 film, *Bird*. For those who many not know, this was a film dedicated to the life and career of Charlie "Bird" Parker, one of the greatest freakin' sax players the world will ever know. A true jazz legend and pioneer. The film was directed by Clint Eastwood (a diehard jazz fanatic) and stars Forest Whitaker as Bird. Might I add, he did a great job, too.

Anyway, there's a scene in the movie where Bird goes into a theater and finds one of his old bandmates playing rock 'n' roll while wearin' a big, bright, glittery suit. Basically, the guy is a sellout. Well, after the show ends, Bird grabs the guy's sax, takes off into the alley behind the theater, and proceeds to belt out a few licks. The sellout and some of his buddies run after him and manage to wrestle the sax back. Apparently, they thought he was trying to steal it! Well, Bird simply replies, "I just wanted to see if it could play more than one note at a time," and then walked away. The sellout just stands there and says nothing. Not a single word. Ouch!

Man, if you woulda told the Bird "one note is enough," well, he probably woulda looked at you and laughed right in your face. Fact is, most great musicians work their asses off and play notes left and right. They are "busy players." Again, my ears had always told me so. When I listen to all these wonderful players, I hear *many* wonderful notes, not just one wonderful note. But when the masses beat you into submission with their so-called "truth," you just kind of accept it. Well, no longer is that the case.

Of course, the problem is not the musicians themselves. They just go out there and play. The musicians are not the problem here, *at all*. For all I care, they could play more notes cuz what they do is fantastic. No, the problem here are the so-called "music experts" and assorted music critics out there who have lied to us and who for ages, continually castigating many brilliant musicians as "overindulgent wankers." Some music fans in general are guilty of this as well. The fact that throughout history everyone from Wolfgang

Amadeus Mozart to Edward Van Halen has been unfairly castigated for playing "too many notes" is absolute, total, and complete bullshit. Man, I think it's just one of those sad cases were perception becomes reality. You know, when you hear something repeated *over and over and over,* eventually, you just accept it as truth.

Folks, if the great Jimi Hendrix had songs with guitar soloing containing more notes than Van Halen's "Eruption," um, then should he be castigated, too. If critics are to slam Edward for playing "too many notes," then shouldn't we say the same thing about Jimi? Well, of course not. Certainly not in my book, that's for sure. They are and forever will be a pair of total bad-asses. However, the fact remains that I discovered two classic Hendrix songs with soloing containing *more notes* than "Eruption." And, you know, a solo is a solo. Regardless whether you solo during an actual song or bust out some wild unaccompanied solo piece, a solo is a solo is a solo. So whether you play 1,000 notes during one solo in a song or play 1,000 notes over the course of two or three different solos in a song, in the end it still adds up to 1,000 notes, period. And if your soloing in a song contains more notes than "Eruption," well, that basically means you are playing more notes than the soloing of every Van Halen song ever written. No other Van Halen solo in history contains more notes than "Eruption." I mean, it's not even close. After "Eruption," the next highest note count I found was in "Spanish Fly," which contains just over 550 notes. Man, you don't even wanna look at some of Edward's most classic and legendary guitar solos. Fact is, the note count is quite paltry.

For example, the "Jump" guitar solo contains just over 110 notes. Folks, that's about the same amount of notes found in the solo of Nirvana's "Teen Spirit," ok? The main solo in "Mean Street" contains just 130 notes, while the outro contains 234 notes. The "Hot for Teacher" solo contains just over 250 notes. Wow, big deal. Man, the solo in Chuck Berry's classic "Johnny Be Good" has more notes than the "Hot for Teacher" solo! "Ain't Talkin' 'bout Love" has two solos, each one containing just over ninety notes. The "Panama" solo also contains just over ninety notes, too. The "Atomic Punk" solo contains just over 190 notes. "Runnin' with the Devil" has two solos, each one containing a staggering fifty-seven notes! The main solo in "Light Up the Sky" contains just over 125 notes, while the outro contains 76 notes. The "Unchained" solo contains just over sixty notes. The "Beautiful Girls" solo contains about sixty notes, too. The "On Fire" solo contains about 100 notes. The "Ice Cream Man" solo contains about 285 notes.

Not millions of notes, not thousands of notes, and not even a thousand notes. Even "Eruption," which is the exception, contains fewer notes than many of the classic solos by other guitar players and assorted musicians.

Man, you can even go beyond "Eruption." Kick back and compare Edward's "Jump" solo to Jimi's "Voodoo Child" solo. When you put most of Edward's classic solos up against "Voodoo Child" or "Come On Pt. 1," well, the difference in note count is absurd. Same thing goes for another Jimi classic, "All Along the Watchtower." Jimi plays several amazing solos during this song that in the end gives us a total of over 700 notes.

In fact, let's look at each of their classic debut albums. I mean, without a doubt, Jimi Hendrix and Edward Van Halen are the only two rock guitarists in history to reinvent the instrument. Therefore, I think it's a great comparison.

For starters, *Are You Experienced?* contains twelve solos and seven outros. Basically, nineteen solo sections. During these nineteen solo sections, Jimi plays a combined total of about 3,200 notes. When you break that down, man, it simply means he's averaging about 168 notes per solo section. Meanwhile, *Van Halen* contains fourteen solos and two outros. Basically, sixteen solo sections. During these sixteen solo sections, Edward plays a combined total of about 2,700 notes. When you break that down, it simply means he's averaging about 168 notes per solo section.

Shhh…do you hear that? Don't hear anything, do you? Wanna know why? Cuz everyone who's ever accused Edward (and every other shredder) of playing far too many notes has now, as of this very moment, shut their pie hole. In a nutshell, and as shocking as this may be to some people, Jimi Hendrix and Edward Van Halen basically played the same amount of notes during their solos on each of their respective debut albums. I mean, *precisely* the same.

Which, you know, makes you wonder what some people are hearing when they listen to Edward's solos. Rather, I should say, what some people *think* they are hearing. It's so funny how some people *truly swear* that Edward plays way more notes than everyone else. I dunno, perhaps they have some kinda sonic schizophrenia or something? Or perhaps they have never even heard a Van Halen album to begin with? Frankly, at this point, I don't even care to know.

However, if you really wanna have some fun, whip out the guitar tab/music for Jimi's masterpiece, "Machine Gun" (*Band of Gypsys,* 1970). The amount of notes flying around during this song's three solos and outro is insane! Put it to you this way: the total amount of notes Hendrix unleashes during his brilliant soloing on "Machine Gun" is about as many notes as you'll find during all the solos on an entire Van Halen album, *combined.* Any questions?

I could go on and on showing you plenty of classic songs with classic solos that contain more notes than most of Van Halen's classic guitar solos. For example, Eric Clapton's killer soloing on the classic "Crossroads" contains just over 675 notes. Which, by the way, is about the same amount of notes Randy Rhoads played during his amazing soloing on "Mr. Crowley." And with the exception of "Eruption," Clapton's "Crossroads" soloing contains more notes than the soloing on every other Van Halen song in history. Pretty sick, huh? Eric Clapton playing the same amount of notes as a shredder? You better believe it. In fact, you could look at "Crossroads" as Eric Clapton's own kind of shredding, really. 'Ole Slowhand was absolutely tearin' it up on that classic. He wasn't slow on this one, *at all*. Dude was rippin'!

Oh, and there are plenty more examples, too.

Jimmy Page's killer soloing on "Heartbreaker" contains over 520 notes. Stevie Ray Vaughan's beautiful soloing on "Riviera Paradise" contains over 1,000 notes, while the soloing on another SRV classic, "Pride and Joy," contains over 700 notes. Carlos Santana's sweet soloing on "Europa" contains over 1,000 notes, while his soloing on another classic, "Samba Pa Ti'," contains over 600 notes. Jaco Pastorius's brilliant soloing on "Donna Lee" contains over 450 notes. David Gilmour's tasty soloing on "Comfortably Numb" contains over 530 notes. B.B. King's smoky soloing on his classic "The Thrill Is Gone" contains over 300 notes. Dickey Betts's sweet soloing on "Jessica" contains over 750 notes. Slash and the boys of Guns N' Roses tear it up during their wicked soloing on the classic "Paradise City," clocking in at over 1,000 notes.

Man, Ed King's brilliant soloing on the classic Lynyrd Skynyrd anthem "Freebird" contains thousands of notes! Seriously, after I got past 2,000 notes, I needed an I.V. of Guinness. Like with Hendrix's "Machine Gun," the amount of notes played during the brilliant "Freebird" solo is about the same amount of notes you'll find during all the solos on a Van Halen album, *combined*. In fact, we can even go back to the *really* old school and check out the great Django Reinhardt! Django's soloing on his classic "Nuages" contains just over 270 notes. His soloing on another classic, "Limehouse Blues" contains over 750 notes. Hell, the great Albert King's smokey, insane string-bending orgy of a solo on his classic "The Sky Is Crying" contains hundreds of notes. Hmmm, I wonder...out of all those notes, which are the two notes that blow Edward Van Halen away? Quick, someone get Joe Walsh on the horn! Hey, in the famous words of Triumph the Insult Comic Dog, "I keed! I keed!" All keed-ing aside, the point I'm tryin' to make is that if two notes were enough, why did he play hundreds?

We can even go outside the world of guitar, too. For example, the genius soloing during John Coltrane's masterpiece "Giant Steps" contains just over 1,400 notes (first solo has 1,200 notes, second solo has 206 notes). That's way more than "Eruption" or any other VH solo, ever. In fact it's way more than the amount of notes found during the solos of most guitar shredders, period. I went and looked up the note count for one most of my favorite shred guitar pieces ever, the amazing "For the Love of God" by Steve Vai. Guess what? The solo in "For the Love of God" contains just about 800 notes. Again, that's much less than you'll find on "Giant Steps."

Look up the music of Charlie Parker, Benny Goodman, Art Tatum, Dizzy Gillespie, and Vladimir Horowitz. Lots of notes flying around, man. And don't even get me started on classical music! Those legendary composers like Beethoven and Mozart certainly played their fare share of notes, to put it mildly. You know, to this day, I've *never* heard a "one-note symphony," ok?

If you wanna have even more fun, please get your hands on the sheet music for anything by legendary Russian composer/pianist, Sergei Rachmaninoff. Talk about a wonderful array of notes played at light speed, man, is it any wonder the dude from the movie *Shine* ended up a few fries short of a Happy Meal? Continue the fun and go look up the music for Nicolò Paganini's 24 Caprices! Man, I've actually seen all the sheet music for that. My local music store has a book of the 24 Caprices and there are tons of beautiful notes exploding all over the place. Much more than any guitar shredder will probably ever play. Man, Nicolò was a monster. I mean, the 5th Caprice alone is insane!

Basically, the point I'm trying to make is this: *No one* makes a living playing one note. Between rhythm playing *and* lead playing, there is a healthy amount of notes being fired off. Sure, you might hit that one single note during a solo that is just *perfect*.

For example, Jimi Hendrix hits one of the sickest, deepest notes I've ever heard in my entire life during his masterpiece, "Machine Gun." This note comes right after the verse at the four-minute mark of the track. Man, Hendrix rings this one note for about twelve seconds and it just absolutely cuts right through you. In those twelve seconds, you see your life flash before your eyes. I mean, this is a note of freakin' biblical proportions, ok? However, that single, glorious, gut-wrenching note is literally swamped by about a couple *thousand* more notes! And while the soloing in "Machine Gun" contains all those notes, to be honest, I don't think a single note is wasted. Sure, that one note blows my mind, but all the other ones are important, too.

The fact that all those amazing players I just mentioned play as many notes and, in some cases, even *more notes* than Edward Van Halen proves they are all the same. There really is *no difference* between eras, genres, instruments, and so forth. For example, one musician might deliver a solo containing 300 notes at a rapid pace. Another musician might deliver a solo containing 300 notes at a slow pace. Meanwhile, another musician might deliver a solo containing 300 notes where they change pace, going from slow to fast to slow again, or vice versa. And another musician might deliver two solos during a song, each containing 150 notes. One musician might deliver those 300 notes in a flurry of notes, while another might deliver those 300 notes one at a time.

What does this all mean? It means that no matter how you dress it up, in the end, 300 notes is 300 notes! Regardless whether you play them fast, slow, fast *and* slow, in a flurry, one at a time, upside down, or whatever, you will still end up with 300 notes, period.

Of course, in the end, all of this is *totally and completely meaningless* as far as the actual *music* is concerned. Hell, even Edward Van Halen himself has always stated that his music is all about sounds, *not* notes. I own tons of Edward Van Halen's interviews, and I honestly cannot recall a single freakin' time when Edward sat there and talked about notes or scales or anything like that. Not that I'm knockin' those things, ok? I'm just pointing out that the man has never really spoken about his playing or his music in terms of notes, at all. So I want to make very clear that my note count was done strictly to show that *no one* makes a living playing one note and that Edward Van Halen plays the same amount of notes as any other great musicians. In fact, Edward actually plays a lesser amount of notes than many of the other greats.

Basically, I wanted to crush the "too many notes theory" into oblivion. And since Edward Van Halen seems to be one of the big, if not *the* biggest target of those who believe in this theory, I knew his soloing would prove, beyond a shadow of a doubt, that he is not an overindulgent wanker. Never has been, never will be. In the process, since he is considered by many to be the "head shred," I knew this would also help clear the name of many other brilliant musicians, especially guitar players, too.

Again, it's not in the note count, cuz in the end, that's absolutely meaningless. All this info is good for is for simply disproving a stupid theory, that's all. I mean, no one counts notes while listening to a solo, ok? Lord, I hope not. If you did, you'd probably be up for a lengthy stay in the rubber room over at Shady Pines Mental Hospital. Either that or you'd end up becoming the odds-on favorite to star as Raymond in *Rain Man II.* "Yeah...Yngwie J. Malmsteen's soloing during 'Black Star' contains 1,642 notes...*definitely* 1,642 notes...Kmart sucks...yeah." All kidding aside, the note count is irrelevant. Fact is it's all in the *delivery,* baby. It's all about every single musician's respective style and touch. In the end, it's not about the three hundred notes, or fifty notes, or one note, or two thousand notes, or whatever…it's all about *what you do* with 'em. Better yet, it's *what you say* with 'em. Besides, if you don't have a great song, who really cares?

Fact is most great musicians have fertile musical minds. In other words, they have tons of great ideas and music coursing through them. This causes 'em to play a healthy amount of notes. There's a great story I've heard about Miles Davis and John Coltrane that confirms this. Just before Miles Davis and John Coltrane finally split, something went down between these two giants. It's a story that's been passed down by musicians for years. Apparently, one day while they were jamming, John went off on one of his long solo trips. You know, this is a man who could sometimes solo for half an hour or more, during which he would certainly unleash a healthy amount of notes. Mind you, we are not just talkin' fingers here, ok? On saxophone, you are talkin' mouth, lungs, *and* fingers! Yeah, no doubt that Coltrane's blazing note-rich "sheets of sound" style of playing he pioneered can basically be considered shredding on the sax, baby.

So John went off soloing into the stratosphere and Miles let him go. When John came back down and finished, Miles went over to him and just started chewing him out. Miles was known to have a dry sense of humor, and he chastised John for playing too long a solo.

Poor Coltrane took Miles's verbal assault on the chin and replied apologetically, "I just get carried away. I get these ideas which just keep coming and coming and sometimes I just can't stop…"

Miles simply replied, "Try taking the motherfucker out of yo' mouth."

Throughout history the "too many notes theory" has been leveled on many of the world's greatest musicians. From Mozart and Coltrane to Van Halen and Vai, that label has been branded on many of these brilliant players at one time or another. Well, no longer will that be the case. You could say that as of 2005, the "too many notes theory" is now officially dead.

Vaya con diablos, beatch…

The Frankenstrat

"I really dug that Eddie Van Halen played the same guitar on stage that he used to record his albums."

— John Mayer

Of all the guitars Edward Van Halen has built, owned, and played throughout his entire life, I believe the single most famous one is known as the "Frankenstrat." Or as Edward affectionately calls her, "Franky." The name is just a term (I don't know precisely who came up with it) that basically means a Strat-style guitar that's been "Frankensteined" together. In other words, it's a Fender Strat-style guitar Edward cobbled together using parts from different guitars. Hence the term "Frankenstrat." Without a doubt, the "Frankenstrat" is one of the most legendary and recognizable instruments in the history of music.

This is the first guitar Edward ever built that had his famous trademark "red, white, and black" striped paint job, but the fact is, it began its life strictly striped black and white. For starters, I'll give you a quick history of Edward's guitars throughout the years, and then we'll jump into the "Frankenstrat." This will give you a solid idea of how *and* why the "Franky" came to be.

Edward began messing around with his brother's acoustic guitar back in 1966. By early 1967, he got his first electric, a $70 Teisco Del Ray four-pickup guitar from Sears in Pasadena. So it's not like he just immediately threw on some goggles, picked up a chainsaw, and started building guitars. What happened is that throughout his teens, he began to experiment with his guitars. In other words, he'd dick around with 'em, big time. He'd tear 'em apart, study 'em, and then piece 'em back together. In the process, he managed to mess up a lot of nice guitars! It wasn't like Edward came out the gate as the Bob Vila of guitars or something, ok? No, creation and innovation can be an ugly process. But hey, that's they only way to do it and that's the only way to learn. So as a teen, he began to dick around with all his guitars. No one ever taught him how to do work on guitars. Everything he learned came through trial and error.

During these early years Edward was actually quite fond of Gibson/Les Paul guitars. It makes sense to me cuz quite a few of his heroes played a Gibson. Eric Clapton and Alvin Lee were both owned and played a Gibson ES-335. No surprise, Edward would get one, too. Jimmy Page obviously was a major Gibson Les Paul user. For my money, that's where Edward really got the inspiration for playing a Les Paul. Even Jimi Hendrix, known primarily for his Fender Stratocasters, owned and played a Gibson, too. Many great players did.

So I believe in 1968, Edward's old man laid down some bread and purchased him a 1968 Gibson Les Paul. Edward had previously owned a Gibson twelve-string acoustic, but it eventually broke due to the fact that he didn't have a case for it. By the early '70s, he would add a Gibson Flying V to his arsenal as well. This was at the time he was in high school, and so this is the time he really began to dick with his guitars. I've heard he actually destroyed a pretty sweet Gibson ES-335 around this time. That guitar may have been the "guinea pig" guitar for him. Apparently, he really tore it apart, or sacrificed it, depending how you look at it, to learn how to repair other guitars. Soon after he sacrificed his Gibson ES-335, he got a 1955 Gibson Les Paul Jr. By the mid 1970s, Ibanez guitars caught Edward's eye and ear. He went out and purchased an Ibanez Destroyer. Man, this is a great guitar. The mid-1970s Destroyer was made out of Korina wood, which is an exotic tone-wood that absolutely sings. The neck was made of rosewood, and the guitar came fitted with two Gibson PAF humbuckers. I believe this is the guitar that truly represented the sound Edward was looking for. He really dug the tone of the guitar and the sound of the PAF humbuckers. This Ibanez Destroyer was a tone machine.

I also believe this might be the very first guitar he ever striped. Edward painted silver and red stripes on this guitar. His striped paint jobs would also become a trademark. Unfortunately, he ended up messing with the guitar too much and screwed it up. In an attempt to make it look even wilder, he hacked a big chunk of the body out of the guitar. The guitar looked wild, but removing that chunk ended up screwing up the guitar's sound/tone, forever. Edward would still use it over the years during shows and on records. Hell, half of that first Van Halen album was done with this guitar. But I don't believe it ever sounded the same again.

After he hacked it up, the guitar earned the nickname "Shark." Now, this could be for a couple of reasons. One, cuz it looked like a freakin' shark made off with a piece of the body! Seriously, the reason being that it gave the body a certain "shark fin" quality to it. Just imagine a standard Flying V, but with the lower side of the V shorter than the higher side. Or if you ever see the Charvel Jackson Randy Rhoads signature model, that seems to be an evolution of Edward's infamous "Shark" guitar. You know, the very cool and sleek "shark fin" look. If you wanna see the "Shark" guitar, check out the cover of Van Halen's *Women and Children First* album.

It was also around the mid-1970s that Edward got interested in Fender guitars. Apparently, some believe Edward made the switch from Gibson to Strat-style guitars after seeing the Jimi Hendrix movie *Jimmy Plays Berkeley* with his friend—and guitar tech at that time—Tom Broderick. Perhaps Edward liked the guitar and the fact that it had a whammy-bar. So Edward went out and got himself a 1961 Fender Stratocaster. I believe he may have also purchased a 1959 Stratocaster as well. While Edward seemed to really dig the feel of these guitars, the rest of the band didn't much care for their sound. The band concluded that the sound of the Fenders was too thin compared to the sound of the Gibsons, which was mainly due to the single-coil pickups found in most Strats. So how do you solve this problem? Well, Edward came up with a very clever idea. He took the pickup from the Gibson and slapped it into the Fender Stratocaster.

You see, Edward had always loved the *sound* of a Gibson. However, he also came to really love the *feel* of the Fender Stratocaster. Along with the fact that a Fender Stratocaster had a whammy-bar, while a Gibson did not. So to get the best of both worlds, he simply yanked the Gibson PAF humbucker out of one of his Gibsons and stuck it in his Fender Stratocaster. Voila! Gibson sound out of a strat guitar equipped with a whammy-bar, baby. Mind you, the Fender Stratocaster is only equipped for three single-coil pickups, *not* for any type of humbucker pickup. To solve this problem, Edward would simply break out his trusty chisel and rout out some more room at the bridge-position to be able to shove that humbucker in there.

Another small problem was that the poles of the Gibson PAF humbucker pickup didn't align properly with the strings on the Fender guitar. You know, the poles on the Gibson pickup were obviously made for Gibson string positions, which happen to be closer together than on a Fender. No problem, Edward routed a little more space and just slanted the pickup a bit until the poles were aligned with the strings! And so that is how the humbucker pickup would end up, screwed into his guitar at a slight angle. If you look close at pictures of the "Frankenstrat," you can clearly see the pickup appears to be at an angle.

Another cool idea Edward used for his pickups is known as "potting." Basically, you take the pickup and drop it into a pot of hot wax! Hence the term "potting." The reason people pot a pickup is simple really. When you drop it into the pot, the hot wax will seep into the pickup. After you take it out and the wax hardens, this really helps to keep the winding inside the pickup from moving around. In turn, this helps significantly cut down on feedback. You just take some good 'ole fashioned surf wax (SEX WAX) and heat it up. When it's all melted and hot, pour it into a pot (like an empty coffee can) and then place the pickup inside. Kids, *do not* try this at home! The reason why is because you can easily ruin a pickup this way. Believe me, Edward Van Halen ruined many pickups before getting it right. Besides, a lot of pickups nowadays already come potted. Whenever you buy a pickup, check the details, cuz it will usually tell you if they have already been potted or not.

Ok, so Edward has potted his Gibson PAF humbucker pickup, routed out his guitar, and placed it in the bridge-position at a slight angle. Now here comes the funny part. Once Edward had fitted the pickup into the bridge-position on his Fender, um, he didn't know how the hell to rewire the guitar for three pickups. Remember, the Fender Stratocaster comes equipped with three single-coil pickups. Edward removed the one single-coil at the bridge-position in order to rout it more and shove that Gibson PAF humbucker in there. Once it was in, he was still stuck with the other two single-coil pickups at the middle and neck-position. How do you solve this little problem? Well, according to Edward, you say "screw it" and simply wire the damn guitar for just one pickup! That's all he did. He figured he didn't even need the middle and neck-position pickups, so therefore he only wired the guitar so the one Gibson PAF humbucker pickup in the bridge-position would operate. He also didn't know how to rewire the "TONE" knob and "VOLUME" knob on his guitar, either. Figuring that he never uses the damn "TONE" knob anyway, once again he said "screw it" and simply wired the volume knob to operate. The funny thing is he actually used the knob that read "TONE" as his volume knob! Now whether this was done as a joke or as by accident, I honestly have no idea.

We now have a Strat-style guitar with one humbucker pickup in the bridge-position and one knob. Folks, without even realizing it, Edward Van Halen had stumbled upon a guitar design that would eventually become the blueprint for how many companies built their guitars for years to come. His "one-pickup, one-knob, Strat-style guitar" would eventually become one of the most recognizable and popular guitar designs on the planet. However, for now he was just a teenager dickin' around in his parents' garage. Finally, in 1975, just two years after graduating high school, Edward Van Halen would apply his "one-pickup, one-knob, Strat-style guitar" technique into building what would become one of the most famous guitars the world has ever known: the "Frankenstrat." You see, around this time, Edward became interested in Charvel guitars.

The Charvel Guitar Company was founded and operated by the very cool Wayne Charvel, out in California. Basically, Wayne was making great "hot-rodded" versions of a Fender Stratocaster guitar. Wayne's guitars were and still are sweet guitars. Well, it was really Wayne and his pal Lynn Ellsworth. These two guys made a helluva team and put together many great guitars, including the body and neck for Edward's "Frankenstrat."

During the mid-'70s Edward began to pop into the Charvel Factory looking for bodies, necks, and so forth. One day, in 1975, Edward purchased the body and neck that would become the "Frankenstrat" from Wayne Charvel himself. Apparently, the body was down under some other bodies in a box of castoffs! It was a Boogie Ash unfinished Strat-style body that Edward paid a mere $50 for. The body had been routed only for the middle and neck position pickups. There was no hole for the bridge position pickup. Well, at this point, that's really not a problem. Edward applied the technique he'd used on his Fender Stratocasters. You know, he broke out his chisel and routed the bridge-position to accommodate a Gibson PAF humbucker. I believe Edward took this particular Gibson PAF humbucker pickup from his 1961 Gibson ES-335 guitar.

I know he eventually took a real liking to the overwound humbucking pickups that Seymour Duncan was hookin' him up with. I also believe Edward practiced overwinding the pickups himself, too. Those overwound pickups definitely brought more bite to the table, baby. I think that was an important element, as far as his overall sound went.

Like the body of the guitar, the neck was also a cast-off. The maple neck was built by Lynn Ellsworth and cost Edward just $80. I believe Edward got it the same day he picked up the body. Right after he got it, Edward attempted to fret the neck himself. He acquired some Gibson jumbo fret wire from Lynn and managed to bond the frets onto the neck with super glue. For the tuners, Edward used Schaller tuners on his "Franky." Another cool touch was widening the nut grooves. This was done so the strings could slide around a bit and not grab. In fact, Edward widened the grooves and then frequently oiled the nut with "3-in-1 Oil" to help prevent the strings from grabbing, as well. The volume pot was taken from an old Les Paul Junior. The brass nut and tailpiece were taken from a 1961 Fender Stratocaster. The pickguard was just a regular 'ole pickguard, but it was actually cut by Edward himself.

The tremolo on the "Frankenstrat" was taken from either a 1962 or 1963 Fender Stratocaster. It was your basic standard bridge. This standard Fender tremolo would remain on this guitar through the recording of the first two Van Halen albums. Many people seem to believe that he was using a Floyd

Rose Tremolo on those albums, but the fact is, he wasn't. Edward would not make a recording using a guitar equipped with a Floyd Rose until the third Van Halen album in 1980! So how in the hell was he able to stay in tune while doing all those crazy bar-dives and shit on those first two Van Halen albums and tours? Again, by widening the nut grooves and oiling them, he was able to stay in tune. Honestly, a whole lot of that has to do with his hands, as well. You know, his *touch*. When you go off on the whammy-bar, you can't just pull it down and then let it go so it just snaps back. No, you have to work it back into place *after* the dive. The fact that Edward Van Halen was able to molest his whammy-bar and stay in tune is a testament to him being a master of his instrument, really.

Anyhow, here's the final tally: $50 Boogie Body (Ash), $80 neck (Maple, by Boogie), Gibson Jumbo Frets, Schaller Tuners, 1 Gibson PAF humbucker pickup (potted) in the bridge-position, 1 standard Fender tremolo, 1 brass nut, 1 tailpiece, 1 pickguard, 1 knob. Reinventing the electric guitar as we know it? PRICELESS…

All kidding aside, the hardware was now in place. So what's left? Why, a cool paint job, of course! Edward's trademark striped design was something that surely came about from experimentation, as was usually the case with just about everything he did. Originally, the "Frankenstrat" was painted all black. Edward then taped stripes all over the body and repainted it white. The technique of taping stripes is used on everything from motorcycles to skateboards. After the tape was removed, he now had black stripes. The paint Edward used was not exactly some fancy-ass super-expensive paint. No, he actually used Schwinn bicycle paint! In fact, he applied several coats of the Schwinn bicycle acrylic lacquer. Apparently, Edward then hung the guitar in his parents' garage so it would dry. Now eventually this guitar would end up being striped black, white, *and* red in 1979. Honestly, the "red, white, and black" striped design would probably become the most recognized design in history, far as guitar designs went. However, the "Frankenstrat" began its life strictly striped black and white. There are plenty of pictures of it with the original striped design from the club days, as well as from the first couple of Van Halen tours. You can also see "Franky" on the cover of Van Halen's first album, too.

The end result was unlike anything anyone had ever seen. After it was completed, Edward took it to the basement of David Lee Roth's parents' home and put the guitar through its paces during band practice. For starters, the band freaked over how wild it looked. No one had ever seen anything like it, really. More important, however, is how good the damn thing sounded and managed to stay in tune. The rest of the band just couldn't believe he was able to go ballistic on his guitar, whammy-bar dives and all, and manage to somehow stay in tune!

So there you have it, the story of the "Frankenstrat." One of the most recognizable and legendary instruments *ever*. Yes, this is the guitar Edward used to record "Eruption," "I'm the One," "Ice Cream Man," "Ain't Talkin' 'bout Love," and many other Classic Van Halen songs. Over the years, Edward's continued to own, play, and record with many different guitars, from Gibson and Steinberger to Fender and Ripley. He's also developed several signature model guitars throughout the years as well. While he continued to work with Charvel all the way through the first two Van Halen albums, during this time, Edward never actually had a signature Charvel model, per se. Throughout his career, he's had four different signature models.

The first came when Edward hooked up with Kramer Guitars in the very early '80s. I believe it was at Kramer that he finally had his first-ever signature model guitar. Well, kinda sorta, really. In all honesty, it wasn't a signature model, per se. The guitar Edward put together with the good folks at Kramer was simply known as the "Kramer Barretta."

Sadly, by the end of the '80s, Kramer Guitars folded. But it wouldn't be long before Edward found another home. In 1990, he began working with Ernie Ball Music Man, and soon after there would be a signature "Ernie Ball EVH Music Man" guitar. The relationship with Ernie Ball lasted about five years, at which point Edward moved on to Peavey. With Peavey, Edward would release his next signature model, the "Wolfgang" guitar, named after his son, Wolfgang Van Halen.

After staying with Peavey until 2004, Edward is now currently working with Charvel, and has released his "EVH Art Series" guitar, which is based on his classic Charvel designs from early in his career back in the late '70s. Meanwhile, his Peavey Wolfgang will now be known as the HP Special, the "HP" standing for Peavey founder, Hartley Peavey. By the way, the 5150 amp is now called the "6505." You know, to celebrate Peavey's fortieth anniversary of being in the biz, 1965-2005.

In the end, all of these respective instruments are very cool in their own right, no doubt about it. However, I truly believe when most people think of Edward's guitars, well, the one that immediately comes to mind is probably his 'ole "Frankenstrat."

The Floyd Rose Tremolo

"Floyd Rose tremolos are pretty incredible. You can get all the sounds that are on the Jimi Hendrix and Van Halen albums without going out of tune."

— Kirk Hammett

For starters, Floyd Rose is actually a dude. I think many people aren't even aware Floyd Rose is actually the name of the man who created this legendary device. He is obviously a guitar player as well. The tremolo system that bears his name is probably one of the most important pieces of equipment to ever come down the pike. I believe he'd been working on this cool device during the mid-'70s, when finally by the late '70s, he had about three prototypes ready to go. In 1979, one of the first three ended up in the hands of Edward Van Halen. The rest, as they say, is history. However, there are people who have no idea, so here's the deal.

Throughout history, one of the biggest problems guitarists have faced is keeping their damn instrument in tune, especially if you have one that comes equipped with any kind of a whammy-bar. Every single guitar player out there knows precisely what I am talking about. You go a bit whammy happy and your guitar seems to go out of tune pretty damn quick. Mr. Floyd Rose came up with a solution. He developed a "floating tremolo unit." Along with the floating tremolo came the fact that you had to clamp the guitar strings down at the nut as well. In order to do this, you simply had to change the nut on your guitar for the nut that came with the Floyd Rose. These two parts work together to accomplish stable and secure tuning. Once the strings were stretched out and properly clamped down at the nut, the Floyd Rose allowed you to whammy to your heart's content. Seriously, you could dive-bomb all day long and your guitar would not go out of tune.

So in 1979, Floyd showed his new tremolo system to Lynn Ellsworth, who was pals/partners with Wayne Charvel of Charvel Guitars, of course. Lynn saw the device and his only advice to Floyd was, "Show it to Eddie." Well, Floyd did just that. They got a hold of Edward Van Halen and presented him with one of the first three prototypes of the Floyd Rose. I believe this was during the fall of 1979, to be exact. Edward routed out one of his guitars for the device and actually road tested it by playing some shows during Van Halen's 1979 tour with it. Did the device work? Absolutely. Once the strings were stretched and clamped down, shit, whammy away all day. However, as is the case with any device – *especially* a prototype – there are always issues. For starters, if you broke a string, you had to unclamp everything at the nut before you could change it. But I believe the main issue seemed to be that what you got in terms of stable tuning, you lost a bit in terms of *tone*. Apparently, Edward found that the Floyd Rose had a very bright sound to it, which in turn made your overall sound brighter, too.

Being the master tonesmith that he is, Edward was not about ready to sacrifice even an ounce of his nice warm tone and overall sound for tuning stability, no matter how much you could whammy away. Man, he'd always managed to do a damn good job of staying in tune with his standard Fender tremolo by having amazing touch, along with widening the groove on the nut and dabbing a little "3-in-1 Oil" on there. I believe he would also put the strings through the hole in the tuner and wind it up instead of down. This way there would be no angle from nut to tuning peg. Very clever, dude.

So in order to make up for the Floyd Rose's bright sound, Edward began doing some heavy EQ'ing on his own sound. On top of that, he began using much thicker guitar bodies made out of wood like mahogany in an attempt to balance things out and get a nice warm tone out of his Floyd Rose-equipped axe. Another thing he did was to mount the Floyd Rose directly onto the body of his guitar. Well, what I mean is the device would no longer be floating. See, when it "floats," it means you can pull it up *and* down. Edward only really pulled it down, so in that case, why even bother to leave it floating? The first idea he came up with was to actually shove a quarter under the trem! This basically leveled out the device and therefore it would not be floating.

Over the years, he would continue to make simple adjustments (removing a couple of springs and so forth), and eventually the Floyd Rose was resting back at a slight angle, flush onto the body of the guitar. Apparently, Edward seems to believe *everything* should be mounted directly onto the body of a guitar, since everything is connected. In his opinion, this helps you achieve greater *tone*. Now this cat is the E.F. Hutton of tone, y'all, so pay attention. Anyway, after road testing it and weighing all the pros and cons, Edward decided the system was definitely a keeper. A little brightness can be corrected, and the fact that you could lock those strings down and stay in tune was truly groundbreaking. It was also a definite plus during live performances. Most people don't realize that playing a concert, indoors and especially outdoors, the elements alone can actually cause a guitar to go out of tune!

To have a unit that allowed you to whammy all day long and not go out of tune was simply too good to pass up. With Edward's aggressive guitar style, the Floyd Rose would definitely more than earn its keep. In the end, he would make the few adjustments he needed to make in order to maintain his amazing overall sound/tone, cuz the Floyd Rose was simply too damn good to pass up.

Edward Van Halen and Floyd Rose struck up a nice relationship and continued to work together into the '80s. I believe Edward may even have helped improve and fully realize the device over these years as well. By the early '80s, the system had fine tuners. You see, once your strings were clamped down at the nut, this renders the tuning heads of your guitar totally and completely useless. I know, you are probably sitting there going, "Hey, but if this thing keeps the guitar perfectly in tune, what does it matter?"

Well, the fact is that no instrument is probably *ever* tuned perfectly. In any event or emergency, so to speak, you would still need to do a bit of tuning, probably some really *fine tuning* just to get it as close as possible. And so that is precisely what the Floyd Rose was still missing: fine tuners. The prototype had no fine tuners. Everything else was in place and the system was operational, but there was no way to fine tune strings once they were clamped down. By the early '80s, this problem had been resolved. I seem to recall an interview Edward did back in the day where he mentioned the fine tuners and his role with them. However, I'm sorry to say, I was simply not able to confirm 100 percent whether Edward developed 'em or not. My bad.

The collaboration between Edward Van Halen and Floyd Rose was a devastating one-two combination. Here you had Floyd Rose, a man who invented a system to help solve arguably the number one problem guitarists everywhere faced. Here you had Edward Van Halen, the new kid on the block, who has rocketed to the top of the pyramid and is being called "the most innovative and important player since Jimi Hendrix." By 1980, Edward and his band were full-blown superstars, so guitarists all across the world were clamoring to learn *everything* about the man, from his style and sound to his gear. In other words, when Edward suddenly showed up with a Floyd Rose on his guitar, um, the rest of the world followed suit. It's the equivalent of what Michael Jordan did for Nike, basically. You know, MJ rocked the Nikes and everyone wanted a pair, period. EVH rocked the Floyd Rose, so everyone wanted one, period. You had *the* groundbreaking new guitar player on the block with *the* groundbreaking new tremolo system. Man, you just couldn't beat that one-two punch.

When Edward signed with Kramer Guitars in the very early '80s, I believe he got Floyd Rose an exclusive distribution deal with them, as well. Basically, all Edward's signature Kramer guitars now came equipped with this groundbreaking new tremolo system. You could also pick up any guitar/music magazine and see pictures of Edward in concert playing a guitar equipped with the Floyd Rose. The union of these three parties would translate into the Floyd Rose exploding into the music world in a huge way.

Mr. Floyd Rose deserves all the credit in the world. It was his invention, 100 percent. However, Edward Van Halen deserves credit, too. The Floyd Rose Tremolo would probably have been successful regardless, but obviously having the endorsement of the world's hottest and most important new guitar player at that time (who was also part of one of the world's biggest bands) did not hurt, ok? In a way, Edward acted as a guinea pig by taking one of the first three prototypes out with him and road testing it during Van Halen's 1979 Tour, as well as by later making some suggestions and so forth. Along with this comes the important fact that Edward officially endorsed the system by using it on his own guitars, as well as making it a standard part of his signature model guitars with Kramer. The fact that he endorsed the Floyd Rose definitely caught the ear of just about every single damn guitar player on the planet! In the end, it was a pretty historic collaboration, but to this day, I am not really certain Edward gets the credit he deserves for his role in all of this.

Quincy Jones Tells Edward to "Beat It"

*"Eddie came down to the studio with two six packs of beer, did a couple of takes, and just **tore it up**."*

– Quincy Jones

It's not an urban legend, folks. That insane guitar solo you hear during "Beat It," Michael Jackson's number 1 smash hit off the legendary *Thriller* album, is indeed none other than Edward Van Halen. In my opinion, this is one of the most important collaborations in the history of music. It was also a huge risk, especially for Edward. Remember, this collaboration with Michael Jackson took place in 1982. That was four whole years *before* the Run DMC/Aerosmith collaboration for the remake of "Walk This Way" in 1986. And in all honesty, Aerosmith really had nothing to lose at that point, anyway. (They'd been struggling for six years and their 1985 "comeback album," *Done With Mirrors,* had stalled.)

Meanwhile, Van Halen was at the height of their powers at the time Edward hooked up with MJ. Man, for a rock/metal guitar player to hook up with someone from the world of pop/R&B/dance was simply unheard of back in 1982. So how does the baddest rock/metal guitarist on the planet of that time end up on a Michael Jackson album? Two words: Quincy Jones.

In 1982, Quincy Jones hooked up with Michael Jackson to produce the album that would become known as *Thriller.* To begin with, this was already a historic collaboration. At the time, Michael truly was the "King of Pop" – especially *after* this album hit the street. Quincy Jones was definitely the king of producers, far as his respective style and what he does. In other words, you already had two kings in the mix and ready to go. Unfortunately, the third king proved to be a hard man to reach. Apparently, one of the things Quincy wanted from Michael was a rock song. *Thriller* was truly an incredibly versatile album. It was chock full of amazing musicians, from Steve Lukather and Jeff Porcaro to Paul McCartney. The album had slow songs, dance songs, and pop songs. However, in Quincy's view, what was missing was a rock song. He'd always wanted Michael to do a rock song and so he made the suggestion. As fate would have it, Michael already had an idea in the works along these lines. This "idea" would become the song known as "Beat It."

"Beat It" flat out kicks ass, period. It was a worldwide number 1 smash hit, easily one of the biggest songs of Michael Jackson's entire career. It has a killer groove, and that smokin' riff was laid down by the amazing Steve Lukather (Toto, ace session man). The riff kinda sounds like the Beatles "Day Tripper" riff on steroids! (Well, to my ears, anyway.) Nice job, Luke.

I believe Steve also played electric bass on this track as well. Other brilliant musicians on "Beat It" include Jeff Porcaro on drums and Greg Phillinganes on Rhodes Synthesizer.

All these men got together for this one track and really nailed it. However, there was something missing. Quincy wanted a guitar solo. Not just any kind of guitar solo, but a serious ass-kickin' type of solo. In 1982, if you were lookin' for a "serious ass-kickin' type of solo," um, there was really only one man for the job: Edward Van Halen. So Quincy got on the horn and personally called Edward up. Now, you would think that a personal phone call from Quincy would seal the deal, right? Well, guess again. Fact is, when Edward picked up the phone and the voice at the other end claimed to be Quincy Jones, well, Edward hung up. Apparently, he thought it was a crank call! Seriously, could you blame Edward? If you were Edward and some dude calls you up outta the blue claiming he is Quincy Jones and that he wants you to play on, of all things, a Michael Jackson album, well, would you believe it?

And so here we have Edward Van Halen hanging up on legendary Grammy Award-winning producer Quincy Jones. I believe he even called Quincy an asshole! You know, like "Stop calling me, asshole!" Again, he didn't think it was the real Quincy. Could you imagine? Man, this cat is so legendary, he doesn't even go by one name. No, he is actually known in most circles by just one letter: "Q." Well, thank God Q is persistent, cuz I believe Edward actually hung up on him a couple of times! It simply appeared that Quincy was getting nowhere. He quickly changed up his strategy and contacted Van Halen's management instead. Once the management contacted Edward and told him Quincy Jones had been trying to reach him, well, you could imagine how bad Edward felt. It had been the real Quincy Jones all along!

Lucky for all of us, no feelings were hurt. You know, Edward just thought it was a crank call. Nothing personal. Fact is, Edward really respects Quincy Jones. I would go as far as to say that, in my opinion, the main reason Edward decided to contribute a solo to "Beat It" was because of Quincy Jones. I really don't know if Edward would have done that for any other producer, honestly. Or if it had even been Michael calling him up. All the credit in the world goes to Q for personally calling Edward to come play on the song, although there is one other person who played an important role in all of this. That person would be Edward's engineer and trusty "extra ear," Donn Landee. It was Donn who actually convinced Edward to take part in the session. So Quincy called Edward up and invited him, but Donn did the convincing. I also believe the fact that Edward's bro Steve Lukather was involved in the session didn't hurt, either.

As fate would have it, Van Halen (the band) was on a short break from the "Diver Down Tour" at the time Quincy was calling Edward. So sometime between August and November of 1982 (I was not able to find a precise date) Edward Van Halen and Donn Landee went to Westlake Studios in Los Angeles to lay down a serious ass-kickin' guitar solo for "Beat It."

Quincy, Donn, and Edward went into the control room at Westlake Studios, sat down at the mixing console, and listened to a rough mix of the track. Remember, "Beat It" was pretty much complete, far as the actual song went. It was only missing a solo. As they sat there listening, Quincy told Edward where the solo should go. Apparently, Q wanted him to solo over a one-chord vamp. Sounds like a cool idea, but Edward had something else in mind. As he listened to the backing track, Edward made a few suggestions and then asked if it would be cool for him to solo over the actual verses, instead? I guess to his ears it would have been more interesting, musically speaking, to solo over the chord changes during the verses than just over a one-chord vamp. Being the brilliant producer that he is, Quincy allowed Edward to follow his musical instincts and agreed to let him solo over the verses. Nice move, Q.

Folks, I believe the time they spent listening to the track and deciding on where to solo took longer than the amount of time it took to actually record the damn thing. Man, Edward showed up to Westlake armed with two six-packs and his legendary "Frankenstrat" guitar, rarin' to go! Of course, Donn was there to have his back, too. When the time came to cut the solo, Edward set up in the studio and played his legendary "Frankenstrat" through an Echoplex and an old Marshall amp (not his legendary Marshall, rather one they had at Westlake).

Now this might shock some people, but Edward knocked the "Beat It" solo out in just two takes. In fact, the entire "session" was done in about one hour. Edward did two spontaneous solos, back to back, and then let them pick the one they liked best – "them" being Quincy and Michael Jackson. Yes, apparently MJ was there as well. The story goes that MJ actually told Edward, "I really like that high, fast stuff you do!" Michael was obviously referring to Edward's wild and super-fluid "hummingbird" picking technique. Edward actually closes out the "Beat It" solo with that precise technique. Out of the two solos he cut, I believe they used the second take.

Man, how can you even begin to describe this solo? Basically, it's Edward. Quincy was smart enough to let Edward be Edward. In other words, the solo is absolutely searing. This solo would have been at home in any Van Halen song. Hell, this solo would be at home in a freakin' Slayer song! Seriously, I've heard that Quincy might have even been a little worried. Not because the solo wasn't good. Obviously, the solo was phenomenal. No, the worry was that it might be a bit too "heavy" for a rock song. Well, for a Michael Jackson pop/rock song, anyway.

I mean, have you heard this solo? The opening of the solo sounds like a damn chainsaw or something? Not surprising considering Edward than proceeds to tear it up in his signature style, unleashing absolutely searing passages, squeaks, full on whammy-bar molestation, harmonics, super-fluid two-hand tapping, and hummingbird picking. The "Beat It" guitar solo is about thirty seconds of pure sonic bliss. No doubt, it's a jaw-dropper, baby.

In the end, everyone decided to go ahead and include it in the song. I believe Steve Lukather had a big hand in this as well. You know, far as the final mix of the song and for assuring Quincy it would fit nicely in the song.

Poor Quincy, man. I just don't think this cat could ever have imagined that solo. Edward definitely did not give Q a cheap shot. No, he went in there and didn't back off one bit as far as his playing was concerned. Edward wasn't gonna lollygag around and play softer or whatever. Nah, he went in there and went ballistic. It's like, "Hey dude, if you want me on your song, um, you are gonna get *me* on your song." Well, that's *precisely* what Quincy wanted.

Anyway, one of the sickest cameo appearances ever laid to tape was done in just a few minutes, over the course of just two takes. Twenty bucks says there's still a hole in the mixing console where Quincy's jaw dropped through it. Oh, and you wanna hear the best part? Edward Van Halen did it for free.

The guy ends up playing on a number 1 smash hit off the highest selling album of all time, *Thriller,* and he didn't make a penny. No, he was *not* ripped off, ok? Over the years, Edward has always explained he did it as a favor to Quincy Jones. He's also joked that maybe one day, as a form of payment, Michael Jackson will give him dance lessons! I honestly believe

Edward just wanted to try something different. The chance to work with a legend like Quincy Jones, who he truly respects, was simply too good to pass up. I also think he was smart enough to know that if he took any kind of payment, the masses would cry "SELLOUT!" Edward was not about to sell his services to *anyone*. It's certainly cool for session players to get paid for playing on someone else's album. There's not a damn thing wrong with that, God bless 'em.

Thing is, if a man in Edward Van Halen's position accepts money for playing on someone else's album – *especially* a Michael Jackson album – hey, the masses will cry "SELLOUT!" Believe me when I tell you that regardless whether he got paid or not, plenty of rockers and metalheads were *not* happy, to put it mildly. Many were flat-out pissed that he played on a Michael Jackson song. Again, times were quite a bit different, you know? But hey, for every one of 'em who got pissed and jumped ship, Edward won two or three *new* fans due to the insane worldwide success of "Beat It" and the *Thriller* album, overall. The funny thing is that after "Beat It" exploded, Edward received tons of offers to play on other people's albums. Well, he turned 'em all down, every single last one. In fact, to this very day, Edward Van Halen *still* receives many offers to play on other people's albums. And yes, he continues to turn 'em all down. When you think about it, it's the smart move. I mean, hey, you just can't top "Beat It," and I think Edward knows that as well.

This collaboration also opened the door for other players to hook up with MJ. Amazing players like Steve Stevens, Slash, and Jennifer Batten would all eventually work with Michael Jackson as well. I'm certain the fact that Edward had already hooked up with Michael didn't hurt. Plus, I'm sure it put their minds at ease. It's like, "Hey, if Edward worked with MJ, well, why not me?" Not to mention the fact that soon after "Beat It" hit the airwaves, you suddenly started hearing ripping guitar solos – complete with two-hand tapping and all – in R&B and dance music. Coincidence? Um, I think not.

Man, if Edward woulda received any kind of a percentage for appearing on that *Thriller* album, the rewards would have been insane. Another interesting fact many people don't know is that Edward Van Halen was actually asked to appear in the classic video for "Beat It" as well. Alas, he once again respectfully declined. If Edward would have appeared in that video, man, that definitely would have been a snapshot of a truly historic collaboration. Instead, we get a well-choreographed fight/dance sequence during the video when his guitar solo comes up.

Who knows, perhaps nowadays the "Beat It" video could have been a video MTV would cite as a "groundbreaking moment" or something? You know, much like they do with the 1986 Run DMC/Aerosmith video for "Walk This Way." I believe it was a mistake for Edward not to appear in the video, but hey, I totally understand why he didn't do it. Again, it was enough of a musical risk to even play on that one song. You simply did *not* see rock/metal dudes doing that kind of thing back then.

Overall, I honestly and firmly believe this is one of the most important musical collaborations, *ever*. Nowadays it's become commonplace to see musicians from different genres and musical styles come together on songs, in videos, and so forth. It's become almost cliché, really. There is nothing really dangerous or groundbreaking about it anymore. But before all of 'em, even before Run DMC/Aerosmith, there was EVH, MJ, and Q. Three kings, baby. The king of rock, the king of pop, and the king of producers! Three men at the height of their respective powers, doing something that had *never* been done.

In the process, "Beat It" helped MJ gain even more steam in helping to break the "whites-only" video rotation there seemed to be on MTV at that time. The "Beat It" music video was a huge smash, just like the song. Surprisingly, the song also got MJ major airplay on rock stations worldwide! The reason? Well, I like to think a lot of it had to do with Edward Van Halen, of course. Without Edward playing on that song, I simply can't believe *any* rock station was just gonna start playing Michael Jackson music, ok?

So I tip my cap to each and every one of 'em for puttin' their ass on the line back in 1982. Thank you to Quincy Jones, Michael Jackson, Edward Van Halen, Steve Lukather, Jeff Porcaro, Greg Phillinganes, and all the other fine musicians involved in the historic "Beat It" sessions.

Randy Rhoads and the Sunset Strip

"Eddie Van Halen is great – I don't want to get near competing with people like him."

– Randy Rhoads

Edward Van Halen and Randy Rhoads were a part of the same Hollywood club scene during the mid-to-late 1970s. It's mind-blowing to think these two totally bad-assed guitarists came from the same scene, at the same time! They were actually less than two years apart in age, and while Edward lived in Pasadena, Randy lived in Burbank. You know, for all the talk you hear about how Clapton, Page, and Beck grew up in the same area and played in the same club scene, I think the fact that Edward and Randy share a similar history seems to get overlooked. They may not have been hanging out and jamming together like those other three did, but nonetheless, it is staggering to think of two such enormous talents out there simultaneously kickin' ass.

Unlike the whole Clapton, Page, and Beck situation, the Edward and Randy situation can get downright brutal. You know, specifically between fans. Some of the most insane and passionate arguments I've ever heard in my life are the "Who's better, EVH or RR?" arguments. I've actually seen people nearly come to blows! I'm not kidding, either. Worse yet are the ones who claim that Edward and Randy were rivals, or who paint them as rivals, I should say. As well as those who paint Van Halen and Quiet Riot as rivals, too. You know, from back in their club days. As if these two bands would meet behind the Fat Burger on La Cienega to duke it out or something? Believe me, there was enough room on the Sunset Strip for both these bands.

Fact is, there was never any kind of rivalry here. There was actually a healthy amount of respect between all parties involved. Yeah, how boring, right? I hate to burst the bubble of all those revisionists out there, but these were two bands and two guitarists who were simply doing their own thing and rarely crossed paths, despite the fact that they were just a town apart and played the same scene. For example, Edward had his band, Mammoth, which was formed in 1972. He then hooked up with David Lee Roth at the end of 1973. By the beginning of 1974, they became "Van Halen" and were playing clubs. Randy had his band, Quiet Riot, which was formed in 1975. By the beginning of 1976, Quiet Riot was playing clubs. Guess how many times Van Halen and Quiet Riot met face-to-face and played a show together during their club days?

Once…

Yeah, quite a rivalry, huh? Not quite Yankees vs. Red Sox, is it? Besides, neither one of these brilliant musicians ever looked at music as a "rivalry." I know that people love to mix it up and compare *everything*, you know? If anything, it was the fans that really got a rivalry going.

Obviously, two great virtuoso players who come from the same scene are gonna draw comparisons. It's just that it's never actually been a competitive thing for either of the two players involved, and that's a fact. Seems some people love to separate the two of them and make it appear as if they competed against each other and all that crap. Nothing could be further from the truth. Rather than separate the two, I think we need to embrace and respect both. Everyone has their favorites, but in the end, the *respect* is what's important.

So, to show what a swell guy I am, I brought in none other than the great Kevin DuBrow to talk about the club days. Kevin is gonna let you know how he met Randy Rhoads and how they came to form Quiet Riot. He's also gonna talk about Van Halen and what it was like to see them back them back in the day, sharing some cool stories and memories. Finally, he will dismiss any b.s. concerning any kind of rivalry between these bands, guitar players, and so forth.

Man, believe me when I tell you that Kevin's memory is absolutely incredible. So much so, I actually asked him when he's gonna write a book! I mean, the dude's got one helluva memory. From the tone of his voice alone, you can totally tell how much he loved the club days and how much he loved making music with Randy. However, before I hand it over to the man, lemme just give you some quick info on the late, great Randy Rhoads.

Randy Rhoads was born on December 6, 1956. He lived his entire life in Burbank, California. His mom, Delores Rhoads, is a music teacher. Randy began his music training at a very early age. I believe he was around six or seven years old. Although he really wouldn't get serious about the guitar till he was in junior high school. But once he did get serious, man, he really dedicated himself to the instrument. As a teenager, he was already giving guitar lessons.

Randy and his best friend, bassist Kelly Garni, would go on to hook up with Kevin DuBrow and drummer Drew Forsyth to form Quiet Riot. They paid their dues on the Sunset Strip through the mid-to-late '70s, although Randy's big break actually came when he quit Quiet Riot and hooked up with Ozzy Osbourne's new band after Ozzy got booted from Black Sabbath in 1979. Out of the many guitar players who auditioned, Ozzy personally chose Randy as his new guitar player. Ironically enough, Randy was not even a Black Sabbath fan growing up!

In March of 1980, Ozzy, Randy, bassist Bob Daisley, and drummer Lee Kerslake would begin recording what would become Ozzy's first solo album. Finally, in September of 1980, the classic *Blizzard of Ozz* album was released and Randy would go on to earn "Best New Talent" in *Guitar World* magazine's annual reader's poll! The funny thing is, Randy had been paying his dues for years with Quiet Riot, but he didn't get to taste the bright light until *Blizzard of Ozz* came out in the fall of 1980. Meanwhile, Van Halen were already full blown superstars by this time. Van Halen had already released three consecutive Platinum albums and were just completing their third tour by the time *Blizzard of Ozz* debuted in September of 1980.

Man, what an amazing time, huh? Van Halen was easily the biggest American hard rock/metal band alive. You could say they were already one of the biggest bands in the world, period. The legendary Black Sabbath had passed the torch to them in 1978 and the boys in VH were definitely kickin' ass and takin' names. Add to that the fact that Edward had reinvented the guitar and basically stood head and shoulders above everyone else, so to speak. Then here comes Ozzy with Randy Rhoads and bam! They hit the scene and began kickin' ass, too! As Randy won "Best New Talent" in *Guitar Player* magazine's annual reader's poll (1981), Edward won "Best Player." That's about as devastating a one-two combination as you'll ever find in your entire life. At this time I simply can't imagine there being two bigger and more ass-kickin' players alive on this planet, especially in the world of rock and metal, than Edward and Randy.

Soon after the tour in support of the *Blizzard of Ozz* album, the band would go back into the studio and record the follow-up, *Diary of a Madman* (1981). It would be yet another successful album and tour. In what could have been a disastrous turn of events, the firing of Ozzy Osbourne from

Black Sabbath actually led to his hooking up with Randy, Bob, and Lee, and recording some of the best material he's ever done. Everything was going great until things came to a sudden and tragic halt on March 19, 1982. That is the day we lost Randy Rhoads in a plane crash in Leesburg, Florida.

Rather than focus on how he passed, let's focus on how he lived, along with the incredible music/guitar playing he left us with. He gave us all some really cool material with Quiet Riot and two classic albums with Ozzy. In the end, it's more than enough to show he was a truly phenomenal musician. Without a doubt, he is one of the greatest who ever lived. And now, ladies and germs, here's the man...

Kevin DuBrow: "I used to hang out at Rodney Bingenheimer's club. That's where I first met Randy Rhoads. Randy and Kelly Garni were in a band with Smokey, this gay singer from Hollywood. So they played Rodney's club a couple times and I used to hang out there. I had just gone to see Humble Pie in San Diego and when I came back my brother had written a message saying, 'Randy from Smokey's band called...wants to talk to you about being a singer in his band.' So I called him and we immediately had a rapport on the phone. The one album we both had in common, which made us want to form a band, was the first Montrose album with Sammy Hagar, *Montrose* (1973, Warner Brothers). We wanted to be just like that first Montrose album.

"So Randy and Kelly Garni came to my mom's house and I played him a whole movie of me playing with a guitar player that later was in the Dickies, and they kinda giggled at it. Then we eventually met up at his mom's house. We ended up forming Quiet Riot in May of 1975. Our first gig was at the La Cañada Country Club in June of 1975. It was for Burbank High School graduation. We did mostly cover tunes, stuff like Alice Cooper, Humble Pie, and things like that, along with some originals, too. Stuff like 'Force of Habit,' which is 'Suicide Solution,' and a song called 'Pistol,' which was later 'Ravers' on the first album. We only got about eight songs into the show and they made us stop because Randy was so loud they were afraid the back windows were gonna break. Our second show was Halloween 1975, at the Machinist Hall in Burbank. We also played shows on November 1st and 2nd as well.

"The first time I saw Van Halen, Randy and I went and saw them. We saw them at the Starwood. Eddie was playing an Explorer [Ibanez]. Yeah, it was a white Explorer. He hadn't gotten into the tremolo bar system yet. I remember a lot of things about them. Alex used a silver sparkle drum kit and Eddie used borrowed amps. In fact, I think he borrowed his amps from Chris Holmes [guitarist for W.A.S.P.]. Eddie and Chris lived down the street from each other and were friends. I remember we were pretty impressed by Eddie. He was doing a lot of stuff that reminded me of Allan Holdsworth. He had just started with the mandolin picking, and he was into hammer-ons, too. He did a lot of really fast stuff that was really done clean, which we were *really* impressed with. Alex Van Halen's drum riser was made out of plywood sheets and milk crates! That was his 'drum riser.' And David Lee Roth, well, no one was really impressed with him 'cause at the time he was just a Jim Dandy clone.

"The songs were solid, but not as great as they ended up being on the first album. Obviously, 'Runnin' with the Devil' was there, but a lot of their songs, like 'House of Pain' and stuff like that, didn't make their first record. Those songs didn't come out till later. I have a CD of the Van Halen Warner Brothers demo, and you can hear different pieces of songs end up in different songs. They just hadn't really fine-tuned themselves, yet. Then Randy and I went and saw them again at the Starwood. Eddie had a brown Strat, and he's just started using the whammy-bar. We were amazed that he used the whammy-bar and it didn't go out of tune! You know, this was before the Floyd Rose. So we figured it was time to meet them. We went into their dressing room and we introduced ourselves. Eddie Van Halen says, 'Yeah, you guys are ok, but you sound too much like Queen!' [laughs] I remember Randy says, 'How did you use the tremolo system so much and it didn't go outta tune?' And Eddie goes, 'Oh, it's a secret. Jeff Beck showed it to me.' We just rolled our eyes and went, 'Ok.'

"David Lee Roth is really nice. I didn't really talk to the other guys. Another time we met was at a club called the Cabaret. It was on Santa Monica and La Cienega, right near where the Fat Burger is. All the bands used to play there. We were in line to see somebody and Eddie and Dave were in line behind us. You know, they were out together, which is kinda strange considering their history.

"We opened for Van Halen at the Glendale College Auditorium on April 23, 1977. This is the only time we ever played a show together. I actually have, in my scrapbook, a newspaper clipping with a picture of us that says, 'This is Van Halen.' [laughs] It was really funny.

"Anyway, so Randy was actually sick that day. At the soundcheck, we actually sat in the audience and listened to them. I remember Eddie was playing Chris Holmes' amp. I was actually talking to Chris about this the other day. They were Chris' amp cabinets and they had all the tolex ripped off and he had refinished them in wood, with black grille cloth. Like, natural colored, wood-colored Marshalls. They soundchecked with 'Feel Your Love Tonight.' Pretty good memory, huh? [*laughs*] We said, 'Wow! We've never heard that one!' It was *really* impressive, *blatantly* commercial, and a *really* great song. We just went, 'Wow!' Eddie's guitar tone sure had improved, too. I mean, it was *always* good, but it had *really* improved.

"We didn't talk to them but Ron Sobol, who was my friend, has pictures from that show. I remember Eddie was playing a black Strat with, like, a white binding on it that night. I actually have a film of us from that show. It's a film of us doing one song, the first song of the show. The show didn't sell that great. It was in the theater, so we were in the theatrical department. That was our dressing room. We all got dressed in drag for photos after the show 'cause there was a bunch of dresses back there.

"I saw them at the Whisky [A Go-Go] a couple of times, without Randy. They played a New Year's Eve show there on December 31, 1977 right before their debut album came out. I don't think they even played that many songs from the album 'cause I think they didn't want anybody to steal their songs or something. [laughs] David Lee Roth and I always had a good connection. I think he's the greatest. I ran into him one time at the Starwood. This was a couple of albums later on, and right before Quiet Riot got signed. We were talking and he goes, 'Man, you're a really good singer. I see you comin' up on my rear view mirror!' Which I thought was a really cool thing to say. I remember when Quiet Riot played the US Festival in 1983. We were the first band that day. You know, we opened the show. Well, when we were leaving the hotel to go to the site, 'cause our show was like at 11:45 A.M., David Lee Roth was walking into the lobby at like 10 A.M. He'd been out all night, getting high and stuff. He just wandered in and was looking real bad [laughs]. Yeah, he was pretty out there that morning.

"Looking back, one of the reasons Van Halen had better songs than Quiet Riot is that Van Halen did a lot of covers, so they learned from the best. They honed their craft by playing tons of covers and eventually learned what worked about those songs by all those different artists –*especially* ZZ Top – and they learned how to write songs better than us. We didn't really play covers. I was already writing originals and our originals weren't that great 'cause we didn't take the time to play covers; to learn. They did a lot of cover tunes, so they could play places that we didn't play. There were a lot of clubs back then, but you *had* to play covers. You know, Top 40 stuff.

They were a better band. We were more image and they were more musical. They were more blues-based than us. Anything that's blues-based will stand the test of time more than anything that's pop-based – in my opinion, anyway. Van Halen was more blues-based. We later became more blues-based. That's why they were a better band and why their songs make more sense. Also, Alex Van Halen knew what 'groove' meant. Our drummer, Drew Forsyth, wouldn't know a groove if it hit him on the head! He just couldn't keep time and he was accenting on every shot, so you couldn't tap your foot to it. Van Halen also played a lot more than we did, so they got to hone their craft a lot better, before we were even out there.

"There was never any rivalry between Van Halen and Quiet Riot, and Randy respected Eddie. I know that after the first Van Halen album came out, Randy's students all wanted to learn that stuff. He had to learn it. To me, they had nothing to do with each other. They coexisted, but Randy came from a different place, musically speaking. It was so much different than Eddie. He was more into doubling and tripling his leads. It was a different philosophy, completely. Visually, Randy was obviously influenced by Mick Ronson. Musically speaking, he was influenced by people like Johnny Winter, Leslie West, and Ritchie Blackmore. I actually got Randy into Jeff Beck. Glenn Buxton [Alice Cooper's guitarist] was a big influence, too. Randy was somewhat into Michael Schenker as well. Later, he became a big fan of Gary Moore." ♪

Man, it's truly amazing how two kids comin' out of the Sunset Strip in the mid-'70s could go on to inspire and touch so many people, even to this very day. From Zakk Wylde and the late, great Dimebag Darrell to Daron Malakian, Tom Morello, and even the mighty Jack Black, you'll find the majority of the great players out there have been influenced and inspired by both EVH and RR. Basically, if you don't own albums by these two cats, um, there's no hope for you.

Along with the fact that they actually shared some of the same influences and how both played with so much fire, too. Hey, they're both virtuosos, you know? While their methods in the studio differed – Randy preferring to overdub while Edward preferred live, raw and spontaneous takes – they were both still able to capture, on tape, the way their fire-breathing styles came across live on stage.

You can also look at how Randy was so into classical music and implemented that into his playing on classic songs like "Revelation (Mother Earth)." Edward began his music career playing Beethoven and Mozart at six years old. From the age of six to twelve, it was all classical piano, remember?

Some of his classical influence turned up on legendary pieces like "Eruption" and "Spanish Fly."

Oh, and both of them were into Charvel guitars as well. Edward began working with Charvel way back since the club days, in 1975. Remember, the bodies for his "Frankenstrat" and other guitars he built were purchased directly from Wayne Charvel, and Wayne continued to hook Edward up all the way through Van Halen's first couple of tours. By the end of 1979, Randy had found his way to Charvel as well. And both of them really dug Les Paul's, too. You'll find plenty of pics from their club days and early tours where both used a Les Paul, on stage and on record. So yes, they did have things in common aside from being two monstrous virtuosos.

Not to mention the mutual respect between 'em. As you can tell by the quote at the opening of this chapter, well, Randy definitely had respect for Edward. Kevin DuBrow even mentioned it, and Randy's own words confirm it. Lord knows I flipped through plenty of music mags to find his exact words. You see, after Randy passed, just about every major music mag – from *Guitar World* and *Guitar Player* to *Hit Parader* – had a Randy Rhoads tribute issue during the '80s. Many continued doin' so into the '90s and right on into the millennium!

Well, not only did these issues have plenty of Randy's own words from interviews he'd done during his time with Ozzy, they also had words from the people who knew him, worked with him, and so forth. For example, in one of the many tribute issues to RR, legendary producer Max Norman recalled how during the sessions for the classic *Blizzard of Ozz* album back in 1980, there only seemed to be one guitarist Randy would ever mention on a regular basis.

Max Norman: "Van Halen was one of the few guitarists Randy would talk about. One day I asked him, 'What guitar players do you like, Randy?' And he said, 'I like Eddie Van Halen.'"

Major respect, baby. In fact, during interviews Randy did back in the day, he would always be cool and respectful towards Edward. Randy seemed like a very cool, classy guy. And he made no bones about the fact that he was quite aware of Edward. Then again, who the freakin' hell wasn't, you know? I mean, just about every guitarist on the entire freakin' planet was aware of EVH when he hit the scene. How could you not be? You'd be stupid to ignore the first and only man since Jimi to reinvent the craft.

So while everyone is entitled to their opinion, in *my* humble opinion, Randy Rhoads was *not* some "EVH clone." That is simply not the case. Randy was his own man. Period.

Was he aware of Edward? Absolutely. Did he respect Edward? Absolutely. Was he influenced by Edward? Well, in a way, I guess he was. Perhaps "impacted" or "inspired" might be a better choice of words, really. To me, "influences" are more the people you grew up listening to, you know? Obviously, Randy didn't grow up listening to Edward, cuz they were about the same age. So, you know, there was no VH on the radio or in stores for him to listen to when he was growin' up!

However, being able to witness Edward play in clubs *waaay* before the rest of the world even knew he existed was definitely an advantage. You know, cuz Edward is the kinda guy who, upon just one listen, can cause you to question *everything* you thought you knew about guitar playing. Shit, just go back to the "Club Days" chapter of this book and see what George Lynch said about seeing/hearing EVH for the first time, ok?

In fact, during an interview with music journalist John Stix back on August 14, 1981 (you can read this amazing interview in the August 2004 issue of *Guitar World*), Randy basically admitted that during his concert solo spot, he did a lot of the same things Edward did. Man, he almost sounded apologetic!

Well, there's really no need to apologize. Like Edward, Randy was a young guy who'd just been thrust into the limelight by joining Ozzy. You know, he simply wanted to make a name for himself. Hell, you can't blame a guy for that, really. He did what he had to do.

Overall, I believe Randy had his own sound and his own approach. So just cuz his solo spot borrowed a bit from Edward's doesn't entitle anyone to brand RR an "EVH clone." That's just stupid. Besides, who on Earth *didn't* borrow a bit from Edward?! Man, everyone and their sister did! And that's fine. You can't blame people for having the good sense and good taste to listen to and borrow from the first and only dude since Jimi to reinvent the craft! You'd be stupid not to. But for my money, I believe Randy was one of the truly great ones, who was able to build upon the blueprint Edward had set. He brought his own ideas and flavor to the world of guitar. And whatever ideas he may have picked up from EVH that turned up in his own playing, whether in concert or on actual recordings, Randy was always able to use them tastefully and in his own way. At least to my ears, anyway. Damn, it woulda been so interesting to see where his musical journey woulda led him!

So I always thought it was cool how, unlike some other big-name players, Randy actually admitted his awareness and respect for Edward. However, that awareness and respect went both ways. You see, Edward Van Halen certainly recognized and respected Randy's talents as well.

For example, in the November 1982 issue of *Guitar Player* magazine, which served as a tribute to Randy after he passed, Edward Van Halen stated the following: "Randy Rhoads was one guitarist who was honest and very good. I feel so sorry for him, but you never know – he might be up there right now, jammin' with John Bonham and everyone else."

During another tribute issue back in the day, Edward Van Halen stated: "I have an immense amount of respect for what he did. Some people say I may have had an influence on his playing, but I never was able to ask him that. If it's true, I'm very honored, because I thought he was very, very good. He was also very dedicated to his playing. I think that showed in his work."

Damn, you gotta love that. But it's not surprising, really. I've always believed that greatness recognizes greatness. Period. So it's really not shocking to see how these two were so respectful and tipped their cap to each other. That is very cool, indeed.

After all, they were, and still *are* one of the most devastating one-two combinations I've ever seen in my entire life. Perhaps *the* most devastating one, ever. For my money, EVH and RR were the "twin towers" of the guitar world – *especially* the worlds of shred and metal. I mean, who do you think represented "metal" guitar playing here in America back in the days before the great Metallica hit the scene, hmmm? Here at home, "metal" guitar was basically EVH and RR. Period. That's it. Sometimes I think people need to be reminded of that fact, you know?

In the end, I'm aware everyone has their personal favorites or whatever. Hey, that's cool. However, I believe that everyone would be better served by listening to the music and guitar playing of both Edward and Randy. For example, I know Zakk Wylde is fond of saying that he believes Edward is the greatest guitar player who ever lived, and that Randy should be in the Top 5. Yeah, that sounds pretty damn good to me. So crank up some *Van Halen,* crank up some *Blizzard Of Ozz,* kick back and realize how after all these years, the music and guitar playing on these albums still kicks the absolute livin' shit out of a whole lotta what's out there today!

Randy Rhoads Discography

Quiet Riot I (released in Japan, 1977)
Quiet Riot II (released in Japan, 1979)
Blizzard of Ozz (1980)
Diary of a Madman (1981)
Ozzy Osbourne: Randy Rhoads Tribute (live album, 1987)
Quiet Riot: The Randy Rhoads Years (1993)

The Greatest of All Time

"When I hear a guitar, I like to hear the other thing. Any guitarist that can transcend the instrument knocks me out. Hendrix is a good example. You don't hear the guitar, you hear the exuberance that goes beyond the instrument and the kind of phrasing he uses. Eddie Van Halen's got that, too."

– Pat Metheny

Who is the greatest guitar player of all time: Jimi Hendrix or Edward Van Halen? Man, if I only had a dollar for every single time I heard this question, I'd be a millionaire. The very first thought that comes to my mind is, "Well, are we strictly talking rock guitar players here?" Cuz the fact is, both Edward and Jimi are *rock* guitarists, ok?

Throughout history, there have been many phenomenal and important players, from Steve Vai to Chet Atkins. However, they are *not* rock musicians. Sure, they can play everything from rock to Bavarian folk/techno (whatever the hell that is), cuz they are *extremely* versatile musicians. But rock is simply not the medium they chose to truly express themselves in. Man, there are just so many damn different styles of music! So how in the hell does one even begin to compare, say, Django Reinhardt to Stevie Ray Vaughan? Uli Jon Roth to Frank Zappa? Eddie Hazel to Buckethead? Les Paul to Michael Hedges?

Alvin Lee: "It's like the different innovators. Django Reinhardt was the greatest guitarist of the forties and Jimi Hendrix was the greatest guitarist of the sixties. The seventies was a bit hazy...and it's a matter of taste. There's no 'Best' guitarist. The eighties, there's so many good guitarists, Joe Satriani, Jeff Healy, Stevie Ray Vaughan,

244

Mark Knopfler, Eddie Van Halen. Eddie is good, he's a very good guitarist; a hot technician."

To even begin to possibly compare players, I believe you have to go by their respective style. I mean, would you compare Michael Jordan to Wayne Gretzky? I don't think anyone compares basketball players to hockey players, ok? Yeah, they are both *"the shit"* as far as their own respective sport is concerned, but I believe you can only truly compare athletes within their own respective sport. Fact is, as far as the world of rock guitar goes, Edward and Jimi are the same player. What I mean is both Edward and Jimi did the exact same thing when they hit the scene: they reinvented the electric guitar and changed the face of rock. Folks, that is an indisputable fact.

In order to fully comprehend how this came to be, well, you got to go back to the man who started it all. While Edward and Jimi reinvented the instrument – key letters there being "re" – they did not invent rock guitar playing, per se. After all, Edward and Jimi are *rock* guitarists. And while the electric guitar has and most likely always will be the main instrument in rock music, well, rock guitar does *not* begin with either of them. It didn't start in 1967 with Jimi's debut and it didn't start in 1978 with Edward's debut.

There have been many terrific and important guitarists throughout the course of music history – especially from the world of blues – who went on to influence rock guitar. After all, the blues gave birth to rock 'n' roll. We can thank everyone from Robert Johnson and Howlin' Wolf to Muddy Waters for that. However, I believe the legendary Chuck Berry is widely considered to be the godfather of rock guitar. Chuck hit the scene in 1955 and laid down the blueprint for rock guitar. Three words, people: "Johnny B. Goode." 'Nuff said.

Everyone who followed *absolutely had* to go through Chuck if they wanted to play rock guitar. People like the Beatles, the Stones, the Who, Ted Nugent, Jeff Beck, Eric Clapton, Dickey Betts, and countless others. Each and every single one of these legendary artists cut their teeth on Chuck Berry records. It's a fact. Yeah, Chuck taught 'em all how to play rock guitar and rock music. As Eric Clapton told *Guitar World* magazine in 1997, "If you wanted to play rock and roll you would end up playing like Chuck, or what you learned from Chuck, because there isn't any other choice. He's really laid the law down."

Other legendary players have issued similar statements. For example, during an interview with *Guitar World* magazine in 2002, the great Dickey Betts stated, "In the Fifties, Chuck Berry was to guitar what Jimi Hendrix became in the Sixties. He played so differently from everybody else; it was a totally new sound for guitar."

In fact, even the late, great John Lennon once stated, "If you were going to give rock 'n' roll another name, you might call it 'Chuck Berry.'"

After Chuck Berry laid the law down in 1955, many great players, from many different worlds of music, continued to push the envelope over the next decade. Players such as: Scotty Moore, Eddie Cochran, Duanne Eddy, Steve Cropper, Link Wray, Bo Diddley, James Burton, Michael Bloomfield, Freddie King, Albert Collins, the Ventures, George Harrison, John Lennon, Keith Richards, Jeff Beck, Dick Dale, Albert King, Pete Townshend, Syd Barrett, Dave and Ray Davies, Buddy Guy, and, of course, the great Eric Clapton.

You know, for all the talk about Jimi Hendrix paving the road for Edward Van Halen and many other modern-day players (which, of course, is absolutely true), people tend to forget all the great players who paved the road for Jimi!

Anyhow, Chuck's blueprint for rock guitar held fast for about a decade. Then, in 1967, Jimi Hendrix hit the scene and reinvented it. After Jimi laid the law down in 1967, many great players, from many different worlds of music, continued to push the envelope over the next decade. Players such as: Jimmy Page, Alvin Lee, Johnny Winter, Frank Zappa, Rory Gallagher, Tony Iommi, Robert Fripp, John McLaughlin, Peter Green, Allan Holdsworth, Harvey Mandel, Ritchie Blackmore, Leslie West, Duane Allman, Dickey Betts, Carlos Santana, Billy Gibbons, Glen Buxton, Buck Dharma, Ronnie Montrose, David Gilmour, Lowell George, Frank Marino, Al Di Meola, Brian May, Jan Akkerman, Michael and Rudolph Schenker, Uli Jon Roth, Glenn Tipton, K.K. Downing, Angus and Malcolm Young, Peter Frampton, Lou Reed, Gary Moore, Eddie Hazel, Ace Frehley, Mick Ronson, Pat Metheny, Steve Howe, Neal Schon, Tommy Bolin, and, of course, the great Ted Nugent.

For my money, Ted Nugent is *the* main link between Jimi Hendrix and Edward Van Halen. The Motor City Madman exploded onto the scene back in 1968 when, at just twenty years old, he released the classic, "Journey to the Center of Your Mind" with his original group, the Amboy Dukes. Since then, Uncle Ted's been kickin' ass in the music biz for almost forty years! I truly believe his primal stage presence and mastery of everything from feedback to playing with his teeth, combined with his killer tone and totally insane blazing chops, is the rock world's truest link between Jimi's and Edward's respective styles. After he went solo in 1975, I believe Ted Nugent was basically at the top of the rock pyramid, far as American rock guitarists went, for the better half of the 1970s. During this time, he released five albums, all of which went Platinum upon release! Here at home, Ted was actually outselling other monster acts of the time, like Kiss and Aerosmith! Along with that, he was also one of the top concert draws around, period. And while all of his 1970s albums are a must listen, well, *Double Live Gonzo* (1978, Sony) is a true classic. If you wanna hear some truly insane shit, um, then this is the album for you. It's *definitely* a must-own, baby.

Anyhow, Jimi Hendrix's blueprint for rock guitar held fast for about a decade. Then, in 1978, Edward Van Halen hit the scene and and reinvented it. Simply put, *no one* has ever done it since. Sure, there have been many great players to come down the pike and continue to push the envelope even further than Edward *and* Jimi. Technically speaking, anyway. However, most of 'em are from outside the rock world, like: Steve Vai, Joe Satriani, Yngwie J. Malmsteen, Jason Becker, Shawn Lane, and Buckethead. In fact, it appears most of 'em happen to be brilliant, otherworldly solo artists. However, you will find a few examples in major bands. Metallica's dynamic duo of James Hetfield and Kirk Hammett certainly comes to mind. As does Children of Bodom's blazing young axeman, Alexi Laiho. No doubt Zakk Wylde always goes ballistic with Ozzy, as well as with his own band, Black Label Society. And, of course, so did his bro, the late, great Dimebag Darrell of Pantera/ Damageplan.

But the fact is, *no one* has ever reinvented the instrument and changed the face of rock the way Edward and Jimi managed to. I mean, it's really not even close. They both changed everything, overnight. I simply can't think of too many other guitar players who have impacted the world of music in general more than these two men, either. You'll find that most great guitar players out there will cite *both* Edward and Jimi as an influence and inspiration. Basically, most great players have been touched by both of these cats, period.

In my opinion, if you had a Mount Rushmore of rock guitar players, three out of the four faces would probably have to be Chuck, Jimi, and Edward. Funny how they are all American, huh? Edward may be of Dutch descent, but he came to America at the age of six and lived his entire life here. In other words, he's American. Rock 'n' roll is *our* music, baby. It came from the blues, which is *our* music, too. Far as I'm concerned, the rest of the world still owes us!

All kidding aside, I'm aware that in the end, people will always have their favorites. However, it's all truly subjective as far as who one may or may not believe is "the best" or "the greatest." In fact, "the greatest" may not even necessarily be "the best." Sure, Edward and Jimi are each considered by many to be "the greatest." But the fact is neither of these two cats *ever* proclaimed themselves "the best" or "the greatest"! I'm one of those guys who believe if you proclaim yourself "the best" or "the greatest" at something, regardless what it might be, then you're probably not (the exception being Muhammad Ali, of course).

For example, Jimi was into many different players, from West Montgomery and Howlin' Wolf to Buddy Guy and Eric Clapton. I know that just before he died, he did an interview where he mentioned that Billy Gibbons was his favorite new player. You know, the Reverend Willy G. from ZZ Top, baby. Edward Van Halen is a major fan of the Reverend as well. Like Jimi, Edward was into many players, from Jeff Beck and Jimmy Page to Eric Clapton and Tony Iommi. However, if you asked Edward who "the best" or "the greatest" guitar player is, he will always and forever say Allan Holdsworth. Sure, his first guitar hero was Clapton, but he's always stated that Allan is the best. In fact, he's been consistently saying it during interviews throughout his entire career. Edward has always stated that, for his money, Allan is *"the man."*

Allan Holdsworth came roaring out of Bradford, England back in the late 1960s. By the early 1970s, he'd hooked up with the band Tempest, and in 1973, they released their debut album, *Up and On* (Bronze). Since then, Allan has been kickin' ass and blowin' minds for over thirty-two years now. In fact, he is still recording and touring as we speak. Allan is a totally independent and uncompromising artist who's always done things on his own terms. Not only has Edward Van Halen stated that Allan is *"the man,"* he's also stated, during countless interviews, that Allan Holdsworth is probably the only player to ever make him say, "How'd he do that?"

I believe the amazing Steve Vai has also pointed to Allan Holdsworth as being "the best." The great Yngwie J. Malmsteen once said that Allan's solo during his classic song, "In the Dead of Night" scared the livin' shit outta him! Many players, from Yngwie to Edward, have cited the "In the Dead of Night" solo as one of the all-time greatest solos ever laid to tape. In fact, when I spoke with Allan for this book, I asked him about that solo. (Shit, I had to!) Well, he chuckled and said, "Yeah, it was all right, I suppose. That was a *long* time ago. It was all right for that time, I guess." Um, can you say "humble"? On top of that, I asked him if that was a first-take solo. After some thought, he almost sheepishly admitted that it was! Freakin' unbelievable.

Anyway, for my money, I believe that in terms of pure chops, Allan is beyond *everyone*. I totally agree with Edward, Steve, Yngwie, and all the other greats who point to Allan as *"the man."* Hey, that's saying something, cuz regardless, dudes like Edward, Steve, and Yngwie are still virtuoso musicians, you know? They are still three of the best players in history, period.

Sadly, someone like Allan Holdsworth will never be considered "the greatest" by the masses because he chose a different medium of music to express himself in. He is known and incredibly well-respected within music circles – *especially* by his peers, of course. Over the years, everyone from Tom Morello and John McLaughlin to Randy Rhoads has proclaimed major respect for Allan's otherworldly ability. But to the rest of the world, he remains a mystery. Add to that the fact that he is simply not into writing material considered "radio-friendly." In turn, this means that he simply will not get much radio play or press. So once again, he remains a mystery to the masses. Nonetheless, check out his music, cuz his playing is astonishing.

In order for someone to be considered "the greatest" at something, *especially* by the masses, I believe you pretty much have to do your thing on a big stage. And really, is there a bigger stage in music than rock 'n' roll? Frankly, there isn't. While hip-hop has certainly pulled up close to it, in terms of sales and popularity, I still believe rock 'n' roll is the single most popular form of music on the freakin' planet. It's why many consider the Beatles to be the greatest band of all time, or why many consider Led Zeppelin to be the greatest hard rock band of all time. It was that insane level of success and popularity in the world of rock music that makes 'em "great." The talent is a given. It's the same reason Babe Ruth, Michael Jordan, and Muhammad Ali are considered by the masses to be "the greatest" in their respective sport. They did what they did on the big stage and they each transcended their respective sport.

I truly believe "the greatest" in anything is usually, if not *always* a larger-than-life figure. Seriously, does anyone believe the Babe would still be a legend and considered "the greatest" if he'd hit 714 homers in Double A? Can you even name me who hit the most homers in a Double A season or career? Yeah, I didn't think so. The fact that the Babe hit all those homers at the Major League level is what made him. Add to that the fact that he hit 'em while winning a bunch of World Series with the most successful and popular baseball franchise of all time, the New York Yankees. Certainly that helped his status as "the greatest," to put it mildly.

So, as far as who is the single greatest rock guitar player of all time, the two names that seem to consistently appear at the top of the list are Edward Van Halen and Jimi Hendrix. Then again, someone like Jimmy Page deserves much consideration as well. He may not have "reinvented" the instrument as Edward and Jimi did, but man, what he accomplished with Led Zeppelin is truly staggering, incredibly important, and vastly influential. On top of that, the guy can flat out wail, too! But since Edward and Jimi changed the face of rock music *and* reinvented the instrument, it always comes down to these two men.

Man, rock music and the electric guitar simply go together hand in hand. I think most people would agree, "No electric guitar, no rock 'n' roll, period." The electric guitar has always been the weapon of choice in rock music. It ain't rock 'n' roll till somebody plugs in and turns up the distortion, baby. And Edward and Jimi are both *rock* guitar players. While they listened to, absorbed, and loved many different styles of music, they chose rock music as the medium they wanted to express themselves in. They are the only two cats in the history of music to change the face of rock *and* reinvent the instrument. And while the electric guitar was obviously their weapon of choice, fact is both could play the living hell out of an acoustic, too. (Hey, last time I checked, both have six strings, you know?)

In fact, those are just a couple of the many things these two giants have in common. The similarities between these two men are actually pretty staggering. Sure, as is the case with anything in life, there are differences between them as well. Let's take a quick look at all those similarities first, before going on any further with this discussion.

*Both came from humble beginnings.

*Both displayed a love of music at an early age.

*Both displayed an amazing amount of talent at an early age.

*Both had fathers who were into music and supported their pursuit of music.

*Both picked up the electric guitar at the age of twelve.

*Both were completely self-taught on the instrument. Neither one ever had so much as a single guitar lesson. They were both blessed with an amazing ear for music.

*Both had tremendous love and respect for the blues. While they loved and listened to *everything* from pop to classical, the blues would be the foundation upon which each of their respective styles was built. Basically, they both started with blues and then eventually turned it into a much more aggressive thing, really.

*Both would eventually choose rock music as their medium of expression.

*Both were obsessive musicians who dedicated their entire life to their craft. These guys took their guitars *everywhere*. Eventually, each would possess an incredible amount of technical ability. Even as teenagers, they were *absolutely killing* people with their playing. While Edward has always been known as a "master technician," I must say Jimi certainly knew his way around a fretboard, to put it mildly. As crazy as this may sound, I honestly believe Jimi's prowess on the instrument is sometimes overlooked. I mean, Jimi had incredible chops and technical ability.

For example, it really pisses me off when people call Edward "technical," then turn around and call Jimi "soulful." Whether the morons who say this realize it or not, that's actually a pretty stupid, racist statement. To me, that is no different then the morons who call black athletes "naturally gifted" while calling white athletes "hard-working and intelligent," or "a student of the game." Yes, Jimi was soulful. No doubt about it. But do you ever notice how Jimi is often called "soulful," while you rarely hear the word "technical" thrown his way? Man, Jimi Hendrix was a "master technician," baby! On the other hand, ever notice how Edward Van Halen is often called "technical," while you rarely hear the word "soulful" thrown his way?

The *Merriam-Webster Dictionary* defines soul as "a person's total self." By that definition, these are two of the most soulful bastards the world has ever known, cuz all these guys did was put their total self into their music and into their craft. In turn, this led to both of these men possessing a vast amount of musical knowledge and complete mastery of their instrument. Hey, being "self-taught" doesn't mean you still don't have to know your shit, ok?

What's really cool is neither of these men let his brain get in the way. In other words, while they each possessed an absurd amount of technical ability, it *never* got in the way of their music. If anything, all that mind-boggling technical ability helped them to better express themselves in their music. Because they were soulful and put their entire selves into their craft, they were able to master the instrument. Both Edward and Jimi proved, without question, that you could be technical *and* soulful.

*Both were tremendous songwriters in their respective styles. While they both received a healthy amount of acclaim for their guitar playing, without those songs they wrote, man, they wouldn't have been anywhere near as big.

*Both paid dues by playing hundreds of shows in clubs and so forth. By the time they were old enough to legally drink, both had a lifetime's worth of live experience under their belt.

*Both of them were discovered by the bass player from other popular rock bands. Jimi was discovered in 1966 at the "Café Wha?" in New York

City's Greenwich Village by the Animals' bassist, Chas Chandler. Edward was discovered in 1976 at the Starwood Club in Hollywood, California by Kiss bassist, Gene Simmons.

*Both were into power trios. Mammoth, the earliest incarnation of Van Halen, was a power trio, with Edward on lead vocals. The Jimi Hendrix Experience was a power trio.

*Both were never comfortable singing. Edward eventually handed the vocal duties over to Diamond Dave. Jimi never really liked the sound of his voice much, but was convinced to stick with it by others.

*Both were huge fans of Cream. I believe this is why both were huge fans of the power trio format, as well. Cream served as a blueprint, early on.

*Both were huge fans of Eric Clapton as well. Edward has always stated that as far as his influences go, Eric is his main man. Jimi liked, respected, and was influenced by Eric, too. In fact, the only reason Jimi finally agreed to go to England with Chas Chandler was *after* Chas promised that he would introduce him to Eric.

*Both released debut albums that would change the face of rock music and guitar, *forever.* Jimi with *Are You Experienced* (1967), and Edward with *Van Halen* (1978). Basically, they both changed the face of rock and reinvented the instrument with their debut albums, period.

*Both were ridiculously young when they recorded their debut albums. Jimi was twenty-four years old, while Edward was just twenty-two years old.

*Both debut albums achieved amazing commercial success, which is pretty rare for groundbreaking musicians. *Are You Experienced* (1967) sold over 4 million copies in America to date. Meanwhile, *Van Halen* (1978) sold over 10 million copies in America to date.

*Both debut albums contained precisely eleven tracks – ten songs, one instrumental, each.

*Both released covers as their first single, Jimi with "Hey Joe" by Billy Roberts, and Edward with "You Really Got Me" by the Kinks.

*Both continued to do covers throughout their career, however, always managing to put their own respective stamp on anything they touched.

*Both were considered *"the man"* during their respective eras. Not only by the fans but, even more importantly, by their peers. On stage, each was considered the most devastating live player of his respective era. Each became the player *other* players came to watch. You know you are *"the shit"* when other great players come to watch you.

*Both were monster showmen. Overall, Edward became known for his amazing nonstop energy and natural, charismatic, infectious stage presence. Jimi had that, too. But Jimi was also known for his flamboyant costumes (everything from skin-tight outfits to feather boas), overtly sexual stage moves, electric hair, tricks (playing behind the back, with his teeth, etc...), destruction of guitars (including sometimes burning them), and the kitchen sink! I believe Jimi learned a lot about showmanship during his stint as a backup guitar player for one of the greatest showmen of all time, Little Richard. Yes, Jimi was a member of Little Richard's band during the mid-1960s. Pete Townshend's stage presence had a big effect on both Edward and Jimi, too.

*Both had a healthy following of dudes *and* women, especially at their concerts.

*Both would mainly become known for using Strats or Strat-style guitars, although they played and recorded with many different types of guitars.

*Both used Marshall amplifiers. Although they'd use different amps to record their music over the years, both became synonymous with Marshall early in their career.

*Both were known to play brutally loud in the studio and on stage as well. On stage, Jimi would usually have two or three Marshall stacks behind him, fully cranked. Edward has been known to use up to two to three times that amount, fully cranked.

*Both were full-on whammy-bar masters *and* molesters, using the bar to coax sounds out of their instrument that most people couldn't even fathom. It's as if they used the bar as an instrument unto itself.

*Both were fearless experimenters, willing to do anything and *everything* to achieve the sounds they heard inside their head.

*Both are considered to be among the top lead players in history. And yes, that is correct. However, they are also two of the top *rhythm* players in history as well. I've read countless interviews they did throughout their career and found that both these men consistently stressed the fact that rhythm, *not* leads, is perhaps the single most important aspect of guitar playing.

*Both were considered the fastest player when they hit the scene. A lot has been made about Edward's blazing speed and the fact that he was even faster than Jimi. And yes, he was faster and more fluid. However, that in no way, shape, or form diminishes the fact that when Jimi burst onto the scene in 1967, he was indeed the "fastest gun."

For example, one of Jimi's heroes and influences was the late, great Albert King. They eventually got to meet, hang out, and even watch each other perform. During an interview with *Guitar World* magazine in July of 1991, Albert had this to say concerning Jimi's speed, "…Jimi was a hell of a guitar player, the fastest dude around—at the time." So anyone who believes Jimi wasn't fast, um, go back and listen to the music, please. Not just his studio albums, go check out his live recordings, too. For example, check out the track "Woodstock Improvisation" off the Jimi Hendrix *Woodstock* album. Then come back and tell me homeboy wasn't ripping, ok?

*Both were considered the "heaviest" cats during their respective eras. Many considered Jimi to be "proto-metal" due to songs like "Foxey Lady" and "Purple Haze." Many considered Edward to be "metal" due to songs like "On Fire," "Runnin' with the Devil," "Light Up the Sky" and, of course, "Eruption."

So while some might chuckle at the idea anyone would ever consider the music and playing of these two as "metal," the fact is back in their time they were indeed the heaviest cats out there, period. Hence, they were often labeled as "metal or "proto-metal." The same thing happened to many other greats like Led Zeppelin, Black Sabbath, AC/DC, and Deep Purple, too. In the end, it makes sense cuz the fact is, most great metal bands/guitar players were influenced by all the people I just mentioned.

*Both achieved a lifetime's worth of success by their mid-twenties. For example, in Jimi's brief four-year career, he released three studio albums: *Are You Experienced* (1967), *Axis: Bold As Love* (1967), and *Electric Ladyland* (1968). Actually, you could say he recorded four albums worth of studio material, cuz *Electric Ladyland* was a double album. Sadly, these would be the only studio albums Jimi ever recorded. The total number of songs on these albums was forty.

Well, if Edward's career had been four years, here's what his legacy would have been: *Van Halen* (1978), *Van Halen II* (1979), *Women and Children First* (1980), and *Fair Warning* (1981). Not bad, huh? Mind you, *Fair Warning* was released just two months after Edward Van Halen's twenty-sixth birthday. Oh, and guess what the total number of songs on these albums is? Forty, baby. So both Edward and Jimi had released precisely four albums worth of studio material (with a total of forty songs) during their first four years in office. Not a bad first term at all.

*Both built their own studios. Jimi had his Electric Ladyland Studios in New York, while Edward has his 5150 Studio in California. Needless to say, both studios are truly legendary. I simply cannot fathom the number of amazing musicians who have passed through the doors of both those studios. I believe Electric Ladyland is available for use. Meanwhile, 5150 is basically up the road from Edward's house, and therefore it is a private studio.

*While both are "giants" in the world of music and guitar, neither one of 'em paints a truly imposing figure. Jimi was about five feet eleven, while Edward is about five feet eight. Fact is, many of the greats were pretty wiry dudes. For example, Randy Rhoads and Kurt Cobain were five feet seven... while Angus Young is even shorter than that. And I think it's safe to say *none* of these cats woulda been tested for steroids, ok? Man, Zakk Wylde's right arm probably weighs more than Jimi and Edward, *combined!* On the other hand (no pun intended) both Jimi and Edward had huge paws. You know, really big and powerful hands (easy ladies...*easy*).

For example, on the high E string, Edward can reach from the fifth fret to the twelfth. And from the twelfth fret, he can hit any note on the fingerboard above.

*Both were masters of sound. Their music was about *sound*, not necessarily notes. Better yet, what was *between* the notes. They also knew how to use effects very tastefully. Frankly, Edward didn't even use many effects. Meanwhile, Jimi had an arsenal of effects, but for the most part was able to control 'em and use 'em quite well.

*Both became rock stars and incredibly famous, but neither one ever really cared for the spotlight. Well, not in that way, anyway. Fact is, both were soft-spoken, even shy individuals who were never truly comfortable with all the attention they got. Basically, they preferred to let their music and playing do the talking.

*Both lived wild lifestyles. Edward has somehow managed to keep himself together throughout the course of a twenty-seven-year career and survive all the excesses that come with super fame, being a rock star, and all that business. You know, all the typical *VH1 Behind the Music* stuff. Aside from Led Zeppelin, a Van Halen *Behind the Music* would put most others to shame. Sadly, Jimi was not as fortunate. He died just two months shy of his twenty-eighth birthday on September 18, 1970. His career was just four years. Then again, Jimi did more in four years than most could do in four lifetimes.

*Both have gone on to impact, influence, and inspire most of the major players to come down the pike since their respective debuts. Even wilder is the fact that they managed to impact, influence, and inspire just about every major player on the scene *before* them as well. Hands down, they are two of the most important and influential musicians in history – *especially* in the world of "shred guitar."

While most people are aware of Edward's impact on shred, the fact is Jimi impacted and influenced shredders as well. Hell, most of the great shredders, from Steve Vai to Joe Satriani, are *huge* Hendrix fans and grew up cutting their teeth on his records. I mean, even Yngwie J. Malmsteen himself has always stated that Jimi Hendrix is the reason he picked up a guitar! So in the end, there is no doubt that EVH and JH inspired and influenced the shred world, big time.

Not so different, are they? For my money, they're the same. Yeah, I know, some of you want a definitive answer. Well, that's about as good an answer as I can come up with. It's just the nature of the beast, man. Jimi blew up the spot in 1967 and took things further than anyone ever had. Edward blew up the spot in 1978 and did the exact same thing. It's evolution, man. Like going from version 1.0 to version 5.0 to version 9.0, you know? We see it in everything from music to sports. For example, Gordie Howe was the greatest hockey player ever...till Wayne Gretzky came along. Sure, Gordie is still a legend and, yes, he paved the way for Wayne. However, if you were starting a hockey team tomorrow and you could pick any player in history, um, who would your first pick be? (And we can't forget Super Mario, either!)

Look at the world of golf as well. Once upon a time, Ben Hogan ruled all...till Jack Nicklaus showed up. Since then, it appears that Jack Nicklaus has ruled all. However, in the late 1990s, a kid named "Tiger" showed up on the scene. Man, before it's all said and done, Tiger Woods might just own 'em all. Hell, he's already in their ranks as we speak. If Tiger retired right now, he's already among the all-time greats. Or, look at track and field. For ages, the great Jesse Owens was *"the man."* Then, one day, a kid named Carl Lewis showed up. The rest, as they say, is history. Shit, back in the mid-'70s, Tony Alva was considered the greatest skateboarder in the world. Well, by the late '70s a kid named Tony Hawk showed up.

Look at the world of cycling, too. In the '80s, Greg LeMond was *"the man."* In 1986, he became the first American to win the Tour de France. He also won the Tour in 1989 and 1990, back-to-back, baby. Overall, he is a three-time Tour de France champion. Well, by the start of the millennium, a cat named Lance showed up. A record seven consecutive Tour de France titles later, Lance Armstrong is now *"the man."*

Hell, the same thing goes for the world of basketball, too. In fact, during the foreword to this book, Brian May likened Edward Van Halen to Michael Jordan. Man, that's a great analogy, cuz I've always felt Edward was the MJ of the electric guitar. For my money, that would make Jimi Hendrix the Julius Erving of the electric guitar. Simply put, we wouldn't have Michael Jordan without Julius Erving. That is a stone-cold fact. Dr. J blew up the spot in the '70s. He paved the road for Michael Jordan and everyone else, for that matter. Man, Julius Erving truly innovated the game of basketball when he hit the scene. Between a handful of seasons in the ABA and eleven seasons in the NBA, he became *"the man."*

I also believe he was the first player to truly defy gravity on the big stage. Yes, the Dr. turned dunking and other aerial feats into an art form. Hell, he could make a simple layup look like poetry in motion. He did things with a basketball that *no one* could ever imagine. Basically, the world had *never* seen anything like Dr. J. He truly elevated and transcended the game of basketball in a way no other player had ever come close to. Up until that point, he was *"the shit."*

Then along came Michael. Fact is, Michael Jordan soared to dizzying heights that no other player – including the legendary Dr. J. – has ever come close to. By the time he retired, MJ had a higher p.p.g. average (the highest of all time, actually), scored more points throughout his entire career, won more MVP awards, and won more championships than Dr. J. (And remember that MJ retired for a year or two during his prime, ok?)

Basically, MJ took what the Dr. did and reinvented it on an even larger scale. Simply put, MJ transcended the game in a way no other player ever has, before or since. That ain't a matter of opinion, it's a matter of fact. Not to mention his impact off the court as well. One word, baby: Nike. Hell,

anything MJ touched turned to gold! On the court and off, he was *"the shit."*
So if you started a basketball team tomorrow and could pick any player in
history, um, who would your first pick be? Regardless, that does not in any
way, shape, or form diminish what Dr. J achieved. Dr. J is still the greatest
player of his era, which in turn makes him one of the greatest of all time. He
is a Hall of Famer, an ambassador of the game, and a legend, period. Besides,
we can go back even further and look up all the greats who paved the way for
Julius Erving! Lord knows plenty of great players paved the road for Dr. J,
MJ, and everyone else. But in the end, I think it's safe to say most people in
this world consider Michael Jordan to be the greatest player of all time. Many
of the greatest players ever will agree.

Well, that's *precisely* how I view Edward and Jimi. Yes, Jimi Hendrix
reinvented the guitar. In the world of rock, he was the first to do it, God bless
him. The guy was a total bad-assed motherfucker! Still is, in my book. But
then Edward came along and reinvented it again. In the process, I honestly
believe Edward Van Halen transcended the instrument in a way that no
other player has ever come close to since – and that includes every style of
music, not just rock.

I mean, it ain't even about better or worse. Both these guys are monsters!
It's really about takin' it to the next level, that's all. And Edward *definitely*
took the instrument to the next level. Hell, some would say he took it up a
couple of levels. Not to mention the fact that Van Halen, especially during
their classic era, experienced a level of popularity and commercial success
the likes of which no American hard rock/metal band and guitarist had ever
come close to. Regardless, Jimi is still Jimi. In no way does that diminish
who he is and what he did. As Zakk Wylde told me, "Jimi is the chosen son
of the electric guitar. You know, he's the Babe Ruth of guitar. And no matter
who hits more home runs, whether in a single season or during an entire
career, the Babe will always be…the Babe!"

I have to agree with that statement 100 percent. But I must add that is
precisely what makes Edward Van Halen's achievements in the world of rock
music and electric guitar even more astonishing. You have to understand
that after Jimi blew up the spot in 1967, *no one* believed we'd ever see the
likes of that again. I think most people believed it would be 100 years before
anyone ever came close to what Jimi Hendrix did on or for the instrument.
His achievements and impact were *that devastating,* ok? So when Jimi died
in the fall of 1970, I don't think anyone could have imagined that just eight
short years later, some baby-faced Dutch kid from Pasadena would release an
album that sent everyone back to the woodshed. It just wasn't supposed to
happen. No way. Not in a million years. How could this be?

What's even sicker is that Edward managed to do this without ripping Jimi off. Edward somehow rewrote the rules of the electric guitar and did everything in his own unique way, without being any kind of a Hendrix clone. Edward had everything from his own unique style to his own unique guitars to his own unique stage presence. Man, Jimi Hendrix is about as tough an act to follow as you're ever gonna get, but somehow Edward Van Halen managed to find a way to do it. And it's not just cuz of Jimi's monster talent, ok? It's just, damn, how do you compete with a ghost? Not that music is a competition, you know, I'm just saying.

However, for all their similarities, there are a few differences – sadly, none of which has a damn thing to do with music – that totally affect how Edward and Jimi's respective legacies are perceived. Never has this been more apparent than in *Rolling Stone*'s "Top 100 Guitarists of All Time" issue (October 2003). Apparently, they feel Jimi Hendrix is the greatest guitar player of all time. Hey, that doesn't upset me, at all. You can make a great case for Jimi being the greatest, so I have no problem with Jimi appearing on the cover and being ranked number 1. However, they ranked Edward Van Halen number 70. No, that's *not* a typo. You heard right, *number seventy,* baby.

Basically, *Rolling Stone* believes that Edward belongs a full sixty-nine spots behind the only other guitarist in rock history to do the same exact thing he did. Oh, and you don't even wanna hear some of the names that occupied those sixty-nine spots between Jimi and Edward. I mean, with all due respect, some of 'em couldn't even tune Edward's guitar, ok? Hell, the fact that some of 'em were anywhere near Jimi freaks me out as well. Mind you, I'm actually a fan of many of those players, but frankly, I can't even fathom them being anywhere near JH or EVH. Not to mention all the phenomenal players, from Django and Vai to Di Meola, who were left off the list!

Overall, this issue caused a major uproar among fans *and* musicians worldwide. And it really wasn't even the fact that Jimi was number 1. Sure, some people will disagree with that. You know, plenty of people will name everyone from Edward to Jimmy Page as number 1. Ultimately, I don't believe Jimi being ranked number 1 was the reason this issue caused such a ruckus. No, it was all the great players left off the list, combined with the fact that Edward Van Halen wasn't, at the *very least*, riding shotgun to Jimi at the number 2 spot that basically made tons of people go ballistic. In fact, everyone from Jason Becker to Zakk Wylde came to the defense of EVH. Man, I think poor Zakk had to be sedated after reading that issue. I'm not kidding, either. Shortly after that issue hit the stands, Zakk Wylde did an interview with the good folks over at *sleazegringer.com* where, among other things, he expressed his desire to pay a visit to the offices of *Rolling Stone* by proclaiming: "I'd just like to go down to the building and burn it down, you know what I mean? Just for shits and giggles."

So how in the world could something like this happen, you ask? Man, especially here at home, in an American publication? Well, as I just mentioned, there are a few differences – sadly none of which has a damn thing to do with music – that totally affect how the legacies of these two legendary musicians are viewed – *especially* by many members of the music press.

For starters, Jimi Hendrix died young and in his prime. Let's face it, the sad fact is that our society loves for 'em to live fast, die young, and leave a good-lookin' corpse. As the great Neil Young once sang, "It's better to burn out than fade away." But at least Jimi was already a legend *before* he died, ok? You know, he was not one of these average musicians who suddenly became a "genius" and a "legend" *after* they got mauled by a pack of rabid weasels. However, his tragic death most certainly turned him into a deity. It's happened to everyone from Robert Johnson to Elvis Presley. While they are all fantastic, legendary, and important musicians, no doubt their passing on at an early age turned them all into deities.

Along with this comes the obvious fact that Jimi Hendrix never got old. Therefore, he never had to deal with changing musical climates and trends the way Edward has had to do over the course of a twenty-seven-year career. Man, it just ain't easy being a "living legend," you know? That's probably the single hardest thing to do. You know, cuz people are constantly asking, "What have you done lately?" That's the whole game, right there. It's always "What have you done lately?" Obviously, Jimi Hendrix is exempt from that cuz he passed away thirty-five years ago. Meanwhile, Edward Van Halen has had to deal with that day in and day out, year in and year out, since 1978.

Oh, how I love it when people question what Edward has done lately. I like to believe that he's probably chillin' at 5150, polishing his crown and keeping the throne warm for the next guy to hit the scene and transcend the game. Problem is, he's been polishing that crown and keepin' that throne warm for over twenty-seven summers now, ya know? Man, when's the next kid gonna show up on rock's doorstep, guitar in hand and shit-eatin' grin across his face, ready to blow up the spot and send everyone back to the woodshed? Dude, we're waitin on ya!

Man, I just think people forget the insane pressure that comes with being in the position Edward's been in for so long now. Hey, I'm certainly not playin' the violin for *anyone* here, ok? I'm simply saying that this man has an incredible reputation to live up to, and that simply cannot be easy on anyone regardless of all the money, fame, and ass he's gotten over the last twenty-seven years. I mean, damn, how on Earth do you live up to that reputation? It's un-fuckin-real, man.

Another interesting fact is that the majority of Jimi's album sales came *after* he died. In fact, it was me and *my* generation – not his – that made Jimi Hendrix a Platinum and multi-Platinum artist. Which makes me wonder if the folks back in the '60s ever truly appreciated this man's genius and music? Did they truly appreciate his musicianship, or were they just there for the spectacle of it all? Sadly, it appears that Jimi sometimes believed it was for the latter.

For example, I've read Jimi Hendrix's final interview. It was conducted by journalist Keith Altham on September 11, 1970, just seven days before Jimi died. Well, during this interview, you can totally tell this was a man frustrated over the fact that he believed many people were showing up solely to see him hump his guitar, play with his teeth, smash his guitar, burn his guitar, and so forth, instead of for the music. In other words, Jimi Hendrix believed many people were coming to *see* him, not to *hear* him (If Jimi were alive today he would absolutely *cringe* at the current state of music, cuz it's almost completely image-driven).

Personally, I don't believe Jimi ever really needed any of that gimmicky, flashy stuff. I'm not talking about all the movin' around and energy he displayed on stage, cuz that was awesome. I'm talkin' about the guitar burning, guitar humping, playing with the teeth, and all that business. It was fun, but I sometimes feel all that overshadows his musicianship. For example, whenever I talk to people about Hendrix, I notice that, quite often, the first thing that tumbles outta their mouth is the fact that Jimi burned his guitar or played with his teeth. Man, it makes me wanna dropkick 'em. This guy was a serious musician and a true visionary. Sadly, many people just remember him for being "the crazy guy who burned his guitar and played with his teeth." It's tragic, really. That's not cool, at all.

Hell, on top of that, you now see people lightin' their guitar on fire in stupid beer commercials. Frankly, I don't think Jimi *ever* could have imagined corporate America co-opting his guitar burning schtick to sell beer some thirty-five years after he passed. (The funny thing is, in that very same commercial, the guitar player actually employs some of Edward's two-hand tapping style, too!) So, in all honesty, I never much cared for all that kinda stuff. In the end, gimme "Machine Gun" (*Band Of Gypsys,* Capitol, 1970). This song is basically Jimi, standing still in one spot on stage, unleashing some of the sickest and most insane guitar playing ever laid to tape.

On the other hand, look at all the hype that's come with Jimi's Woodstock appearance. In my opinion, "Machine Gun" kicks the livin' shit outta *anything* he ever played at Woodstock. Hell, I own plenty of bootlegs where his playing is far above what he unleashed at Woodstock. Although the concert was obviously historic, the set certainly did have its moments and, of course, his "Star-Spangled Banner" was a monster statement. What's really trippy is that most of the crowd had left by the time Jimi played! I mean, what the hell? From over a half million people who attended Woodstock, I believe there were about fifty thousand people scattered around the grounds on the morning Jimi closed the festival. Man, who the hell leaves before Jimi plays? I don't care what the conditions were, man. I woulda given my left nut to see that dude play and it boggles my mind to think anyone would leave before Jimi took the stage!

Regardless, the fact is that Jimi Hendrix became *waaay* bigger by dying. If he were alive today, I honestly don't know if he'd be half as big. His passing on at an early age basically froze him in time, keeping Jimi in his prime, forever. I believe the modern-day equivalent of that is the late, great rapper, Tupac Shakur. While he was alive, 2 Pac released four studio albums that produced combined sales of over 8 million copies in America. Pretty damn good. However, guess how many he sold *after* he died? Over 25 million, baby. No bullshit. After 2 Pac died on September 13, 1996, his seven studio albums that were released posthumously sold a combined total of over 21 million copies. Along with the fact that an album he released just a few months before he died, *All Eyez on Me,* sold another 4 million copies after he passed, too. Put it all together and you've got over 25 million copies sold here in America after he passed. Unbelievable. The poor guy wasn't able to even enjoy that success. Hopefully, his family has.

Man, the sad fact is that for both 2 Pac and Jimi, dying – *especially* dying young and under tragic circumstances – was actually the best career move they ever made. Hell, look how many movies and books have already been made about Jimi and Pac (You don't see any movies about Edward's life, do you? And his life reads like the American Dream!). What's even wilder is the fact that both these men have somehow managed to release more albums *after* dying? For example, Jimi Hendrix recorded three studio albums and one live album before he passed. Basically, he gave us four classic albums during his all-too-brief four-year career. Guess how many albums have been released *after* Jimi died? Hundreds. Since he died on September 18, 1970, Jimi Hendrix has somehow managed to release hundreds of albums. Tragically, this man's brilliant legacy has been dirtied and diluted by the release of hundreds of albums, many of which are straight garbage. You know, a lot of compilations and sub-par live performances. Hell, soon they'll be releasing albums of Jimi tuning his guitar and changing the battery in his wah pedal.

On top of that, you can now purchase everything from Jimi Hendrix incense and coffee mugs to Jimi Hendrix boxer shorts. Gee, I can't wait for the Jimi Hendrix condom to hit stores. Thanks to Cynthia "Plaster Caster," we know it'll make the Trojan Magnum look like a freakin' pinky warmer. All kidding aside, that sucks. Edward experienced a bit of that as well, but nowhere near the insane level Jimi has. It's just sad to see a musical genius turned into a product.

So while his early passing led to immediate sainthood, everything from boxer shorts to coffee mugs, and countless Platinum and multi-Platinum albums, in my opinion, it may have also led to Jimi becoming the cliché answer to the question "Who is the greatest guitar player of all time?" Sadly, many people today will simply recite his name, maybe even buy the T-shirt, without owning a single album or being able to name you a single song other than maybe "Purple Haze" or "Foxey Lady." I mean, if every single person who said Jimi was the greatest would *actually own* at least one Jimi album, well, he'd easily be the highest selling artist of all- time. Tragically, that is not the case. Man, I often wonder if some people just say Jimi Hendrix is the greatest guitar player ever cuz, well, that's what they believe you are *supposed* to say. It would be tragic if this man became the cliché answer to a freakin' question, cuz there was absolutely *nothing* cliché about Jimi, at all. Apparently, if you don't say Jimi is the greatest, well, you have committed total and complete *blasphemy*. In turn, you should be doused with holy water and immediately deported. Damn, and I thought we had freedom of speech in this country!

Hey, I am not saying anything against Jimi Hendrix. I love and respect Jimi Hendrix. Hell, we're talking about him in the middle of a freakin' Van Halen book, you know? Nah, I'm strictly talking about our society and all the lemmings out there that mindlessly recite Jimi's name without knowing a damn thing about the man and his legacy. Meanwhile, many people seem to view Edward's legacy much differently than Jimi's, despite the fact that they both basically accomplished the same damn thing.

For example, when Edward hit the scene in 1978, he exploded the boundaries of the electric guitar. Like Jimi, Edward did things on the instrument and drew sounds from the instrument most people had never heard and, frankly, didn't even know were possible. Basically, he reinvented it. And while the entire first Van Halen album is groundbreaking, well, "Eruption" *alone* is, technically speaking, way beyond *anything* that anyone had ever freakin' heard in the world of rock and on the electric guitar up until that point. Simply put, *no one* had ever done that on a guitar until Edward did it. People thought Jimi Hendrix had maxed the electric guitar out. Well, Edward Van Halen proved 'em wrong.

Up until 1978, the term "electric guitar" meant Jimi Hendrix. They were one and the same, period. But after Edward hit the scene, the term "electric guitar" meant Edward Van Halen. And that's not a matter of opinion, that's a stone-cold fact. Edward wasn't the best in the game. No, he *was* the game, just as Jimi had been in the late '60s. And since 1978, Edward's been spilling his guts on stages across the world for twenty-seven years, all the while battling constantly changing musical climates and trends. Not to mention the toll of life on the road, inner band turmoil, personal issues, and so forth. Frankly, I'm amazed that *anyone* could survive that long, really.

The amount of time Edward has spent in the bright light of the music biz is almost seven times longer than the amount of time Jimi spent in the bright light. There's a classic saying, "Heavy is the head that wears the crown." Well, Jimi Hendrix wore that crown for four years. Meanwhile, Edward Van Halen has worn that crown for twenty-seven years. Man, if Edward was president, he'd be reaching the end of his seventh freakin' term (mind you, you're only supposed to get two terms, max). However, it always appears that "what could have been?" seems to win out over "what *has* been" – *especially* to many in the music press. Man, when you start dealing in those terms, well, it's a slippery slope, indeed.

Now, had he lived, perhaps Jimi Hendrix *may* have gone on to do some of these things. Then again, had he lived, maybe Jimi would have dropped out of the music biz entirely by the early 1970s! Before he passed, this was a man who had quickly grown sick of it all. The pressures and demands of the music biz ate at this man's soul. These are the same crummy pressures and demands that have eaten at Edward's soul for twenty-seven years now. So when people speculate that nowadays Jimi would be "ruling the world" or whatever, I simply laugh at them. Personally, I like to believe Jimi woulda gotten the hell outta the music biz entirely. You know, on the "corporate" side of things, anyway. He already had his own studio, Electric Ladyland, and I like to believe he eventually would have started up his *own* record label, like, an indie label. How freakin' cool would that have been? You know, so he could release all of his music whenever he damn well pleased, much like the late, great Frank Zappa did.

Perhaps nowadays, Jimi Hendrix would be living in London, playing clubs, and maybe even releasing some of his music online. And instead of playing a Strat through a Marshall, maybe he'd be playing an Ibanez through a Budda? Who knows, right? It's so tragic, really. And I know that it's human nature to focus on "what could have been?" instead of on "what *has* been." So while both Edward and Jimi reinvented the electric guitar and changed the face of rock when they hit the scene, the fact that Edward's life has been about twice as long as Jimi's has obviously enabled him to build up quite an impressive resumé. But hey, should we punish the dude for that? Sometimes I feel like Edward needs to apologize for living past the age of twenty-seven?

Not to mention the sad reality that many people, for whatever reason, view Van Halen as an "'80s band." Never mind the fact that they formed and debuted in the '70s and enjoyed major success through several different decades. And I think we know how many people – *especially* those in the music press – view the '80s. Basically, it's been written off as a sorry, useless decade of music. This is totally and completely unfair, especially when you consider all the great bands and guitarists who hit the scene during that time. Meanwhile, the '60s is presented as the greatest musical decade, ever. Flat out, we are constantly sold on the fact that decade (and it was a phenomenal decade, *especially* for rock music) is *"the shit."* Basically, we've been taught that anyone who didn't get to experience the '60s should apologize for having been born too late.

In a perfect world, none of this would really matter, cuz the indisputable fact is that Edward and Jimi basically accomplished the same damn thing. You know, as far as reinventing the instrument and changing the face of rock music when they hit the scene. They both transcended the instrument, as the great Pat Metheny said. However, when you check Edward's resumé, well, I simply can't think of too many people who can compete with that, period. Then again, it's never been about who's better or anything like that. Music is *not* a competition. Fact is, these two cats mastered the instrument in a way that few human beings will ever comprehend.

I mean, surely both Edward and Jimi surpassed what Chuck Berry could ever do on the instrument, you know? But that doesn't diminish who Chuck Berry is and what he accomplished. His legacy is intact. Regardless how many great players take the instrument further, Chuck will always and forever be the "godfather of rock guitar," period. God bless him. Just because Edward Van Halen took guitar to the next level does not in any way diminish or dwarf Jimi's accomplishments. That's just life, baby. Again, it's a natural evolution that you see in everything from music to sports. For example, a lot of people today claim that Jimi Hendrix is still "the best." They will sit there and wholeheartedly tell you that to this very day *no one* comes close to Hendrix. And yes, even by today's standards Jimi would still be pretty damn amazing. But in all honesty, a whole lot has happened in the world of guitar since he passed. To say Jimi Hendrix is still "the best," technically speaking, is like basically saying the guitar has not advanced a single inch over the last thirty-five years! Seriously, can anyone look me in the eye and tell me the guitar has not advanced a single inch since Jimi Hendrix passed away almost thirty-five years ago? That would be a truly ridiculous statement. The guitar has advanced by leaps and bounds over the years, baby. In terms of chops and overall technical ability, yes, people have surpassed Jimi Hendrix.

In fact, the same thing goes for Van Halen, too. I can't look you in the eye and say, "Yes, Edward Van Halen is still the best guitar player alive. No one can touch him. Yeah, no one even comes close, even to this day!" Man, I'd be lying out my ass if I said that. Sure, no one has come close in terms of reinventing the instrument, changing the face of rock, and transcending the game. But in terms of chops and overall technical ability, yes, there are people who've pushed the instrument further. So I can't sit here and tell you that Edward is still, technically speaking, the best. Basically, that would be like saying the instrument has not advanced a single inch since 1978!

Yes, Edward is still a total bad-assed motherfucker and he is still better than most. Hey, once a virtuoso, *always* a virtuoso. But the fact is there are players who have come down the pike since Edward hit the scene who have continued to push the envelope and managed to come up with some absolutely brilliant shit on the guitar. It's all about evolution. That's life, baby.

I mean, hello, have you heard people like Steve Vai, Joe Satriani, Yngwie J. Malmsteen, Jason Becker, Shawn Lane, and Buckethead? Man, those guys are absolutely phenomenal! Once again, we must also mention Metallica's Hetfield and Hammett, along with Children of Bodom's Alexi Laiho, too. Oh, and of course, Zakk and Dime should *always* be mentioned. And you know what? Dream Theater's John Petrucci should *definitely* be mentioned with all these cats as well. That dude is freakin' sick. Period. Oh, and as long as Allan Holdsworth is still breathing, well, pretty much every freakin' guitarist on the planet is still havin' conniption fits.

Wow, what a shocker, huh? You know, to actually admit there have been guitarists who've come down the pike *after* Edward and continued pushing the envelope? Um, yeah!

What, just cuz this is a Van Halen book, I guess I'm supposed to sit here and tell everybody that the guitar begins and ends with EVH? Man, please. All those cats deserve credit, dammit. I mean, if I didn't give 'em credit, I'd be no better than the people who keep insisting the guitar has not advanced an inch since Jimi passed away. So all those cats, and many more, deserve credit. No doubt about it. Hell, I could sit here and tell you how everyone from Tom Morello to The Edge kicks some serious ass, too. Man, I could go on forever.

However, I'm smart enough to know it all comes down to each and every single person's respective opinion. Lord knows that many fans of music and guitar are downright militant about who they believe to be "the greatest." Twenty bucks says that right now, someone is probably reading this going, "You asshole, the greatest guitar player of all time is Stevie Ray Vaughan!" Hey, if that's who *you* believe it to be, so be it. You picked a great one! Man,

I could *never* hate on someone for proclaiming the late, great Stevie Ray Vaughan "the greatest." Rave on Ray Vaughan, baby!

Regardless who you like better or who you believe to be "the greatest," the fact is both Edward and Jimi changed the face of rock music and reinvented the instrument. It always comes down to the simple fact that Jimi Hendrix and Edward Van Halen are the only two rock guitarists in history to ever do that. It's indisputable. Basically, they are the same player. Different eras, but they accomplished the same damn thing went they hit the scene. To me, they are they "dynamic duo" of rock guitar, and should be joined at the hip, forever. You know, it's like there's this *very* exclusive club – and they are the only two members of that club. Basically, if you held a convention of the greatest guitar players of all time, walked up on stage, stepped up to the podium and stated, "Will all the players in the history of rock music who've reinvented the electric guitar please step forward," well, only two dudes could stand up and take the stage: Jimi and Edward. Meanwhile, everyone else would just basically have to sit there and clap.

So in the end, of course, all of this begs the following question: Why did *Rolling Stone* rank Jimi Hendrix number 1 while ranking Edward Van Halen number 70, hmmm? Yes, that's the $64,000 question, right there. Anyone? Ola? Bueller? Hellooo? Frankly, I can't believe anyone is *that* uninformed, so obviously there were other factors and motives at play. There is simply no logical reason for that, you know? As I stated earlier, I have absolutely no problem with Jimi being ranked number 1. Like many people, I've become quite used to that. Sadly, almost comfortably numb to that. Jimi Hendrix is the expected, safe choice, really. What trips me out is the fact that Edward was cast down towards the bottom third of that list, a full sixty-nine spots behind Jimi. Gimme a break, man. To me, that would be like Wayne Gretzky passing Gordie Howe to become the all-time scoring leader, only to then be ranked number 70 on the all-time scoring list. Man, would that make any freakin' sense to you?

To be perfectly honest, I don't even believe in ranking guitar players. There are too many great players, too many different styles. And I certainly don't need some magazine to tell me that Jimi, Edward or anyone else is "great," for that matter. However, if you're gonna do it, then *please* do it right. I mean, it's not rocket science, ok? Far as rock goes, Jimi was the greatest of *his* generation, and Edward was the greatest of *his* generation. Folks, is that so damn hard to comprehend? Basically, each man has been given ownership of an entire decade. In Jimi's case, his work during 1967, 1968, and 1969 was enough to make him the top dog of the 1960s.

Meanwhile, Edward's work from 1978 on the through the entire following decade was enough to make him the top dog of the 1980s. Hell, *Van Halen* or *1984* alone pretty much guaranteed his ownership of the '80s, you know? In fact, *Guitar World* magazine named Edward "Player of the Decade" for the 1980s in their February 1990 issue. So each of these bad-asses was the greatest of his respective generation/era. In turn, this earns both of 'em a seat at the table, so to speak, among the all-time greats.

Again, they are the only two men in the history of rock to reinvent the guitar and change the face of rock, period. Basically, as far as rock music goes, you have the first king, which is Chuck Berry. Then you have the second king, which is Jimi. And then you have the last heir to the throne, Edward, who became King III. While many great players are "rock royalty," for my money, these are the three kings of rock guitar. Just try to imagine the world of rock guitar without Chuck, Jimi, and Edward. And if you're lookin' to choose between Jimi and Edward, hell, flip a coin. Either way, you come up a winner, cuz they are both kings.

I mean, choosing between Jimi and Edward is like chosing between Jessica Alba and Eva Longoria. You know, cuz at the end of the day, shit, both of those women are *smokin'*. The point being, of course, that you really can't go wrong either way! Feel me?

The funny thing – or sad thing, depending on how you look at it – is that we're all still waiting for King IV. Man, to this day *no one* has matched Edward, you know? Again, not talking chops here, but rather overall impact, influence, and reinventing the guitar. Fact is, there is yet to be a rock guitarist – since Edward hit the scene in February 1978 – to transcend the game the way he did. For my money, Edward Van Halen is *"the one,"* like Neo in *The Matrix*.

Actually, you could say he is very much like Katsumoto. You know, the great Ken Watanabe's character in the amazing Tom Cruise flick, *The Last Samurai*. Cuz Edward really is the last one of his kind. He is *"it."* In the entire history of rock guitar, only two men have reinvented the instrument. One tragically passed away thirty-five years ago. The other one is Edward.

Basically, Edward Van Halen is the only living rock guitarist to have ever reinvented the instrument. Period. In other words, *respect* and *recognize* who and what he is. Cuz when that man leaves this world, *"it"* leaves with him. And there will *never* be another.

Man, that's the best, most honest answer I can give, cuz frankly, I have yet to discover any kind of formula for determining who is the single greatest of all time. For example, over the years, I've actually heard many people say Jimi Hendrix should always be number 1 simply due to the fact that he was first. In my opinion, that doesn't do the man justice. Nor does it make much sense. There has to be more to it than the simple fact he came first. For example, apply that line of thinking to other fields. So Dr. J should always rank higher than Michael Jordan cuz he came first? And Gordie Howe should always rank higher than Wayne Gretsky cuz he came first? And Ben Hogan should always rank higher than Jack Nicklaus cuz he came first? Hell, if we're gonna think like that, then the Ford Model T should always rank higher than the Ferrari Maranello cuz it came first. I guess Atari should always rank higher than the Sony Playstation and X-Box cuz it came first. And the VCR should always rank higher than the DVD player cuz it came first.

All kidding aside, that's a pretty childish attitude to have, you know? I'd like to believe that most human beings are capable of expressing a much more heartfelt, intelligent, in-depth explanation as to why they believe Jimi Hendrix should rank as the number 1 guitar player of all time, other than, "Well, uh, Jimi came first." Man, that's pretty pathetic. Jimi deserves better. Besides, by that line of thinking, well, Chuck Berry should rank higher than Jimi, cuz the fact of the matter is that Chuck came first. Hell, Chuck paved the road for Jimi, Edward, and everyone else!

You know, by that line of thinking, Eric Clapton, Jeff Beck, Buddy Guy, Pete Townshend, Albert King, and many others would have to rank higher than Jimi, too, cuz they came first and paved the road for Jimi. Hell, if not for Clapton, would Jimi even have a career? Remember, besides the fact that Cream served as a major influence, inspiration, and blueprint for Jimi's own band, the Experience, well, the only reason Jimi even agreed to hook up with Chas Chandler and go to London was *after* Chas promised him that upon their arrival in London, he would introduce him to Eric Clapton. In the end, by that line of thinking, Chuck Berry should rank higher than *everyone,* cuz he paved the way for all and invented rock guitar, period.

Who knows, perhaps one day someone can figure out and explain why Edward Van Halen was ranked sixty-nine spots behind the only other guitar player in rock history to accomplish the same exact thing he did? Till then, I'll just kick back and enjoy the music of both these cats. Cuz in the end, the greatest guitar player (or players) of all time is whoever the hell *you* believe it is, *not* who some magazine tells you it is… which is really the point of this entire chapter. There are so many great guitar players out there from many different worlds of music. Look at all the great players I mentioned during this chapter alone!

So I'll say it again. In the end, the greatest guitar player of all time is whoever the hell *you* believe it is. In other words, if you believe that it's Chuck, then it's Chuck. If you believe that it's Jimi, then it's Jimi. If you believe that it's Edward, then it's Edward. If you believe that it's Stevie Ray, then it's Stevie Ray. If you believe that it's Allan Holdsworth, then it's Allan Holdsworth. If you believe that it's Jimmy Page, then it's Jimmy Page. If you believe that it's Steve Vai, then it's Steve Vai, and so forth.

Hey, it's not like the "music police" are gonna come to your home, break down your door, and arrest your ass because you proclaimed Vinnie Vincent the greatest of all time, ok? If you believe the "Egyptian Warrior" rules all, then hey, more power to you. Besides, last time I checked, there wasn't any kinda "Greatest Guitarist of All Time" championship belt or something, you know? You can't just throw all these guys in a ring, UFC style, and have 'em duke it out till there's one clear winner. So in the end, the greatest guitar player of all time is whoever the hell *you* believe it is.

Spandex and the '80s

*"I think Van Halen really defines the '80s and I think they were the greatest thing the '80s made. They were great. I mean, if you listen to those records their **still** great."*

—John Mellencamp

Ah, spandex. Once upon a time rock stars, like professional athletes, martial artists, and superheroes, were actually in good enough shape to wear spandex. In this day and age, you'd probably pay most of today's rock stars *not* to wear spandex. Seriously, if you ever have a really bad hangover and want to induce vomiting, um, just picture many of today's so-called "rock stars" wearing spandex. (Man, somebody get me doctor!)

Anyhow, over the years, many in the press and music critics alike have pointed their bony finger at Van Halen and deemed them the "Godfather of Spandex Rock" or whatever the hell you wanna call it. Fact is they are absolutely 100 percent *wrong*. Frankly, I don't know precisely who invented the whole "spandex rock" thing, but it certainly was *not* Van Halen.

I totally understand that the terms "spandex" and "'80s" go hand in hand. No doubt that spandex was all over the place during that decade. And hey, it's cool. Frankly, I don't have a damn thing against spandex! It's just I'm a stickler for the facts, and I believe credit should be given where it's due. Van Halen was not and never has been a spandex band. If anyone can produce a *single* picture where all four members of Van Halen are posing in spandex, um, I'll owe ya a case of Guinness.

However, I must admit that Diamond Dave was known to rock the spandex from time to time, no doubt about it. I believe during Van Halen's third tour back in 1980, DD broke out the spandex for the very first time. From then on, he would continue to wear spandex during their concerts.

Not all the time, but some of the time. Frankly, it was for mobility more than anything else. I mean, why do you think many athletes use spandex? Hey, running around on stage in a pair of jeans or leather pants is cool. Lord knows Dave did a lot of that, too. But for someone as physical as Diamond Dave, well, spandex was the perfect complement. After all, this was a guy who was in perpetual motion, on stage, for two hours a night, complete with flying leaps off the drum riser and all! Try pulling that shit off in a pair of leather pants or jeans, ok?

Hell, Van Halen was a very physical band, period. Lots of energy, baby. Frankly, I'm surprised the rest of the band didn't rock the spandex as well. I guess you could say many people point to Diamond Dave, specifically, as being the "Godfather of Spandex Rock" or whatever. So while Edward, Alex, and Mike were pretty much "spandex-free" throughout their entire career, 'ole Dave was never shy about occasionally putting on a pair of pants so tight they reveal what religion you are (or, depending on the rock star, what brand of sock you're using).

Well, I did my homework and was able to locate some of the earliest cases of spandex or spandex-like material in rock music. Surprisingly, one of the earliest examples came in the form of none other than the great Jimi Hendrix. 'Ole Jimi certainly didn't mind rocking the skin-tight outfits. Hell, Jimi had a wardrobe collection that woulda made Outkast's Andre 3000 jealous!

Honestly, I don't know if some of Jimi's outfits were spandex per se, but they were pretty damn close to it. This was in the mid to late '60s, of course. By the early to mid '70s, everyone from Steven Tyler of Aerosmith and Freddy Mercury of Queen to Big Jim Dandy of Black Oak Arkansas was rocking some kind of spandex or spandex-like outfit. The boys in Kiss definitely had 'em, too. And I believe even the great Mick Jagger rocked the spandex as well.

Eventually, the whole spandex thing would go on to explode in the '80s. Everyone from Axl Rose to Ozzy rocked the spandex at one point or another. But the fact is, the practice of rock stars wearing spandex began way before the '80s. In other words, Van Halen, or I should say specifically David Lee Roth, was *not* the first rock 'n' roller to wear spandex. In the end, Diamond Dave simply may just be the most famous one. Over the years, Dave has often stated that his outfits were a cross between Bruce Lee and Batman. And yes, at times, they very much were!

Frankly, I have never understood why there appear to be so many misconceptions about Van Halen's image, especially during their Classic era. Like, why does the press seem to lump Van Halen in with all those hair bands? Honestly, I have never seen a picture, not a *single* picture that shows all four members of VH posing with big hair. Not once. It appears quite a few people, *especially* in the music press, have deemed VH as the "Godfather of Hair Metal," too. Once again, they are 100 percent *wrong*.

Yes, VH had hair. No different than everyone from the Beatles to Metallica. Yes, they had long hair. No, they most certainly did *not* have huge Aqua-Netted hairdos that threatened the ozone layer. For a reference point, go look up pics of Mötley Crüe or Poison. *That*, my friends, is "big hair." Hey, not that I have a damn thing against any of the "hair bands," ok? The Crüe is cool as shit! But the fact remains that Van Halen was not and never will be a bunch of hair-farmers. Man, if anyone can produce a picture, and I mean a *single picture* of all four members of VH, together, posing with big hair, um, I'll owe ya two cases of Sierra Nevada Pale Ale *and* a bottle of Smoking Loon, ok?

Not to mention the fact that the boys of Van Halen never, and I mean *never* wore makeup. So why some in the press refer to VH as "glammy" or "glam rock" is also beyond me? Sure, Diamond Dave was a colorful character, but never did a single member of VH ever go on stage lookin' like a guy in drag. Not once. Hey, not that I have anything against glam. Hell, some of the greatest bands and artists ever, from Aerosmith and Kiss to the N.Y. Dolls and David Bowie have had their glammy elements, to put it mildly.

I mean, everyone from Guns N' Roses and Mötley Crüe to Poison has always stated how much '70s Aerosmith influenced and inspired them. That's not surprising, really, cuz the boys from Beantown were pretty glammy back in their heyday. After all, Aerosmith hung out with and played shows with the N.Y. Dolls, you know? So Lord Tyler and his crew *definitely* picked up a few pointers from the Dolls.

Anyway, Van Halen simply doesn't fall into that category. Maybe cuz Diamond Dave was colorful, a lot of people assumed the rest of the band looked that way too. You know, since DD was their frontman and all. I dunno, man, but the fact is that Van Halen was *never* glam.

It just appears that so much has been said and written about their image. Unfortunately, most of what's been said and written is by people who can be considered legally "brain dead." Like, for whatever reason, Van Halen also appear to get bunched in with a lot of the acts from the '80s. Although I kinda understand this line of thinking. After all, VH was one of the biggest acts during the '80s. Hell, some would say they flat-out *owned* that decade. Much like how Led Zeppelin owned the '70s and Nirvana appears to have gotten ownership of the '90s. Many in the press often refer to VH as the "ultimate '80s band" or whatever. Hey, that's a wonderful thing, you know? To be crowned *the* band of an entire decade is insane!

Especially a decade like the '80s, cuz that was a *killer* decade of music. Sadly, however, I don't think Van Halen being deemed "band of the '80s" is always meant as a compliment. Unfortunately, the '80s is viewed by many critics as somehow being worse or less important, musically speaking, than just about all the other respective decades. Man, that's such bullshit. Don't believe the press, critics, or even music channels when they tell you that the '80s was basically Flock of Seagulls and Winger, ok?

Yeah, that may have been the '80s for *some* people. However, as a child of the '80s, it appears *my* '80s was a slightly different, much better experience. My '80s was all 'bout Van Halen, Metallica, Guns N' Roses, AC/DC, Megadeth, Slayer, Ozzy w/Randy Rhoads, Ozzy w/Zakk Wylde, U2, the Clash, Prince, the Beastie Boys, Public Enemy, Eric B and Rakim, Run DMC, the Cars, Billy Idol, Mötley Crüe, Skid Row, Anthrax, Stevie Ray Vaughan, Def Leppard, Bad Religion, Black Flag, the Bad Brains, Steve Vai, Cheap Trick, the Police, Art of Noise, John Cougar Mellencamp, Michael Jackson, the Cult, Iron Maiden, the Red Hot Chili Peppers, Faith No More, Pantera, Sonic Youth, Hüsker Dü, the Flaming Lips, My Bloody Valentine, Living Colour, and the Pixies. Well, to name just a few, anyway (Hey, I'm diverse – so sue me).

You know, all the amazing bands that debuted in the '80s, or all the amazing bands that debuted on the cusp of the '80s (VH, the Police, the Clash, and so forth) that rolled right on into the '80s and continued to explode all over the map by releasing tons of killer material during that decade. In fact, many people believe the '80s actually began with Van Halen's 1978 self-titled debut, *Van Halen.* Well, that may just be the case. To this very day, many people out there believe the '80s started with the release of VH's debut album. Hell, I know I'm one of 'em.

Now, in all honesty, I have to admit the '80's was an absolutely horrible time to have grown up. Frankly, I don't know how I survived and managed to come out such a swell guy. Holy shit, could you imagine the horror of having to grow up listening to that lot! Man, especially having to listen to guitar players who could...are you ready for this? Who could *actually play their guitars.* What's even more shocking is the fact that a lot of those guys could actually solo? Mother of all creatures good and sane, why Lord?! It was hard enough to sit through an entire VH or Metallica song, but to have to sit through one their solos, too? Or to have to listen to Stevie Ray single-handedly bring the blues back? It's amazing I didn't end up a mental misfit. Yeah, *none* of that compares to what's out there today.

Ok, so I'm pouring the sarcasm on pretty thick. Screw it, you know? I'm just truly over the fact that the '80s has been relegated to "cheese status" among the masses, especially among many of today's music critics in general.

And to see the mighty Van Halen sometimes named the "head cheese" of the "cheese decade" hurts even more. Fact is that was an incredibly diverse decade of music, and Van Halen was right at the top of it. Again, some would say they owned it.

The '80s gave us everything, baby. I mean, look at all the bands I mentioned earlier. If you break 'em down, you'll see this decade had everything. You want pop? Here's Michael Jackson and Madonna. You want hard rock and metal? Here's VH, Metallica, Iron Maiden, Guns N' Roses, Pantera, Slayer, Megadeth, Ozzy (solo), Mötley Crüe, Def Leppard, Venom, Skid Row, L.A. Guns, and Anthrax. Not to mention AC/DC with the amazing Brian Johnson at the helm, continuing on in the name of Bon. You want hip-hop? Here's Run DMC, Eric B and Rakim, N.W.A., and Public Enemy. You want indrustrial? Here's Ministry and Nine Inch Nails.

Want more? Fine, here ya go. You want punk? Here's the Clash, Bad Religion, Bad Brains, and Black Flag. You want blues? Stevie Ray Vaughan single-handedly brought blues back in the '80s, baby. You want rap-rock? Here's the Red Hot Chili Peppers and the Beastie Boys. You want alternative/indie? Here's the Talking Heads, R.E.M., Hüsker Dü, the Cure, Sonic Youth, My Bloody Valentine, Soundgarden, Jane's Addiction, and the Pixies. Man, and how in the bloody hell do you even begin to label a band as freakin' brilliant as Faith No More? They blazed a path for everything from alternative to rap-rock to you name it! Or, like, U2. How the hell do you label them? Or, like, the Cars? Or Devo? How do you label them?

Oh, and you want killer guitar players? Well, you've come to the right decade, brother!

Here's Edward Van Halen, Randy Rhoads, Zakk Wylde, Dimebag Darrell, Steve Vai, Joe Satriani, Eric Johnson, James Hetfield, Kirk Hammett, Dave Mustaine, Chris Poland, Marty Friedman, Jason Becker, Dave Murray, Adrian Smith, Slash, Izzy Stradlin', Kerry King, Jeff Hanneman, Scott Ian, Dan Spitz, George Lynch, Prince, Stevie Ray Vaughan, Jimmie Vaughan, The Edge, Michael Hedges, Steve Stevens, Yngwie J. Malmsteen, Dr. Know, Vito Bratta, Steve Lynch, Mick Mars, Jennifer Batten, Alex Skolnick, Warren DeMartini, Nuno Bettencourt, Neal Schon, Warren Cuccurullo, George Thorogood, and Dave "Snake" Sabo.

Whew, lemme catch my breath. But wait, we ain't done yet! Here's Andy Summers, Elliot Easton, Jeff Healy, Dave Navarro, Hillel Slovak, John Frusciante, Jim Martin, Steve Lukather, Phil Collen, Steve Clark, Vivian Campbell, Richie Sambora, Brad Gillis, Jeff Watson, Rik Emmett, Michael Fath, Tony Macalpine, Vinnie Moore, John Petrucci, Mark Knopfler, Jake E. Lee, Dweezil Zappa, Michael Angelo Batio, Ty Tabor, Tracii Guns, Paul Gilbert, Jeff Mantas, Kai Hansen, Thurston Moore, Lee Ranaldo, Frank

Black, Robert Smith, Kevin Shields, Bob Mould, Wayne Coyne, J. Mascis, Kim Thayil, Vernon Reid, Peter Buck, Greg Ginn, Johnny Marr, Rick Nielsen, and Brian Setzer.

Well, to name just a few, anyway. I mean, if I kept goin', I could probably put an entire book together. Now, seriously, should I or anyone else actually feel bad or be embarrased by the fact that we grew up listening to all those cats? Yeah, right. Man, the '80s was an incredibly versatile decade, chock full of great bands, great music, and absolutely insane guitar players. No doubt, Van Halen was right at the forefront. But as huge as they were during this decade, I simply wouldn't refer to them as an "'80s band." VH formed in 1972, as Mammoth. They paid their dues playin' clubs during the mid-'70s and got signed in 1977. Then they released two albums in the late '70s, rolled right on into the '80s, and got even bigger. Then they rolled on into the '90s with Sammy at the helm and continued their insane success. Fact is, from 1978-1996 Van Halen had a dozen consecutive multi-Platinum albums. They also managed to score five number 1 albums, two in the '80s and three in the '90s. In other words, this band experienced mind-boggling success during the '70s, '80s, *and* '90s. So in the end, why would I relegate 'em to a single decade? They are just a great rock 'n' roll band that kicked ass through several different decades.

But if you'll allow me to play devil's advocate here, damn, you could make a terrific argument for Van Halen owning the '80s. I mean, Diamond Dave was arguably *the* rock star of that era. No doubt Edward was *the* guitar player of that era as well. Many consider *1984* to be *the* album of that era, too. Along with the fact that 1978's *Van Halen* pretty much ushered in the '80s and served as a blueprint for tons of people. That's a fact, baby.

And as a band, well, VH certainly weren't second to *anyone* in terms of talent, songs, popularity, album sales, concert attendance, influence, and overall success during this decade. Considering how many great bands and guitar players were on the scene during the '80s, shit, that is nothing to be ashamed of, to put it mildly. If anything, you could say VH was *the* '80s band or whatever, not just "an" '80s band, you know? That's a big difference, right there.

For example, as of 2005, here in America, Van Halen has actually sold more albums than Def Leppard and Mötley Crüe – *combined*. Pretty sick, huh? Especially when you consider those two bands were incredibly successful. Not to mention the fact that each of those two bands has often been proclaimed as *"the"* band of the '80s by many in the music press. As huge as Guns N' Roses and Bon Jovi are, well, Van Halen has outsold both of 'em here at home, too. Oh, and not by a small margin, either. In fact, VH outsold each of 'em by more than 20 million copies! Man, all of those bands I just mentioned have been very successful. So the fact that VH put up those kinds of numbers makes you realize just how freakin' insane their success has truly been.

As far as overall success, impact, sales, popularity, influence, concert attendance and so forth—especially here in America—I believe the only band from the '80s that can truly stand shoulder-to-shoulder with Van Halen is Metallica. That's it. I truly believe that next to Edward Van Halen, the most important and influential guitarists of the last quarter century—especially in the world of hard rock/metal—have been Hetfield and Hammett. That's my opinion, anyway.

I mean, seriously, how many fuckin' kids on this planet picked up a guitar and wanted to form a band after hearing Edward, James, and Kirk? Jesus H. Christ, the numbers are probably staggering. Flip through any guitar magazine and you'll see that, even to this very day, kids are still claiming those three cats as the reason they wanted to play guitar and the reason they got into rock/metal and wanted to form a band. It's un-fuckin-believable.

For my money, as much as I love everyone from U2 to Guns, I truly believe VH and Metallica are the big dogs of the '80s. Between the two of 'em, the only reason I'd probably give the title to VH is cuz Metallica simply wasn't as high-profile as VH during the '80s. I mean, it really wasn't even close. Obviously, the boys of Metallica were way more "underground," for lack of a better term. So, in the end, I dunno if you can even hand over an entire decade to one band? But damn, you sure could make a terrific case for VH. No doubt about it. Absolutely. If Led Zep owned the '70s and Nirvana the '90s, well, Van Halen may just own the '80s.

Quien Es Más Macho?

Dave or Sammy? It's become the "Ginger or Mary Ann?" of the music world, hasn't it?

Man, you can walk up to just about anyone and say "Dave or Sammy?" and they will know *precisely* what you're talkin' about. No last names necessary, baby.

However, when it comes to the Van Halen legacy, it appears one of the biggest misconceptions is that they somehow got bigger or sold more albums with Sammy Hagar. Man, I wish I had a dollar for every time I tuned into a show on one of the big music channels and was subjected to some wannabe metalhead (wearing a vintage Motörhead shirt they probably just bought on eBay in a sad attempt to appear legitimate) tellin' me that Van Halen was much bigger and sold more albums with Sammy. So, in the end, *quien es más macho: señor Dave o señor Sammy?*

Well, I give VH and Sammy all the credit in the world for what they accomplished. It was truly mind-boggling and I honestly don't believe any other band ever pulled it off the way they did. To make a lead singer change, score four consecutive number 1 studio albums, and continue to pack arenas for over a decade?! Shit, that's unreal. I tip my cap to 'em. And I'm man enough to admit I like plenty of their songs. Having said that, however, I must now point to the facts.

Ladies and germs, the fact is Van Halen sold more albums with David Lee Roth, period. Well, I should say they sold more during their time with David Lee Roth, really. Cuz in all honesty, those monster sales had as much to do with the music the band wrote during that era as anything else. If Dave was the only reason these guys sold albums, well, they wouldn't have sold any

278

with Sammy, would they? And I don't think Diamond Dave sold 34 million albums as a solo artist, either, ok? Cuz that is precisely how many albums Van Halen sold during their Classic era here at home! The six albums Van Halen released during their Classic era sold over 34 million copies in America alone. Two of those albums, *Van Halen* (1978) and *1984* (1984), have earned a Diamond Award for selling over 10 million copies in America, each.

Meanwhile, the five albums Van Halen released during their time with Sammy (four studio albums and one live album) sold over 18 million copies in America. Hey, that's nothin' to sneeze at, ok? You wanna know how freakin' big that is? Put it to you this way: the Who sold 20 million albums in America during their *entire career*.

Regardless, VH sold more albums here at home with Dave than with Sammy. Man, it ain't even close. I mean, we're talkin' almost two to one here! I think the fact that the band scored four consecutive number 1 albums with Sammy obviously throws a lot of people off. Yes, they did enjoy bigger chart success with Sammy, but the chart success of their Classic era was pretty damn impressive, too. Beginning with their 1978 debut album, the six albums of the Classic Van Halen era charted at the following peak position: number 19, number 6, number 6, number 5, number 3, and number 2, respectively.

As you can clearly see, each album with Dave charted higher than the previous, and they were well on their way to the top of the charts before Sammy came on board. In the end, both eras are insanely successful. Every single album from each of the eras is multi-Platinum. Between these two eras, you have a dozen consecutive multi-Platinum albums! As far as hard rock and metal goes, I believe only Led Zeppelin has more.

So the fact of the matter is that Van Halen was bigger and sold more albums during their Classic era. Plus, the overall aura and mystique surrounding this band was simply much bigger during the Classic era as well. In the end, I guess we have to say that *señor Dave es más macho!* All kidding aside, both eras were truly phenomenal in their own right. It's just that the Classic VH era was, and still *is,* truly insane.

In closing, if an average, everyday schmuck such as myself can simply cruise on over to *www.riaa.com* and score this information in a freakin' matter of seconds, well, all those big music channels, along with the music press in general, have absolutely *no excuse* to keep gettin' it wrong year after year, ok? Fellas, you guys get *paid* to know this shit. I don't. So for crissake, get it right. I'm certainly not tellin' anyone how to do their job. I'm simply tellin' 'em to please do it *right.* Thank you.

Edward Van Halen's Ear

How good is Edward Van Halen's ear? Insane. Flat out, his ear is *absolutely insane.* As I mentioned earlier in this book, I don't believe Edward Van Halen has what is known in most music circles as "perfect pitch." This is the ability to hear a piece of music one time and then basically turn around and play it, *verbatim.* I don't believe Edward has this per se, but I know whatever ability he does possess can't be that far off, either.

To show what an amazing ear Edward has, I could easily point to the fact that he was playing Beethoven and Mozart at the age of six. Or the fact that he was mastering Clapton and Hendrix tunes by ear back in junior high. Along with the fact that he was completely self-taught on the guitar, there are plenty of other examples of how good his ear is. However, my favorite is a story I came across during an interview with the founder of Peavey Electronics, Hartley Peavey. I located it over at the official Van Halen Web site, *www.van-halen.com,* in the "Interview" section.

As you may or may not know, Edward Van Halen and Peavey forged a very successful partnership in the early '90s that lasted all the way till 2004. It was a great partnership that produced Edward's legendary signature 5150 amplifier series and signature guitar, The Wolfgang. Well, apparently when Edward hooks up with a company, he doesn't just toss his name on something and then sit at home waiting for the check. No, he is a total hands-on type of guy. It was not uncommon for Edward to fly down to the Peavey Factory in Mississippi and get his hands dirty, so to speak. Basically, he was personally involved in every aspect concerning the building of his 5150 amps and Wolfgang guitars. In other words, those products were not leaving that factory until his ears told him they were ready. It's an admirable quality, but I'm sure the dudes on the assembly line must have been going bonkers!

Well, one day Edward and Hartley were working together building cabinets for his 5150 amp series, when Hartley discovered just how insane Edward's ear truly is.

Hartley Peavey: "Ed and I were building cabinets and Ed was telling me what he thought the cabinets should have in them. Peavey is one of the largest users of plywood in the Southeast, and we have a lot of these little cutoff strips from when we're sawing out various panels and so on. We use these strips as braces, since plywood is pretty stiff. Ed could hear the difference, with his ear, between a plain wood brace and a plywood strip brace. I would have bet you ten thousand dollars and never worried that he couldn't do that. Nor could anybody do that. And I would have lost because he could do that consistently. So we had to go to solid wood braces instead of plywood braces and we still do."

Um, any questions?

Check the Stats

Record sales. For years, arguments have raged over whether or not record sales count. You know, far as determining an artist's talent and so forth. Well, frankly, they don't. Record sales do not automatically equal talent. However, there are times when talent does equal record sales. So the fact that some vacuous, assembly-line pop star may sell millions of albums should not take away from the amazing commercial success of any *true* artist. In the end, I know there are people out there who are into the numbers and all that business. If that's the case, well, this chapter is for you.

When it comes to determining an artist's popularity and career consistency, album sales are really the only way to go. Well, concert ticket sales are quite telling, too. But honestly, when is the last time you saw a chart with concert attendance stats? Basically, it comes down to album sales and chart positions. Rather than look at 'em in a negative light, people should understand that album sales are basically how many people you've touched with your music. That's really what they represent, when you think about it? Album sales = the number of people you've touched with your music. So if you go to the official R.I.A.A. Web site and look at the top ten selling bands in America, well, their sales will make total sense, cuz they are all incredibly influential artists.

The Beatles – 168.5 million
Led Zeppelin – 107.5 million
The Eagles – 89 million
Pink Floyd – 73.5 million
AC/DC – 66 million
Aerosmith – 65.5 million

The Rolling Stones – 64.5 million
Bruce Springsteen and the E Street Band – 61.5 million
Metallica – 57 million
Van Halen – 56.5 million

Honorable mention would go to U2 with 50.5 million sold here at home. Now, when you look at that list, it makes absolute sense. For example, if someone impacts and influences you, chances are you went out and bought their albums. More often than not, I truly believe this to be the case. Well, at least until the late 1990s, before illegal downloading exploded, anyway. From the beginning of rock back in the 1950s until the very late 1990s, people bought records, tapes, CDs, and so forth.

So while the concept of anxiously awaiting a new album and counting down the days till its release date may be completely foreign to many people under the age of twenty-one, the fact is that up until the late '90s, that's how it was done, baby. That's how you got your music, period. And if you were influenced, impacted, and inspired by a certain artist, well, your only choice was to go down to the store and buy their album. Then, of course, you take the album home and play the damn thing over, and over, and over again until you've mastered the songs, licks, solos, and so forth. Simply put, that's the way it worked. I'm certain many people still do that today, but now, with the explosion of music downloading, well, music is just a click away. In the end, how the hell else are you gonna learn someone's stuff, you know? Basically, if you are influenced and inspired by a certain artist, chances are you probably bought their albums and cut your teeth on them. The point being, you absolutely have to get your hands on their music to learn their stuff, period.

Anyway, let's take a look at Van Halen's stats. I will simply list all their albums, along with how many copies were sold here in America, and their peak chart position. You know, the highest position each album hit on the Billboard Album Chart. By the way, all of these stats are available over at the official R.I.A.A. Web site *(www.riaa.com)*.

Van Halen (1978), 10 million, number 19
Van Halen II (1979), 5 million, number 6
Women and Children First (1980), 3 million, number 6
Fair Warning (1981), 2 million, number 5
Diver Down (1980), 4 million, number 3
1984 (1984), 10 million, number 2
5150 (1986), 6 million, number 1
OU812 (1988), 4 million, number 1

For Unlawful Carnal Knowledge (1991), 3 million, number 1
Live: Right Here, Right Now (1993), 2 million, number 5
Balance (1995), 3 million, number 1
Best Of, Volume 1 (1996), 3 million, number 1
Van Halen 3 (1998), 500,000, number 4
Best Of Both Worlds (2004), 1 million, number 3

Man, those are pretty devastating stats. When you add those up, you're staring at 56.5 million albums sold in America. Folks, that's basically a wall filled with 56 Platinum awards and 1 Gold award. Not bad, huh? (Remember, Platinum = 1 million copies, Gold = 500,000 copies.)

Another astonishing fact is that from 1978 to 1996, Van Halen scored a dozen consecutive multi-Platinum albums (despite a lead singer change). To put that in perspective, Led Zeppelin has thirteen multi-Platinum albums in their entire career. I believe that as far as hard rock and metal goes, Led Zep is the only band with more multi-Platinum awards than Van Halen. The legendary Aerosmith has a dozen multi-Platinum awards in their entire career, too. And while they weren't consecutive, hey, that's still a staggering number and good enough to tie them with Van Halen. Overall, Van Halen and Aerosmith are two of the top three selling American bands here at home, as far as hard rock and metal goes. The third, of course, is Metallica. Of the three, the boys from Beantown rank first, followed by Metallica, and then Van Halen.

From 1973 till present, Aerosmith released twenty-five albums (fourteen studio, four live, five compilation, two Box) that have sold a combined total of 65.5 million copies here at home. They have a dozen multi-Platinum albums, two number 1 albums, and one Diamond Award for *Aerosmith's Greatest Hits* (1980).

From 1983 till present, Metallica released eleven albums (eight studio, one live, two compilation) that have sold a combined total of 57 million copies here at home. They have ten multi-Platinum albums, four number 1 albums, and one Diamond Award for *Metallica,* aka "the black album" (1991).

From 1978 till present, Van Halen released fourteen albums (eleven studio, one live, two compilation) that have sold a combined total of 56.5 million copies here at home. They have a dozen consecutive multi-Platinum albums, five number 1 albums, and two Diamond Awards for *Van Halen* (1978), and *1984* (1984), respectively.

Um, should this really surprise anyone? Monster bands and monster talent = monster sales numbers. It's not surprising at all. And if you combine their insane U.S. album sales with their album sales from overseas, well, that would bring both Aerosmith's and Metallica's total sales to over 100 million albums, each. Meanwhile, that would bring Van Halen's total sales to over 75 million albums. Basically, that's a wall filled with 75 Platinum awards. Not bad, boys.

What these three bands have accomplished is truly staggering. As I mentioned earlier, please, do *not* allow the monster sales of some vacuous, assembly-line pop star to diminish what these three bands, and all those other great bands, accomplished. That's like comparing apples and oranges. Aerosmith, Metallica, and Van Halen are three of the top American bands, period. All the bands in the Top 10 truly deserve to be applauded for the level of success they have achieved. Hopefully, they continue to touch millions of people with their music and musicianship.

The Impact and Influence of EVH...

"Eddie Van Halen was probably the most influential."

– Tony Iommi

Right off the bat, I'd like to point out that any attempt to even begin to measure the insane impact and influence of Edward Van Halen is truly a futile exercise. While I have tried my damndest, how in the world can I begin to cover it all?

I mean, aside from all the major musicians and bands he touched, there are also the millions upon millions of people worldwide who also picked up instruments and formed a band cuz of this man. Edward's impact and influence, so incredibly vast, stretches off into just about every kind of music imaginable. After all, he is one of only a few musicians in history to reinvent an instrument. So basically, Edward is one of those rare musicians who not only inspires people to pick up the instrument, but he actually inspires those who already play to want to get better and truly dedicate themselves to their craft.

However, aside from all his amazing feats on the instrument itself, Edward Van Halen also managed to change the entire guitar industry, period. In other words, his impact and influence definitely go beyond dive-bombs and solos. For starters, companies everywhere began, um, "borrowing" everything from his one-knob one-pickup configurations to his striped paint jobs. Also, amp builders began using his legendary "Brown Sound" as a model for the overdrive channel on their own amplifiers. In fact, many still do to this very day. Oh, and whenever Edward hooked up with company and created a signature series of products, well, they flew off the shelves at light speed. I guess this is one of the reasons why, like many, I consider Edward to be the Michael Jordan of the guitar world. Basically, he transcended and affected the world of music offstage like no other guitar player has ever done. Hell, even if he wasn't "officially" hooked up with a company, he still brought them major credibility.

For example, while he never had a signature model with them per se, Edward helped put Charvel on the map. Remember, he'd been workin' with Wayne Charvel since 1975, a full three years before VH's debut album came out! Edward's collaboration with Charvel set off a "do-it-yourself" craze that lasted from the late '70s all through the '80s. Hell, to this very day, many people build their own guitars, in part because Edward did. And while he never had a signature model with Marshall Amplification per se, Edward's Marshall (100-Watt Plexi Super Lead, 1959 model – circa 1966-1967) is certainly one of the most legendary pieces of equipment, ever. The fact that this amp was a big part of his early, classic "Brown Sound" certainly didn't hurt the folks over at Marshall, know what I mean?

Over the last twenty-seven years, Edward Van Halen popularized and brought major credibility to Kramer, Ernie Ball, Floyd Rose, MXR, and Peavey. Hell, his 5150 amplifier series *alone* is legendary, owned and used by everyone from Buckethead to Aerosmith's Brad Whitford. And again, don't even get me started on all the companies – which, of course, shall remain nameless – that ripped off everything from his pickup designs to his guitar designs. Yeah, you know who you are, rat bastards. Man, so many people got filthy stinking rich off many of the things Edward Van Halen created. It's absurd. Oh, and please ask any of the folks over at *Guitar Player* magazine or *Guitar World* magazine what Edward Van Halen has done for their popularity and credibility. For example, the March 1980 issue of *Guitar Player* is still, to this very day, their highest-selling issue of all time. Coincidence that this was the first time Edward Van Halen was ever featured on the cover? I think not.

As if all that doesn't make for quite a sick resumé, don't forget that Van Halen, the *band,* was an incredibly influential entity in its own right. Diamond Dave, Sammy, Mike, and Alex influenced and inspired an insane number of musicians as well. Yes, the members and music of Van Halen were extremely influential. Man, if I began to research all of these aspects, I simply never would have completed this section. So I realized the smartest thing I could do is to simply focus on Edward Van Halen and all the major (big-name) guitar players out there that he influenced and inspired.

However, we need to address a couple things before we dig in. For starters, I believe the one major misconception concerning "influence" is that a musician absolutely has to sound like the musician(s) they are influenced by. In reality, nothing could be further from the truth. The fact is, most musicians – *especially* the great ones – make a conscious effort to *not* sound like their influences. This is why determining the overall impact and influence of a certain musician can prove to be so damn difficult. For example, I bet no one would ever imagine that newer cats like Mike Einziger of Incubus and Mike DeWolf of Taproot were influenced by Edward Van Halen, you know? Well, they were. In fact, both of them have stated Edward is the reason they play the guitar. Yeah, funny how some people actually believe EVH's influence ended when the '80s ended, huh?

> **Mike Einziger:** "I was grooving to Van Halen when I was six. I tried to play then, but my hands were too small and it hurt. So I played drums, flute and piano instead. Then when I was twelve, I was at a friend's house and I saw his older brother playing 'Eruption.' He was really good, and I thought it was the coolest thing I had ever seen. So I told my mom I had to have a guitar and, being totally cool, she went out and got me one the next week."

Mike DeWolf: "The reason why I got my guitar was Eddie Van Halen. I knew that I would never play like him, nor did I want to, but that's what inspired me. He's just amazing and he's doing something that he created pretty much on his own and that's something that I want to do. Growing up, I'd play solos over Metallica and Pearl Jam tunes, but Eddie Van Halen was the main man."

So you see, it's just not as simple as finding a bunch of wannabes who borrow a couple of techniques from Edward, or that even go as far as trying to be an Edward clone. For my money, that is *not* influence. Nah, that's a freakin' joke. Not just as far as Edward goes, but any musician, for that matter. I'm not talking about the brilliant players who followed Edward's lead and implemented certain aspects of his style into their own respective style in a tasteful manner. Nah, I'm talking about the cheap imitators and rip-off artists. During an interview with *Guitar World* magazine that appeared in their April 1987 issue, the late, great Frank Zappa summed up the whole EVH-clone fiasco of the '80s, as only Frank could.

Frank Zappa: "If you don't sound like Eddie Van Halen, then apparently you don't actually play guitar anymore. I have no intention of ever sounding like Eddie Van Halen, and, uh, it makes you wonder why you would even bother to play the guitar, because the current audience would listen and go, 'That's not a guitar. It doesn't go wee wee wee wee, wee wee wee wee.' So why do it?

"I'm not saying anything against Eddie because I think what he's done for the guitar is wonderful. But the thing that's tragic about the marketplace is that *everybody* decided they were all going to do *that*, and then the competition is not musical. It's gymnastic. Okay, they say, 'I want to sound like Eddie, but in order to be better than Eddie I have to be faster than Eddie.' That seems to be the aesthetic operating procedure in the marketplace. Meanwhile, Edward probably sits back and goes, 'These guys are really stupid.' Because I don't think that's what he had in mind when he developed the style."

Unfortunately, most great artists have clones. For example, after John Coltrane hit the scene, man, it wasn't long before tons of JC clones emerged. Many are still around today! Lord knows everyone from Led Zeppelin to Jimi Hendrix have had plenty of people cop their trip. And, of course, Edward experienced this as well. But hey, none of these artists can be held responsible for that, you know? I mean, really, once someone sets a blueprint, just about anyone can come after and learn it. Hell, I've seen small children who have mastered Beethoven and Paganini, for crissake! Man, these kids can play all of that classical music *verbatim*. When you see something like that, you realize it's possible for any artist in history to be copied. So frankly, with all due respect to George Lucas, screw the clones. A small faction of wanabees should not in any way, shape, or form, diminish the accomplishments or legacy of any artist. Nor can that artist ever be held responsible.

Man, if that was the case, well, then every great artist in history would have to be castigated for the sins of their clones, beginning with the Beatles for flooding this world with tons of awful boy bands! Then we'll blame Elvis Presley for flooding the world with Elvis impersonators! All kidding aside, man, you just can't do that. The proper way is to look for musicians who were so blown away by Edward Van Halen, they were inspired to do their own thing. King's X guitarist Ty Tabor is a prime example of that.

> **Ty Tabor:** "When Eddie Van Halen came around, he blew me away so bad that the last thing I thought of doing was trying to copy his style. Van Halen really messed me up, but since his style was so new and huge, he inspired me to go in the other directions and seek out my own voice on the guitar, instead of trying to copy him like so many others did."

Tom Morello of Audioslave is another phenomenal guitarist who ended up sounding *nothing* like his influences, despite the fact that during his college days, he spent countless hours a day practicing, listening to, and copying people like Edward and Randy Rhoads.

> **Tom Morello:** "During the time I was practicing so much, I started to sound like other contemporary players. When I had a love for Randy Rhoads, I was sounding like Randy Rhoads. At one point I started copying Al Di Meola too much. What draws people to the instrument is the love for guitar players that play a certain way. I mean, even though it wasn't intentional, it was hard to avoid copping Eddie Van Halen. He was basically *'the shit'* back then."

For my money, it's all about going deeper and finding the people who have truly been touched by a certain musician, like all the great players I just mentioned. Inspiring someone to get into music and pick up an instrument is about as deep as it gets, you know? And Edward has had that effect on tons of people. So for me it goes further than simply copping his trip. Besides, just cuz someone hits dive bomb or plays a simple tapping lick does not even necessarily mean they are "influenced" by Edward Van Halen, ok? Who knows, it could just mean they heard those ideas and borrowed 'em from him to try and sound cool or whatever. To me, that *does not* qualify you as having been influenced by EVH.

In the end, the person who sounds absolutely nothing like you may just be the one who's actually been most influenced and inspired by you. Mike Einziger, Mike DeWolf, Ty Tabor, and Tom Morello are all major examples of that. It makes total sense, when you think about it. Many of today's guitarists, including some of the ones I just mentioned, grew up during the '80s. And, I mean, if you grew up during that decade, well, of course you're gonna be aware of Edward and touched by him. Hell, how could you not be? For these players, as I'm sure has been the case for millions more, Van Halen become one of those artists who is a "rite of passage," you know?

Basically, you could say Van Halen was the "gateway drug" for millions of kids. You know, musically speaking. I mean, you might end up playing nu-metal, alternative, thrash, and so forth, but VH was the man and the band that made you wanna pick up an instrument and form a band. It's like, if you were into rock or metal, and if you were into guitar, you absolutely had to own and listen to those early Van Halen albums. That's a fact, baby. Boatloads of people wanted to pick up a guitar and form a band after hearing Van Halen. Hell, for some, the desire to want to pick up a guitar and form a band even came from just seeing a Van Halen music video. This was the case for Taking Back Sunday guitarist, Frank Meneschino.

Frank Meneschino: "I started playing guitar because of Van Halen's videos for the *1984* album. I'm mostly a fan of the band's David Lee Roth era. I always felt that when Eddie Van Halen soloed he was actually trying to say something. A lot of guys who imitated him weren't saying anything 'cause they just didn't have that in them. What I took from Eddie was the idea of using fast pull-offs and employing all your fingers equally."

Green Day's Billie Joe Armstrong is another musician who sounds nothing like Edward. Nor does his band sound anything remotely like Van Halen. Yet, like countless others, Van Halen was a rite of passage.

Billie Joe Armstrong: "Mike Dirnt [Green Day bassist] and I lived about a mile from each other when we were growing up in Rodeo, California. We put together out first band, Truant, when we were eleven. We played hard rock like Van Halen's 'Runnin' with the Devil,' AC/DC's 'Back in Black,' and Def Leppard's 'High 'n' Dry.'"

Another great example of someone who does not sound anything like his influences would be none other than Edward Van Halen himself. As I pointed out earlier in this book, Edward's main man was Eric Clapton. That was and will forever be his biggest influence. Yet he sounds absolutely nothing like Clapton, does he?

If you look at his other really big influences, like Jimmy Page, Jimi Hendrix, and Pete Townshend, you'll find that Edward sounds absolutely nothing like them, either. While he grew up mastering all of their shit, he turned that around, innovated, and came up with his own unique, signature style and sound. To this very day a lot of people shake their head when they hear that Edward's main influences were cats like Clapton, Page, Hendrix and Townshend, cuz they search and search for similarities between their respective styles and simply come up empty-handed.

Another big misconception is that a musician only influences those who come after him.

Again, nothing could be further from the truth. I actually believe there are two different ways to impact and influence, and they are:

1) You can impact and influence those who come *after* you.
2) You can impact and influence those who came *before* you.

Now you see why this can prove to be such a difficult task. It's hard enough to try and find the musicians influenced by someone who came *after* that person, but to also find the ones who came *before* makes it all the more difficult. That's a whole lot of ground to cover, baby. On top of that, a musician can influence people at any stage of their life, as well. What I mean is, you don't necessarily have to grow up listening to someone since you are like five years old to be influenced and inspired by that person. For example, you could pick up the guitar at age seven, be playing for like fifteen years, and then one day at twenty-two you hear someone who totally blows your mind! At the very least, you've been "impacted." I don't know if "influenced" is the right term for this situation, but anyone who makes you reassess the instrument is definitely impacting you, to put it mildly.

As the great Brian May mentioned during the foreword to this book, seeing Edward Van Halen during the first VH tour in 1978 made him reassess everything he thought he knew about guitar playing. Mind you, Brian May had already been playing guitar for many years, and Queen were already full-blown superstars who had been on the scene a full six years *before* Van Halen. Folks, when someone like Edward causes a truly legendary and phenomenal musician like Brian May back to reassess *everything*, damn, what else can you really say? Well, you could say he touched many other greats, like Mountain guitarist, Leslie West.

Leslie West: "Eddie Van Halen is my favorite guitar player and he is a really good friend of mine. I learned so much from him, especially when I stopped playing guitar for a while in the late '70s. I went to see him play and he inspired me again. He is a great guy."

Man, Leslie West is a truly brilliant guitar player. The guy is a legend who even managed to meet and jam with none other than Jimi Hendrix! I mean, who doesn't know the riff to his classic song, "Mississippi Queen," you know? Regardless, the fact is that Edward influenced and inspired Leslie. In all honesty, it's not that surprising. Van Halen is simply devastating live in concert, very powerful and inspiring. So the fact that anyone would be blown away by a VH show is not surprising at all. However, a simple Van Halen backstage warm-up session can be a near religious experience as well. Legendary guitar master Pat Metheny can testify to that.

Pat Metheny: "I think he is a really great player and someone I always enjoy hearing. There was a time I went to VH shows as much as possible just to check him out. One time, I got to go backstage before a show and hear him warm up – which was absolutely mind-blowing – he played more incredible music in that thirty minutes of warmup time than he did in all the VH 'shows' that I heard rolled together. He is so creative – it would be great to hear him expand into other areas... Eddie is more like a jazz guy anyway to me – he is always searching for sounds and ideas it seems."

Basically, Edward Van Halen ended up touching, influencing, and inspiring many of his own influences. Another great example would be none other than Pink Floyd's David Gilmour. Just one year after the release of *1984,* when Classic VH was ruling the world, David did an interview with *Guitar Classics* magazine that appears in their January 1985 issue. During the interview, he made a few interesting comments concerning Edward Van Halen.

David Gilmour: "These days I don't look to other people with the objective of trying to steal their licks, although I've got no objections to stealing them if that seems like a good idea. I'm sure that I'm still influenced by Mark Knopfler and Eddie Van Halen as well... I can't play like Eddie Van Halen. I wish I could. I sat down to try some of those ideas and can't do it. I don't know if I could ever get any of that stuff together. Sometimes I think I should work at the guitar more."

Ok, lemme get this straight. Eddie made David believe he should "work at the guitar more?" Man, that's just wrong. I mean, are you freakin' kidding me? David Gilmour is one of the truly great and legendary players in history! On top of that, he's a member of Pink Floyd, a truly great and legendary band. When you send someone like David Gilmour back to the woodshed and even cause the man to wonder aloud about his own abilities, well, you should be made to serve jail time. Man, at this point I don't know if Edward Van Halen is influencing and inspiring people, or in fact tormenting them?

All kidding aside, it goes to show just how vast Edward's influence truly is. Oh, and you can add one more of his influences to that list as well. ZZ Top's Billy Gibbons is a legendary musician who's been payin' his dues since the late 1960s. Not only did this cat get to jam with Jimi Hendrix, Jimi actually professed that Billy was his favorite new player! Billy is one of those rare players who got to meet and jam with both Jimi and Edward. Well, you could say Edward made a decent impression on Billy, too.

Billy Gibbons: "If you had a guitar poll, I'd put Edward Van Halen in the first five slots and then the next five would start opening up."

However, I think the most amazing example of this comes from Edward's own guitar hero, Eric Clapton. During a 1985 interview with the *Boston Globe*'s Steve Morse, Clapton made a pretty stunning statement. The article, titled "**Eric Clapton: A Rock Star Mellowing Out**," appears in the June 23, 1985 issue of the *Globe*. Here's the part of the article I'm referring to:

As for other contemporary guitarists, he admires Eddie Van Halen and Toto's Steve Lukather, but says they might "blow me away quite easily" if they were to jam together.

Man, that is shocking. Well, the fact that Clapton said he admired Edward and Luke is not shocking at all, really. What is shocking is to hear someone like Eric Clapton admit that they could blow him away quite easily. That is just staggering, cuz it's not often you'll hear a legend admit that they could get schooled by some of the new kids on the block, you know? It's no wonder some of the "old guard" were pissed off at Edward and many of the other new cats. Shit, many are still pissed to this day! I mean, when "GOD" admits that young guns like Edward and Luke could "blow me away quite easily," well, talk about being crushed.

Brian May, Leslie West, Pat Metheny, David Gilmour, Billy Gibbons, and Eric Clapton are all obviously legendary players. They also all happened to be on the scene *before* Van Halen. Nonetheless, each of these monster musicians was touched by Edward Van Halen. What's even sicker is that Edward didn't just influence, impact, and inspire guitar players, either. While the focus of my research was indeed to see just how many major guitar players he touched, I came to discover that Edward has influenced and inspired all kinds of different musicians. For example, Mötley Crüe's Tommy Lee comes to mind. While Tommy is known, rightfully so, as a slammin' world-class drummer, the fact is he plays guitar, too. When Tommy was growing up, there were really two people who inspired him to become a musician. One was Kiss's drummer, Peter Criss. Take a wild guess as to who the other one was?

> **Tommy Lee:** "Eddie Van Halen's guitar fucking freaked me out. Eddie Van Halen had me air-guitaring, and Peter Criss's drum set flipped me out. That got me doing the cardboard boxes and setting up these pretend drum sets and thinking I was just the full-blown rock star. I was that guy, jumping up and down on my bed in the mirror thinking I was Eddie Van Halen or with my drumsticks up in the air like I was Peter Criss."

The same thing goes for former Rage Against the Machine and current Audioslave drummer, Brad Wilk. While the drums became his instrument of choice, the fact is, Brad actually started on the guitar. Take a wild guess why he asked his parents to buy him a guitar.

> **Brad Wilk:** "For some reason my parents didn't want to buy me a drumkit; they thought it wouldn't last. I had begun on guitar when I was eleven. I heard Eddie Van Halen, so that's what I wanted."

Oh, and aside from drummers, we got bass players, too. For example, legendary bassists like Billy Sheehan and Michael Manring cite Edward Van Halen as an influence and inspiration, as well. And ex-Dream Theater keyboard player Derek Sherinian has always cited Edward as his main influence. Hell, if you turn to the "Tribute" section of this book, you'll see that even world-renowned violin virtuoso Mark Wood cites Edward as a major influence, too. Man, twenty bucks says that somewhere in this world, there's a triangle player trying to play "Eruption" as we speak (poor bastard). All kidding aside, I could go on citing musician after musician. However, the true focus of this section is guitar players. So here, in no particular order, are a few guitar players who've been influenced and inspired by Edward Van Halen:

Steve Vai, Slash (Guns N' Roses/Velvet Revolver), Brian May (Queen), Kirk Hammett and James Hetfield (Metallica), Zakk Wylde (Ozzy/Black Label Society), Dimebag Darrell (Pantera/Damageplan), Randy Rhoads (Ozzy/Quiet Riot), Kerry King and Jeff Hanneman (Slayer), Jason Becker (Cacophony/DLR Band), Joe Satriani, Daron Malakian (System of a Down), Mike Mushok (Staind), Jon Donais and Matt Bachand (Shadows Fall), Billy Corgan (Smashing Pumpkins/ZWAN), David Gilmour (Pink Floyd), Mark Tremonti (Creed/Alter Bridge), Leslie West (Mountain), Tom Morello (Rage Against the Machine/Audioslave), Kenny Wayne Shepherd, Jack Black (Tenacious D), Kai Hansen (Helloween), Dr. Know (Bad Brains), Dave Navarro (Jane's Addiction), Jennifer Batten (Michael Jackson), Mike McCready (Pearl Jam), Kurt Cobain (Nirvana), Dweezil Zappa, Scott Ian (Anthrax), John Frusciante (The Red Hot Chili Peppers), Johnny Rzeznick (The Goo Goo Dolls), Jimmy Bruno, Dave Mustaine (Megadeth), John 5 (Marilyn Manson/DLR Band), Richie Sambora (Bon Jovi), Josey Scott (Saliva), Mike DeWolf (Taproot), Meegs Rascon (Coal Chamber), Ty Tabor (King's X), Buckethead, Jerry Cantrell (Alice in Chains), Dave "Snake" Sabo (Skid Row), Kenny Chesney, Steve Stevens (Billy Idol), Jon Schaffer (Iced Earth), Justin Hawkins (The Darkness), Dino Cazares (Fear Factory), Beck Hansen, Jonathan Kreisberg, Ramon Ortiz (Puya), Akira Takasaki (Loudness), Pat Smear (The Germs/Nirvana), Chris Holmes (W.A.S.P.), Mick Mars (Mötley Crüe), Stephen Carpenter (The Deftones), Trey Azagthoth (Morbid Angel), Chris Duarte, Tom Dumont (No Doubt), Morgan Lander (Kittie), Billie Joe Armstrong (Green Day), Tony Rombola (Godsmack), Wes Scantlin (Puddle of Mud), Phil Collen and Vivian Campbell (Def Leppard), Vito Bratta (White Lion), Yngwie J. Malmsteen, John Petrucci (Dream Theater), Carl Bell and Brett Scallions (Fuel), Jeff Mantas (Venom), John Connolly (Sevendust), Rivers Cuomo (Weezer), Shane Theriot, Mark Chapman (A.), Jake E. Lee, Alex Skolnick (Testament), Paul Gilbert (Mr. Big/Racer X), Warren DeMartini (Ratt), Wolf Hoffman (Accept), Steve Brown (Trixter), Michael Angelo Batio (Nitro), Greg Howe, Nuno Bettencourt (Extreme), C.C. DeVille (Poison), George Lynch (Dokken/Lynch Mob), Michael Fath, Steve Morse (Dixie Dregs/Deep Purple), Rich Ward (Stuck Mojo), Trey Spruance (Mr. Bungle/Faith No More/Secret Chiefs 3), Birèli Lagréne, Mike Einziger (Incubus), Mike Tempesta (Powerman 5000), Frank Meneschino (Taking Back Sunday), Allison Robertson (The Donnas), Matt Scannell (Vertical Horizon), Greg Camp (Smashmouth), Frank Hannon and Tommy Skeoch (Tesla), Tommy Shaw (Styx), Damon Johnson (Brother Cane), Michael Eisenstein (Letters to Cleo), Rusty Cooley, Noko (Apollo 440),

Arjen Lucassen (Ayreon), Mike Turner (Our Lady Peace), Ron Thal, Timo Tolkki (Stratovarius), George Bellas, Larry Lerlonde (Primus), Neil Zaza, Toshi Iseda, Joy Basu, Mark Kendall (Great White), Paul Crook (Anthrax), Reb Beach (Warrant/Dokken), Brad Gillis and Jeff Watson (Night Ranger), Vinnie Moore, Chris Impellitteri, Mick Sweda (The Bullet Boys), Blues Saraceno, Johnny Hiland, and Brian Young.

Yeah, I know, some of the names on that list caught you off guard. I'm pretty sure there is one name in particular that most people didn't expect to see on there, and that's Kurt Cobain. Well, believe it not, the head of the "alternative nation" was apparently quite the little hard rock and metal fan growing up. While he discovered pop music as a child and was later introduced to punk rock at the age of sixteen by the great Buzz Osbourne, Kurt spent most of those years in between listening to a whole lotta hard rock and metal. Judas Priest, Iron Maiden, Kiss, Led Zeppelin, Aerosmith, Cheap Trick, AC/DC, and Black Sabbath were just some of the bands he was into. And yes, Classic Van Halen was very much in the mix, too.

In fact, about a year or two ago, I caught one of those VH1 shows about Nirvana. I believe the show aired at the same time the very first Nirvana greatest hits album was released. Anyway, one of Kurt's closest friends was Dylan Carlson, former member of the band, Earth. During the show, Dylan mentioned how one night, when they were hanging out, Kurt began to recite all these facts about Edward Van Halen. Apparently, Kurt even went into detail about the kind of pickups Edward used, how many times he wound them, and so forth. It blew me away, cuz these are things the casual fan is simply *not* gonna know, ok?

Not long after seeing that show, I came across a new book titled *Heavier than Heaven*. In my opinion, this is the most honest and accurate Kurt Cobain/Nirvana book ever written. The author of this fine book is Charles R. Cross. So, of course, I contacted Charles and asked him if Kurt was really into VH growing up. His response was swift and precise, and confirmed what I'd always suspected.

Charles R. Cross: "Kurt Cobain as a teenager was obsessed with Eddie Van Halen. He had Van Halen records in his collection and worshipped them. That was in part due to Eddie's guitar playing, but also because of the role that VH played to any kid growing up in that era in America. He wrote a bit about Van Halen in his journals, but frequently copied the VH logo on notepaper, probably while he was in class." ♪

This might be a shocking revelation to some, but to me, it really isn't. Kurt Cobain turned eleven years old the very same month Van Halen debuted, February of 1978. And I believe he got his first electric guitar just about two or three years later. So it makes total sense to me that Kurt would be into them. At this time, VH hit the scene and quickly became the greatest American hard rock/metal band around. Hell, one of the greatest bands worldwide, period. If you were a kid growing up in America during the late '70s and throughout the '80s, man, chances are you were very aware of Van Halen and touched by them – *especially* if you were a kid who played guitar. Hell, how could you not be, you know? Fact is, Edward Van Halen became *the* guitar hero to millions of kids, overnight.

Basically, Kurt was no different than any other kid in America at that time. He owned all those Classic VH albums and he cut his teeth on them. Yes, little Kurt sat in his bedroom, guitar in hand, and played along to "Eruption," "Ain't Talkin' 'bout Love," "Unchained," and many other VH classics, just like everybody else did. For example, I believe we've all seen the classic video for "Teen Spirit," right? You ever noticed how during the guitar solo, Kurt is actually *not* playing the solo? Rather, he is tapping on the neck of his guitar, kinda spoofing the two-hand tapping Edward put on the map. Well, how do you think Kurt knew about that? Cuz EVH was his hero growing up, that's how. Man, it's pretty wild that, once upon a time, Edward Van Halen was the guitar hero to a kid who would go on to become the head of the "alternative nation." So while it never really turned up in Kurt's guitar playing and music, nonetheless, that was the case.

However, if you look at Kurt's guitars, you'll find a subtle hint that confirms just who his guitar hero once was. For example, Kurt favored Fender Mustangs and Jaguars. Well, if you look closely, you'll notice he removed the original pickup and placed a humbucker in the bridge position of many his guitars. His signature model, the Fender Jagstang, contains a humbucker in the bridge position, too. Gee, where do you think Kurt got *that* idea from, hmmm?

In the end, this is all just a tiny fraction of the incredible impact and influence of this man and his band. Oh yes, it goes *way* beyond the '80s and solos and shred guitar, baby. (And y'all thought "Six Degrees of Kevin Bacon" was fun, huh?) Basically, what it all comes down to is this one simple fact: If you are not directly influenced by Edward Van Halen and his band, well, then you are probably influenced by someone who was.

Tribute...

How do you pay tribute to someone like Edward Van Halen? It's like the old question, "What do you get the man who has everything?" It would appear that Edward has lived a pretty blessed existence, to put it mildly. He's managed to survive all the general excess and madness that comes with livin' in the bright light of rock 'n' roll throughout the course of a twenty-seven-year career that spans four decades. In the process, he and his brother Alex formed the nucleus of one of the baddest and greatest rock bands the world will ever know. They sold over 75 million albums and managed to sell out every big joint from the Forum and Madison Square Garden to the Budokan. Lord know's they had a whole lotta fun in the process, know what I mean?

However, I don't view Edward as a saint, sinner, "God," or whatever. Fact is, he's human. You know, a normal jerk who happens to play guitar, as he's always been fond of saying. Those closest to him point out the fact that after all these years, he's still just...Ed.

In January 2005, the man turned fifty, which in and of itself is truly a monster feat for any rock 'n' roller. And, of course, he got himself a shiny new hip and managed to kick cancer's ass at the turn of the millennium, too. Let's see, he's done everything from change the face of rock and reinvent the guitar to kick cancer's ass? Yo Edward, I hear the superhero business is accepting applications.

All kidding aside, Edward Van Halen has given us some of the most amazing rock music and sickest guitar playing the world will ever know. In return, there are a few people who would like to say thanks. Simply put, over 100 of the world's finest musicians have come together to pay their respects to the man and his band. Within this amazing group of musicians, you will find the world's greatest guitar players. I figured, what the hell, if you're gonna honor one of the best, then you have to bring in the best, period. Anything less just wouldn't do.

So basically, you can take everything I've written up till this point and rip it out. I'm serious, too. As heartfelt and honest an effort as this book has been, what I've written up to this point means absolutely squat compared to what you are about to read.

You see, I've always felt that in the world of music, as in any field, what matters most is what your peers think of you. When people look back at Edward's life and career years from now, one of the most important factors, if not *the* most important factor, is gonna be what his peers thought about him. And while I could have easily done a cut-and-paste job (as I did throughout most of the rest of this book), I knew this section had to be special. That is precisely why I personally contacted each and every single one of these fine people. I wanted it to be personal and I wanted fresh commentary. In the end, I just thought it would be cool to pay tribute to someone while they are actually still around to enjoy it, you know?

Well, one by one, they came. Like James Hetfield, who hit me up from the road right smack in the middle of Metallica's 2004 summer tour! And Ted Nugent, who got back to me while on safari in Africa! Man, you gotta love Uncle Ted. In fact, I was able to bring in phenomenal musicians from the world of rock, hard rock, pop, heavy metal, thrash metal, death metal, bluegrass, country, jazz, blues, shred, hardcore, fusion, rap-rock, punk, gypsy, and alternative. You like classical? No prob, we got Grammy Award-winning classical guitar virtuoso Sharon Isbin too. All of these fine people provided heartfelt commentary.

However, the biggest surprise was just how many of them have actually managed to meet and jam with EVH over the years. Some of them can even call themselves his friend. Man, I never knew how much this dude gets around!

Now, in all honesty, I was just lookin' to get a few words from each of these people. You know, your basic "Eddie Van Halen kicks ass!" type of quotes and so forth. Well, it turns out many of 'em had a helluva lot more to say than that.

In fact, aside from talking about him as a musician, many of these people simply chose to speak about what kind of human being Edward is as well. As much as they enjoyed speaking about his musicianship, music, and band, they really seemed to enjoy speaking about what a cool and generous dude he is. Oh, and many of 'em gave their two cents about Van Halen, the *band*, too. You know, about the band as a whole, certain members, their music, their live show, and so forth. Overall, it paints a pretty clear portrait of who this man is.

Meanwhile, some of 'em have even been in bands that toured with and opened for Van Halen. Lucky for us, they were more than willing to share what that experience was like. For example, Steve Lynch's former band, Autograph, earned the coveted opening slot on VH's legendary 1984 tour. Well, Steve was cool enough to talk about that experience. Along with Snake Sabo, Randy Bachman, and Mark Tremonti, all of whom are members of bands that have toured with and opened for Van Halen, too.

Man, I had so much amazing material that I simply didn't have the heart to chop it all down. For example, when someone like Edward's old pal Allan Holdsworth takes time out of his life to personally call me up and speak to me, the least I could do is honor his words and not chop an entire phone call down, you know? Rather, I took everything given to me and simply threw it in the back of this book. It's the equivalent of when your friends signed the back of your yearbook in grade school, only these people are great musicians and have far less acne. Besides, they simply don't make "thank you" cards big enough to contain all this material. So I had to write an entire book instead. Yeah, thanks a lot.

All kidding aside, it's quite an amazing collection of talent. Some of the greatest guitar players (acoustic, electric, slide, banjo, etc.), bassists, drummers, frontmen, pianists, harmonica players, Stick players, and even violinists all came forward and participated. Edward Van Halen and his band have truly touched people from all the different worlds of music. While some offered a few succinct words, others actually had stories to share. Be it of meeting Edward, jammin' with him, seeing him in concert or back in the club days, and so forth.

I was absolutely blown away that so many people would take time outta their lives to participate. Whether you gave one line, one paragraph or one page, every single word counts and is truly appreciated. Your generosity and class surpass your amazing musicianship. You've truly made this project complete, so I thank you all.

Oh, and there are also a few cool bonuses, too. Alan Paul of *Guitar World* magazine had some words to share. So did the gentleman who provided the killer cover shot for this book, legendary rock 'n' roll photographer, Neil "the Zloz" Zlozower. Man, the Zloz shot the entire Classic VH era! Former MTV VJ Iann Robinson gives us his two cents on Edward and his band, too. I truly respect Iann cuz he genuinely knows his shit and doesn't pull any punches. Basically, he gives it to you straight, and that's precisely what I was lookin' for.

I also brought in legendary music journalist Jas Obrecht. Back in the summer of 1978, Jas was able to score the very first Van Halen interview. Well, this turned into a friendship with Edward that lasted all through the classic VH era and then some. Basically, Jas was one of the privileged few who got to see and know Edward Van Halen onstage, backstage, and offstage. Being a total class act, he took some time out to share what that experience was like.

And finally, since I know Van Halen is a band that has always possessed a terrific sense of humor, I brought in Kevin Booth. Basically, Kevin was a lifelong friend and partner in crime of the late, great comic genius/philosopher, Bill Hicks. He is also the co-founder of Sacred Cow Productions and maintains the official SCP Web site as well. The man is a comic *and* musician, along with the fact that he also happens to be a damn fine producer, too. Well, Kevin was kind enough to take some time out and share everything from how he and Bill were fans of Edward's growin' up to how the music of Van Halen actually served as the soundtrack to the very first keg-party fight they ever witnessed! And believe me when I tell you that his description of the classic "Brown Sound" is worth the price of admission, alone.

So that's the deal. Oh, and I've listed everyone in alphabetical order. Appropriately enough, this means the tribute opens with none other than the late, great Dimebag Darrell. I acquired these words from Dime just a few months before he passed, thanks to the wonderful folks over at Bass Management down in Texas. After what went down in December 2004, Vinnie Paul, Zakk Wylde, and many other wonderful people got together to give the man a proper send-off. Apparently, Edward Van Halen was there, too. He spoke a bit about Dime, who he had finally met for the first (and only) time backstage during one of the final shows of the 2004 VH tour.

Well, aside from having grown up a huge VH fan, Dime was also a huge fan of Edward's black-and-yellow-striped Charvel guitar. You know, the one that's on the cover of the *Van Halen II* album? So much so, in fact, that when they finally met, he actually asked Edward if he could hook him up with one of his new Charvel EVH Art Series replicas of that guitar. Of course, Edward agreed. Hell, he even told Dime that he would stripe the guitar for him personally.

However, once Dime passed, one would think this was no longer possible, right? Well, think again. You see, Edward actually showed up to the send-off with a black-and-yellow guitar in tow. Well, not just "a" black-and-yellow guitar, but rather "the" black-and-yellow guitar. Yes, the original one that appears on the cover of the *Van Halen II* album. Basically, Dime was holding this guitar when he was laid to rest. Amen, brother. And I hope yer gettin' yer pull on with Bon, Randy, Cliff, Jimi, Jaco, Bonham, Stevie Ray, and everyone else up there, man.

In the end, I humbly speak for myself and for all the fans and musicians around the world when I say, thank you, Edward...

"Dimebag" Darrell Abbott

When I first heard Van Halen, this was something far beyond anything I'd ever heard before. I fell in love...when I first saw Ed on the cover of VH1 with his custom white and black pinstriped axe, I knew he was the cutting edge. As I learned more about Edward and how he customized all of his guitars and gear, it all just kept gettin' cooler and cooler. But most of all, it was the way he played, it was so carefree, but yet so perfect. It was true magic caught on tape. From his feel, licks, tricks, and massive brown sound, to knowing just which effect, how much to use, and when to use it. Ed truly has it all!

Edward Van Halen, by far, is the most innovative and bad-assed guitar player to date, and has managed to harness this magic for over twenty-five years. To this day, I still turn to my VH records for ideas and inspiration. Long live Edward Fuckin' Van Halen!!! ♪

R.I.P. Dime (1966-2004)

Miriam Akkerman

Jan remembers Eddy living in Friesland, where I believe his father was a teacher and marching band leader, which must have influenced Eddy's sense of harmonical structure in music, which Jan rates highly (Jan himself started on accordion). He later found out that Eddy was attending Jan's gigs. Jan played in a group called Brainbox and later Focus, of course. He must have realized, or his father did, that in Holland there's no real rock scene, as Jan always stated in interviews later on, and took the wise decision to leave Holland in order to start a career in the U.S. with great success and well deserved, too, 'cause Jan liked his playing and is proud of the man. So as a rock musician Jan rates Eddy highly, if not one of the best coming from this small country Holland. Jan says hi and "Dag Eddy" and keep it up. He gives his warm greetings from a cold country. ♪

Tommy Aldridge

I consider Mr. Van Halen a genius…both of them, actually. He's got it all, chops and creativity – just like Randy Rhoads.♪

Vinny Appice

It's great to see two brothers make great music together for all these years and still sound on fire today. ♪

Kenny Aronoff

I love Eddie Van Halen's playing. He is amazing. He reinvented rock 'n' roll guitar like no other guitar player has ever done. He invented his own style and it wasn't all about technique. Yes, he is technical, but he is musical also. I love his playing. Alex is also special. He invented his own sound and is one of the great solid rock drummers. ♪

Randy Bachman

I had the privilege of touring with Bachman-Turner Overdrive as opening act for Van Halen on the 5150 tour in 1986. Sammy, Alex, Michael and Edward became like brothers to us. They and their whole crew were like family. People got married, some got divorced, some babies were born and everything else possible happened, as is the case when over a hundred people band together as a touring entourage for almost a year.

Eddy was particularly a really great guy. He welcomed my kids, who visited the tour, with open arms. He kind of "adopted" my son Tal who idolized him. He would put on Tal's hat while he soundchecked, let Tal play his guitar while he drummed, and he hung out a lot with all of us. On the last day of Tal's visit, when he came to say goodbye to Eddy, Eddy told Zeke his guitar tech to go on stage and get number 2. Zeke did and Eddy gave his number 2 Kramer Red/White/Black guitar to Tal. He autographed it to him, and we took a bunch of photos. This was one of those unforgettable moments in one's life that will always be talked about as life changing. Edward certainly changed Tal's life at that point as he did mine.

I had my own precious moment in Knoxville, Tennessee when after the gig about 3 A.M., my room phone rang and a voice said, "Randy, this is Edward. Can you come to my room, 313 right away?" I hung up, got dressed and walked to room 313. Eddy was outside the room sitting on the floor in the hallway, playing guitar. He told me that a friend of his had just passed away (committed suicide) and that he couldn't get to the funeral and wanted to make up and play a song for his friend right then and there, and would I listen to it. I listened to it and told him I was sure his friend heard it too and appreciated the song was "just for him." I wish I had a tape recorder with me as this was the most beautiful and emotional guitar playing I'd ever heard. I'll never forget that moment.

In soundchecks and dressing room warm-ups, Eddy would play the most incredible guitar things that were totally far over the top of what he played on stage. He was a master. He still is. He pioneered that style of hammer-on/pull-off guitar playing, taking it into pop/rock music and making it listenable and commercial. To this day when I hear a VH song on the radio, I always crank up the solo, as it's unforgettable. It's part of the joy of the record and of everyone's life.

Eddy once told me that he didn't care about being remembered for his guitar playing but that he'd rather be remembered as a great human being who was kind and considerate of others. I must say that I will always remember him as both. I'm sure that everyone who got to know him will remember him as a great person who played incredible guitar! Rock on Eddy! ♪

Ginger Baker

I am flattered that the Van Halens were inspired by Cream. ♪

Kofi Baker

Their music is very cool and they are very good musicians. I have gotten into a lot of their music. ♪

Jennifer Batten

Van Halen represented the highest musicianship, creativity, innovation and energy of rock in the '80s for me. Eddie often added much more listener interest to their songs (than what was out at the time) by including a separate soloing section that went into another key. So many rock songs seem so predictable and boring to me in that, by the time you've heard a verse and a chorus, you know the rest of what is to come so there are no surprises. Van Halen always had surprises and fresh news up their sleeve.

When *1984* came out, I called the record shops and stayed on top of the release date because I was so anxious to see what was next for them. The only other time I've done that is when Jeff Beck's *Wired* album was due for release. I was in Tower Records when I heard *1984* for the first time and still remember the feeling from that. I transcribed and wrote out every solo for that and they were the hardest I've ever had to do because of his odd grouping of notes. As he's said in interviews, he has no idea what he does between the bars but always manages to land on his feet. It's that kind of rhythmic tension that really adds to the excitement in his solo. It's like watching someone on a tightrope with no net.

I also clearly remember the first time I heard the "Beat It" solo. I was at a band rehearsal and it came on the radio and the whole band stopped what they were doing and were stunned. I tried to learn that solo and gave up four times before I got it. Needless to say, my persistence paid off several years later when I duplicated it for three world tours with Michael Jackson.

Although the note choices, feel, tone quality and clarity, wicked bends, squawks and screams, and of course the tapping is what most guitar players focus on as "what made Van Halen," it was much deeper than that. There was a band energy that easily resonated with people. Eddie was the first player in years that you would see smiling in photos. It really took the edge off the overly macho tough guy image of rock guitar and made them seem friendlier than other bands. Roth also added a lot to that. There was a very healthy sense of humor in the band. They didn't come off like they were trying to prove they were bad-asses. The talent was a given, and they were up there to share and have fun. ♪

Jason Becker

You hear so much about Zeppelin, AC/DC, Kiss, Pink Floyd, and other old bands like that (rightfully so), but to me, far above them all was Van Halen (mainly the first six albums). Doesn't anyone remember how they completely made other bands look like wimps? And as for Eddie, no guitar player since him has even come close to touching his little toe. Everything about his playing was unique, mind-blowing, and full of emotion. ♪

Adrian Belew

In 1977 I had my first big break being discovered by Frank Zappa. Three months were spent in Los Angeles rehearsing for Frank's world tour. My friend [now guitarist for The Bears] Rob Fetters came out for a weekend visit. We spent one unforgettable evening walking up and down Sunset Boulevard engrossed in conversation about life in general and music in particular.

We loved to talk guitars. At the time we thought we were the only two guitarists in the universe who had discovered a secret technique: playing the fretboard with your right hand. We walked and talked for hours and suddenly we were in front of the famous Whisky A Go-Go. We had to go in. After we settled in our seats an unknown band strutted on stage and began to wail. The guitar player was incredible, playing up and down the neck with his right hand. Rob and I looked at each other in amazement, "Wow, he's using the secret technique like we do!"

Of course, the band was Van Halen, as yet undiscovered or signed to a record label. I loved hearing such a fresh guitarist. It was a thrill to watch him play. That night, my first exposure to Eddie, is a night I will always remember. ♪

George Bellas

I remember quite clearly, the very first day I heard Van Halen. I was in seventh grade and over at this girl's house. Her older sister said, "Check this out!" and then proceeded to put on Van Halen's first album. "Runnin' with the Devil" played and I was immediately captivated (I stopped everything I was doing and hovered inches above the record player), and then came on "Eruption" – my jaw hit the floor!

I was so incredibly inspired it was almost beyond belief. I kept putting "Eruption" back on, over and over and over! That was a great night! Not only did I get lucky with hearing Van Halen for the first time, my girlfriend's older sister became super friendly that evening as well! Hearing Van Halen play guitar that evening changed my life forever.

All through high school I was totally immersed in Van Halen's music. The emotion and attitude Eddie packed into high guitar playing, not to mention his groundbreaking unique techniques, were a constant source of inspiration for me. I bought every album the put out, but seemed to really the albums *Van Halen, Van Halen II,* and *Women and Children First.* Wow, those tunes rocked my world! All the rest of the albums that followed were nothing short of spectacular, but those first three albums hit me like a brick upside my head! It's rare that a player like Van Halen comes along and just turns everybody over on their ears. His playing is so easily recognizable and extremely unique. I also think Eddie has always had a really great attitude, it seems like he is always smiling, and that charisma just shines through in his playing.

Awesome guitar playing, great songs, nice attitude, and killer stage presence make up a great guitar player that deserves front row in the rock history books. Thanks Eddie, for some of the best music and guitar playing the world has ever heard! ♪

Jeff Berlin

Back in 1982 I hooked up and jammed with Edward Van Halen. Our playing together was simply amazing. It was the next generation of Cream. I brought harmony and jazz chops and blended it with his stunning rock playing. Nothing existed like it before or since. If we had played together publicly, we would have changed the rock rhythm section forever. Eddie was great and his brother was absolutely my favorite rock drummer for years. Great time!

I regard Eddie as important to rock guitar playing as John Coltrane was to jazz saxophone. His influence extended to such a range that until Nirvana changed rock music, almost every guitarist in rock played like him. It simply was impossible to find a guitar player who didn't tap or try to get those stunning great rock lines that he came up with. But, Eddie was also the best comping guitarist in rock music, hands down. His background guitar parts were simply brilliant and often caught my ear. They were as important as his solos were. ♪

Kevin Booth

Sometimes people took what Bill Hicks said too literally. In Bill's later years he would sometimes categorize Eddie Van Halen with some other crappy artists just 'cause he was trying to make a point about, like, um, bad pop music in the modern age. So sometimes he would make the comment that Eddie Van Halen was no Jimi Hendrix. That Jimi Hendrix had a dick like a buzz saw and that there will *never* be another man like Jimi Hendrix!

So Bill would say shit like that, but at the same time when we were in our high school band, Stress, one of the first songs we learned to play – like I'm sure many other people did – was the Van Halen version of the Kinks "You Really Got Me." Bill played guitar and I played

bass. And, of course, I had friends back then that when Van Halen hit the scene with that were like, "Man, the Kinks do the *real* version of it." But I'd be going, "Dude, I like the Van Halen version. It fuckin' rocks!" And they would go like, "Oh, that's kinda, like, the queer side of you that likes that crank-it-up thing."

Thing is, Eddie Van Halen is one of the pioneers of that concept of rock. Maybe Jimmy Page had done it before, but Eddie came in with a technical side and a sound, a *tone,* an ability no one had ever matched. To this day no one has. Sure, there are plenty of great players out there that can move their fingers fast and do all that technical stuff, but they'll never have the *balls* of Eddie, you know?

There were many times Bill and I were either tripping on acid or had done a little blow and we definitely got inside of what Eddie used to refer to as the "Brown Sound." The only way you could really experience the "Brown Sound" is if you were playing a really loud, distorted instrument that kind of, like, harmonized inside of your brain at a certain frequency that just felt like a narcotic. Actually, coupled with the narcotics in your brain, you almost had to *be* on a narcotic to totally understand it. It was almost like a visual thing where you'd actually *see* the color brown in front of your eyes if you hit a certain harmonic.

Bill was trying to chase down that "Brown Sound." If he coulda he woulda. He had a Big Muff pedal and a Stratocaster that actually belonged to Bachman-Turner Overdrive. He had an overdrive preamp with batteries installed inside of the Stratocaster. If he could have afforded it, he would have really gone after it. Bill was definitely intrigued with the concept that Eddie used a step-up transformer (Variac) to put higher voltage levels to his amplifiers. Bill really loved the fact that Eddie was known to burn out an amp at almost every single show.

One night, Bill had done a show in Houston and he was on one of his "holier than thou" rants. He was goin' on about how Jimi Hendrx, *that's* a rock star. John Bonham, *that's* a rock star. He was like, "You know, these people think Eddie Van Halen is great, but that's *nothing* like Jimi Hendrix!" So he said all that on stage, but then we get in the car for like a three-hour drive to the next gig and he pops in a cassette of Van Halen's *1984* that he'd just bought! And he played that song "Top Jimmy" to me. As we listened, Bill was air-guitaring along to the song. Bill just *loved* that kind of dissonant finger-picking and all the kinda crazy harmonics that Eddie would throw out there that would make the hair on the back of your neck stand up, you know? "Top Jimmy" was just one of those songs, I think, that no one had really paid attention to. It wasn't like, hey, let's listen to "Runnin with the Devil" or "Panama." We'd listen to "Top Jimmy" and realized here's one that many people, including us, never really paid attention to. Bill and I loved "Top Jimmy."

A cool story that I always remember is from when Bill and I were in high school. We were just kids and we went to a keg-party. And I'll always remember there was this high school house band playing and they were rockin' out. It was a garage band, really, but they had good chops. They had every note down and you can tell they'd done their homework. Well, this keg- party had the first big high school keg-party fist fight Bill and I had ever witnessed. And the fist fight broke out during the guitar solo to "Runnin' with the Devil!" It was almost like the entire brawl, with all the people punching each other and throwing chairs and everything, was like *perfectly* in time with [sings solo for "RWTD," note-for-note]. We died laughing! Bill and I re-enacted that scene over and over again after it happened [*laughs*].

We were both big fans of the Classic Van Halen era. In fact, my manager, Gary Stamler, used to be Van Halen's attorney. He went on to be one of their personal managers as well. Later on, he represented Sammy during the break-up. Gary is still my manager today. He almost managed Bill back around 1991 or 1992. One time, Gary was over at Eddie's house. Him and Eddie were just sitting around on the sofa talking and Gary was like just kind of shuffling through all the papers on Eddie's desk and he found two checks that hadn't been cashed. One was for $80,000 and the other was for, like, $70,000. They were just like heaped in a pile of various papers and junk mail and stuff like that. And Gary was like, "Dude, you didn't cash these checks?!" and Eddie was just like, "Oh, dude, I forgot about it."

Another cool story is when Bill opened for one of our major influences, Eric Johnson. You know, Bill opened the show as a comedian and then Eric went out there and played. Well, Bill got really drunk backstage with Eric Johnson and he was lecturing Eric saying, "You know Eric, if you wanna write some *real* hits, you need to drink some beers or eat some meat or something...put some hair on your chest!" 'Cause Eric doesn't drink and is a vegetarian. So Bill keeps on, "You know Eric, Eddie Van Halen has all the moves (chops) but he can pop out a hit. It's not all just technical ability. Eddie has the ability to make everybody's dick get hard with the right chord at the right time!"

I tell you man, Eric *does* need to eat a burger and drink a beer! The whole "vegan thing" don't work if you're a guitarist. It's, like, pick up a flute...just get it over with already. In fact, Bill used to joke that Eric's guitar sounded like a clarinet! [*laughs*] There are all kinds of crazy stories about

Eric. I remember one story where I heard Eric would *swear* that he could tell the difference between Eveready batteries and Energizer batteries – in terms of when he used them in his effects pedals. He swears he could tell the difference between the two batteries! Or, like, Eric could tell the difference whether a patch cord was goin' this way or that way? [*laughs*] All kinds of crazy fuckin' shit! He was like *super* anal.

Bill was more into the Van Halen thing. You know, that *rawness* and *balls*. In fact, this guy named Ron, who produced my band back in '87, has also worked with Ted Templeman as an engineer. Bill and I were really into the fact that Van Halen could go into the studio and basically just bang it out like a live concert. Ted had the ability to keep it like if they were walking into a live show. They could all be in the same room together, they could all have their amp set the way they wanted…it wasn't like, "Oh, we're in the studio, so we gotta have everything like *this*." And, you know, kinda fuck up their ability to interact with each other.

Personally, I was more in the Classic Van Halen era with Dave. I mean, you know, Dave was a comedian! He had comedic timing. And he was a martial artist, and Bill was into that. Just like Elvis was a martial artist, you know, Dave had all the timing. There was such a raw chemistry between those guys during the classic era that I always liked and I know Bill liked very much, too. We actually went and saw VH in concert back around 1982. They were just the coolest.

You know, even though Van Halen went through the whole "'80s thing," and you see all those television shows now making fun of that shit, Eddie was *still* cool. He got his hair cut at the right time, you know? [*laughs*] He always had a cool sense of humor and the way he handled himself was always very cool. I just don't think there was ever another guy like him. I know he had studied classical music and had been trained as a pianist. Bill and I both appreciated that because we had both studied some classical music. In fact, Bill's dad was a classically trained pianist. Bill was foremost setting out to be a guitar player at first, not a comedian. And Eddie Van Halen *definitely* had a strong influence on him. ♪

Bill Bruford

Eddie Van Halen is a master of the guitar. ♪

Jimmy Bruno

Eddie plays with tremendous passion, fire and energy. It is not hard to be touched and influenced by his guitar playing. Good music is good music, regardless of the style. For me, I tried to copy his energy. ♪

Ernie C.

First time I saw Eddie was back in the '70s, probably around '76. They used to play up and down the strip here in Hollywood. They played a place called the Starwood. They also played a place called Gazzarri's, and I saw them there, too. I saw them play and I thought he was really good. And then, of course, they got a record deal and ended up being the biggest thing of the '80s. Well, late '70s and '80s. When that first record came out, Eddie played some neat stuff. When he played "Eruption" I was like, "What? How's he doin' that?" There were many guitar players out then at the time, but Eddie was at the head of the crop. To me, he was *"the man."*

So a few years back I produced a Black Sabbath record. And I know Tony Iommi, so I took some pictures of me with Tony. You know, pics of me with Tony arm in arm and all that kind of stuff. So Tony says to me, "When you see Eddie, go say hi to him." So one day Van Halen is playing here at the Forum in L.A., and I went down there. I didn't have any tickets or passes or anything like that. Basically, I just showed up, you know? But I knew security and I knew that they were gonna be really cool. Well it turns out security was very tight for this show. But when I got there I ended up seeing those two guys, Mark and Brian. You know, they have a radio show. They were heading out kind of early 'cause, you know, they have to do a morning show. I asked them if I could get a pass and they hooked me up.

So I walked in through security and all that, and I see Matt, Eddie's guitar tech. I say, "Hey Matt, I wanna see Eddie and say hi to him." Matt's like, "Well, you know, Eddie doesn't really like seeing anybody. You know how Eddie is, really quiet." And I'm like, "Ok, cool." I end up just hangin' back there. I even ran into a manager friend of mine. So while I'm back there I see Eddie walking and smokin' a cigarette, doin' the "Eddie Van Halen thing," you know? [*laughs*] His brother was out there, too. So I say hi to his brother and then I went up to Eddie. I had the picture of me with Tony Iommi on me and I said, "Hi Eddie, my name is Ernie C. You probably don't know me. I'm in a band called Bodycount, but I produced a Black Sabbath record and Tony Iommi told me to say hi to you." Eddie looks at the picture and he's like, "You produced a Black Sabbath record?" I'm like, "Yeah." And he's like, "Well, if Tony Iommi says for you to say anything to me, then you're a friend of mine!"

Eddie gave me a hug and he gave me his number, and it wasn't a "Hollywood-thing" either, you know what I mean? He gave me his number and said, "Here, give me a call. Here's the number to my house, here's the number to my studio, and here's the number to my beach house," you know? And I'd call him up from time to time. I believe this was during the time he was getting cleaned up. I've been wet my whole life, so I know how that is.

So I'd call him up and he'd talk to me for, like, hours on end. And I was like, "Damn, I got Eddie Van Halen talkin' to me on the phone!" [*laughs*]

Eddie is great. I remember when I wanted a left-handed Ernie Ball guitar, and Eddie was with Ernie Ball at that time. So I called up Ernie Ball and they wouldn't make me a left-handed one. Man, I *really* wanted this guitar. So I called up Eddie and I was like, "Eddie, they won't make me a left-handed guitar." I say, "Man, this is *your* guitar, but they won't make me one?" And Eddie was like, "Man, they'll make you a guitar. If they made one for John McEnroe, they'll make one for you." Needless to say, they made me a left-handed guitar. Eddie's *"the man."* He's such a nice guy. I can't say a bad word about him. ♪

Emmett Chapman

Edward came over to my home studio on Yucca Trail in the Laurel Canyon Hills and spent a couple of days trying out a ten-stringed, standard tuned Stick. That was in January 1987 and he wanted to record rhythm section tracks with his brother Alex on trap drums, playing simultaneous bass and melody from both stereo sides of The Stick.

He played most of the day, each day, and I became acquainted with him from a most unusual perspective, that of nonstop musical creation. He was working on songs, his own way, improvising on a particular groove until it crystallized into something thematic, structural and repeatable. He seemed never to lose a beat, and when he was talking, the music seemed to continue right on inside his head, having a life of its own. Driving bass lines, counter-melodic riffs, upbeat chords, percussive rhythms, all became elements of an embryonic song which began to take on a living form. He bought two Sticks, but I guess his project was never carried to completion. His instruments just sort of disappeared from circulation and as far as I know, he still has them.

In my studio he played according to the Stick technique, both hands perpendicular to the fretboard, and seemed to understand it well, tapping bass lines and lead riffs counter-rhythmically. On guitar, however, Edward plays a different kind of two-hand tapping method than the one I discovered on my nine-stringed guitar in 1969. He holds his right arm and hand more nearly parallel to the strings, with his guitar more horizontal, always ready to switch back to regular picking/plucking techniques. Of course his left hand and fingers remain in normal guitar fingering position, at right angles to the neck and strings, thus orienting the fingertips in a "line of attack" across successive frets as guitarists do (good for scales and melodies). In contrast, his right hand and fingers are parallel to the neck and strings (and at right angles to the other hand). This is good for melodic arpeggios and pedal points, and Edward uses this hand orientation for an inexhaustible supply of amazing two-handed melody lines, the right hand embellishing what the left hand does.

The Stick technique puts both hands perpendicular to the neck and strings, each hand approaching the fretboard from opposite sides, the hands and fingers parallel to each other. It encourages "drumming" of all eight fingers to execute scales, pentatonics and guitar type melody lines and chords in both hands equally. It also encourages independence between the hands, allowing simultaneous bass and lead lines plus chords.

Edward forged the way and popularized the alternative approach to two-hand string tapping, with graceful and expressive rock styled lead lines. If you want to play guitar type scales and melodies with just the right hand alone, however, his "line of fingertip attack" is ninety degrees off, running across the strings instead of along the frets. Drumming your fingers in this right hand orientation will play the instrument's tuning itself rather than the successive notes in the fret spaces, and you have to move your entire right arm at the shoulder joint to play right hand scales and lines. He seems to have no interest in tapping simultaneous lines and has always concentrated on his blazingly focused, single-note rock lead lines. But of course he has his old standby, the standard right hand guitar technique as a counterbalance, where he often gets two independent riffs and patterns going at once – a nice complimentary blend of methods!

Beyond the tons of publicity circulating around him since the early '80s, Edward is truly a creative artistic force and a gift to American rock 'n' roll. (When you're a gift to the world, performance flows easily.) I hope he will live to be a ripe old age so that we can see where his musical journey finally leads. ♪

Metal Mike Clasciak

Eddie Van Halen is an amazing example of a unique guitar player. Here's a guy that not only has his own trademark style, he *develops* new styles to be copied by thousands later. Of course his sound is also extremely trademark. All these things I respect very, very much. I came into the guitar world a bit late, around 1986, and immersed myself in Yngwie and Steve Vai as my early heroes. However I will confirm that every time I hear early Van Halen records now I get that awesome "This Rules!" feeling and I immensely enjoy Eddie's guitar playing. I'm sort of glad it happened this way, because it allows me to go back and still discover incredible talent. ♪

Rusty Cooley

I think Eddie is a completely brilliant player, always adding something new to the guitarist's arsenal. Eddie really helped pave the way for today's guitarists. ♪

Steve Cropper

Yes, Eddie is a great player. I've only been with him once, shooting a video for Hank Jr. some years back. I have always liked Eddie's style. He always seems to throw in a little taste of R&B in his music and I like that. I'm sure he could do more if the songs call for it and maybe one day he will. I've always enjoyed watching him. He really puts himself into it, he's not just showing off 'cause he can. ♪

Bob Daisley

Regarding Van Halen, the band, I must say that they were the epitome of the beginning of the "'80s guitar-hero rock." As for Edward Van Halen, well, I just love his precision and taste in his playing and choice of notes – a true guitar "hero." He seems always to make a valid musical statement in whatever he does. I know he was an influence on Randy Rhoads and I'm sure on many other players too. I wouldn't say I was a huge fan of the band, Van Halen, but I do have a "Best Of" album that I like to play from time to time. I have great respect for Edward as a player/musician and for the band for opening avenues in music as they did. I think Edward and the boys deserve high acclaim and praise always. ♪

Craig DeFalco

I've known Ed for over twenty years now. One thing I really love about him is he's never been influenced by any kind of music or any kind of musician out there. Other than having respect for Eric Clapton and Jimmy Page, but never sounding like them when he plays. He's always had his own signature sound. A lot of people try to change with the times, with their music, when they play and record. Instead of going with the trends, he sets the trends! Ed is so tuned into his own creativity…he's like an opened channel when he plays!

He is one of the greatest and doesn't show it to the people close to him. I love the guy as a human being as much as I do as a guitar player. Ed puts his family and his friends first in his life. And he really proved that to me when he took my band, Laidlaw, out on the Van Halen 2004 Summer Tour as the opening act. He not only gave me the opening slot but put us in a tour bus, as well. He just blows my mind. And just last week we all lost Dimebag Darrell to a senseless death. Darrell was a huge Edward Van Halen fan, and Edward took that to heart and went to and spoke at his wake for Dimebag's fans and friends. I love the guy...he has a huge heart! ♪

Buck Dharma
Eddie Van Halen is the Jimi Hendrix of his generation. ♪

Al Di Meola
Eddie was an absolute original and innovator in his world! ♪

Chris Duarte
I saw Van Halen in San Antonio back in 1978. I was about fifteen at the time. I think this was their first tour and they were opening for Black Sabbath. I can remember I was all the way across on the other side of the San Antonio Convention Center. Eddie was playing "Eruption," and I could still make out his spidery long fingers. I could see them almost all the way across the convention center! Mind you, the SACC was the biggest venue in San Antonio at the time. It held about ten, maybe fifteen thousand people.

The show was really great. Van Halen had a huge buzz goin' around and their first album was so successful. It was just this remarkable thing. Nobody had ever heard a rock guitar coming across like this. You know, it was crazy. Besides the fact he was bringing back some real work with the whammy-bar. Jeff Beck was about the only one around that time that was really doing work with the whammy-bar. You know, real pioneering work.

Van Halen was obviously going places. They had youthful exuberance behind them. But when you really get down to it, it's always been Eddie. Even in hindsight I can look back at it and you can put Eddie with *anybody*. He's so unbelievable. Eddie's gonna make any band sound good. At the time the chemistry was right for them. Nobody really minded David Lee Roth's antics back then 'cause he was just a way over the top performer! I remember they did "Ice Cream Man" at that show. Dave come out with the acoustic and did it and it was over the top.

You know, Dave was jumpin' around and they were all jumpin' around. It was just way cool. Funny thing is, Black Sabbath is the reason I was there. I was a *huge* Black Sabbath fan. Now I look back and I feel honored and privileged that I was there to witness Van Halen's first tour. I saw AC/DC on their first big tour, too. Those were the glory days, back then.

For me, it always comes down to the fact that Eddie changed rock guitar. And you know he'd be a competent sideman, 'cause his "Beat It" solo is legendary! It's a truly remarkable solo. As far as rock goes, there's hardly anybody better. He's definitely somebody *way* above the rest of us, at what he does. His legacy will last for a long time. I've always been reverent of Eddie and his band. When I'd hear VH on the radio I'd always go, "Oh yeah, that's Eddie Van Halen – *bad-assed motherfucker.*"

Along with the guitar playing, his songwriting is great, too. And that band had great vocals. That's another thing that the music of Van Halen transition smoothly into the pop format. They had these great harmonies, man. When a guitar player can provide competent background vocals, that's something. In Eddie's case, it's exemplary background vocals. I remember when I saw them live and they did "Runnin' with the Devil" and "Jamie's Cryin'," man, they sang it just like on the record. It was flawless! You know, that's not easy to do. When I saw them on that first tour the seed had been planted that, well, this is the King of rock guitar, right here. ♪

Aynsley Dunbar

First off, Alex Van Halen is quite an innovative drummer. I really respect his playing, have always enjoyed listening to him play, and I still do. It really was exciting to have Van Halen open for Journey for our Infinity tour. It gave me great pleasure to watch Van Halen do so well on our tour and then soon become one of the greatest rock bands of our time. They are *excellent* musicians, so to me, they quite honestly deserved it. ♪

Dave Ellefson

Only a handful of times in history has there been a band that completely changed the course of music history. In the late '70s Van Halen was one of those bands. Whatever was goin' on in rock and roll didn't really matter once their debut album came out. Every track was blistering and let's face it, "Eruption" got every guitar player flustered as they tried to figure out how to "play like Eddie." People were even trying to modify their amps to sound like him, hoping that there was a secret weapon hidden somewhere but apparently it was all in his hands.

In fact, VH music could be credited with the early foundings of Megadeth. Back in 1983 I moved from rural Minnesota to Los Angeles. A couple days later, on one early morning, I began playing the bass line to "Runnin' with the Devil" in my shoebox-size apartment. My upstairs neighbor, who was still sleeping, was fit to be tied by my thundering bass line and screamed down at me to "shut up" and then threw a flowerpot on my window air conditioner as an exclamation point to his fury! That neighbor was Dave Mustaine and within days Megadeth was born. ♪

Rik Emmett

When Van Halen burst onto the scene, it was really all about Eddie, as far as I was concerned. It was an "Eruption," and it changed the face of rock lead guitar forever.

He was the quintessential American guitar hero, with the cigarette dangling, the cocky show-off licks and tricks, the smirk, the rock star jumps and California surfboard customized wowie stick guitars. But he was also clearly the real deal. He could *play,* with a really beautiful, solid sense of time that revealed the true musicianship in his DNA and belied the shallow rock star imagery. He had really good hands, coupled with that gift, that knack, for choosing the right notes at the right times. And my goodness, could he ever fire off the runs and arpeggios and the trademark hammer-ons and and pull-offs that made his solos seem like a pyrotechnical display that was blazing, spinning wildly, shooting off out of control, only to resolve them in ways that made you realize that everything came out exactly as he intended it, in that big huge fat Brown Sound that said, "Hey there kiddies, I am Eddie Van Halen. I am the best American Rock Star Guitarist you have ever heard."

Alas, I've never had the pleasure of jamming with him, or even meeting him. It's true that we were on the bill together at the US Festival in '83, but VH had their own backstage compound, and we had our own little trailer area, and I was not (never really have been – probably never will be) much for backstage fraternization anyhow. Plus, those boys had, um, quite the party going all afternoon and evening, with the (relatively) local Hollywood and L.A. people out in full force.

I once went to see a Van Halen concert in Toronto at Maple Leaf Gardens, early '80s, Roth era, and actually got comp tickets to experience it from the house. I had some dude beside me who was puking, almost all over my shoes, and had people running around me screamin' in my ears, with the secondhand dope smoke thick as a Marshall cabinet grill cloth scraping up my nostrils... I also heard one of the loudest bands whose P.A. I ever made the unfortunate mistake of getting in front of (other top contenders are Motorhead and Aerosmith). They were so loud that night that I had to leave early, because the P.A. was literally making me dizzy and nauseous (well, that and the thick smoke mingling with the aroma of vomit).

Anyway, I saw a band (and stood as part of a crowd) that revelled in the excesses of rock and roll. But Eddie was having a good night, so I also got to bear witness to two amazing guitar solos (the extended "Eruption" and the one with the echo repeats and volume knob swells). I also heard some terrific, classic rock songs delivered by one of the greatest American Rock Guitar heroes, in his prime. Which made it all worthwhile. ♪

Michael Fath

I remember hearing Jeff Beck in the Yardbirds, specifically the song "Shapes of Things," for the first time, when it was all happening, and saying to myself, 'That's what I am going to do!' Jeff will always have a special place in my heart for his influence and inspiration, as many other rock players have similarly affected my countenance, but there were only two rock guitarists, that upon hearing their notes grace the airwaves, completely took me by surprise, in a much different fashion. Something more akin to a religious experience, and that was Jimi Hendrix and Edward Van Halen.

The similarities between these two are uncanny, and I am not talking about the obvious. Yes, both were technically different and somewhat superior to many of their peers, both were flashy in their deliveries and presence, and Jimi and Edward were extremely "comfortable" with their respective instruments. My own personal amazement, however, was their superlative grasp of rhythm and phrasing, in other words, they grooved like no other!

Music is a funny thing, and playing guitar can be quite "combative" and challenging, sometimes "deadly," especially if one is competing in the same professional arena with some of the aforementioned players, and also the stellar craftsmen and women of today. I do compete, surviving thirty-plus years, and I am still standing today.

Jimi came out when I was a kid and a decent player, and I was amazed but not so threatened, as I was still "minor league." Edward came out when I was a pro, and still I was truly impressed. Even though I was gathering my own momentum and such, he blasted his way into my heart, and influenced not only me, but also a kazillion others. Again, it was the "reverential" experience, all over again. And for this, I am very grateful, as I will take *any* profound experience and influence, and absorb whatever I can, to be the player that I am.

I've met Edward a few times, participated in guitar ads with him, and have even shared a concert stage. We're not friends, but I do smile when I think of certain tunes, especially Van Halen's early years, and will not forget one of the world's truly best. ♪

José Feliciano

When I first heard Eddy tapping on the guitar strings in a percussive way, it reminded me of my own personal version of a technique that developed out of necessity, really, many years ago in Greenwich Village. I performed solo in coffee houses and at times, while in the middle of a song, I'd feel my shirt tail slipping out from the back of my pants. I'd tuck it back in while continuing to play with the other hand and found that this simple maneuver would get a great reaction from the audience. I decided to make this technique a part of my performance ever since. So I say to Eddy, "Right on! Go for it! It worked for me and it obviously works for you, as well!" He does a great job; Eddy is super! ♪

Anton Fig
Eddie Van Halen is a fantastic guitarist and great musician. ♪

John 5
I started playing guitar when I was seven years old. Not long after that, *Van Halen* was released. I bought *Van Halen* 'cause my friend told me Gene Simmons had been a part of it. Yes, I actually bought that album just because it said "Gene Simmons" in the liner notes. I hadn't heard anything about Van Halen, but I was so into Kiss that I just bought it 'cause it had Gene's name in there. And, you know, I hadn't been playing guitar all that long.

So I put it on and it was an epiphany. Of course everybody probably says this, but it was really like a whole door was opening. It was a sound, a feeling. It's so weird that you could get such a *feeling* from the sound of a guitar, you know? It was like, "Oh my God!" It just sounded *so mean* and *so good*. Even as a little teeny kid, I knew back then. I was like, "Wow, this is unbelievable!" So from then on I was totally sold.

I had this guitar teacher, and it was very strange 'cause he was, like, seventeen and he was so good. He could actually play all of that stuff. I mean, he was my guitar teacher but he was still this kid as well. He was only a few years older than me. He played keyboards, too, and would actually play guitar lines while playing keyboards. It was incredible. He taught me all the Van Halen stuff and I was just sold. For a while all I played was Van Halen. I remember saying to myself when I was thirteen years old, "All I wanna do in my life is play with David Lee Roth." That was my dream. I was such an Eddie fan, and so I wanted to play with Dave. I remember thinking, "If I could be anybody in this world, I would be Eddie Van Halen."

You know, he married Valerie Bertinelli, who was on *One Day at a Time*, and I *love* that show! I just felt that Eddie Van Halen had it all. Well, my dream came true when I started writing for David Lee Roth. I was sitting on my friend's couch, not really doing much, and I saw the book *Crazy from the Heat*. I was playing with Rob Halford at the time. I sat up on the couch and I said, "You know what? I'm gonna call David Lee Roth's manager and see if they need any songs." I knew Dave wasn't really doing much at this time. You know, this right after the whole Vegas thing.

So I called over there and said, "Hi, I'm John Lowery. I just wanna know if Dave needs any songs? I play with Rob Halford right now," and blah blah blah. They told me they weren't really looking for anything at the moment, but that I could go ahead and send them something if I liked. Hey, I felt like at least I'd gotten my foot in the door. You know, at least I can send something to the manager. So I wrote these Van Halen-esque sounding songs. I tuned 'em down just like they did and put that cool reverb on 'em, just like they did. I knew that style so well 'cause I'd studied it my whole life. So I sent it to them and a few days later the manager called back and said, "Yeah, we like these. Can you send us three more?" I was like, "Wow!" Man, I was so over the moon! It was like someone had just told me I'd won the lottery. I was so happy. I could have gone on off just that phone call, alone.

Well, I went in there and wrote three more songs, and it's hard to come up with three songs to please David Lee Roth, you know? Well, the manager calls me back and says, "We like this batch, can you send us more?" And I was like, "Um, no. Well, you guys, I gotta talk to Dave. You know, I have to get some kinda confirmation from him that he's getting these songs. For all I know, you guys could be getting these songs." The manager agreed. He called up Dave and a meeting was arranged at Dave's place. So I went over to Dave's house and he said, "Hey John, nice to meet ya!" I was over the moon! You know, I used to wait at the hotel for Van Halen and stuff like that. This is my first time really meeting David Lee Roth. He's a hard guy to meet. He's actually a very secluded kinda guy. You just didn't see him out a lot back in the day. And he says, "Yeah, we're gonna do a record and we're gonna do it live, like Van Halen used to do it. These are perfect songs for that." And I said, "Well, Mr. Roth, I'm playing with Rob Halford in the day, so, um, can we do it after I rehearse with Rob Halford? 'Cause I'm supposed to go and tour Europe with Rob." And Dave says, "No, son, I want you first. Our downbeat will be six in the mornin', that's when we're gonna start. 'Cause I want you first and I'm not takin' you second."

Like a few days later we get this band together and started playing. And our downbeat was 6 A.M. The first song we recorded was "Slam Dunk." Dave said to everybody in the room, "If you can't do it in two takes, you can't do it. Roll it!" So we played. Well, the version of "Slam Dunk" that you hear on the DLR Band CD was a first take. It's completely live. Man, that was really cool.

The funny thing is, I actually met Eddie before I met Dave. The first time I met Eddie Van Halen was when I'd just moved to California. It was, like, 1987, maybe 1988. I was at the Guitar Center and Ed was there for something. I can't even really remember what it was. Robert Knight, the photographer, was there as well. Robert knew I was a big Van Halen fan, so he called me up and said, "Oh, um, Eddie's down here. Why don't you come down here and we'll take a picture of you two?" Needless to say, I *ran* down there.

I got upstairs, 'cause he was in the upstairs office of Guitar Center, and I met him. And then Robert took a picture of us. That was pretty much the first and last time I met Ed. I remember when the DLR Band album was getting a lot of radio play at that time, as was the *Van Halen 3* album. Both albums were out around the same time. And, you know, Eddie was doing interviews about the album and stuff. Well, they asked him if he'd heard the David Lee Roth record? And Eddie said, "Yeah, I have. And, you know, that John Lowery guy, Dave should hold on to him 'cause he's good." Man, that was pretty cool.

So I met Eddie in the late '80s and I met Dave in the late '90s, but I'd actually seen Van Halen in concert before then. First time I ever saw Van Halen was on the 1984 Tour. Thank God, you know? I was like fourteen or something. You know, I was little but I got a chance to go. I mean, I knew *all* the songs. I knew 'em all and I knew how to play 'em all. I can still remember it to this day. I was on the main floor, about twenty-four rows back. It was just *incredible*. They were *on fire!* They were so good and *so tight* and so on their game. I was blown away. I was in awe, really. I just couldn't believe it! It was just *perfect*.

I remember my good friend JT was there with me. We lived in Grosse Point, Michigan, which is like this upper class place in Michigan. Well, Van Halen was there on a school night, and I remember at 2:30 in the morning he came over to get me in his mom's car. Mind you, we're fourteen years old. He took his mom's nice Cadillac out, picked me up, and we drove *downtown* to the worst, most dirty part of Detroit. These two rich kids, in this nice car, in downtown Detroit, to go meet Van Halen, at 2:30 in the morning! We knew they were leaving that day, you know? Well, we got down there and they were already gone. We were like, "Ugh!" But it's good memories.

I went on to catch several VH tours. Aside from the 1984 Tour, I also got to see the 5150 Tour and the OU812 Tour. Oh, and I just saw them on this last tour, too. You know, the Best Of Both Worlds 2004 tour. And they did a lot of Sammy material, of course. But I have to say it was so good. The songs they did with Sammy were really hit, hit, *hit* songs, you know? They were just *great* songs. We were listening to them live and we're like, "These are *great* songs!" 'Cause I'm a songwriter, you know? I've written songs for all these various artists. So I'm listening to them going, "God, these are such good songs!" They were well-constructed, well-written and melodic. It's great music. So yeah, they did some really great music with Sammy as well.

My buddy Mark Friedman does publishing for Van Halen, on the David Lee Roth side. So he got us such good seats. I mean, they gave us fourth row! We were so close I got a chill. It was so awesome to be so close to them again. Even with all the stuff I've been through. You know, like, hangin' out with all these rock stars and movie stars, and playing with so many different people. I still wasn't jaded. I still got that chill when I was there. I was like, "Wow!" What's even wilder is that my bodyguard is their bodyguard now. So after the show we went backstage and I got to talk to Al. I talked to Mike, too. Unfortunately, Ed had already taken off. But it was great to see them. It was a cool night. ♪

Bela Fleck

I think Eddie is awesome. It's amazing that after all this time no one has touched him at what he does. He is truly an original and a staggering musician. ♪

Marty Friedman

Actually I was not influenced by Eddie Van Halen. That's because when he came out, his playing was so freaking cool that I had no idea where to start to figure out what he was doing. Before you knew it, every guitar player in town was copying Eddie big time so I figured that one more Eddie clone was not necessary so instead of working my fingers to the bone struggling to learn his playing, I just enjoyed listening to it.

Looking back, that was probably one of the best decisions in my career because it forced me to diversify my influences. The first three albums were the soundtrack to some of the best moments of my adolescence. I'd love to hear some new stuff in the vein of "On Fire," "I'm the One," "Atomic Punk," or "Romeo Delight." That music captures such a fun period of time. ♪

Paul Gilbert

I was twelve years old when I heard the first Van Halen album. If I live to be 100, I don't think I'll ever be blown away like that again. Then I saw them live in '79 on the second album tour. It was absolutely life changing. Those guys were having such a *good time.* I'm too young to have seen the Beatles on *The Ed Sullivan Show.* But I saw Van Halen with David Lee Roth in 1979. I have *lived.* ♪

Trey Gunn

The first impact of Van Halen on me wasn't the guitar. It was the smack of the band as a whole. And then...then I began to listen. And really listen.

What was I hearing? Is that a guitar? Is that just a guitar? Is that just *one* guitar? Hold on. Back that up and let me hear that again. That is just one fucking guitar. Playing along with just a bass player, a drummer and a singer. A real power trio! There isn't even a rhythm guitar dubbed in under the solo. Could this be for real?

And then I really began to wonder. What kind of guitar player is that? How is he doing that? Wait a minute. Is he really doing that? Back that track up again. Damn, if he isn't really playing all of that. And I bet...I bet that he played that in one take. Who is this guy? And where is he? Because I think I'm going to have to kill him. But let me hear that track again, first. ♪

Scott Henderson

I think Eddie Van Halen is a great innovator in the world of rock music. Given that so much had already happened in music before he came along, that's really saying a lot. Eddie put so many different things together. He combined technique with the soul of blues. Few guitarists had really ever put that together. The whole merging of chops and feel. Before him there were some chops players and some feel players, but he really excelled in both.

He's a great musician. It's a shame that so many guys felt they had to copy him. In a way, that led to the sorry state that we're in now in rock music. But it's just not those guitarists to blame. It's also the record companies, too. They put out music with fast guitar playing that totally lacked the *feel* and the *soulfulness* that Eddie had. Very few guitarists came after him have that combination of chops and real blues feel that he has. I can understand how people got tired of hearing guys play so many notes, without any real regard for tone and phrasing. Eddie's great tone, feel, and phrasing are what separated him from all those other players who tried to copy him. It's like in the fusion world where a lot of players jumped on the Holdsworth train and played a lot of notes, but without the melodic sense that Allan has.

I kind of lost touch with the rock scene in the '80s, 'cause I had really gotten into jazz at the time. But you couldn't help notice a great player like Eddie come along. It was just like, "Whoa! Man, this guy plays his ass off!" It doesn't matter what kind of music you're into. I mean, anybody, whether a classical musician, jazz musician or whatever, would recognize talent in any field. I have bootleg tapes of Eddie from before he ever came across that two-handed tapping technique, and he sounded amazing then! It proved that he had it then, you know what I mean? I think he would have done great in his career if he'd never even brought two-hand tapping to the table. He is an important player, anyway. Very few players have the chops, soul and musicality of Eddie Van Halen. He really is a special player. That's the total package right there – that's *"the shit."* ♪

James "Papa Het" Hetfield

Picture a bored schoolboy in his suburban bedroom, listening to his clock radio very late one night. Listening this late is against his parents' wishes, of course. It is waaay past "Lights out," you know? Well, he is still not interested in what he hears when, "And now, a brand new song from local band Van Halen," was calmly announced. Instantly "And the cradle...the cradle will rock..." proceeded to punish the tiny speaker. What a sound! He could not believe stuff like this was *on his radio!* From that moment on, this somewhat less bored schoolboy started a neverending quest for the *crunchiest guitar sound known to man.* It still drives me today. ♪

Johnny Hiland

When I think of Edward Van Halen, I see a man of great might with an "out of this world" style of guitar, whose tapping technique flipped this generation on its ears. I have always admired his person on stage because he delivers his style of guitar with an excitement and enthusiasm that is unbeatable, yet he can drag a smoke, stand in one spot and knock the fire out of you with his virtuosity. He gave players like myself finger tapping and a new distortion tone to reach for and still continues to kick ass with his band, even today.

I just recently had one of the best times of my life. I went to see Van Halen for the first time, with my manager, in Cincinnati, Ohio. It was a mind-blowing experience, to say the least! I have been a Van Halen fan for a long time and always considered Eddie a hero of mine. Within the past year of 2004, I have been blessed with getting to know Sammy Hagar, lead singer and frontman of Van Halen. He had me come perform at the grand opening of his new Cabo Wabo Cantina in Lake Tahoe, Nevada. What fun we had!

He is an incredible man with enormous talent who loves life and his fans. It is a sincere pleasure to walk on stage with him. It was a dream come true. He'll put a smile on your face from the moment he greets you, until the time you leave and beyond that. I'll honestly tell you that Michael Anthony is the same way. I did not get the chance to meet Eddie or Alex on this trip, but I am in hopes that one day it will happen.

Van Halen as a band has had so many incredible hits from "Jump" to "Panama," from "Poundcake" to "Summer Nights." Their show is absolutely unbelievable. The musicianship is fabulous! All four members are adept players and performers and the vocals are unmistakable. They will tear you in two with a ripping show. They performed for over two hours with nonstop hits and individual solos from each member. Just unbelievable!

Edward Van Halen set a new standard for rock guitarists with his tone and technique and yet managed to set a new standard for all guitarists with his personality on stage and showing his love for the guitar. He is still a hero to me and always will be one who inspires me every single day. He has made his musical footprint that will continue forever! God love Van Halen! ♪

Wolf Hoffman

I remember very well when I first heard Eddie Van Halen, I thought, "How on Earth does he do that?" I had never heard anything like it! He was incredible and still *is* one of the top players. In those days, the early eighties, he influenced me immensely and I tried hard but could never get anywhere near his style, it never felt like me. So I eventually drifted away, turned to other things and found my own style of playing. One thing if for sure: Eddie influenced a whole generation of players like nobody else in the eighties! ♪

Allan Holdsworth

The first time I ever really heard Edward was when I was on tour with U.K. back in 1979. We played some festivals together. You know, shows where you have three or four different bands on there. Van Halen was the headliner and we were further down the pipe. That's how I first met him and heard him. He was great. I always thought Edward was great. He's a fantastic guitar player. The thing that I always loved about Ed was that he was a really organic player. You know, like, a naturally talented musician. In a way he kind of reminds me of Jan Ullrich, the German cyclist. Jan is one of the most naturally gifted cyclists ever, and I kind of feel that way about Eddie.

I used to spend quite a bit of time with Eddie and I really miss him. I haven't seen him in a bit. The last time I saw him was when Van Halen played San Diego in 1998. He got my daughter and I backstage, and she was really stoked!

Back in 1982, after I split with U.K., I moved to California and started with my own band. We played the Roxy a couple of times and he came down there to watch us play. Ed is really a nice guy, a real sweetheart. He even managed to get us a deal with Warner Brothers. In turn, they brought Ted Templeman in to produce the album. It didn't work out for various reasons, none of which had to do with Ed. All he tried to do was help us. I just kind of had a hard time with it 'cause I thought I'd been signed to do something like what I had been doing, but it turns out they wanted it to be completely different than what I wanted it to be. So I was banging heads with Ted Templeman the whole way through. In the end, Ted just decided I was just too much of a pain in the butt and he says, "You're off the label!" [*laughs*]

The funny thing for us was when I got bounced off the label, the contract said they had to allow us to do one more demo before they would get the right of refusal. So we did a demo, which they then refused, and that demo was *Metal Fatigue!* Yes, *Metal Fatigue* was the demo for the next Warner Brothers record, and they turned it down. So I took that record and gave it to Enigma, which was owned by Bill Hein back in those days. It was kind of lucky for me because they paid for the recording and then I just gave it to somebody else. It was kind of a drag, really, because it was so much better than *Road Games*, you know? But like I said before, none of this was Ed's fault in any way, shape, or form. All Ed did is try to help us. The whole thing was so unfortunate. I ended up having very little input. That's why on the record I put "Produced by circumstance," because I was supposed to produce it as well, but it didn't happen that way. Basically, my hands were tied.

Ed's always been a great. He's a terrific songwriter, too. His guitar playing and songwriting are all part of the same thing, in a way. What he does, and the environment he puts what he does in, is balanced. Otherwise you would be like Elvis Presley sings Thelonius Monk or something. What he does fits perfectly in the area that he's working in. And I know that he can do things outside of that, too. I like his songs. It's hard to write popular music, you know? It's not easy. I mean, I don't think I could ever write anything that would sell *anything*. It just doesn't come out like that [*laughs*]. I remember there was one thing that I wrote and Ed liked it. But the funny thing is if you had given that same thing to him, he woulda turned it into something that would have probably sold. Whereas when I was finished with it, *nobody* wanted to hear it [*laughs*].

I've always liked his music. Although, like many, I think it would be interesting to hear him do a solo record. I think it would be great, actually. Now might be a good time for him to start doing something like that. Who knows, perhaps we could get together and do something? I mean, I'd love to do something with Ed. Absolutely. He could make it sort of like a merging of two sort of overlapping things. I think it would be a lot of fun.

I remember when we got together and jammed at the GIT back in the early '80s. I've actually heard a recording of that jam and it was pretty hilarious [*laughs*]. We were having some fun, for sure. It was just a jam and there was not much regard for the structure of the music, really. If we got together now, we'd obviously have to consider what the structure of the music was and so forth. So, you know, it would be where we could both meet, *together*. As opposed to putting it either in his world or in my world, it would have to be, like, an overlapping worlds thing. It would be a challenge, and I think it would be really cool. I love Ed and I love what he does. There aren't too many people I've come across that I can relate to, you know, musically speaking. But he is one of them. ♪

Steve Howe

When Van Halen appeared, Ed's guitar work certainly reinvigorated the rock guitar world with the excitement of high-speed playing and dazzling techniques. He brought together many of the developments happening at that time, from across the guitar spectrum.

Once again the union of singer (rather two singers) and a guitarist combining their efforts won over the masses but through this, it has earned Edward a credible position in the "All-Time Greats of the Guitar." ♪

Scott Ian

From the first note I heard Eddie play on *Van Halen,* I knew the world was about to change. Eddie revolutionized guitar playing and influenced more people than anyone else before him. I know it's blasphemy to not say Hendrix, but to me Eddie is the undisputed king of guitar. ♪

Chris Impellitteri

Edward Van Halen is one of my biggest influences. The reason I play a Stratocaster is because of Van Halen. "Eruption" and "Spanish Fly" completely changed the way I approach the guitar. Edward showed me I could be technical and yet reckless and get some really amazing guitar solos. I hope to achieve the originality of Van Halen. ♪

Sharon Isbin

Van Halen's virtuosity and creativity sets you on fire. With a gutsy instinct and fine-honed intelligence, his playing is wild, inspired, heartfelt and ravishingly compelling. A true inspiration. ♪

Alphonso Johnson

I do remember the day that I met Eddie (I believe it was in St. Louis) while I was on tour with Santana. In fact, Leslie West was there as well. The thing that impressed me the most was during our time together in that hotel room (I think it was Leslie's room) he showed me how to use his tap style on my bass. He played my bass so effortlessly, even though the action was high, and sounded great. He even gave me a lesson showing me how to play tap and pulling harmonics.

Eddie invited us to his concert that night and introduced me to the guys in the band and they were all really unpretentious and really friendly guys to hang out with. I also remember that Eddie was not very happy with being a rock star because he felt the audience sometimes would respond with applause when he was not playing his best. I think he wasn't sure if they were really listening to what he was trying to say musically or if they were going through the motions because that's what they were programmed to do. ♪

John Jorgenson

I still remember reading about Eddie, this amazing new guitarist, in reviews of early VH gigs in So Cal-based music mags. I lived seventy miles east of L.A., in Redlands, so I didn't get in too often to L.A. unless one of my bands was playing somewhere. I was very jealous of all the great press he got, and thought to myself, "This guy can't be all that great!" Boy, was I wrong!

The first time I really realized the impact he was having was when I attended a big Festival at the L.A. Coliseum in '78. I was playing bass in a band that was managed by Kiss management at the time, so we were able to finagle some backstage passes to the show. On the way from the parking lot to the stage door, "Eruption" was blasting out of almost every car stereo I passed. I had never heard such intensity and technique in a rock guitarist before. This was the dawning of a new age of guitar playing. VH hit the stage with all the fire of a rising star, and gave the audience a stunning combination of musical power and finesse, served up with just enough showmanship from Roth to keep the nonmusical audience members rockin' right alongside the rows of slack-jawed guitar players, who were hearing Eddie do things that they never even imaged could be done!

Many years later in the mid '90s I was working with Elton John. One night we found out that VH was playing in Atlanta, where we were. Big time roadies all know each other, so bassist Bob Birch and I went to our tech to see if he could score some tickets for us. As luck would have it, his buddy was Alex's drum tech, and he got us backstage passes. Alex couldn't have been nicer as he visited with us in the green room.

Eddie popped in for a moment, and told me he was trying out a new prototype guitar for the first time on stage, and was a little worried about it. Then he asked us if we wanted to watch the show from behind the monitor desk, which of course we did, as it was on Eddie's side of the stage. We had a great view of this modern master of the guitar, as he effortlessly coaxed that beautiful tone from his guitar. We watched in awe as Eddie "magically" palmed his pick to reach up and do his trademark tapping, never seeming out of control for even a second as he fired off amazing riffs, squealing pinched-harmonics, diving whammy chords – you name it, he did it!

When it came time for Alex to do his drum solo, Eddie came over to us as he headed off the stage to take a break, and offered to get us a beer! I said, "Aren't you a little busy right now?" He responded only with his familiar sly smile, the one he gets after he plays something that even surprised him! We thanked him so much for the great concert, as we knew that the band would likely be rushed off stage back to their hotel. He was gracious and self-effacing, the model of a great artist who does what he does because he loves it.

Over the years, I have been lucky enough to be in the presence of greatness several times – chatting with Cab Calloway between sets, sharing a 4th of July picnic with Archbishop Desmond Tutu, listening a few feet away from Stephane Grappeli's violin ...watching Eddie Van Halen that day was another one of those times, one that I will always remember not only for the great artistry, but for the kind human as well. ♪

John Kalodner

Eddie Van Halen is one of the greatest rock guitar players of all time. And with his brother Alex and Michael Anthony they make one of the greatest rhythm sections in modern-day rock music, on par with Led Zeppelin and Aerosmith. Both singers were great frontmen, each with their own distinct style. Van Halen is one of the only bands ever to be viable with two completely different singers. ♪

Phil Keaggy

I remember back in the '80s when I first heard Eddie's guitar playing. Not only did he turn the heads of a generation of guitar players, but mine as well. His overdriven sound was distinct and well-defined. One of the things I enjoyed about Eddie's style was that he was having so much fun doing it. That was obviously infectious. He also demonstrated his virtuosity when he played in clean tones. So you knew he had the goods. Eddie will always be remembered for that great solo on "Beat It," but he has contributed a wealth of great guitar playing on all his recordings. ♪

B.B. King

I met Eddie at the Les Paul Tribute show years ago and he seemed like a very nice young man. I'm often asked what I think about guitarists outside the world of blues, you know, far as rock guitar players like Jimi Hendrix and Eddie Van Halen. I've always believed that Jimi, while he was alive, became the number one rock 'n' roll guitarist of all time. Having said that, I must also say that I believe Eddie is a close second. After Jimi died, that's when my opinion went to Eric Clapton as the number one guy. Next to Jimi Hendrix and Eric Clapton, I can't think of too many people who've done more for rock guitar than Eddie Van Halen. ♪

Kerry King

First time I heard Van Halen was back when the first record came out. I grew up in L.A. and "Runnin' with the Devil" was all over the place. So I went out and got the record. It's always the same for me, you hear a song that gets you off and then you gotta go do your homework about it and find out more about it. Then you get the album and you hear the stuff he's *really* doing, like "Eruption," like "I'm the One," and all that crazy shit!

But I never got to see them when they toured behind their first album. From the second album till *Fair Warning,* I saw them like six times in a row in L.A. I remember the first time I went to see them they opened with "Light Up the Sky." It was pretty cool 'cause, you know, I was young and getting into music. They were using all those lights, and the lights are cool. Then when they get to the part where they sing "Light Up the Sky," everything fuckin' lit up! It's just one of those things I'll never forget. Let alone all the crazy fuckin' whacky guitar playing.

When I started playing guitar, Edward was definitely an influence. Obviously, I'm one of those people that likes the first two records, especially, and then the third one and fourth one, too. After that they became more of a pop band. I mean, they were always a rock 'n' roll band, but after *Fair Warning* they kind of became a pop band. Every time they came to L.A., I had to go see them because I knew I'd be blown away by whatever they played. Whether Ed did a ten-minute solo or a two-second solo, you know you'd be fulfilled because whatever he played was what you wanted to hear. Man, when they played it's like the whole building shook. It was a cool time to be a guitar player coming up, watching somebody just gettin' on stage and rippin' ass! ♪

Dr. Know

Eddie's definitely an interesting one. I can relate. You know, what he's been through with singers [*laughs*], and being a guitar player in a popular band, for lack of a better term. I have a lot of respect for Eddie and for his playing 'cause he's always tried to do something different. He's so fresh. Man, I really hope he's doin' all right, as far as his health goes. You know, with what he went through just a couple years back. I hope he's doin' great.

It's just, man, being in a band is not easy. And, you know, people have these expectations, like, "Oh well, Sammy Hagar is not David Lee Roth." Or, like, "Israel is not H.R. or whatever." It's, like, that's not what it is, you know? Whoever, or whatever, is what it is. People just have a tendency to be very closed-minded. They're used to what they're used to. Everybody has their preferences. But hey, if the shit was the other way around, what would they be saying? [*laughs*]

Another one of the many reasons I really respect Eddie is 'cause he was just so raw. You know, he just let it rip. He wasn't fuckin' skinnin' up [*laughs*], you know what I'm sayin'? He's like, "Aight, whoooaaaeeerrrgghhhh!" You know, just like how he feels. Keepin' with the spirit, my brotha. That's cool, 'cause I approach music and guitar playing the same way. Like, a lot of times, after I play a solo, I have to go back and analyze it and be like, "Oh yeah, I did this, this, and that. Ok, now I gotta go play the gig, lemme learn what I did." I know Eddie comes from that school, too. You know, that whole "go with the flow" thing. It's very inspirational. You know, go with the flow and make them fingers go. 'Cause if you start thinkin', then you're *thinkin'*.

The funny thing is, once it's documented on record, everybody wants to hear that shit *exact*. Like, every little nuance, the same way. Then I find myself embellishing on that. Whatever is the theme, I'll take it somewhere else. It's like, "Ok, it's the obvious theme, and here's the other part everybody wants to hear, but I'm gonna flip it *like this*." 'Cause, man, you can't do a cover of yourself [*laughs*]. It's a gift, and you just can't take that for granted. I'm sure Eddie goes through that, and I know I do, too, so I can relate.

I remember how Van Halen came out just after we had formed the Bad Brains. Well, back then we were known as Mind Power. This was when we all hooked up in Washington, D.C., back in '77. I believe the first time I heard VH was, like, when they came out the following year, in '78. Man, I remember people were like, "Yo, you *gotta* hear this fuckin' Van Halen band!" You know, all rah rah rah and this and that. I was like, "Yeah? Lemme hear it." [*laughs*] After I heard it, I was like, "Yeah, ok. Uh huh." [*laughs*]

Eddie definitely had an influence on me as far as being raw and open and just fuckin' *rip it*. Which, you know, that's what I was doin', anyway. But, for lack of a better term, they were more "commercial" than we were. So it's like, here's a "commercial band" with *big balls* and just, like, out there *doin' it*. So just keep on doin' what you're doin' [*laughs*], you'll be all right. Whether you end up being commercially successful or not, you gotta do what you gotta do to feel good in your spirit and in your heart, you know?

Man, he's just so innovative. You know, he's *always* lookin' for the next thing. Like, the whole "Brown Sound" thing is, like, "Tweak this amp! Make that shit do somethin'! Gimme somethin' *different*." In fact, I just had a guitar made. You know, a new guitar that was made for me. I was just lookin' at it and it kinda resembles one that Eddie had. It actually looks like one of his Ernie Ball EVH Music Man guitars. I was actually gonna buy one of those, too! I have played one and I like that guitar. So anyway, I had this guy make a guitar for me and it kinda resembles that guitar. 'Cause it's, like, you want this, you want that, you want this, you want that...then this is what you get [*laughs*]. 'Cause, you know, you want the best of all the worlds. You want to be versatile and you want it be comfortable. You want it to have the maple in it and you want it to sound "tele," "stratty" and everything. So it looks a bit like that guitar.

But while the gear and all that is cool, when it all comes down to it, it's in the fingers. I mean, two people can use the same amp, same guitar, everything, and sound absolutely different. You know, 'cause it's in the fingers. Your attack, bone structure, or whatever. A lot of people makin' amps these days are still incorporating the components of the "Brown Sound." You know, where you can dial it down to lower wattage, as a power section more, to make that amp fuckin' swell and growl. It's like, "Weeeaaaarrrggghhhhhh!"

Yeah, Eddie's always lookin' for something different. Even, like, on that song [Poundcake] when he put that doggone thing on the pickups and went, "Zing!" You know, the power drill? It was like, "Whoa! Here's a new toy!" It was something different. It's all 'bout not being conventional. It reminds me of when people would come out with a new effect, back when everything was still analog, and it was, like, "What if I did *this*? Oh, ok, this is the typical setting, lemme go diagonally to that and see what happens," you know?

Man, the messed up thing is I've never gotten to see him play live! There's been a couple of times when I could have actually gone and shit happened and I didn't. I'm kinda pissed about it. I've seen plenty of footage of him, though. And all my buddies are like, "Yo, yo, you *gotta* see Eddie!" For years now, they've been on me about that. But I've never had that opportunity. A lot of that just has to do with being a musician, you know? Always being on the road and so forth. It's like everybody's touring at the same time [*laughs*]. It's like, "Oh shit, next week so-and-so is playing. Damn, I'd love to see them!" But you can't 'cause you're doin' your thing.

Anyway, no doubt, Eddie had an influence on me. Absolutely. Totally. Definitely. We're kinda in the same mode, like, "Let's do this!" [*laughs*] Hearin' him doin' what he was doin' was like, "Oh, ok, so shit...I can do this. He don't give a fuck, so I don't, either!" [*laughs*] You know, and when Van Halen hit the scene, they took it back to straight up rock 'n' roll. Like, back to the Hendrix school. We gonna play music, we gonna play guitars, we gonna play rock 'n' roll, we gonna have some fuckin' *sounds*, and we gonna have fun!

I can really relate to that 'cause that's what the Bad Brains were like, you know? We were young and very excited and like, "This is what *we do*." We didn't give a fuck who liked it or who didn't. This is what we doin' and we love it. Van Halen had that, too. So you can *hear* the commitment. To me, that's probably one of the most important things. It's not about all the playing or singing or the music per se or whatever. As far as I'm concerned, it's about the elements. There's the technical side, but then there's the *feeling*, you know?

And it could be in a few notes, or it could be one freakin' note. But if you feel that note, that's it. In the end, space is important. 'Cause the shit *breathes,* you know what I mean? Eddie definitely understands that, too. You can hear it in his music and in his playing. Space allows the music to breathe and to flow. Unfortunately, a lot of people don't get that aspect. Or, like, Eddie's amazing rhythm playing. I've always been very aware of that aspect, too. But again, unfortunately, I think a lot of people just don't get it. You know, as a player, you have to cover all bases. There are just so many different aspects, and Eddie does all of them really well.

For me, I just think it always comes down to the fact that he did his own thing. Man, that's something you don't really see much now. It's just so tough these days. You know, with the current state of music and all. On top of that it's, like, everything's been done. Man, there really ain't nothin' new under the sun. We're in the last chapters here. It's so hard for someone to come up with somethin' new the way Eddie did, 'cause it's, like, "Eddie did this and that!" You know, "Eddie already put the drill on the fuckin' thing!" You know, that's played. You can't do that. So, like, it's all been done. Or, "Oh, Hendrix did this and that!" Or, "Wes Montgomery did this!" Or "Holdsworth did this!" You know, Holdworth's crazy. He's outta his mind. Forget about it! I have all his records, like with Tony Williams, U.K., and all that stuff. Man, he fucks shit up all the time! Like, all those crazy, dope, *dope* players leave me dumbfounded. You know, Jimi, Eddie, Wes, and so forth. Allan Holdsworth is in that category, too. He leaves me dumbfounded. It's like, "What the fuck?"

As a player, I feel that all players have a certain respect for one another, you know? When you're on that side of the ball, you know what it's like. And, you know, there's not that many people who are on that side of the ball. For me, it always comes down to doin' somethin' different. In the end, you gotta do you. No doubt, Eddie Van Halen did that. ♪

Wayne Kramer

Ed Van Halen is one of the singular musical identities of our time. He carried the art of the electric guitar to a new sonic dimension. In jazz days, there were a small group of saxophonists everyone tried to sound like, such as Coltrane, Ammons, Prez and a couple others. Today, Eddie holds that same status. He has his own voice. ♪

Wayne Krantz

I didn't really get in on the first waves of Van Halen; I think the first record I bought was *1984,* which I loved. Somebody gave me a copy of *Fair Warning* sometime after that. Of course the guitar was stunning; electrifying. It cut you right to the quick but it had such an organic, warm feeling; something the imitators never got. The context set the guitar up perfectly – with David Lee Roth's cartoon thing contrasting all the musicianship in the rhythm section the balance was dead on; everything in that band mattered. I remember how shocked everybody was at the intensity of it, the completeness of it. It kicked my ass and inspired me. And it still sounds as good as it did then. ♪

Robby Krieger

I definitely believe that EVH is a musical genius. He invented a new way to play guitar that many have tried to emulate, but few have succeeded in doing so. I know because I've tried myself. The trick to playing his tapping style is to get the proper sound. You've got to have the proper amounts of feedback, echo, chorus, and a few other things in the right proportions. That's the easy part. Then you have to learn how to use your right hand all over again. This innovative style is only part of the package. He is also a great arranger, producer and writer. ♪

Jonathan Kreisberg

Eddie was obviously a true natural, making the difficult appear effortless. I have no doubt that whatever style he would have chosen to play, be it classical, jazz, flamenco, etc. – he would have been a monster. The beauty in his choosing of the rock arena is it exposed an entire unsuspecting generation to a great virtuoso while they were partying their asses off. He was never alienating people with his musicianship, he was drawing people into his world of positive possibilities. ♪

Bruce Kulick

Eddie and Van Halen are huge influences on me, and the rest of the rock world. His guitar playing is soulful and quite often brilliant. The band, in all its forms, had terrific material and made you feel good. That is what a band should do, make you wanna move. And Van Halen did that best. ♪

Biréli Lagrène

Eddie is a great master and a monster for us guitar players. I have a big respect for him. ♪

Albert Lee

I first met Eddie through our involvement with Ernie Ball/Music Man. I've been involved with the company for thirty years and was around when Sterling Ball was kicking ideas around for a new guitar. They eventually brought out the Silhouette, which I was very happy to play for a while. In the meantime, they designed a guitar called the Axis, which was to become my favorite guitar. Sterling talked of putting it on the market but got involved with Eddie so my guitar had to wait a while.

They worked very hard on his guitar. I believe they made twenty-six prototypes before he found what he wanted. They copied the neck from his original guitar, which was thinner on the treble strings and a little fatter on the bass edge of the neck. They had a little more trouble duplicating the sound of his pickup and took it apart to discover that the windings were broken and they were trying to copy a broken pickup!

Anyway, the guitar eventually came out with his name on it and when production was under way the brought out my guitar. It was around this time that we did a number of gigs together. We did a warm up at a bar in Malibu with Steve Morse and Steve Lukather. It was a lot of fun and even though the bulk of the music was not exactly what Eddie was used to playing, he shone as he usually does. I remember him being reluctant to solo on my song, "Country Boy." He said he didn't know what to do on it. I told him to just be himself and of course it was great. We later did a jam at the NAMM show with the same players. People always remember that night and I doubt if it will ever be surpassed. We did another gig at the Hard Rock Café in Los Angeles not long after and that was also a lot of fun.

One funny moment I remember well was driving Eddie in my old Ferrari to the MTV studios in L.A., we were to meet up with Spinal Tap. It was one of those hot summer days and my car was overheating so I put on the fan to cool down the engine. Eddie was so uncomfortable he bailed out of my car and rode with some of the other guys we were following. The car still overheats.

The guitar that had Eddie's name on it now is called the Axis. Even though he moved over to Peavey, I have a feeling it's still one of his favorites. I've played with a lot of great pickers over the years, but I never get nervous anymore because I've been on stage with Eddie, Steve M. and Luke and held my own. I figure that it's easy from now on. ♪

Tony Levin

I've always been an admirer of Eddie's playing – the two encounters I've had with him both confirmed to me what a dedicated and talented musician he is.

Years ago, when I was recording at A&M studios in L.A. (with Pink Floyd) I ran into Sammy Hagar in the studio hallway. He told me that Eddie was inside one of the studios, working on his solo album, and playing bass on it. It seems, Sammy said, Eddie was an admirer of *my* bass playing, and had been practicing a part I'd played on a Peter Gabriel track. This amazed me, since I'm not the speediest of bass players, and Eddie... well, it turned out that the part was one (on "Big Time") where I'd had the drummer playing his sticks on the strings while I merely handled the left hand notes. Who else but Eddie would try doing that himself? When I met and spoke to Eddie I joked with him a bit about it ("Oh, you think that part is hard?"), but then had to reveal to him that it took a drummer with two sticks to do the original part.

Some time after that, Eddie was one of the guests at a Les Paul tribute television show, where I was in the band accompanying all the guest guitarists. Most made do with a perfunctory rehearsal, or came into town just for the soundcheck and show, and did some sort of jam. Eddie, though, had written a new piece for the occasion, and we spent hours working it out in the rehearsal studio (hard hours, but extremely satisfying for me) to give the show something he thought worthwhile. And playing that piece live for the television show was one of the magical musical experiences I've had. Like I said before, he combines talent with unusual dedication, and we're the lucky recipients of the great playing it's produced. ♪

Steve Lukather

The only thing greater than Ed's musical talent is his HEART! It seems like we have known each other for many lifetimes! Same goes for Alex. My respect and love for these guys as men and as musicians has no peers. It just is... I am honored to call Ed and Al my soul brothers. Love to *all* the guys but there is a special bond I feel for the VH brothers. A class act and it's all fucking real! It's inspirational to be near greatness like that. Turn it up and learn something! ♪

Steve Lynch

I remember exactly how Autograph came to open for Van Halen on the legendary 1984 tour. We were rehearsing at a place called Victory Studios in North Hollywood. To be honest, we weren't even really a band, we were just kinda jammin' together, not sure whether it was even gonna become a band because we were all playing in other projects. You know, in other paying projects. Kerry Richards was playing in a group called the Coup on A&M Records. Steve Isham (the keyboard player) and I were playing in a group with Holly Pinfield on Dreamland Records. Steve Plunkett, the singer, was playing with Earl Slick in a group called Silver Condor, on Columbia Records. And Randy Rand, the bass player, was playing with Lita Ford.

So we were all playing in paying gigs. We kinda got together more just to jam. But then we started writing songs together and we kinda liked the way it sounded. Andy Johns, the producer/engineer, came down to one of our rehearsals and he really liked the songs. He said to us, "Hey, I've got some free time down at Ocean Way Studio on Sunset, in Hollywood." So we went in and banged out five songs, real quick, over just a couple of days. Well, that demo tape ended up in the hands of David Lee Roth! Kerry Richards, our drummer, was friends with David Lee Roth. He and David used to go jog together up Sunset Boulevard every morning. You know, they would meet together every morning around 8 A.M. and go jogging. Of course, David was interested in what Kerry was doing. So Kerry tells David he's in a group called the Coup and ended up playing him some of their stuff. David seemed to like it and thought it was ok.

But then he played him some of the stuff we had. Well, David really liked it. He told Kerry, "Hey, we're lookin' for somebody to open up for us on the '84 tour." Kerry was like, "Um, lemme go ask the guys." Of course, we *jumped* at the opportunity! We were all in paying gigs, but we had all completed our commitments at that time. It worked out perfectly 'cause we had time to go out on the road for a few months. So we got together back at rehearsal and wrote some more songs because we didn't have enough songs to play a whole set. David heard them and he liked those songs, too. He invited us out on the tour and the rest is history. Mind you, we didn't even have a record deal at the time. I mean, we didn't even have a band name! We actually came up with the name "Autograph" when we were driving a Winnebago from L.A. to Jacksonville, Florida for our first gig on the '84 tour. You know, we had to have something to put up on the marquee, so that's how we came up with the name. As silly as it sounds, that's how it happened.

RCA came out and saw us. Warner Brothers, A&M, all those record companies started to see us. You know, down at the Omni in Atlanta they started a little bidding war. Then, of course, it kinda ended up at Madison

Square Garden with RCA offering us a deal. We actually ended up going out on tour with Van Halen for about three or four months. Then we actually quit the tour because there was no need for us to be out there. You know, we weren't promoting a product. So RCA wanted us to quit, and we wanted to get into the studio. We new this was a good opportunity. I believe we'd played in front of a couple million people by that point. You know, we were playing four or five nights a week in front of twenty thousand a night. Over about a four-month period, well, you do the math. Since we weren't really promoting anything, we figured we'd just go back to L.A. and start on the album.

The opportunity to open for Van Halen on their '84 tour was amazing. That was one of the most legendary tours in rock history. Definitely one of the biggest tours of the '80s, that's for sure. To this day, I'm indebted to them for that.

Opening for Van Halen on that tour, was, um, scary [*laughs*]. They were the biggest band in the world at that point, you know? Overall, I just looked at it like it was great. I've never been a competitive player, so to me it was just great. Van Halen was selling out everywhere they played, every night. Some of the cities they played, a Van Halen concert was about the biggest event of that year. Their fans were pretty cool to us, and the members of Van Halen were all cool to us, too. I remember Mike Anthony was always in our dressing room. He is just the most down to earth guy. Throughout their entire career, it's just never affected him, at all, as a person. Edward and Alex were very nice as well. Then, of course, there's Diamond Dave.

Dave was crazy and animated. He was always the center of attention and very outspoken. Dave is the total party guy, and very witty. We went to a strip club with him once. It was the Cheetah Three in Atlanta, as a matter of fact. We'd gotten done playing and it was still fairly early. Dave was back in our dressing room and he says, "Hey, let's go to the strip club." So we all piled in a couple of limos, but then we end up getting out of the limos and taking the subway there. Which was kinda fun, actually. We all jumped on this late-night subway. I believe it was when the new Atlanta subways had just opened up. We took the rapid transit out there and we went to the Cheetah Three and we had a gas out there.

There was a comedian up on stage and he didn't know who David Lee Roth was. There was an entourage of about twenty of us that sat at this long table that they put together for us right next to the stage. Well, this comedian just got on Dave. That was a *big* mistake. Dave got up on stage, took over, and totally ripped this comedian apart! [*laughs*] He won! The comedian actually laid down on stage and Dave put his foot up on top of him and the whole place was up on their feet cheering Dave on. Man, you just can't get over on this guy. You know, you just can't! He's used to talking in front of twenty thousand people and here's this comedian trying to get over on him. Dave just went up there and ripped him apart. It was hilarious.

Dave was a star from the get-go. He had so much personality. Nowadays, a lot of that "rock star" thing is so contrived. There was a time when people really *lived* the rock 'n' roll lifestyle. They were really *rock stars,* you know? Without even really trying to be, it's just that's what they were. I think Guns N' Roses was the end of that. Van Halen had that, as did Mötley Crüe, and I think Guns was the last band to really live that rock 'n' roll lifestyle.

So yeah, I had a great time on that tour. It's pretty amazing when you realize that Van Halen was less than a year away from breaking up. I have to admit there were signs of that on the '84 tour. You know, backstage and so forth. Sometimes the vibe was so heavy you could cut it with a knife. Why do you think Mike Anthony was in our dressing room every night? [*laughs*] It's a shame. Maybe they just shoulda taken some time off to rethink some things. Hey, hindsight's always 20/20, right? I know David went on, like, a Tibetan adventure. He went on an Amazonian adventure, too. You know, to try to really air his head out. I remember one time we were talking about when he went to Tibet. When he came back, he didn't even wanna be in a band anymore. I mean, I can totally understand how spiritually, that would change you.

Sure, you might be in the biggest band in the world, but it's nothing compared to the size of this world and this universe. All of that angst that went on backstage during the '84 tour, well, I really won't get into it 'cause that's their business, you know? I feel they are the only ones that can really talk about that. But I will say that when they went out on stage you didn't see *any* of that. On stage it was complete camaraderie. Those guys were *consummate professionals.* When the vibe got like that backstage, honestly, I'd just find a little corner to go practice in and put my headphones on.

It's just, man, it was wild. All those months on the road, playing gigs, partying and so forth. Oh, and then there's the women. The groupie scene around this band was *insane.* You know, women were thrown at 'em like Frisbees! It was an extremely chaotic time. Not just with the band, but with their crew and what went on backstage. Man, it was insane. Their crew did not enjoy people trying to bootleg stuff, to put it mildly. You know, like T-shirts and stuff. So they *definitely* took matters into their own hands when it came to that. It was a whirlwind. I look back at it and just shake my head. I look back at all those things we did, like touring with Van Halen, Mötley Crüe, Aerosmith, Ronnie James Dio, and Whitesnake. It was wild times, man.

Van Halen and the Crüe were the wildest. The '86 tour we did with Mötley Crüe was just as insane as the '84 Van Halen tour. It was overboard! After that tour I quit drinking for about five years. Basically, I didn't remember that much of that tour [*laughs*]. I mean, we would wake up on their tour bus, and they would wake up on our tour bus. It didn't matter 'cause we were all going to the same city! But it was absolute mayhem. Utter chaos. If they ever did a VH1 *Behind the Music* on Van Halen it would probably have to be, at the very least, a two-hour special. And that would be the "edited" version, ok?

It was over the top. Van Halen were definitely in the ranks of Led Zeppelin, Mötley Crüe, and any of those bands that had a complete overkill of backstage activities, so to speak. The things they were pulling in hotel rooms was complete madness! On top of all that, the '84 tour is when Dave had his mini-bodyguards. You know, the midget bodyguards? Or as some referred to it, his "little man security detail." They would be in on some of the action, too. Dave would get those guys laid all the time. In fact, the midgets probably got laid more than anybody! [*laughs*] And here we are, on our very first tour, right in the middle of all this pandemonium. I still look back and go, "What the hell was that?" I mean, that was a great, *great* part of my life. But would I get back on a tour bus and do it over? Um, no [*laughs*]. It was insane!

I remember that with the VH show they would have this whole section backstage of all women. It's funny 'cause when their road crew would go and hand out backstage passes, they would tell the girls, "Is that your boyfriend? He doesn't come back. No guys backstage. Sorry." It was only women, unless it was someone from the press or something like that, of course. Other than that, it's only women, period. And so, of course, most girls left their boyfriends behind. It's like, "Hey, if I could go backstage and have sex with David Lee Roth, see ya later!" I quickly came to realize what the whole bodyguard thing was all about. You know, why they needed bodyguards around them all the time. Most people never think about it, but there are a lot of jealous boyfriends and husbands that wanna kill these guys 'cause they may have ruined their relationship, marriage or whatever just by breezing through town one night.

These women would dress in the skimpiest outfits and, no matter what cost, place themselves right at the front of that stage. They made sure they were seen, whether by someone on stage or by one of the crew guys. Sometimes I'd walk out on stage and forget my guitar parts! I'd just be standing there goin', "Oh my God, look at all the eye candy!" Van Halen drew tons of fine lookin' women, and every chick out there wanted to jump those guys.

Again, without getting into too much detail, I will simply assure you they were livin' the rock 'n' roll lifestyle. It was absolutely goin' on, 100 percent. Man, everything you've heard and a lot more. A *whole* lot more. There is stuff that went on that nobody even has a clue about. It was totally over the top. Van Halen and Mötley Crüe were definitely the wildest, baddest bands out there. I went on tour with both of these bands during their heyday. I was a part of two of the wildest tours in rock history: the '84 Van Halen tour and the '86 Mötley Crüe tour. I witnessed both of those tours and I just went, "My God!" They were livin' the ultimate rock dream. ♪

Harvey Mandel

Eddie's a great player. I call him a *"slickster."* He's sharp, like a gunslinger. Like a young guy who was fast and wild. You could tell he was good. I'm not really into that kind of music, per se. But as a guitar player, I really respect him. He's a good musician. To be honest, I wasn't even that thrilled when I heard him on record. You can't always tell on record, you know? You hear a record and think, "Yeah, ok, that's cool." But then I saw him play one time in person. When you hear someone play for an hour, and you watch him do all kinds of wild shit, then you really know what they are capable of doing. Being the guitar player that I am, I can tell by looking at him and just watching him play in person how good he really was. ♪

Michael Manring

Eddie was a big influence. Although some people might criticize Van Halen's music for being commercial, there was just no denying the passion and creativity Eddie brought to the guitar. His blend of technique and energy was inspiring and infectious. In fact, I think he was probably one of the most influential musicians of our time. It was funny because at the time they were popular my main gig was with Windham Hill records, doing lots of very mellow music. It may seem odd to have been influenced by someone who was sort of at the other end of the spectrum, but the way Eddie opened up the instrument and expanded its potential transcended genre and style.

Every once in a while someone comes along who shows you that an instrument is much deeper and more expressive than was previously thought. It's always a unique thrill when that happens and it gives you the sense that the world is full of extraordinary possibilities. Eddie is definitely that kind of musician. ♪

Jeff Mantas

I remember the first time I heard Eddie play. I took my brand new copy of *Van Halen* out of the packaging and eagerly placed it on the turntable, cranked up the volume and let it rip. What hit me was so unexpected, it left me stunned. My next reaction was to look at the guitar standing in the corner of my room and think, "What the hell is this guy doing?!"

At this time in England there was all these rumors going around the metal scene about this American guitarist who was amazing, who had taken metal guitar to another dimension. I still don't think that prepared anyone for just how damn good the guy was! I was hooked!

The first time Van Halen came to England, I believe they supported Black Sabbath. I'm sorry to say that I missed them that time around, but when they came back to headline I was there. They played the City Hall in my hometown of Newcastle. The air was electric with anticipation. I was a few rows from the front of the stage and I remember the guys in the balcony who could see behind the curtain yelling down to us how many speaker cabs Eddy had on his side of the stage.

When the curtains went back and they hit the stage, you could hear the collective jaws of the audience hit the floor. The City Hall had *never* seen anything like this before. Then it happened... "Eruption!" All eyes on Eddy as every guitarist in the crowd was fighting to get a better view of what the master was doing. It looked effortless as he smiled his way through it, and I am proud to say I was there to see it.

Saturday afternoon in Newcastle and every budding young rock star would hit the music stores to try out all the guitars they couldn't afford. I was no exception. One thing that became apparent was that the old standard of picking up a guitar, plugging in and, much to the dismay of the music store staff, annoying everyone with your best rendition of "Smoke on the Water" was being replaced with would be right hand hammer-ons and tapping techniques, courtesy of you know who. One music store in Newcastle actually had a sign up which read: "Anyone playing Smoke on the Water will be forcibly ejected." So I think Eddy did the music store a favor, ha ha!

Every young guitarist had his own version of "Eruption," none of which were probably right. Debates would rage about which notes he was playing and how he was doing it. But what is most important is that he introduced us to something that was essentially new. He may not have been the first guy on the planet to use right hand hammer-ons and tapping, but he certainly was the first guy who we all would acknowledge as bringing it to the mainstream.

Eddy's impact on rock and metal guitar was and remains huge and massively influential. Which guitarist out there can honestly say they haven't taken or tried a little bit of what Eddy has done or created? Whilst I would never claim to have risen to the dizzy heights of technical perfection that everyone so easily associates with Eddy, I have to admit borrowing a few ideas here and there. Things that without listening to Eddy's playing, I probably would not have even thought of doing.

As a guitarist I have always thought of myself as being adequate for what I am doing at any one time, so, when we recorded "Welcome to Hell" almost twenty-five years ago, that was the absolute best I could do at that point in time with the knowledge that I had. Just as when I recorded "Zero Tolerance" almost twenty-five years later, the same ethic applied. I have always considered myself more of a songwriter than a lead guitarist, and believe that a guitar solo should be able to take a song to another level, not just be there because the formula dictates so. This is one thing that I think Eddy does so well. His solos are not just there as another texture. They are musical pieces in their own right and become an integral part of the song. One solo that I can attribute directly to Eddy's influence was the solo I played on a song called "Western Days" many years ago which consists entirely of right hand hammer-ons and tapping. Another piece is the opening to a song called "Cry Wolf," which is all octave harmonic tapping of a chord structure.

Whilst imitation is the sincerest form of flattery, remember, Eddy was original. You may be able to play "Eruption" note for note at a million miles per hour, but you will *never* be Eddy! As musicians I believe we should always strive to have some form of originality, something that is uniquely you. My point being is that you know it's Eddy when you hear him. That's a rare gift only a few achieve. Then again, Eddy is a unique talent, and one that the world of guitar should be grateful for. Long may he continue... ♪

Frank Marino

I certainly think Eddie Van Halen is an excellent guitar player, and I also certainly think a lot was made of the hammer-on thing. But that doesn't mean that he made that happen for himself by some kind of dishonest trickery. Not in the least. Look at it this way…If you take a guy like Hendrix and then see what became of his fame when he rose, you could easily point to burning guitars and antics and the like, and say that was what made him famous, and you'd be quite right. Hendrix was truly made famous as a guitarist by things that had *nothing* to do with guitar. But that says more about critics and the listeners than it does about Hendrix. It's almost as if I would say, "Too bad that such a great talent had to be noticed for all the wrong reasons." But isn't that usually the case in our business?

Eddie Van Halen rode the "hammer-on" trick, Hendrix rode the "burning guitar," and I rode the "second coming of Jimi" bullshit, but all of these were simply in the public mind, because that's what the press played up. But that doesn't and shouldn't discredit the actual musician in question, or delegitimize what they did, played, or stood for. Because each of these guys, myself included, was simply a musician who honestly wanted to play music for people, and did it to the best of their abilities. But for the press it's always about hoopla, never about music, except for a few exceptional journalists. That is the terrible thing about our industry, it always has to come down to the lowest common denominator: entertainment for the masses. We could easily say also (and I have said so) that Eddie's fame was helped as much or more by his singer. Do we really think a rock band like Van Halen would have become the powerhouse that they did were it not for David Lee Roth's over-the-top personality? Or how about Keith Richards? Would he have been as noticed in the long run without Mick Jagger? Or Joe Perry without Steven Tyler? So I hope you get the point.

No, Eddie is a good player and probably a great guy (I don't know him). But all of us who share this business also share the luck-of-the-draw odds that some journalist or media group will take notice and publicize our work, to our credit and hopefully not to our degradation. In my own case it has always been more degradation where the media was concerned. But I was fortunate enough to have had fans that didn't care about all of that malarkey, and they stayed with me to this day. I don't know, maybe it was because the more I got pilloried the more I made the same kind of records, fame be damned. So after some people saw that I certainly wasn't getting rich off this music thing, they must have figured I was honest about it all along. 'Cause if pulling the wool over anyone's eyes had ever been my motivation, I certainly would have changed courses (like a savvy politician) as soon as they started writing that I was a graverobber and the like. It became clear that I certainly wasn't benefiting from the press coverage, that's for sure.

And so it is with Eddie, although he did make a whole lot more out of the business in a material way. But that shouldn't disqualify him in anybody's mind when it comes to his talent and/or sincerity. Like every other one of us, he learned the guitar, played it well, joined a band, got lucky because of certain things, and made it to the top. Good for him! Everybody wanted that to be the script for themselves. I wish that all the guys who went through the same thing would have made it as well. And I wish that anyone doing it from here on in would also make it to the top. The only guy I don't wish that upon is myself, 'cause I really didn't want to be "at the top," and never really wanted it in my heart. Certainly I'd like to have money for my work, that will come or it won't...nothing I can do about it. But right now I just want to have fun making music, rich or poor. Fame I'll leave to the politicians. ♪

John McLaughlin

I've always liked Eddie Van Halen. He is a great, revolutionary guitar player! ♪

Chris McLernon

So my friend Len says, "Dude, you gotta hear this band." It was late fall, 1978. Something new had hit his ears and he had to share. We rent to his room and he handed me an album cover while the LP spun on the turntable and he dropped the needle. He might as well have dropped a bomb. The sound of backwards car horns permanently pushed their way onto my musical highway and launched into "Runnin' with the Devil." I looked at the cover. What the hell is this? Four guys, kinda blurry, and the guitarist has some sorta candy cane guitar I'd never seen before. Hmmm... Cool song titles... How is that singer bending backwards like that? Gene Simmons gets thanked...odd. Then "Eruption" started. And everything changed.

I had heard of these guys. American Top 40 had spotlighted the Van Halen brothers the summer before, with their cover of "You Really Got Me." I loved that, but had never found the album in the small town that I was from. And these four guys sound like twenty. It sounded like a band I wanted to be in. It was huge, it was fast, fun, powerful and and before I knew it, side one was over. From there, I made sure I got every other LP. I saw them five or six times and when I moved to L.A. in 1985, I hoped that they'd be someone I'd see there, too. You know, in person, instead of in concert. I never ran into the band, but I ran into Ed. Literally. He was producing a band in the same recording studio my band rehearsed in, and I loudly and blithely drowned out a phone call he was having. His hair was really bushy, and I didn't recognize him as *him*, but went over and apologized. Then I saw *he* was him.
"How ya doin'? I'm Ed."

Whoa...

I apologized for being so loud, introduced myself and from there, we jammed, we bowled, drove around the valley listening to Deep Purple, all the things that dudes do when they play music to play it; to enjoy it. No pretense, all personality and honesty. When we jammed, it was Zeppelin, AC/DC, and Sabbath, with Ed doing dead-on imitations of his favorite guitarists. When we bowled, it was one big insult after another. No wagers, though. Purely for exhibition's sake, I assure you. Man! This guy would have fit in with us as we listened to those loud guys from Pasadena in 1978! He would have jumped and yelled like we did, eating up the sonic adrenaline.

It's odd – I don't care that he's famous. I always told him we'd be bros if he worked at the gas station down the street. We just got along. It didn't matter to me who he was after the shock of our meeting. You meet some of your influences on the way to your own fame and fortune and some are complete and utter pinheads. Luckily, some are guys who you really do wish were in your band, or in your neighborhood. And he's one of them. Don't get me wrong, he's aware of what he's accomplished, and what his influence is, and we both knew this. No false modesty there. Instead of being a burden, it fits him like an old pair of Earth Shoes. It's not a garish birthmark he wants everyone to look away from. Nope. Quite the opposite, actually

And when we did talk music (it was mostly bad jokes and bowling taunts), he always mentioned the band. The Band. THE BAND. Oh, and one other guy. Alex. Most people probably don't know how much the younger looks up to the elder. Maybe Al doesn't. But if you are around Ed for five minutes, you'll realize that while he may be the soul of the band in the public's eyes, in Ed's eyes, Alex is the engine, the airframe, the navigation system and the power that leaves everyone else lost in the Van Halen jet stream. Mike? "The guy you always want in your band," he said. Singers were coming and going at that point, and will probably continue to do so. But he was always consistent. Whatever I heard in a conversation, he would repeat verbatim in the press, so, no candy coating (as I'm sure everyone has seen by now).

Hanging around with him that summer taught me a lot of things, but I still remember this the most: Music is the great equalizer. We both picked up instruments and played them because it was something we had to do. He might be more able than most, but he never threw that gauntlet down. He paid me a huge compliment by telling me I had the ability to fall down the stairs and land on my feet. Knowing that was his main outlook on life, I was flattered and inspired. In 1978, it was cool enough that he could share his music with a kid in a New Jersey dormitory. It was even better a dozen years later to find out that we both remembered the reason why music spoke to us. I'll bet if I ran into him tomorrow or ten years from now, it'd be exactly the same – still bros, still laughing and playing music. And you can't beat that. ♪

Steve Morse

I was immediately impressed with his smooth, musical instincts when we were playing together. He seemed to pick supporting parts that were solid, simple, but had some rhythmic variation. When he took a solo, it was always fluid and natural. When we played out first gig, he invited us to his home to hang out from sound check until gig time. He and his wife were very gracious. I particularly like playing with very talented people, and he has tons of talent! ♪

Dave Navarro

I grew up listening to a lot of Jimi Hendrix, Led Zeppelin, and Cream. You know, a lot of that '60s rock music. When I was in about fifth or sixth grade, I heard *Van Halen.* I was already a guitar player at that time. Soon as I heard "Eruption" it was just so completely mind-blowing. I knew that this was the *"new shit."* Of course, I've been a fan ever since.

Throughout the history of rock guitar playing, I think of there being two major reinventors of the craft. The first, of course, is Jimi Hendrix. Since Jimi Hendrix, I would say there has never been a greater reinventor than Eddie Van Halen. I think Eddie's totally reinvented the instrument and the sound, and he managed to do it in a way that was tasteful. There are a lot of guys out there who do a lot of tricks, but Ed really had his own thing.

I've seen Van Halen live a number of times, back around *Women and Children First, Fair Warning,* and *Diver Down.* Yeah, I saw all those shows and they were great. I've never seen them with Sammy Hagar, but I met Ed last year and it was just amazing. He's just fuckin' awesome, man. He's Ed – the guy can do no wrong. ♪

Ted Nugent

EVH is certainly one of the top innovative virtuosos in history. His sense of musicality and rhythm is truly gifted. The man has immense soul and primal feel. His explosion on the music scene was a pivotal reminder to me to let 'er rip. Though I had no shortage of rip, it's good to be prodded, and that he did. He also opened up certain sounds and harmonic windows to break, that all musicians appreciated.

It was refreshing to witness the hyper energy of their spontaneous vitality out the gate. DLR was an immediate classic and between EVH's dynamo guitar fire and Alex and Michael's incredible tight rhythm slam, it was, and is, some of my favorite R&B and R&R intensity ever. The boys gots the shit. They move me. ♪

Jas Obrecht

I met Eddie Van Halen in July of 1978. I'd just gone to work for *Guitar Player* magazine a month before, and I was standing there the day the first Van Halen album arrived. We put it on the stereo in the main editor's office, which was a gentleman named Don Menn. When the song "Eruption" came on, we were kinda dumbfounded because we couldn't figure out what it was. I remember Don Menn saying, "Is that a keyboard or a guitar? If it's a guitar, I've never heard anybody play that way." So it was *really* different. Also, he had this fire-breathing tone that just seemed to leap right off the vinyl. It didn't sound like any of the records that were coming out around that time.

In terms of guitar technique, it stood head and shoulders above anything that had come out since Jimi Hendrix.

So about a month goes by and I get sent on my first rock 'n' roll interview, which was Pat Travers of the Pat Travers Band. It was one of Bill Graham's "Day on the Green" concerts. It was the very first time the Van Halen band had ever played in northern California. On the ticket was AC/DC, Aerosmith, Pat Travers, and maybe one or two other bands. Anyway, I go there to interview Travers and I had my tape recorder and all my stuff. It's my first big gig at a big stadium. When Travers gets done with his set, I go into the dressing room and he's busy partying with these party girls he had there. He kinda waved me away and said he didn't wanna talk to anybody right now and let's do it another day. I was unhappy about this, you know?

So Graham, bless his heart, he used to have these beautiful spacious setups backstage for the artists and the journalists. They would have, like, pinball machines, food, pitchers of margaritas, and so forth. On this particular day he had, like, a half basketball court. So, being kinda angry at Travers, I start playing basketball. After a while, this kid walks up and says, "Hey man, can I shoot with ya?" I said, "Sure." So we played one-on-one for about fifteen or twenty minutes. When we get finished, we went to the side of the basketball court to cool off, 'cause it was a hot summer day in California. And this kid says to me, "Hey, what band are you in?" I said, "I'm not in any band." He goes, "What are you doing here?" I said, "I came to interview Pat Travers for *Guitar Player* magazine, but he blew me off." I'll never forget, the kid goes, "Pat Travers blew you off? I can't fuckin' believe it! Why don't you interview me? No one ever wants to talk to me." I said, "Well, who are you?" He goes, "My name's Edward Van Halen." I went, "Sit down!" 'Cause I'd just heard the record, you know? So we sat at the edge of that basketball court and did his very first interview.

So the first story came out in the November issue of *Guitar Player* in '78. Eddie calls me up and says, "Hey, I really like this, man. This is nice." We did another interview, when he did his second album, on the phone. Then Edward called me up one day and said, "Hey, everybody wants to sound like me. You know, everybody's always buggin' me. So I'll make you a deal. If you put me on the cover of your magazine, I'll tell you all the secrets to my playing." Naturally, I jumped on it and said yes. So that was the April 1980 cover story – best-selling issue of *Guitar Player* magazine, *ever*. It flew off the newsstands!

Anyway, I went down to L.A. to interview Eddie for this cover story, which was his first cover, and we did it at Neil Zlozower's photo studio. Zloz was there to take photographs of his hands, to shoot Eddie and this and that. During the course of the afternoon, Eddie gave me this really detailed explanation of how he performs his techniques. Like, finger tapping and finger tapping with the right hand moving below the left hand, as he hammers on and things like that. While this was going on, Zlozower took photos of it.

I remember when I first met Eddie in June of '78, he was playing this black and white Strat-style guitar he'd made himself with a Charvel body and neck (I forget the combination). It had something really unusual about it, which was that up at the nut, where the string goes across to the tuner, he had cut the slots extra wide. I'd never seen that *before or since.* You know, where a string would be flapping around so loose in there. But he played with kind of a light touch, and was able to play the guitar without throwing it outta tune.

I remember also, during that interview for the 1980 cover, Van Halen played me an unplugged version of "Eruption." He didn't have his guitar plugged in and he played "Eruption" for me then and there. Man, it sounded *identical* to the record. Without the amplification, without the dive-bomb effect or any of that, it still was, you know, recognizably "Eruption." That was an *amazing* experience. It taught me that the beauty of Van Halen's playing comes from his hands. He has powerful hands. I think that's what really sets him apart. Like, Jeff Beck has those hands that are like baseball mitts, sort of really strong mechanic hands. Van Halen has really strong hands, too. Stevie Ray Vaughan had similar hands as well.

When I first met Eddie in '78, I remember he was real muscular, kind of a pimply-faced kid, and *really* passionate about his music. That was the thing. The other guys seemed like they were into the "rock 'n' roll dream" and all that, but Eddie was just focused on music, music, music. He's just one of these guys where every fiber in his body is musical.

So after we get done with the Zlozower interview, Eddie's driving me back to the airport in his Toyota Land Cruiser. We're on this street in Hollywood that's got a light and maybe six or eight cars between us and the light. And I'm running late for the plane. Eddie looks over at me and goes, "Hey man, hang on!" I said, "Ok." He wheels the car up onto the lawns of the houses and tears off! We're going down the street over all these people's lawns at about three in the afternoon, driving a Toyota Land Cruiser. Then we got to the edge of this curb and he slams down into the street and takes off. Then he screeches his brakes on and asks me if I could loan him five bucks 'cause he's gotta buy a pack of cigarettes [*laughs*]. I said, "Sure, man," and gave him the money. He runs in, runs out, throws me the pack of cigarettes.

For some reason, we started talking about financial stuff. I was surprised to learn that Eddie had made less than I had that year. I don't remember the figure, but it was not a lot. I was like, "I can't believe this? You've got, like, three Platinum albums! How can you not be a millionaire?" He goes, "Well, you know, we split everything four ways, and they tell me they put all our money back into lighting and trucks and stuff. All I know is I never see it." I thought that was quite a revelation 'cause at that time, Eddie was the most important guitarist in rock 'n' roll. He was certainly the most visible.

Eddie was one of those rare characters who introduced a new vocabulary into the language of rock guitar. Only a few people have actually done that. You know, the main guys: Chuck Berry, and Hendrix, especially. Then there's Eddie Van Halen, and there's really been no one quite like him before or since. The Edge brought in a whole new way of playing. You know, his limitations became his strengths. He played simple figures with repeat echoes. At the time the Edge came out and at the time Van Halen came out, all the local music newspapers would have ads, you know, like for "Van Halen style guitar" and for "The Edge style guitar." Eddie's impact was *immediate*. It echoed through the upper echelon of the guitar world, almost overnight.

I heard rumors in 1980 that some of the world's greatest and most famous guitar players were dumbfounded by Eddie Van Halen's playing. When I actually got to interview some of these players – who shall remain nameless – they'd ask me about his pedalboard. They'd ask me about his equipment secrets. They'd ask me if he sped up his playing on the tape so it sounded like he played faster [*laughs*]. I remember Danny Kortchmar, this New York-based studio guy, saying to me, "Yeah, I go into gigs now and everybody wants me to sound like Eddie Van, Eddie Van...that's all I hear is Eddie Van!" I think Eddie caused a lot of pain to a lot of up-and-coming guys, too. I've heard stories of famous guitar players who were coming up when Eddie did, who would have, like, crying fits and nervous breakdowns, simply because they assumed that *they* were gonna be the "God in ascension." Once Eddie came on the scene there was no question – this is *"the cat."* There's nobody else like him. He's number 1. He's the most visible guy and he had the talent to back it up.

I remember that Eddie used to call me up like at two or three in the morning, while he was on the road, just to shoot the breeze. This was in the days before he was with Valerie. I'll never forget one time he wakes me up in the middle of the night and we start talking. I was always happy to hear from him 'cause I just liked him as a human being. He says, "Hey man, we're in Detroit today, and I went to this music store and I bought a Wurlitzer organ!" I said, "Oh, cool." Remember, I'm like, half asleep. He goes, "Yeah, I already wrote a song on it. Listen to this." He puts the phone down by this organ and he starts to riff for me for about four or five minutes. I remember trying to stay awake. Like I said, I was awoken from a deep sleep.

So, he gets all done playing me this thing and we talk for another half an hour or so. Then we say goodbye. You know, I didn't think about it. Then about two or three years later, 'cause this was around 1980 or 1981, this guy I work with asked if he could borrow all of my Van Halen tapes to run safety copies of. I said sure, that's a good idea. So I gave him eight or twelve, maybe fifteen cassette tapes. A week or so later he comes walkin' into my office holding this one tape in his hand and he goes, *"Do you know what's on here, man?!"* I said, "Van Halen, right?" He goes, "Do you remember the time, years ago, when he called you in the middle of the night from Detroit and he'd bought this Wurlitzer organ thing?" I said, "Yeah, I remember that." He goes, "Do you remember that song he played you?" I said, "No." He goes, "It's 'Jump,' three years before they recorded it!" So he had written "Jump" the night he bought the keyboard. I remember him telling me at the end of playing it that he thinks it's a cool song, but he's afraid to show Dave 'cause Dave's gonna put him down.

Eddie was a very sensitive guy – especially back in the early days. I read an article in *Interview* magazine a long time ago, and I later talked with Valerie about this. *Interview* magazine asked Valerie Bertinelli if she remembered the moment she fell in love with Eddie. She goes, "Yeah, I'll never forget it." She said that they were playing somewhere and Eddie got a call from his friend at *Guitar Player* magazine – which was me – that he had just won the best overall guitar category in the reader's poll for *GP* magazine. In other words, he was considered the best guitarist on Earth for that year.

The way Valerie told the story, and later told it to me a second time, was that Eddie got really upset because things were bad with Dave. Apparently, Dave was freakin' out because Eddie was gettin' all the attention, and that *profoundly* bugged David Lee Roth. I don't care what anybody tells you, it bugged the hell outta him. So he and Eddie had just had some kind of an argument before Eddie came back to the hotel. Then Eddie gets a call from me saying, "Hey man, you won! You're number 1. You beat everybody!" Valerie told me that after he got off the phone, Eddie looked at her and starts to cry and says to her, "Why does all the good stuff always have to happen to me?" Then he looks at Valerie and he says, "I love you." I believe it was the very first time he'd ever said that to her, apparently. And Valerie said, "How can you not fall in love with a man at that moment?" I've always thought that was a cool story.

Then when I ran into Valerie in about '85, I asked her about it. She said they actually took the cover off that first EVH cover story I did, framed it, and hung it in their living room. She asked me if I could send her another copy, 'cause she wanted a complete copy with the cover still on it, for their files. Of course, I sent her a copy. ♪

My "Six Degrees of Separation" from Eddie Van Halen
By Terry Oubre

Although my style was formed by the blues/rock pioneers of the sixties, and the jazz/fusion of the early seventies, I have always kept my ears open for something new and progressive. In 1979, I first heard about Eddie through Harvey Moltz, owner of Rainbow Guitars, in Tucson, Arizona. He told me about this amazing guitar player, who had come by his shop the previous afternoon, and played a Martin acoustic with unbelievable technique. Right away I knew this guy had to be good, because the acoustic guitar doesn't lie. He also said Eddie could play the solo from Cream's "Crossroads" note for note.

Eddie would up buying a vintage Stratocaster, and to show his appreciation, Harvey offered to take Eddie out for a pre-concert dinner. After suggesting a few upscale restaurants in the area [to Harvey's surprise] Eddie said, "Let's go to McDonald's." Clearly this guy is unpretentious and down-to-earth. Not your average rock star.

With my curiosity piqued, I soon purchased *Van Halen II*. My first impression was, yeah, this guy's got the fire in his belly. His tone was great, and his playing captured a spirit that had long been missing in rock guitar. Plus, he maintained a progressive edge, even in the context of the pop/rock songs in the band's repertoire. I remember various critics hoping that Eddie would eventually align himself with musicians that would challenge him more. While this might sound like a good idea to some, Eddie flatly rejected it. I have a bootleg tape of Eddie jamming at a club in L.A., with Allan Holdsworth and band, circa 1982. And although the playing is spectacular, the music isn't. In his heart, Eddie is a rocker, and deep down inside, so am I. Whenever I see Eddie perform, it makes me want to play rock exclusively. The more I found out about Eddie, it only confirmed that the guy is a totally dedicated musician, who, like some of us, obsesses over his tone.

For instance, he built many of his first guitars, and through experimentation, found the "voice" he was looking for. He preferred the sound of output stage distortion, rather than a stomp box. He is a minimalist, who squeezes out a universe of harmonically rich tones, with a single bridge pick-up, straight into his amp. Like all great musicians, Eddie's tone is primarily in his hands, but when the "off the shelf" tools were available, he made his own. Add to that the fact that he did his own fret jobs, potted his own pick-ups, and basically was into all the minutia that adds up to great tone.

Which leads my to my late sixties Marshall stack. Yes, I said *my* stack. In 1983, I decided that although they were too loud, too big and too impractical to gig with, I had to get myself an old Marshall stack. So I started looking in earnest and found an ad in the Los Angeles "Recycler" which stated: Marshall 100 Watt stack – early English model. So I go to this guy's house, and there it is, in all its splendor. Immediately after playing a couple of phrases, I was hooked. I asked how he acquired the amp. He said he traded his van for it. Then he said, the amp had been serviced recently by a tech (Jose Arredondo, of Arrco Electronics, who worked on Eddie Van Halen's Marshalls), and the tech said that Eddie wanted the head, but not the stack.

The only reason that amp belongs to *me*, and not Eddie, is because the guy didn't want to sell the head separately. And just for good measure, I keep the amp crankin' with those good old Sylvannia 6CA7's that Eddie prefers. ♪

Alan Paul

Eddie Van Halen is one of a handful of players to completely change the course of electric guitar playing. Many imitators have focused solely on Eddie's impressive technique but they're missing the boat. Theoretically, anyone who puts enough hours into practice can master that aspect and certainly some have. But Eddie combined that technique with endless passion, ingenious creativity, scorching tone, dashes of humor and an incredibly listenable, even addictive hard-driving rhythm guitar style, which is too often overlooked, but played a central role in making his music so damn good. In short, he emerged into the public eye with a completely formed style that included every element of what you look for in a great guitarist. ♪

Chris Poland

When I first heard Eddie Van Halen, I felt like I had a connection with his tone and I didn't realize it till later that it was because we had a lot of the same guitar heroes that we both listened to – and one was Clapton when he was with Cream. When I first moved to California, I was really into Allan Holdsworth and a lot of fusion players, but when I heard Van Halen's tone, I was really drawn to it and part of my playing was kinda in that style – I occasionally go into that sound which is a big part of my sound I feel in some spots. So, yeah, he is a really big influence. ♪

Jean-Luc Ponty

I am really not familiar enough with his playing to give an honest opinion. I remember hearing one of his solos on radio in the '70s-80s and like his style, great sound. He slided like Holdsworth, of whom I knew he was a fan for seeing him backstage after a show by Allan in Los Angeles. ♪

Bonnie Raitt

I've always appreciated Eddie Van Halen's guitar playing and his band's music. ♪

Mich Ralphs

To me, Eddie is simply the best in that genre of guitar playing, rising mountains above all those other what I call "widdley-widdley" players. Eddie has a lot of soul and musical understanding, which one can hear in his tone and style.

His solo on "Jump" was stunning. I was on the road with my mate David Gilmour (Pink Floyd) at that time and if we were in a bar (which we always were) we would both stop yakking and listen to it. The boy is a monster player, plus I really appreciate his melodic and tasteful approach to music, not just the guitar, I may add. Give him my love and best wishes. I would love to make contact with him – I like his style! EVH is COOOL! ♪

Elliott Randall

Edward Van Halen – what can I say? A spectacular guitarist with an abundance of technique and great musical sense of humor – an unbeatable combination when used with extreme taste – which he does! ♪

Iann Robinson

I was hanging out with a friend of mine recently when he said to me, "You know what somebody told me?" I said no, and he said that his friend "knows exactly when the death of rock 'n' roll began." Intrigued I pressed him for this marvelous reason and my friend said his buddy told him straight out "The day David Lee Roth got off the Van Halen bus," and there it was.

So much has been said recently about what Van Halen has become, the war of words with David Lee Roth, The Sammy here, gone, and back here again, and the alcohol and so on and so forth that people sometimes forget that Van Halen was one of the most crushing forces in rock to ever hit the stage. They had everything, the rock attitude, the killer live show, the insane lead guitar player and the man with the voice – you couldn't fuck with Van Halen in the seventies and early eighties, it just wasn't possible. To be 100 percent honest here, I didn't get into Van Halen until the *1984* album, mainly because the "Hot for Teacher" video caught my attention and even after that Van Halen never got under my skin the way Sabbath did. That being said, what can you say about Van Halen's early works that isn't totally complimentary?

For starters, Eddie Van Halen is a killer guitar player and for myself (a drummer) Alex fucking rocked as well. I still don't think he's ever received the credit he deserves. To this day I still can't pull off the opening drum part on "Hot for Teacher." Then you had Dave, the consummate frontman. The man who showed that rock could be a party. Remember, in the seventies, Sabbath and Zeppelin were much more involved with darker themes and imagery, so were most of the bands. Other than Grand Funk Railroad, I'd be hard pressed to find a bigger party band than Van Halen. When they burst on the scene, they pushed it uphill, some saying they did two or three shows a night in shitty clubs to get the name out there. A friend of mine recently got his hands on the demo that the band did with Kiss demon Gene Simmons and it kills. It's funny because on the demo tape, bassist Michael Anthony is playing his ass off and on most of the albums he's the one-note kid – a decision I'm guessing they made to spotlight Eddie and keep the rock groove going. I kind of equate it to what Phil Rudd and Malcolm Young do in AC/DC so Angus can shine.

After I heard *1984* I decided to delve deeper into Van Halen so I bought *Van Halen* and *Van Halen II*, both of which fucking rocked. I remember being sold on the opening bass and drum line on "Runnin' with the Devil" – so simple but so rock. Then came Dave's voice and the party couldn't help but start. I never cared much for his lyrics, in truth I stopped trying to find them after I heard the first album, they were simple and unimportant. Mainly it was the feeling and the vibe Dave was trying to get across. I started buying the rest of the albums and each one had its own little gift. That was another amazing thing about Van Halen, they rocked so hard that people still argue over their best records. Some say *Van Halen II* and *Fair Warning* are their best, others swear by *1984* and their first album – some even say all the albums with Roth are equally awesome in the rock arena. I guess when you're that big and that good and that young, trouble is bound to slap you around. It hit both Van Halen and David Lee Roth when Dave decided to leave – dumb move. Since then Diamond Dave hasn't been able to mount much of a career save for *Eat 'Em and Smile*, which in my opinion should have been the Van Halen album that followed *1984*. The band hasn't been able to rise to the occasion, either.

Dave's replacement Sammy seems like a good guy, but like Ric Flair says, "To be the man, you gotta beat the man," and there's no way Sammy could beat Dave as a frontman, no way on Earth. It's sad because as time went on it seems that all the amazing work they'd done has become lost in the forest of Sammy Hagar, Gary Cherone, and David Lee Roth acting the fool when he's around.

True, the hardcore fans know of the Van Halen legacy, but most young fans only see the "Right Now" video and all the soap opera bullshit. For my own head I'd like to see them break up the band and just let it die with dignity, instead of beating it into the ground. I gotta be one of the only humans in the world not lusting for a David Lee Roth/Van Halen reunion. Be honest though, do you think that nowadays Dave leaping around singing "Jump" would be cool or silly? I know which side of the fence I'd be on with that one. None of it really matters though; most bands can't muster two good albums and Van Halen have six that are as close to perfect as you can get. For that alone they should remain legends in the pantheon of rock. ♪

Henry Rollins

I will always consider myself lucky for being teenage when the first Van Halen album was released. I had heard about it before it came out. Someone told me about a song called "Runnin' with the Devil" and that it was really cool. It was probably getting some airplay and I had not heard it yet. I was in California at a skate contest I think it was and heard a song with that lyric over the PA system. It had to be them. It was. I bought the album the first chance I got.

I was stuck right in the middle of high school. It was a gulag. One of the only things that kept me going was the music I was listening to. Van Halen was in the mix. I remember the night before *Van Halen II* was released, the played the album in its entirety on WPGC-FM in Washington DC, where I lived. I listened. We all listened. I taped it by putting my very bad tape recorder up to the radio and sat very still. It sounded horrible but I played it a few times before I bought the album.

I forget what year it was but I made my annual trip to the arena to see Ted Nugent. It was the best show you saw that year, every year. His band was lethal, and Nugent had amazing tone with that hollow body Gibson. What a show, what songs, what a man. On the third voyage to the Nuge there was a great change. There was an opening band that actually stayed in the memory. Usually the opener was a blur but this time it was a band called Van Halen. I remember they hit the stage and went into "Runnin' with the Devil" after Diamond Dave made his drum riser leap. He acted like his band was the headliner and there was no other band on that night. I remember very well when Eddie performed "Eruption" and the whole place was in disbelief. At the end of it, he looked down at his hands and shook his head like he didn't know what came over him. It was amazing. The set was a monster. Nugent came on a while later and a few songs in, people were chanting "Van-Ha-

Len!" over and over and waving newly bought VH T-shirts until the Nuge came to the front of the stage and yelled, "Fuck Van Halen!!!" He then retreated to his cabinets and played the rest of the show looking down at his wedge monitors. Move over, Ted!

In 1983, when I encountered Diamond Dave at an art gallery in Los Angeles, I told him this story and he shot back the date, location and how many people were at the show. To this day, I can't think of a better interview to read than one where David Lee Roth is full on, which means any interview of his you can find will do. He's the mouth that scored. You wonder how he keeps it all stored in there. He's the most quotable man in the business.

To this day, perhaps some of my most played records that I own are the Van Halen albums with Dave. They still work. To transmit on a critical level for just a moment here, let me say this; Van Halen's perfect synthesis of bone-crunching riffs and almost Beach Boys backing vocals is one of the most irresistible and potent concoctions I have ever heard in music. Perfect for radio without selling out or being wimpy. How the hell can you do that?! Something for the guys, something for the ladies. Adding to that, the presentation was second to none. That was a show. Diamond Dave really needed an arena to realize his vision and when he got one, he wasted no time. Van Halen was like the circus coming to town, like the biggest block party you've ever seen and you're on the invite list.

The proof of the band's rock-solid place in history can be found in all the bands that came immediately after VH broke. All the Eddie clones, Warner Brothers' attempt to make another Dave/VH with the ill-fated Bullet Boys, how guitarists changed their approach to solos. Every frontman in any hard rock band has a little bit of David Lee in him no matter what they say. Some of the stories around the band are the stuff of legend and are known the world over. Brown M&M's – 'nuff said.

The records themselves have lost absolutely no speed after twenty-plus years. Actually, now that I think about it, seeing where music is these days, perhaps those records have picked up a little speed! Hail the Mighty (with Dave) Van Halen! ♪

Rev. James A. Rota II

The thing about Eddie Van Halen that always amazed me (besides the fact that he basically took over the world at age twenty-two) was the fact that he never plays traditional "chords" or "riffs." He phrases his rhythm parts the way a jazz player would. His leads are legendary and his tone is monstrous, but for me it's all in his phrasing. No one has ever been able to emulate it. ♪

Gregg Rolie

Van Halen was a difficult band to follow. What I remember most was one time, prior to a show, I was in Van Halen's dressing room where Ed was warming up. Most people know him for his solos, some of which are classics, but it was the rhythm playing that impressed me the most. The reason why he is such a good soloist is because his sense of rhythm is so in the pocket. He's completely inside his music. ♪

Jim Root

I first heard Van Halen when I was probably twelve or thirteen years old. A friend of mine played "Eruption" for me. Man, at that time I'd never heard *anybody* play like that or make a guitar sound like that. When you're that age, you're kind of impressionable, anyway. And to hear something like *that* coming out of a guitar was kind of mind-blowing, you know? It just makes you think of the guitar in a different way.

Eddie's absolutely a great player and they wrote some really great albums. *Women and Children First, Fair Warning* and albums like that were so guitar-oriented. You know, the pre-Hagar Van Halen. The things he was doing with the guitar, songs like "Little Guitars" and things like that, were just really amazing. I thought *1984* was a brilliant album as well. That was actually one of the first albums that I actually bought on my own, that I didn't, like, steal from my parents or anyone, you know? All of the songs were great, but for some reason I always liked "I'll Wait." There was just something about that tune, you know? "Drop Dead Legs" was great, too. It had a cool guitar riff at the beginning of it. ♪

Jordan Rudess

Eddie Van Halen was key in the evolution of modern-day guitar playing. I think "Eruption" changed us all! ♪

Dave "Snake" Sabo

First time I heard Van Halen was in 1978. Their first record had just come out. What I used to do back then is I would purchase albums based on their album cover. I loved their album cover, and I'd also read in *Circus* magazine, or something like that, that Gene Simmons had worked with them. Immediately I knew I had to check this band out. If the "God of Thunder" is workin' with 'em, my Lord! So I picked up the record and I went straight over to one of my friends' houses. He was a high school buddy of mine, about a year older than me. We used to skip school together and go back to his place 'cause his parents worked. So we'd hang out at his house and crank albums out of his upstairs window, [*laughs*] and put on, like, an air guitar concert. We sat there and just started listening to this record. You know, drinking beers and whatnot, at one o'clock in the afternoon. Mind you, I'm about fourteen years old. And I hear "Runnin' with the Devil" and I thought it was awesome.

Then I heard "Eruption." I'm sure my story is no different than anybody else's. When I first heard that, I had never, *ever* heard anything like that in my life! I had just started playing guitar. I mean, literally just started. I could not understand what this guy was doing. There were all these debates about, you know, whether he's using a delay on this or that. And I had *never* heard of finger tapping or anything crazy like that. Then I start to hear stories about Mammoth and that Eddie used to turn his back to the audience when he did this because he didn't want anybody to pick up on it. Man, I thought that was just, like, the heaviest thing in the world! It's just so cool. Immediately, I knew there was a new hero, as far as guitar players go, in the realm of Jimi Hendrix. I knew he was someone that would change the face of guitar playing, forever. It was so obvious. It's not that I was so intuitive, you know? It was just so damn obvious!

This guy was doing stuff that I, as a guitar player, had never heard before. I grew up listening to Joe Perry, Ace Frehley, Michael Schenker with U.F.O., Jeff Beck, Billy Gibbons. Along with Judas Priest, Iron Maiden, and all those bands. I had still never ever heard *anything* like it. The closest thing I'd heard to it, and it's still not even close, was the solo to "Hell Bent for Leather." That sounded something like the finger tapping thing.

I remember sitting there reading every article I could about Van Halen. It was all so crazy. You know, the fact all the music on that first record was recorded in six days. And his sound! Man, that guitar tone. It was unlike anything I'd ever heard. Everything about it was like nothing I'd ever heard. The songs, the energy, everything! Far as Van Halen, the band, they changed the landscape of music much in the same way Guns N' Roses did. I mean, this was about a decade *before* Guns did it, but they both changed the landscape of music when they came out.

The one thing I think people didn't realize, that I picked up on right away, is the fact that not only was Eddie a one-of-a-kind virtuoso, prodigy guitar player, he is a great rhythm player as well. I don't think some people ever mention that. From that first record, I knew it. Like, just the riff to "Jamie's Cryin'" alone makes you realize what an in-the-pocket, solid rhythm guitar player he is. Along with being just the most amazing lead player as well! So intuitive and, man, it's just so difficult to put into words [*laughs*]. He really is an absolute original. Eddie invented and created something that is yet to be touched.

The very first thing that stands out on that first album, from a guitar player standpoint, is "Eruption" and all the solos. The very close second, for me, was the songwriting. 'Cause for me, it was always about songs. That's what drew me to bands, you know? All through my youth when I was growin' up and to this day. I mean, you can have great guitar players out there such as Yngwie [Malmsteen] and so on and so forth back in the day and even to this day. But to me, as a musician, it always comes down to the songs.

And man, everything he did was just so tasteful. I mean, Eddie coulda sat there and ripped on every song. You know, he coulda done over-the-top shit on every song if he wanted to. But he didn't. The solo to "You Really Got Me" is so completely different to "On Fire," you know? He played *within* those songs. It made his solos an extension of those songs. All my favorite guitar players do that. When I listen to Van Halen and the solo comes up, I always say to myself, "Man, that's *exactly* what should be played." It's like David Gilmour from Pink Floyd. I can never listen to a solo of his and ever question it, at all. Every note is *perfect*.

The first time I ever saw Van Halen in concert was on their 1984 tour. I actually had tickets to see them back around '78 or '79, opening up for Black Sabbath in Asbury Park. I wanted to go so bad and I was with an older friend of mine, 'cause I was only like fifteen at the time. But I so desperately wanted to get into a club as a minor and drink that I sold my ticket so I'd have money to get a fake ID and to get into the club! So I get into the club and a couple hours after I was in there, one of the club owners, who's actually a friend of mine now, recognized that I was *barely* pubescent and said, "Look, if I see you with another drink I'm gonna break your fingers!" It was a great experience, although I probably would have been better served going to see Van Halen that night [*laughs*].

So the first time I saw them was on the 1984 tour in the Meadowlands in New Jersey. It was such a great, over-the-top, positive show. No downer – *nothing* like that. Their songs were heavy party music. They made you want to just stand up, shout, scream and stuff. It was such a great experience! There wasn't one moment where you're sittin' there goin', "Wow, what a downer. My life sucks." They were completely about escapism, you know? There was no big long thesis behind what they were doing. It was straight up and all 'bout havin' a good time and jumping around and the energy. Really, *really* performing.

They were very instrumental in sort of molding me as far as how to get out there and put on a show for the audience. It wasn't just about standing around, you know? It was about really feeling the energy of the music and passing that along to the audience. Making it such where it wasn't the band and the audience, it was *everybody*. Hence the term "in concert." It's like everyone's all in it together for those two or three hours to really leave everything behind and just enjoy the moment. You know, enjoy life. At the end of the day I've always wanted people to leave with a smile on their face. A lot of that came from seeing VH. They always made people feel a part of what was going on on that stage. They were never sitting on a pedestal above everybody. Even with the outrageousness of David Lee Roth and Sammy Hagar and their over-the-top frontman antics, they were always able to make the audience a part of that. It was never a pompous thing.

Skid Row actually toured with Van Halen on their 1995 Balance Tour. Man, what can I say? I am truly one of the luckiest guys in the world to be able to meet and become friendly with so many of my heroes and idols in the music business. You know, so many different and great bands. Opening for Van Halen is one of those things were you're just so intimidated by the enormity of their success, along with the enormity of their influence and power that they have – *especially* Eddie. Man. I'll tell you what, that guy was just so, *so* kind to me and to Scotty [Hill]. I mean, he's the guy. He's the reason why I play 5150's, because he gave me one as a gift! And in New Jersey, no less! It was mind-boggling to me. At the end of the day, I'm a fan, you know? Yeah, I play in a band and whatever and all that, but I'm a fan, man. I was out in front of their stage *every night* watching that band perform. People can say what they want about Sammy Hagar, but he's *awesome*. Freakin' phenomenal.

I remember one day, we're sittin' there in Eddie's dressing room. Eddie always said hi to me every day. We'd hang out and talk. He'd let me hang out on stage while they soundchecked and, you know, not a lot of bands do that. He would talk to me about his tone. I remember the first thing we talked about. We were checkin' out his amps and I was like, "Hey, are these modded out?" And he was like, "Not at all, man. These are *exactly* what we designed, straight from the factory." Then he told me he'd get me one. Honestly, I didn't think anything of it 'cause a lot of people say that, you know?

So then we're in his dressing room and he had one of the 5150 combos. Eddie was like, "Here man, take my guitar and play through it. I'll set it up for you." I'm like, "Are you freakin' serious?" Now, I don't get intimidated very much in life, but that was one of those instances where I'm goin', "Oh my God, please, *please* don't suck really bad right now." I remember thinking,

"Just play and make sure that you don't make an idiot of yourself." So he's settin' up the amp and one of the funniest things happened. Scotty, who was there as well, says, "Man, these things sound *really* good. Do you know anybody that could help me get one?" And Eddie goes, "Yeah, maybe this guy right here," and he points to his signature on the front of the amp [*laughs*].

We played with Van Halen at the Blockbuster Pavilion in Camden, New Jersey. We all drove our own cars to the show 'cause we were all still livin' in New Jersey at the time. I knew I was gonna have a lot of people down there, so I showed up and Eddie was there before me. He calls me over. Funny thing is, he would never call me Snake. He would call me Dave. Which was pretty wild 'cause he was one of the few people who called me Dave. Even my wife calls me Snake. So does my mom. So he's like, "Yo, Dave, come here!" He brings me into his dressing room and he's got two 5150 combos sittin' there. He's like, "Here you go, bro." And I'm like, "What?" And he goes, "These are for you, man." The reason he had two was because one was for me and one was for Scotty. And I was like, "Are you kidding me, man?" Sure enough, once again he goes, "Here, take this guitar." It was the Wolfgang, and he goes, "Lemme plug it in and I'll set it up for you the way I like it and you can write down the settings and so forth." It was absolutely unbelievable!

On that tour, I also became really friendly with Michael Anthony as well. We would go out and play golf together. Every night he'd have "Michael Anthony's Bar" set up behind his backline. So, you know, we're drinkin' Jack Daniel's every night. Mike and I were total drinkin' buddies. It was all 'bout having fun, and we were having a blast. You know, maintaining that youthful attitude. It was tremendous. Touring with them was definitely one of those life-affirming experiences. Everybody on that tour was so great. From the band to their management to their crew! I'm so thankful for that moment in time.

One of the coolest things was you'd be sittin' out there watching the whole show, and then after the show you go backstage and you see Eddie and go, "Man, your solo spot was great today!" And he'd be like, "Nah, it really wasn't. I missed this and I missed that..." And I'm thinking, "Wow! What an incredible thing it must be to be on that level!" you know? Man, just to be on that level where you're arguably *the greatest rock guitar player that ever lived,* and yet you're still humble enough to critique yourself in a very honest way.

He's one of those few artists that are just truly, truly, *truly* gifted. There aren't very many people like that, you know? Prince is one of them. Edward, obviously, is one of those guys. They are few and far between, man. Stevie Ray Vaughan is one of those guys. With Edward, it's just all encompassing.

Check that guy's resumé. Man, how many hits did that guy write? It's unbelievable! As a kid, from a guitar player's standpoint, he was the rock star I wanted to emulate, as far as onstage persona and so forth. You know, he's always *inside* of the music. ♪

Joe Satriani

Eddie's got the best right hand in the business, drop-dead timing and tone for days. He's a master guitarist and a great songwriter. He dropped by the studio back in '92 when I was recording *The Extremist,* hung out for a bit and commented on what we were up to. Man was he wired! It was 11:00 A.M. and he was chain smoking and knocking back beers and talking a mile a minute. Standing next to him, you could tell he was special, a real star with the goods to back it all up. I will always be a big fan of his extraordinary playing. ♪

Michael Schenker

Edward has been my favorite guitarist since the release of Van Halen's first album. ♪

Rudolph Schenker

I have known Edward since 1979, when Van Halen played in Hamburg while supporting Black Sabbath (a great concert). Klaus and I were sitting in the fourth row, and Eddy came directly to us and immediately took us backstage, where we had a great time with the other band members. We then found out that during their club days in Los Angeles, they covered a few of our songs, like "Speedy's Coming" and "Catch Your Train." At midnight, we celebrated David's birthday with the other members of Van Halen in the club, where David got the cake in the face from the band. It was a fantastic evening, and we enjoyed it very much. Ten years later, in 1988, we were invited to their studio in L.A. to talk about the "Monsters of Rock" tour, where we were slotted as the special guest. The tour was a great success, and we had many great times talking about guitars and guitar techniques.

To me, Edward is one of the best guitar players in the world. He influenced many other guitar players with his style. I was shocked when I heard the first Van Halen album, 'cause I couldn't believe what he did with his guitar. Eddie – nice one! ♪

Earl Scruggs

The interesting thing about Edward Van Halen is that he created an entirely new style, which he popularized, and is credited as one of the greatest guitarists of all time. He saw no boundaries in his music or style. What he has done with his guitar style is what I have attempted to do with the five-string banjo, and that is to create an entirely new style, widen and broaden its appeal, and to eliminate its being confined to one category of music. And as far as the band, "Van Halen," it is one of the most innovative, stylistic and creatively moving rock bands in the history of rock 'n' roll. The influence their band has generated is limitless and will always be considered a true cornerstone of rock 'n' roll.

I recorded an album for MCA Records in 2001 titled "Earl Scruggs and Friends." I re-recorded one of my signature tunes instrumentals, "Foggy Mountain Breakdown." When we were in the process of planning the session, my son, Randy Scruggs, who produced the album, spoke to Eddie and his manager to try to arrange a time when Eddie could play on the instrumental. Eddie was receiving medical treatment at the time and we were not able to work out a schedule. The instrumental went on to win a Grammy Award and I would have felt very honored to have had Edward Van Halen's participation on the recording. Hopefully, perhaps we will have an opportunity to get around to recording something together sometime in the future. I would like that. ♪

Kenny Wayne Shepherd

My most definitive memory of Van Halen was when "Hot for Teacher" came out. I'm, like, just a little kid in grade school and I see this video on MTV, right? And I remember seeing the kids jumping all over the desks in school and the teacher's dressed all hot and shit. Dude, I'd *never* seen anything quite like that on television before, especially far as rock music. That really gave me a serious hard-on for some serious rock guitar. To a young kid, it definitely translated the sexual appeal of guitar based rock 'n' roll and hot chicks! It blew my mind, man.

My dad was in radio long before I was even born, and I was born in '77. He was playing all kinds of music and Van Halen was definitely a staple of his format of rock that he played. I actually saw Van Halen come through Shreveport, Louisiana when "Jump" was their hit single. That was just amazing. You know, watching David Lee Roth jump in the air, doin' the splits and all that crazy stuff. It's been cool to see them evolve over the years. I saw the OU812 Tour, and I got to tour with them in 1998 when Gary Cherone was in the band. I've followed them through every year and lineup change. Man, I've always been a big fan of Eddie's, and now I'm fortunate enough to call him a friend.

Eddie and the band were definitely an influence. Man, *everybody* played some air guitar to one Van Halen song or another! Back in the '80s they did so many things that were so influential. I mean, between his music and all the hits that they had. On top of that, he plays on "Beat It," which is off one of the highest-selling records of all time, *Thriller*. The exposure was ridiculous. This guy was just all over the place. It was like if it was *"guitar,"* it was Eddie Van Halen. Eddie is one of those guys that is just so innovative, people are gonna try and recreate what he does and be frustrated trying to do it. You know, there are certain people who come along every couple of generations that have an impact on the instrument like he had. He approached the instrument in his own way and really in a way that nobody has ever put that kind of twist on it. Eddie has influenced many people and will continue to do so.

When I toured with Van Halen in '98, I had a blast. I look forward to doing it again. I really enjoyed myself and became very good friends with all the members of the band. They are all very personable guys, very nice guys. Down home, down-to-earth, just like to rock 'n' roll! ♪

Derek Sherinian

When I first heard *Van Halen* when I was twelve years old, my life changed. In Edward's playing, I made the distinction that you were able to translate your soul and personality through your instrument, and document it on a record for the whole world to eventually enjoy. Edward's approach to the instrument has been a blueprint for me. God Bless Edward Van Halen!!! ♪

Eddie Van Halen: My Lost Guitar Hero
By Alex Skolnick

I heard Eddie for the first time in 1982, when I was about thirteen years old and a friend played me the first Van Halen album. It was the warmest guitar sound I've ever heard. The tone was extremely crunchy and had a stronger presence than most other music. It sounded like each chord was on the verge of feedback, yet still under control. The rhythms weren't smooth and polished like much of the current rock music on the radio at the time. Instead, there were squeals, pick slides and other odd noises, all of which were a perfect complement to the music as a whole.

I never knew the guitar could make so many sounds. I was sure nothing could take my breath away more than these rhythm parts. That is, until I heard the guitar solos.

Eddie's solos took the best licks of rock and blues guitar and completely electrified them. He bent the strings so far that it seemed downright impossible. He spit out melodic runs that had the speed, precision and elegance of flamenco guitar. In between there were short bursts of noise and even full-on explosions. Sometimes he'd play the same pattern all the way across the strings, regardless of scale notes, and it seemed to work perfectly. In addition, there were harps and chime like sounds, which I'd never imagined. I later found out that these sounds were called "harmonics," and had been used before (jazz guitarists Tal Farlow and Lenny Breau, for example, as well as bassist Jaco Pastorius), but as far as I could tell, Eddie was the first to apply these techniques to rock. As if all that wasn't enough, Eddie somehow managed to squeeze in licks that resembled a Bach harpsichord concerto. This type of playing, which I later found out was called "two-hand tapping," forever changed the vocabulary of rock guitar.

To this day, my favorite track is "I'm the One"; nothing prepared me for it. The attitude of the whole band was ferocious, but none more so than the guitar playing. Just when you thought his playing couldn't get any more intense, it did. It was like every great lick from the first album, packed into one song! When the song ended, it was like you'd just gotten off a roller coaster. Suddenly I saw myself on stage playing Eddie's lead guitar parts. I had always dreamed of becoming some sort of singer/guitarist/rock star like Paul Stanley. Now I only wanted to be a lead guitarist and a serious musician. My life had changed.

There were other cool things about Eddie besides his playing. For one thing, he had the coolest looking guitars. I found out that he'd actually put many of them together himself and designed the striped patterns. I always loved the photo of him with the pickaxe, standing above his guitar collection. I dreamed of having a collection like that one day.

The other thing was his hair. Eddie had the best hair, long and thick, and perfectly layered. I wished I could have had his hair stylist and remember many trips to Supercuts with a rock magazine in my hand, explaining that I wanted my hair cut exactly like Eddie's.

I also liked the fact that he seemed so happy. He always had that huge grin and seemed to be having so much fun playing. To read interviews and hear him talk about his love for music and his close relationship with his family was inspiring.

One day I realized that, despite overwhelming artistic success, commercial and financial success, universal acknowledgment from fans, musicians and critics alike, Eddie didn't sound happy. No longer the young devoted musician overwhelmed with his newfound success but committed to developing his art, his interviews reflected a troubled soul plagued with problems: health issues, alcohol abuse, personal difficulties, feuds with ex-band members and other associates... I couldn't believe this could happen to someone whom I and countless others considered to be a national treasure. I'd felt he was invincible. But through him I realized that no one is.

I met Eddie once in 1991. I was rehearsing at the Power Station in Los Angeles for a tour with bassist Stu Hamm. Across the hall from us, the group Toto was rehearsing. Guitarist Steve Lukather dropped in a few times, we got to be friendly. One day, I saw Steve wrestling with someone in the hallway and just figured he was goofing around with his roadie. But then I noticed the sneakers on the other guy; they were colored like a Van Halen guitar, red with black and white stripes. Suddenly I remembered reading somewhere that Steve and Eddie were friends. I looked at this other guy's face again and oh my god...it was Eddie.

I froze and my heart started pulsating. I went around the corner. After collecting myself for a few minutes, I went back to the hallway just in time to grab Steve's arm as he followed Eddie into Toto's rehearsal room.

"Is that who I think it is?" I asked. He smiled.

"He's one of my best friends. Come on, I'll introduce you."

We walked back into Toto's studio and there he was, showing his new Ernie Ball guitar to some of the crew of Toto.

"Eddie, this is Alex Skolnick. He's a good guitarist." I nervously said hello and he shook my hand.

"Who do you play for?" he asked.

"Have you heard of Testament?" I responded timidly.

"No," he said.

"We're a metal band, kinda like Slayer."

"Like who?" he responded.

"Uh, never mind. I'm here rehearsing with Stu Hamm." I mentioned that Stu was Joe Satriani's bassist and that rang a bell. He let me try his new guitar. The neck felt really smooth and fluid in my hand. I imagined this must be like his early guitar, which had a neck made by the company Charvel. I had always dreamed of having a guitar like that but they were quite rare. Therefore, I thought I was paying the highest compliment when I said that the neck reminded me of an old Charvel.

He shot me a strange look and muttered, "No way man. That's my design." I was a bit taken aback. I hoped I hadn't offended him. I realized he was a bit drunk, sipping a bottle and slurring his words (it was one thirty in the afternoon). I asked him about the new Van Halen album which had just come out.

"Our new album is called 'Fuck,' man," he said. He was referring to their album 'For Unlawful Carnal Knowledge.' He signed a book of matches for me and he wrote "To Alex: FUCK Eddie Van Halen." His signature was completely illegible.

A year or so later these matches were thrown away by a girlfriend of mine who found them, couldn't read Eddie's signature and wondered who on Earth would write 'FUCK' on a book of matches.

I'm one of those stubborn ones that only considers the first six albums, ("Dave era" Van Halen) the true Van Halen. Some of my young friends encourage me to give "Sammy era" Van Halen a chance, just thinking of it as a different type of band. I suppose that's true but I just can't make the separation. It's not necessarily because of David Lee Roth or Sammy Hagar as vocalists. It's because you can hear a huge change in Eddie's tone and playing. On a purely personal note, it just doesn't connect with me.

As the years have gone by, his playing on those first several album has never lost any of its magic. It's been a bit frustrating at times to encounter young guitarists who only know the "Sammy era," and I feel blessed to have felt the influence of what I consider the true Van Halen. I've enjoyed sharing the Eddie Van Halen I remember and seeing the reaction (usually something to the effect of "I knew he was good, but...wow.") This happens not just with young guitarists, but with accomplished musicians from other areas of music.

For example, an acoustic bassist, brought up mostly in jazz and classical, heard the *Fair Warning* album and commented that he could imagine Eddie working with the great Miles Davis in one of his electric bands. A Middle Eastern world music artist, unfamiliar with American hard rock, heard "Spanish Fly" (*Van Halen II*) and was surprised to learn it was not some modern Gypsy guitarist from Europe, but Eddie playing a nylon-string flamenco guitar in 1979.

In addition to Eddie's explorations of different guitar styles, Van Halen the band always spiced up each album with the occasional off the wall foray into other territory such as boogie woogie ("Ice Cream Man"), vintage swing ("Big Bad Bill"), barbershop quartet ("Happy Trails") and more, and made these styles hip and cool for all the young, stubborn rockers like myself.

This diversity was a big part of what made Van Halen special and helped inspire me to explore other styles of music.

But with the coming of the mid- to late '80s, MTV became more influential and hard rock music became more image-based. Suddenly, hard rock seemed to have more in common with Michael Bolton than Led Zeppelin, and the new version of Van Halen (with Sammy Hagar on vocals) fit this climate perfectly. Their album sales multiplied, but at a price: most of the spirit, diversity, originality and musical explorations of the early albums was gone.

Meanwhile, Van Halen imitators appeared by the hundreds or thousands, turning what had once been a display of the height of artistry into self-parody. These hordes of imitators focused only on the tricks and flash; the two-hand tapping licks had become a gimmick and found their way into countless forgettable songs by bands that had lost sight of what the original Van Halen had brought to the table in the first place: great hooks, strong grooves, live energy, spontaneity, a sense of where rock 'n' roll had come from and where it could go next. It was a small wonder that alternative music took over with an anti-establishment agenda that unfortunately dismantled much of the musical precedent Van Halen had set.

These days, I look to artists such as Pat Metheny and Jim Hall for inspiration; these artists are continuing to push themselves and break new ground with each new album, much like Eddie used to do. I wouldn't have related to their music as a teenager but at this stage of in my life, I get it. No matter how much older these guys get (Jim Hall is in his seventies), they're helping me grow as a musician, in the same way that Eddie Van Halen once did. However, I won't be cutting my hair like Jim or Pat anytime soon.

While I respect Eddie for who he is, I look back on who he was and I am saddened. I know it's selfish, I have no right to judge him. My expectations are irrelevant.

But I often wonder what happened to the Eddie I remember. No one since has ever been such an inspiration on so many levels. He was my first hero. Whenever I hear Paul Simon sing "Where have you gone, Joe DiMaggio?" (from the song "Mrs. Robinson"), I think of Eddie. ♪

Mike Smith

Eddie Van Halen, great musician, made many great records. I've never met him but have enjoyed his music. I'm extremely flattered that the DC5 had such a big influence on him. It's nice to know that we helped bring such a talent to the record buying public. I hope he continues making music for many years to come. ♪

Trey Spruance

I wouldn't have had the guts or the desire to start playing guitar if it hadn't been for *Fair Warning* and *Women and Children First*. All I cared about before that was Devo, which I also value greatly now. What was amazing about those two VH albums is their fluidity. One being thrown together, the other being a cultivated production, they both reflect the same spontaneous spirit. Eddie's playing on them is as a total musician – he's never been a guy who just plays a riff the same way every night and then does a solo. He's a true improviser.

I think from an early time, for my own playing I never cared as much about solos and all that, as I did about using the guitar to make a band sound good. It might seem ironic that I could credit Eddie Van Halen for that, since so many people think of him exclusively as a shredder. But there are so many intangibles to his playing. Listen to the opening of "Mean Street," or the fucking unbelievable effortless off-the-cuff riffing on "Push Comes to Shove." What is that shit? Obviously, it's all in *how* you play it, not what you play.

Every pecker and his brother played "Unchained" on the guitar. But did it ever in a million years sound like Eddie himself? Was it the Echoplex, the Marshall amp, the Charvel guitar? Fuck no... the guy had a magic touch if ever an electric guitar player did. Plus, Van Halen were a product of the '70s. Ok fine, for stadium rock, Led Zeppelin had more soul and depth as musical expression, but you can't deny that Van Halen as a band had a sophisticated spontaneous chemistry, and that as an improviser, Eddie is unparalleled in hard rock.

Like many, I fucking do not like the Hagar period. It wasn't just the tone that changed, or the producer. Something else changed – the chemistry, a lot of other things probably. I don't know. To bring back the big phrase of the '80s, "shit happens." So whatever – those first five albums are enough. I'll always respect Eddie Van Halen as an electric guitar player more than anyone else. He's still underrated in my opinion. I know that sounds nuts... probably is. ♪

Mike Stern

I've always been a big Eddie Van Halen fan. Of course, he's got an amazingly fluid technique and a very cool sound all his own, but more than that, the energy and the vibe in his music has always been really strong and soulful. Eddie rocks his ass off! ♪

Joe Stump

The first time I heard *Van Halen* and "Eruption" came on I just couldn't believe it. The tone, the playing, all of it was so huge. Like everyone else I was picking my jaw up off the floor. Just brilliantly played and so musically put together. To this day it certainly hasn't lost its impact and remains the benchmark to which all other great guitar cadenzas are measured. ♪

John Tardy

Van Halen is Van Halen and there is no other band like them! Their wide range of songs and styles is as unique as it gets. The biggest reason why is the guitar playing of Eddie Van Halen. The drum style of Alex and the screams of David Lee Roth were a perfect complement to one of the heaviest rock bands ever! ♪

Shane Theriot

After you play the guitar for twenty-plus years and become somewhat proficient on the instrument, it's easy to become jaded and lose the passion for the guitar. You have to work harder and search more to keep the inspiration going. I think that happens to most "working" musicians. When I hear Eddie play, even after all these years, it makes me feel like I'm twelve years old again and that whole feeling of amazement and awe all comes pouring back in. Attitude. Conviction. Rawness. It reminds me of why I picked up the damn thing in the first place. To just say Eddie Van Halen was an influence would be an understatement.

Eddie is the reason that I lived and breathed the guitar when I was learning. He was a huge part of my passion for the instrument. In my opinion, as an improviser he is just as influential as Coltrane or Bird. The whole idea of stretching boundaries and always creating, changing – that is really what I got from him. Sure, I learned the solos and riffs, like everyone, but his soul and energy – the rawness and attitude – these are the things that have kept me a big fan after all these years. But if you want to strictly talk guitar, I could go on for days. Tone? Check out the riff to "Drop Dead Legs." Then again, just about anything of his has great tone. Solos? Listen to "So This Is Love?" "Somebody Get Me a Doctor," or "Full Bug." Rhythm chops? Try "Panama," "Beautiful Girls," or "Unchained." "Spanish Fly" still blows my mind. "Eruption" is like "Donna Lee" or something as monumental. There are so many moments that just do it for me. Thanks Eddie for giving me so much joy through your music. ♪

Toots Thielemans

I know only vaguely about Van Halen's music. But his very special technique really impressed me at the time. Please give him my best regards. ♪

Mark Tremonti

I believe the first time I ever heard Van Halen is when I heard "Runnin' with the Devil" on the radio. It sounded so much more modern and different than everybody out there. I wasn't even playing guitar yet, but it was bad-assed. I'd say Eddie became an influence later in life. When I first started playing guitar, I was more influenced by bands like Kiss. You know, bands that I could play. I was like eleven or twelve years old when I first started playing guitar, and at the time, Van Halen was so over my head, you know, I couldn't really be influenced by it! But once I got to be a better guitar player later on, I became a larger fan of Eddie's. You know, when I could actually take some of his stuff and learn it. For me, Kiss was the introductory thing that would get you to want to pick up a guitar, and then Van Halen was the guy you aspired to be.

If I ever want to push myself, I just listen to some Van Halen and get some inspiration. I just recently bought *The Van Halen Story: The Early Years* on DVD and it was amazing to watch how they proved themselves live, every night. They were so undeniable and full of so much energy. There wasn't a band out there that could say they were a better live band.

In 1998, Creed opened two shows for Van Halen at Madison Square Garden and that was an incredible experience. I remember we had this plan that we weren't gonna open for any bands. All we were gonna do was play our own shows and headline our own shows and build our fan base. You know, 'cause we never wanted to be in a room full of people that weren't our fans. Well when the topic of opening for Van Halen came up, all that's out the window! [*laughs*] It was like, "Hell yeah, we'll open for Van Halen!" That's one of the few bands in the world that no matter what, anytime, anywhere, we'd do it. Before the MSG shows, we actually met up with them at the Palace in Detroit. I remember walking down to watch their soundcheck and Eddie asked, "Who's the guitar player?" I raised my hand, and he showed me his amp and his entire rig. I met his guitar tech, too. I told Eddie I liked the guitar he had designed and he said, "Well, what color do you want?" And then he says, "Ok, when we play Madison Square Garden, I'll bring you a black one."

So we're in the dressing room at MSG and we hear a knock at the door. We blew it off 'cause we're having a band meeting and we thought whoever it was could just come back. They knock again, and once more we blow it off. Finally, the door opens and Eddie peeks his head in and says, "Hey guys, excuse me..." We were like, "Oh, shit! Yeah, come on in!" [*laughs*] So Eddie comes in with a guitar case, pulls out the guitar, taps on it a little bit, says, "Feels good to me," and then hands it over. Man, that's one of the greatest moments ever!

The coolest part is that after the MSG concert, he had his son Wolfgang and his ex-wife with him. You know, at the time they were still married. Backstage there were hundreds of people just waiting to get a glimpse of Van Halen. So they had a minivan waiting for them and they kind of rushed through the crowd. He had his kid and his wife with him, so he really wanted to get in the car. But he caught us out of the corner of his eye and he walked through the entire crowd to come over. He gave me a hug and told me, "Hey, to really get the guitar *exactly* how I have it, you have to take off one of the springs in the back. You gotta loosen this spring and..." Man, I can't remember exactly what he said 'cause I was, like, in awe. It was all kinda going in one ear and out the other [*laughs*], 'cause I was just like, "Holy shit! He just walked through all those people just to come tell me this!" I tell everybody that story.

Eddie's style is so different. When you get into learning his stuff, you find he has a really cool, different, unique style that I don't think anybody else has ever really tapped into. Overall, I'm really influenced by the mood he sets. You know, the energy. Along with his whole attitude when it comes to writing songs and playing guitar. You know, making a good song but making it very interesting musically. I think that's always been my number 1 goal. To make the song the best it can be, but make it as interesting as it can be at the same time. Van Halen *always* did that.

I think Eddie Van Halen is the Godfather of shred guitar. He is *"the one."* You know, Randy Rhoads was great and a great composer of songs, but I think Eddie was the best shredder. If you threw him out against any other guitar player of his time, on the spot, he would outperform *anybody*. I remember when I asked him about the solo on "Beat It," he said he walked in there, knocked it out in an hour, and left. I mean, that was just off the top of his head?! He said he played through it once or twice and that was it, then he left. He's a maniac! ♪

Steve Vai

Edward raised the bar on rock guitar playing. Actually, he most certainly reinvented it and that happens only three or four times a century. When a person plays an instrument, they wear their personality on their sleeve. There has always been an inspired yet intimate simplicity to Edward's musical expressions, not to mention a little iron ore, too. ♪

The Ventures

We, Bob Bogle and Don Wilson, formed The Ventures in 1959. In June of 1960, we recorded "Walk, Don't Run" – Bob played lead guitar and Don played rhythm guitar on that recording. As of this date – August 2004 – we are still together, still recording, and still doing concert dates.

We feel very flattered and happy to learn that we were one of Eddie Van Halen's early influences. Without a doubt, Eddie is one of the most incredible guitarists of all time. We're so glad to hear he has survived his battle with cancer. We wish him the very best of continued health and success. ♪

Carl Verheyen

I grew up in Pasadena and went to Pasadena City College around the time Van Halen was getting started. We had rival bands and would play lunchtime in the quad at the school, as well as the local dances. One night when we were both double-billed Eddie broke a string and borrowed my Les Paul. For an eighteen-year old kid, this is a prize possession, but I lent him my instrument and hung out until our set started. When he finished playing, he walked over to our stage and dropped it into the case from about three feet off the deck. I said, "Hey Ed...those Gibsons don't really bounce well," to which he replied, "Sorry, man. Nice guitar."

Years later, Robben Ford and I were hanging out at my house and I played him the "Panama" solo. We both thought it was his most soulful playing to date, the musicality of the man had surpassed the unbelievable technical side of his playing. I list him as one of the Top 10 most original, homegrown players in the history of the instrument, right up there with Wes Montgomery and Albert King. ♪

Tommy Victor

When VH came about, I was playing bass. I never figured out any VH per se, but I saw them open for Sabbath at The Garden in NY. To me they were the heaviest American band at the time. To this day I believe the "Dead or Alive" riff to be one of the heaviest, greatest riffs ever. It's all needless to say: Eddie is the best American rock guitarist ever. ♪

Dick Wagner

I met Eddie only twice and we got on very well. He is, of course, the most influential rock guitarist of the 1980s and certainly one of the all-time great rockers. His influence was felt by many young players, and his style was copied but never truly mastered. ♪

Jeff Watson

I consider Edward a good friend and a great player and influence on the world of guitar. He taught the public, via MTV, that it is okay to smile and play great guitar at the same time. He brought a sense of humor to the craft earned only through hard work and true talent and innovation. Eddie also had sense enough to never take himself, or this business of rock stardom, too seriously. I believe, as I'm sure most of the musical community does, that EVH has graciously blessed us all with his attitude and abilities, while shunning the seemingly requisite ego that accompanied most virtuosos of the past. ♪

Hank Williams III

Yes, I liked the original Van Halen and Eddie as a guitarist ruled! I'm the reason Bocephus [Hank Jr.] got into Van Halen at all. He had never heard them until I showed him an interview where they mentioned Bocephus. Yup, Eddie kicks assssssssssssssss. ♪

George Winston

It is great to finally have a book on Eddie. He is an inspiration to so many – for his innovative guitar techniques that are used by so many guitarists in different genres to more fully express themselves, for his courage and surviving his bout with cancer, and also who he is personally. ♪

Mark Wood

So in 1976 I was accepted into the Julliard School of Music on violin. I had a full scholarship and on my way to being the next Jascha Heifetz. But then in 1978, the first Van Halen record came out. I had grown up on the Beatles, Allman Brothers, and Led Zeppelin. I was very familiar with rock 'n' roll. I loved it. But when I heard Eddie, that changed everything for me. I had only been in Julliard about a year or two but I was badgering my violin teacher to teach me how to play like Van Halen! But of course the teachers there looked down upon that kind of music so much that I was almost kicked out for encouraging them to teach me these other styles from Hendrix to Van Halen.

When I heard Van Halen that was when I started to develop my electronic violins. I made a six-string violin and a seven-string violin! I put frets on them as well. And I began transcribing Eddie's solos, which changed my whole way of playing. Because I felt that without question, Eddie didn't play the cliché guitar technique. He really developed more of a classical technique, more so than, say, a jazz technique. His influences, from what I heard in his playing, were more *rock*. It was more *from the gut,* which I find to be much more appealing emotionally than, let's say, a jazz guitar player. You know, with the whammy-bar and the hammer-ons. It was like those arpeggiated hammer-ons were classical, "Mozart-ian" type of playing.

Obviously, growing up with classical music, I understood it very quickly. So I was transcribing his solos and they fit so much nicer on a violin than on a guitar. Although I didn't play guitar, it seemed that guitar players that tried to imitate Van Halen never, *never* figured out what he was doing to a tee. Where I felt as a violin player, I really absorbed his musicality far quicker. With his musical background – his dad being a clarinetist and having also been exposed to classical piano – it's amazing how Eddie applied and adapted all that into his guitar playing. And then, of course, when I saw him live, running around and bouncing off his amps! He is the *consummate musician.* Eddie combined virtuoso playing with great showmanship, just as Nicolò Paganini was doing 200 years ago. Eddie was not just standing alone and still, but really putting forth an effort, not only into his playing and great writing, but also into his performance.

Basically, I had found my mentor. Whereas violin players went, there was nothing. As much as I love Jean-Luc Ponty and Jerry Goodman, um, you know, they still were not thinking "outside the box," so to speak. When I heard Eddie I was like, "*That's* the one violin players should listen to and be influenced by!" So that is when I started gravitating towards guitar players. And then, of course, Eddie spawned everybody from Warren DeMartini to George Lynch and all the other great guitar players.

So without question, Eddie spoke to my classical roots. And he also helped me figure out a way to survive in this industry as a violin player, not as a guitar player. I think it's really important to point out that Eddie influenced and inspired many different types of musicians, not just guitar players and rock musicians. Oh, and you can't overlook his songwriting skills. His songwriting skills are *amazing*. His pop and rock songwriting skills are, to me, on the level of an Elton John, the Beatles, and other greats. Even on "Eruption" and "Spanish Fly," where the solo guitar pieces are *absolutely virtuoso*, he was leaning more towards how Paganini showcased his technique within the context of music. ♪

Zakk Wylde

I remember the first time I heard "Eruption." I wasn't even playing guitar then. I think I was about ten years old. I had a buddy who was older than me who played. Well, he played "Eruption" for me. I was just like, "Is that a *guitar?*" I didn't even know whether it was a guitar or what it was. This was around the time I'd just started gettin' into Sabbath and everything like that. Then I heard "Eruption" and I just couldn't believe what I was hearing, you know?

Then I remember hangin' out at a buddy's house one night. We were all hangin' out in the backyard, just chillin' out, and we were listening to *Van Halen II*. That was the first time I heard "Spanish Fly," and I remember thinking, "How can anybody get that fuckin' good?" It was *beyond insane*. I didn't think it was physically possible to play like that! It was ridiculous! Man, to this day, it still holds up. It'll hold up forever 'cause it's that brilliant. Far as I'm concerned, Eddie's the complete package. Technique aside, his rhythm playing, feel, songwriting, tone, riffs, leads – man, it's all there. It's like the best tasting beer you ever drank in your life!

It's just, you know, all the great ones write their own shit. Like, certain players are great songwriters that happen to play guitar. Then you got certain guys that are amazing guitar players, but they can't write a song worth a shit! Eddie does it all. He's the complete package, man. That's the greatest thing about him – he does it all. Even as far as tapping, he's always used it tastefully. He was able to fit that into cool rock songs, as opposed to it just being in some insane musician level. Another really cool thing about Eddie is he *always* mentioned Eric Clapton, Allan Holdsworth, and all the guys he dug, you know? Oh, and far as speed goes, Ed's not just about playin' fast. He can play slow shit, too. He can do *anything*. He's a great songwriter, crafts great riffs, has amazing tone, and his solos are insane, too! I've always looked at solos as the icing on the cake. But you gotta have a cake, you know?

To this day, Eddie is a major influence and inspiration. I got his pictures in my music room and out in my garage, when I'm liftin' weights and jammin'. Before we go out on stage, we'll just crank early Van Halen. Like, on the tour bus, we'll just crank that shit and it gets us all fired up – *especially* if you're a guitar player, you know? It's like, "Oh, think you can play? Listen to this shit!" [*laughs*]

When I look at Van Halen as a band, they were lethal. Man, especially the original. They've always kicked major fuckin' ass, but the original was insane. Ozzy's always told me that when Van Halen came in, it was the changing of the guard. VH opened for Sabbath back on their first tour in 1978 and Ozzy always says to me, "Zakk, they just fuckin' crushed us every night!" They had that fire, man. They were just undeniable. It was just sick-ass fuckin' greatness.

I remember when I was growin' up as a kid, a lot of jazz players and other players looked down on a lot of the rock players. Basically, they felt rock players couldn't really play worth a shit. You know, they thought most rock guitar players *sucked*. Well, I can put on "Spanish Fly" and they'll go, "Who's that? That guy's really fuckin' good!" And I'd go, "That's fuckin' Eddie Van Halen." They'd be like, "Who? Get the fuck outta here! That ain't Eddie Van Halen!" I go, "Uh, yeah, it is."

Back when I was in high school, I remember reading this article with John McLaughlin. I believe it was in *Guitar for the Practicing Musician,* or something like that. In fact, I actually told Eddie about it years later. They were doin' "In the Listening Room" with John McLaughlin. You know, where they bring in a great musician, play him some songs, and then they basically share their thoughts. Well, they play "Spanish Fly" and McLaughlin was like, "Oh, this sounds very flamenco influenced. This guy is a phenomenal player! Who is he?" Obviously, John had no idea it was Ed. I remember telling Eddie and he goes, "Really? He fuckin' said that about me?" Ed had no idea. John McLaughlin was sittin' there going, "This guy is phenomenal! He has amazing technique!" I mean, John plays with Paco De Lucia, so I think he knows a thing or two about an amazing sick-ass flamenco guitar player, you know?

That's why that whole *Rolling Stone* magazine "Top 100 Guitarists" issue drove me nuts. Man, what a fuckin' debacle! That shit pissed me off so bad. The people who voted on that just don't understand. I mean, Eddie Van Halen at number 70? Randy Rhoads at number 85? Yeah, right. If you're gonna have Jimi Hendrix number 1, well, obviously Jimi's a rock guitar player. He didn't play jazz, ok? I mean, he did other things but he is a *rock* guitar player. Man, I love Jimi. I named my son after Hendrix! My son's name is Hendrix Halen Michael Rhoads Wylde. I totally get that Jimi is the chosen son of electric guitar. But if you're gonna put Jimi Hendrix number 1, then number 2 *has gotta* be Eddie Van Halen. If not, put Eddie Van Halen number 1.

It's like with the whole home run thing in baseball. People talk about Barry Bonds goin' for the all-time record, but when you pick up a magazine you see the Babe on the cover. Well, doesn't Hank Aaron own the all-time record? So it should really be Hank Aaron on the cover, you know? But then they'll argue Hank played longer and Babe had less at-bats [*laughs*].

I mean, if you're gonna do an issue about the greatest guitar players of all time, ask guitar players! Seriously, call Edward Van Halen up and ask him for his Top 5 players of all time, you know? Then call Allan Holdsworth and ask him for his Top 5. Get it polled by great players. Then figure out if you're goin' rock, jazz, and so forth. I mean, someone like Al Di Meola is one of the greatest guitar players ever. But Al and John McLaughlin and Paco De Lucia are a different genre, you know? That's how I woulda done it, anyways.

The first time I ever saw Van Halen live was with Gary Cherone in 1998 in Japan. I never got to see VH with Dave or Sammy. I was actually over in Japan with Black Label Society at the same time they were. You know, we were over there doin' promotion, interviews and all that stuff. We hooked up and got shit faced all night in Eddie's room! The best part is that Eddie was playin' me all these fuckin' Led Zeppelin licks. Jimmy Page licks, you know? Sometimes he'd play the entire fuckin' song, too. Man, he'd play all types of shit while we were gettin' blasted. I think I was hung over for about two days after that. Funny thing is, I had to do interviews, like, the next day. And here I am, totally fuckin' blasted! I swear, I was drunk for about two days after.

Well, Van Halen did three nights at the Budokan, so we all went down there and watched 'em. Man, Eddie played his fuckin' ass off! That was the first time I ever saw 'em in concert. I had actually met Eddie way before that. Back when I first joined Ozzy, Steve Lukather actually took me over to Ed's house. Ed is fuckin' awesome. He's a beautiful guy, man. He's good people. Without a doubt, Eddie Van Halen is the greatest guitar player who has ever lived. ♪

Neil Zlozower

I first heard Van Halen in 1978. I was working in this office along with three other photographers and I heard the beginning of "Runnin' with the Devil." I was like, "Oh my fuckin' God! What the hell is *that*? That's killer!" Then I heard Dave's voice and the guitar and everything. Man, it was insane. You gotta remember that in '78 we're comin' off the Village People, Donna Summer, *Grease, Saturday Night Fever,* and the Bee Gees. I wasn't really into any of that shit, you know? I heard this rock 'n' roll and, you know, *no one* sounded like Eddie Van Halen back then. It was just so raw and brutal. It was a straightforward attack, right in your face. Man, I loved it!

I'd actually seen 'em before while they were playing clubs in Hollywood. My girlfriend at the time kept telling me about this amazing band with this insane guitar player that I had to go see. So, you know, we went to go check 'em out. Unfortunately, uh, I couldn't remember shit 'cause those were the "Quaalude days" and I had popped one before their show started!

Anyway, at the time their first album came out, we were working with this company called Mirage, which the other three photographers had formed. Well, I got hired to shoot the very first Texxas Jam, which was held at the Dallas Cotton Bowl. Where most photographers get clearance to just shoot through the first three songs, we were cleared to shoot all the bands through their entire sets. At least in our mind, anyway! So instead of just shooting through the first three songs, like most did, we'd stay there and shoot *all* of Journey, *all* of Heart, *all* of Aerosmith and whoever else was playing that day.

So it's about time for Van Halen and I'm standing on the photo ramp. All of a sudden, this little short guy shows up. He's about five foot three, wearing a black leather coat, black leather pants, detective belt, handcuffs, black leather gloves, and Peter Fonda *Easy Rider* motorcycle glasses. You know, basically the most intimidating human being I'd probably ever met in my life up to that point – *especially* considering he's only five foot three.

So he comes up to me and says, "What are you doing?" I'm like, "Well, my name is Neil and we're with Mirage. We're cleared to shoot all the bands and..." He cuts me off and says, "Well, I'm sorry, *no one* shoots Van Halen. We haven't approved it, you can't shoot it and you have to leave *right now!*" I'm like, "Whoa! Ok!" You know, I didn't wanna mess with this guy 'cause he seems like he's got somewhat of an attitude [*laughs*].

Basically, that was my first experience *trying* to shoot the band. It failed, so I just went out in the audience and watched them. Man, they were great. In the early days, they were just phenomenal. They just couldn't be beat. In their day, Van Halen was just unstoppable. They were the most brutal live band out there, period. So, you know, I was sorta bummed that I couldn't shoot 'em. Later on, I found out that the company doin' their publicity was Bob Gibson and Associates. Well, I was pretty good friends with them and knew all the publicists who worked for Bob Gibson. So I made an appointment to go down there and basically let 'em know I wanted to shoot the guys. I think they did a gig at Long Beach Arena that I went and shot. A day or two later, they played in San Diego, and I also drove down and shot that show.

The first time I ever really worked with them on a one-to-one basis was when they were doing the Day on the Green Festival out in Oakland in '78. I believe Journey, Aerosmith, and AC/DC were on the bill, too. I flew up there and did like a ten-minute backstage photo shoot with the guys against this green, orange, and yellow fence there. You know, this plastic shit was set up there so people on the outside couldn't look into the compound. We did this shoot there and I guess it was the first time they had any photographer of my caliber working with the band.

A couple weeks after the photo shoot, I took the photos down to Bob Gibson and Associates. The band was there, too. They looked at 'em and they loved the photos. The guys in the band and I got along really cool, too. You know, back then they were the same age as me, so we got along good. They saw I wasn't some stuffy, stupid little punk photographer. We just started hangin', almost as friends, you know? We kept workin' together and I shot a few more shows. Did some more photo shoots, too. That's pretty much how I got started with Van Halen. I ended up shooting them from '78 through '84. Basically, I shot their entire classic era.

Man, life on the road with Van Halen was a great experience. Each guy had his own vices, so to speak. You know, I've been on tour with Poison. I've been on tour with Mötley Crüe. And, you know, these guys are supposed to be the "bad boys" of rock. Supposedly, they do the nastiest things and so forth. And they were pretty damn wild, you know? But as far as I'm concerned, *nothing* will ever touch the things that I saw and that we did with Van Halen. Man, it was crazy back in '78, '79, and '80. The whole classic era was insane, really. There was no shortage of girls. Let's just say we all lived life to the fullest, put it to you that way. Far as I'm concerned, Van Halen puts 'em all to shame. Man, I don't even know if the guys in this day and age even know how to have fun.

All the guys in the band are great, and I'm still in touch with Dave to this day. Dave's a great guy. He's a total professional. To me, he's probably the greatest frontman that ever lived. I mean, you got Mick Jagger and a couple others, but Dave is just a *master* entertainer. I think Dave would consider himself an "entertainer" more than he considers himself a vocalist. And yeah, the older people will say that Frank Sinatra was the greatest entertainer.

To be honest with you, there's one guy that I think is right up there with Dave, and that's Louis Prima. To me, Louis Prima is just amazing. I have an old video of the guy and as far as an "entertainer" goes, man, he was just phenomenal. I see a lot of Dave in Louis Prima. And, you know, Dave did Louis' "Just a Gigolo" song back in the day. But to me Dave wins, hands down. He's got 'em all beat. And he's my favorite person to work with as well. ♪

Acknowledgments...

Man, where do I begin? While I basically put this book together on my own, that certainly does not mean I did it alone. Were it not for the kindness and generosity of many different people – as freakin' cliché as this is gonna sound – this book would not have been possible. I mean that sincerely, too. The existence of this project truly depended on the participation of all these fine people – *especially* for the "Tribute" section.

Basically, if none of 'em had taken time outta their lives to participate in this project, well, this book would not be. You are all total class acts and I can never repay you for being so cool and generous. It was a privilege to be able to speak with all of you and to have you on board. So please allow me a moment to say thank you to all of the following people:

"Dimebag" Darrell Abbott (R.I.P. Dime), Miriam and Jan Akkerman, Tommy Aldridge, Vinny Appice, Kenny Aronoff, Randy Bachman, Ginger Baker, Kofi Baker, Jennifer Batten, Jason Becker and the entire Becker Family, Adrian Belew, George Bellas, Jeff Berlin, Kevin Booth, Jimmy Briscoe, Bill Bruford, Jimmy Bruno, Ernie C., Emmett Chapman, Metal Mike Clasciak, Rusty Cooley, Steve Cropper, Bob Daisley, Craig DeFalco, Buck Dharma, Al Di Meola, Chris Duarte, Kevin DuBrow, Aynsley Dunbar, Dave Ellefson, Rik Emmett, Michael Fath, José Feliciano, Anton Fig, John 5, Bela Fleck, Marty Friedman, Paul Gilbert, Trey Gunn, Steve Hackett, Scott Henderson, James "Papa Het" Hetfield, Johnny Hiland, Wolf Hoffman, Allan Holdsworth, Steve Howe, Scott Ian, Chris Impellitteri, Sharon Isbin, Alphonso Johnson, John Jorgenson, John Kalodner, Phil Keaggy, B.B. King, Kerry King, Dr. Know, Wayne Kramer, Wayne Krantz, Robby Krieger, Jonathan Kreisberg, Bruce Kulick, Biréli Lagrène, Albert Lee, Tony Levin, Steve Lukather, Steve Lynch, Harvey Mandel, Michael Manring, Jeff Mantas, Frank Marino, Brian May, John McLaughlin, Chris McLernon, Steve Morse, Dave Navarro, Ted Nugent, Jas Obrecht, Terry Oubre, Alan Paul, Chris Poland, Jean-Luc Ponty, Bonnie Raitt, Mick Ralphs, Elliot Randall, Randy "Rare" Resnick, Ian Robinson, Henry Rollins, Rev. James A. Rota II, Gregg Rolie, Jim Root, Jordan Rudess, Dave "Snake" Sabo, Joe Satriani, Michael Schenker, Rudolph Schenker, Earl Scruggs, Kenny Wayne Shepherd, Derek Sherinian, Alex Skolnick, Mike Smith, Trey Spruance, Mike Stern, Joe Stump, John Tardy, Shane Theriot, Toots Thielemans, Mark Tremonti, Steve Vai, The Ventures, Carl Verheyen, Tommy Victor, Dick Wagner, Jeff Watson, Hank Williams III, George Winston, Mark Wood, Steve Wozniak, Zakk Wylde, "X," and Neil Zlozower.

I'd also like to thank all the good people who handle the management and PR duties for all of the musicians I just mentioned. Believe me, I'll never forget the fact that without y'all passing word of my project along, none of these fine people would have heard about it and been able to participate. Special thanks to all the wonderful people at AuthorHouse, especially Dave Pruet. You rock, Dave! I truly appreciate all your help and support.

Much love, respect and thanks to Alan Paul and all of the wonderful people at *Guitar World* magazine. Your kindness and support was unbelievable, and the interviews/articles that appeared in your fine magazine provided much needed factual information. Major thanks also goes out to Steven Rosen. Your kind words of encouragement were invaluable to me. Thanks for takin' the time to answer all my stupid questions and for all your generosity. Oh, and I still think you are the only one qualified to do an EVH bio, dammit! Man, I also have to send major love and respect to my bro, J.C. Gonzalez. Dude, we did it! Who woulda thought, huh? Man, you're the one who told me I should write a VH book, and for that, I dunno if I should thank you or freakin' dropkick you! All kidding aside, thanks brotha man.

Much love also goes out to Richard Copper. Dude, I'll always consider you a bro and one of the last *true* remaining metalheads on Earth. Shit, you're probably listening to Helloween right now, aren't you Richie? Once again, major thanks to the Zloz for that fuckin' *killer* cover shot! And thanks to Jeff Hausman, creator of the baddest VH fanzine of all time, *The Inside.* I truly appreciated your feedback and kind words.

Finally, I am forever grateful to Michael Anthony, Gary Cherone, Sammy Hagar, David Lee Roth, Alex Van Halen, and Edward Van Halen. To this very day, whenever your music comes on the radio, I still crank that shit up. Thanks for writing the soundtrack to my life.

Text Quotations

"The Switch"
Martin Clarke (*Guitar World*, Mar. 2003)
Rudy Leiren (*Guitar World*, Mar. 2003)

"Mammoth"
Mark Stone (*The Van Halen Story: The Early Years*, DVD)
Rudy Leiren (*Guitar World*, Mar. 2003)
Dennis Travis (*The Inside*, Issue 1, Spring 1995)

"The Club Days"
Slash (*Guitar One* magazine, Apr. 2000)
Mick Mars (*Guitar World*, Mar. 2003)
Rodney Bingenheimer (*Guitar World*, Mar. 2003)
George Lynch (*Guitar World*, Oct. 2004)
Gene Simmons (*Guitar World*, Mar. 2003)
Ted Templeman (*Guitar World*, Sept. 1991)

"1978 Rookie of the Year"
Leslie West (*Guitar World*, Jan. 1987)
Les Paul (*Guitar Player*, Dec. 1977)
Jimmy Page (*Guitar World*, Oct. 1999)
Ozzy Osbourne (*Guitar World presents Guitar Legends*, 2004)
Kirk Hammett (*Guitar World*, Aug. 2001)
Joe Perry (*Boston Globe*, 2004)
Steve Tyler (*SPIN* magazine, 1997)
Susan Masino (*The Inside*, Issue 14)
Billy Corgan (*Guitar Player*, Jan. 1996)
Yngwie J. Malmsteen (*Guitar World*, Jan. 1987)
Slash (*Guitar World*, Nov. 2000)
Jake E. Lee (*JakeELee.com/interviews*)

"Classic VH '78 – '84"
Kurt Loder (*MTV's 20 Years of Rock*)
Damon Johnson (*www.aol.com/chat/chats/brothercane.html*)
Billy Sheehan (*The Van Halen Encyclopedia*, 2001)
Mikal Gilmore (*Guitar World*, Mar. 2003)
Jimmy Briscoe (personal interview by phone, 2004)

"Sayonara, Dave"
Jeff Beck (*Guitar World,* Oct. 1999)
Brian "Head" Welch (*Total Guitar,* Aug. 2002)

"Enter Sam-man"
Neal Schon (*ClassicRockRevisited.com/interviews*)

"Van Halen '85 – '96"
Rob Thomas (*MTV's 20 Years of Rock*)

"Welcome Back?"
Billy Corgan (1996 *MTV Video Music Awards*)

"Don't Call It a Comeback"
Eric Johnson (*EricJohnson.com/interviews*)
Nick Perri (*The Patriot Ledger at SouthBoston.com,* Feb. 9, 2005)

"Discography"
Trey Azagthoth (*roughedge.com/interviews*)
Stephen Carpenter (*Rolling Stone,* June 2000 and *Guitar World,* Sept. 1998)
Billy Corgan (*Guitar World,* Apr. 1996)
Daron Malakian (*Guitar World,* Mar. 2002)
Tom Morello (*MTV's 20 Years of Rock*)

"The Elements of a Great Guitar Player"
Paul McCartney (*Guitar Player,* July 1990)
Kim Thayil (*The Inside,* Issue 16)
Dweezil Zappa (*The Inside,* Issue 16)
Dweezil Zappa (*musicforpets.com/interviews*)
Nuno Bettencourt (*Guitar for the Practicing Musician,* Sept. 1993)
Ritchie Blackmore (*Guitar,* Sept. 1996)
Mick Jones (*Rolling Stone,* Sept. 21, 1989)
David Gilmour (*Guitar,* Sept. 1995)
Rory Gallagher (*Guitar for the Practicing Musician,* Aug. 1991)

"The Classic VH Sound"
Dave Mustaine (*The Sam and Dave Show,* VH1, 2002)
Richard McKernan (*Guitar World,* Mar. 2003)

"Eruption"
Mike Mushok (*Guitar World,* Jan. 2002)
Billy Corgan (*Guitar World,* Apr. 1996)

"Tapping"
Jeff Beck (*Guitar World,* Oct.1999)
Steve Hackett (personal interview via e-mail, 2004)
Harvey "The Snake" Mandel (personal interview by phone, 2004)
Randy "Rare" Resnick (personal interview via e-mail, 2004)

"Too Many Notes"
Joe Walsh (*Guitar Player,* 1988)
Neil Young (*Guitar Player,* Mar. 1992)

"The Frankenstrat"
John Mayer (*Guitar Player,* Feb. 2004)

"The Floyd Rose"
Kirk Hammett (*Guitar World,* Oct. 1999)

"Quincy Jones tells Edward to 'Beat It'"
Quincy Jones (*VH1's Top 80 Songs of the '80s*)

"Randy Rhoads and the Sunset Strip"
Randy Rhoads (*Guitar Player,* 1981)
Kevin DuBrow (personal interview by phone, 2004)

"The Greatest of All Time"
Pat Metheny (*College Musician, Vol. 1, No. 1, Fall 1986*)
Alvin Lee (*NEON,* 1989)

"Spandex and the '80s"
John Cougar Mellencamp (*VH1's Top 80 songs of the '80s*)

"Edward Van Halen's Ear"
Hartley Peavey (*van-halen.com/interviews*)

"The Impact and Influence of EVH"
Tony Iommi (*Guitar for the Practicing Musician,* May 1994)
Mike Einziger (*Guitar World,* Nov. 2000)
Mike DeWolf (*Guitarist,* 2001)

Frank Zappa (*Guitar World,* Apr. 1987)
Ty Tabor (*The Inside,* Issue 16)
Tom Morello (*Guitar One,* June 1998)
Frank Meneschino (*Guitar World,* Sept. 2004)
Billie Joe Armstrong (*Guitar World,* Sept. 2000)
Leslie West (*ClassicRockRevisited.com/interviews*)
Pat Metheny (*PatMethenyGroup.com/Q&A*)
David Gilmour (*Guitar Classics,* Jan. 1985)
Billy Gibbons (*The Inside,* Issue 16)
Tommy Lee (*Rolling Stone*)
Brad Wilk (*RATM.org/interviews*)
Charles R. Cross (personal interview via e-mail, 2004)

"Tribute"

Every single word that appears in the "Tribute" was personally acquired – by phone and via e-mail – from each and every single person who participated. All of these interviews were conducted over the course of 2004 and 2005 by the author of this book.

Web Links...

Official Van Halen site:
www.van-halen.com

Official Michael Anthony site:
www.madanthonycafe.com

Official Sammy Hagar site:
www.redrocker.com

Official Cabo Wabo site:
www.cabowabo.com

Official David Lee Roth site:
www.davidleeroth.com

Van Halen News Desk:
www.vhnd.com

Van Halen Store:
www.vanhalenstore.com

Van Halen Links/Forums:
www.vhlinks.com

Van Halen Mailing List:
www.vhml.com

Van Halen Bootleg Discography:
www.vhboots.com

Unofficial Eddie Van Halen site:
www.EddieVanHalen.com

Classic Van Halen:
www.classicvanhalen.com

Best Friggin' VH Cover Band Alive:
www.theatomicpunks.com

David Lee Roth Army:
www.dlrarmy.com

Official Charvel/EVH Art Series Guitar site:
www.charvel.com

Official Peavey site:
www.peavey.com

Official MXR site:
www.jimdunlop.com

As a bonus, I figured I'd throw in the Web sites for all the wonderful people who participated in this project. I can never truly repay any of 'em, but it's the least I can do. There are quite a few people involved, and I'm aware that some readers out there may simply not recognize each and every single one of 'em. So this way, if you see a name you may not recognize, just hop online and check 'em out!

Official "Dimebag" Darrell Abbott sites:
www.damageplan.com

www.dimetribute.com

If you'd like to make a donation to help the families of all the victims involved in what tragically went down in Ohio back in December 2004, here's the address. Thank you.

Dimebag Darrell Memorial Fund
110 SW Thomas
Burleson, TX. 76028

Official Jan Akkerman site:
www.janakkerman.nl

Official Tommy Aldridge site:
www.tommyaldridge.com

Official Vinny Appice site:
www.vinnyappice.com

Official Kenny Aronoff site:
www.kennyaronoff.com

Official Randy Bachman site:
www.randybachman.net

Official Kofi Baker site:
www.kofibaker.com

Official Jennifer Batten site:
www.batten.com

Official Jason Becker site:
www.jasonbecker.com

Official Adrian Belew site:
www.adrianbelew.net

Official George Bellas site:
www.georgebellas.com

Official Jeff Berlin site:
www.jeffberlinmusic.com

Official Kevin Booth site:
www.sacredcow.com

Official Bill Bruford site:
www.billbruford.com

Official Jimmy Bruno site:
www.jimmybruno.com

Official Emmett Chapman site:
www.stick.com

Official Metal Mike Clasciak site:
www.planetshred.com

Official Rusty Cooley site:
www.rustycooley.com

Official Steve Cropper site:
www.playitsteve.com

Official Charles R. Cross site:
www.charlesrcross.com

Official Bob Daisley site:
www.bobdaisley.com

Official Craig DeFalco site:
www.laid-law.com

Official Buck Dharma site:
www.buckdharma.com

Official Al Di Meola site:
www.aldimeola.com

Official Chris Duarte site:
www.chrisduartegroup.org

Official Kevin DuBrow site:
www.kevindubrow.com

Official Aynsley Dunbar site:
www.aynsleydunbar.com

Official Dave Ellefson site:
www.davidellefson.com

Official Rik Emmett site:
www.rikemmett.com

Official Michael Fath site:
www.michaelfath.com

Official José Feliciano site:
www.josefeliciano.com

Official Anton Fig site:
www.antonfig.com

Official John 5 site:
www.john-5.com

Official Bela Fleck site:
www.flecktones.com

Official Marty Friedman site:
www.martyfriedman.com

Official Paul Gilbert site:
www.paulgilbert.com

Official Trey Gunn site:
www.treygunn.com

Official Steve Hackett site:
www.stevehackett.com

Official Scott Henderson site:
www.scotthenderson.net

Official James Hetfield site:
www.metallica.com

Official Johnny Hiland site:
www.johnnyhiland.com

Official Wolf Hoffman site:
www.wolfhoffman.com

Official Allan Holdsworth site:
www.therealallanholdsworth.com

Official Steve Howe site:
www.stevehowe.com

Official Scott Ian site:
www.anthrax.com

Official Chris Impelliteri site:
www.rapture.net

Official Sharon Isbin site:
www.sharonisbin.com

Official Alphonso Johnson site:
www.embamba.com

Official John Jorgenson site:
www.johnjorgenson.com

Official John Kalodner site:
www.johnkalodner.com

Official Phil Keaggy site:
www.philkeaggy.com

Official B.B. King site:
www.bbking.com

Official Kerry King site:
www.americanrecordings.com/slayer/

Official Wayne Kramer site:
www.waynekramer.com

Official Wayne Krantz site:
www.waynekrantz.com

Official Robby Krieger site:
www.robbykrieger.com

Official Jonathan Kreisberg site:
www.jonathankreisberg.com

Official Bruce Kulick site:
www.kulick.net

Official Biréli Lagrène site:
www.lagrene.com

Official Albert Lee site:
www.albertlee.co.uk

Official Tony Levin site:
www.tonylevin.com

Official Steve Lukather site:
www.stevelukather.net

Official Steve Lynch site:
www.stevelynch.info

Official Harvey "The Snake" Mandel site:
www.harveymandel.com

Official Michael Manring site:
www.manthing.com

Official Jeff Mantas site:
www.venomlegions.com

Official Frank Marino site:
www.mahoganyrush.com

Official Brian May site:
www.brianmay.com

Official John McLaughlin site:
www.johnmclaughlin.com

Official Chris McLernon site:
www.chrismclernon.com

Official Steve Morse site:
www.stevemorse.com

Official Dave Navarro site:
www.janesaddiction.com

Official Ted Nugent site:
www.tnugent.com

Official Terry Oubre site:
www.kendrick-amplifiers.com

Official Alan Paul site:
www.guitarworld.com

Official Chris Poland site:
www.chrispoland.com

Official Jean-Luc Ponty site:
www.ponty.com

Official Bonnie Raitt site:
www.bonnieraitt.com

Official Mick Ralphs site:
www.mickralphs.co.uk

Official Elliott Randall site:
www.elliott-randall.com

Official Randy "Rare" Resnick site:
www.resmo.com/rare/english.shtml

Official Iann Robinson site:
www.metal-sludge.com

Official Henry Rollins site:
www.21361.com

Official Rev. James A. Rota site:
www.fireballministry.com

Official Gregg Rolie site:
www.greggrolie.com

Official Jim Root site:
www.slipknot1.com

Official Jordan Rudess site:
www.jordanrudess.com

Official Dave "Snake" Sabo site:
www.skidrow.com

Official Joe Satriani site:
www.satriani.com

Official Michael Schenker site:
www.michaelschenkerhimself.com

Official Rudolph Schenker site:
www.the-scorpions.com

Official Earl Scruggs site:
www.earlscruggs.com

Official Kenny Wayne Shepherd
site:
www.kennywayneshepherd.net

Official Derek Sherinian site:
www.dereksherinian.com

Official Alex Skolnick site:
www.alexskolnick.com

Official Trey Spruance site:
www.sc3music.com

Official Mike Stern site:
www.mikestern.org

Official Joe Stump site:
www.joestump.com

Official John Tardy site:
www.obituary.cc

Official Shane Theriot site:
www.shanetheriot.com

Offical Toots Thielemans site:
www.tootsthielemans.com

Official Mark Tremonti site:
www.alterbridge.com

Official Steve Vai site:
www.vai.com

Official Ventures site:
www.theventures.com

Official Carl Verheyen site:
www.carlverheyen.com

Official Dick Wagner site:
www.wagnermusic.com

Official Jeff Watson site:
www.wireonfire.com

Official HankWilliams III site:
www.hank3.com

Offical George Winston site:
www.georgewinston.com

Official Mark Wood site:
www.markwoodmusic.com

Official Zakk Wylde site:
www.zakkwylde.com

Official Neil Zlozower site:
www.zloz.com

Contact the Author...

Any comments or questions? All feedback—be it positive, negative, or downright vicious—is most welcome. I created the following e-mail specifically for this book, so knock yourselves out. Believe me, I'll read everything y'all send.

VanHalen101@hotmail.com

Printed in the United States
40155LVS00003B/28